A Calendar of Modern Poetry

Subscriptions (six issues):
£24.50 ($49.00) individuals
£30.00 ($60.00) institutions
to *PN Review*, 402–406 Corn Exchange,
Manchester M4 3BY UK

Copyright © 1994 POETRY NATION REVIEW
All rights reserved

ISSN 0144-7076
ISBN 1 85754 095 6

General Editor MICHAEL SCHMIDT
Co-ordinating Editor NEIL POWELL

EDITORIAL OFFICE
The Poetry Centre · Department of English
University of Manchester
Manchester M13 9PL

Manuscripts should be sent to the editorial office and cannot be returned unless accompanied by a self-addressed and stamped envelope or, for writers living abroad, by an international reply coupon.

Typeset in Monotype Ellington
by XL Publishing Services, Nairn, Scotland.

Printed in England
by SRP Limited, Exeter.

Subscribe to P·N·Review

Order form

I should like to subscribe to *P N Review* for

1 year 6 issues

	PERSONAL		INSTITUTIONAL	
	£24.50	US $49.00	£30.00	US $60.00

ADD £12 OR US $25 FOR AIRMAIL

2 years 12 issues

	PERSONAL		INSTITUTIONAL	
	£46.50	US $93.00	£58.00	US $116.00

ADD £24 OR US $50 FOR AIRMAIL

Specimen copy £4.50 US $9.00

NAME

ADDRESS

POST CODE

I enclose a cheque / PO made payable to *P N Review* for £

I wish to pay by ACCESS / VISA (*delete as applicable*):

☐☐☐☐ ☐☐☐☐ ☐☐☐☐ ☐☐☐☐ EXPIRY DATE

NAME ON CARD SIGNATURE

to *P N Review*, 208–212 Corn Exchange, Manchester M4 3BQ, UK

Editorial

A poetry magazine is defined by its contributors. If it survives for two decades plus, its trajectory defines rather more than its editor's vagaries of taste.

Brian Cox, with whom I set up *Poetry Nation* in 1972, was of the opinion that a 'little magazine' was by definition an enterprise with a death wish: it had its moment, made its mark, and perished. *PN Review* remains a little magazine. It has had its moments, religious, political, critical, all at root poetic. Devoted to appraisal, reappraisal and discovery, it has insisted on the centrality of poetry in cultural life and on the necessity for critical engagement with poems at a technical as well as a thematic and theoretical level.

This issue celebrates the contributors who shape and reshape *PNR* at a time when establishing continuities is as urgent and necessary a task as that of discovery: new writers who emerge through *PNR* seem to me to share common ground with figures of earlier generations who, when the magazine began, were neglected or misvalued in this country. A serious magazine provides a validating, even a legitimising context. *PNR* has been serious in that respect. There is a readership, not a market; there are poets whose work it remains a privilege to publish. After what seemed a lean period in the late 1980s, new writers of moment are emerging.

This anthology in its range of contemporary writing has turned out to be among the most ambitious since Michael Roberts's 1936 *Faber Book of Modern Verse*, with its run from Hopkins to the 1930s. There are ideological affinities with that compilation, so formative of the taste of my generation of readers. It insists on the *responsibility* of poets to language, to subject, to the poem, and therefore to readership. This is not Leavis's moralism but more complex and challenging. Clearly Roberts did not believe that poetry makes nothing happen: it has effects in and on the reader, and on the language which follows it. A poem 'may change the configuration of the mind and alter our responses to certain situations: it may harmonize conflicting emotions…' He adds a caveat: 'the poetic use of language can cause discord as easily as it can cure it.' This view is shared, in different degrees, by many poets of his and later times. Two figures formative to *PNR*, Laura Riding and Edgell Rickword, from very different political perspectives, would have seconded Roberts's declaration. Indeed, Laura Riding claimed to have had a hand in drafting it.

Roberts's *moral* approach – that loaded word must be used without quotation marks – defines in a general way the 'prepoetic' ground of this diverse anthology which is unusual (as Roberts's book was) in blurring the markers between generations. Roberts would not, however, have taken the step I did in this issue. For over twenty years I have chosen work I like by poets I respect. Here I asked them to edit themselves, to select a clutch of poems, or extracts from longer poems, to 'characterise' their work. This abdication has been instructive to me, as it will be to readers at large. The poets choose unpredictably, yet what they say about their selections gives credence to Thom Gunn's argument in *PNR* 98 that we no longer have opposing camps but a continuous spectrum within which poets can be located. *PNR* has been dedicated to this hopeful possibility from the outset, talking of pluralism, fighting shy of 'post-modernism' and other -isms, of endorsing one school or movement. The rhetoric of pluralism gives way here to a manifestation of it: there are poems, and poets writing about the work they do, the world they do it in, the connections they make. It is a way of defining – as I'm often challenged to do – what *PNR* is about.

It would be wrong not to start this anthology with a writer and editor who inspired *PNR*. Though he had stopped writing verse long before the magazine began, he contributed to our debates and was the subject of an early special issue. Edgell Rickword edited several magazines with death wishes, including *The Calendar of Modern Letters* with its famous Scrutinies. As an oblique tribute we adapt the title of his magazine for this issue. In later years he thought of starting a literary and political journal: *PNR* he welcomed, despite its cloudy political definition. His widow Beatrix Hammarling selects his poems.

Three other poets who died during the lifetime of *PNR* need to be remembered. Laura Riding, like Rickword no longer writing poetry in 1972, was a severe and generous presence. Robert Nye, her editor, selects from her work. There is W.S. Graham whose poetry *PNR* was instrumental in re-appraising. His widow Nessie has chosen his work. Finally, George Barker – a supplement was devoted to him and *Anno Domini* appeared in full in our pages – has a place: Elspeth Barker makes the selection. These poets remain large presences. So does David Wright, who died while *PNR* 100 was at press. Many of the poets included here sought his approval of their work before they exposed it to the public. He remains a defining creative presence, through his own work and, invisibly, through the work he did for others.

The largest presences for me are those of C.H. Sisson and Donald Davie. Without them the magazine would have had less focus – or fewer focuses – than it has done. They opened my eyes to many writers. To them this issue is dedicated.

Few of the writers represented here are 'mainstream' in any useful sense. I cannot claim that this issue is 'representative' of the new, reflects a demographic reality or is just in gender distribution. I do say that it celebrates continuities, that these are poets whose work I love, or like, or respect, in different degrees, writers who make the poetic and critical debates that have filled the columns of this magazine for 22 years real: in the end the practitioners of an art, not its critics, theorists or editors, enliven our habits of hearing and feeling, our instinctive and analytical appraisals.

MICHAEL SCHMIDT

ACKNOWLEDGEMENTS

The poems of George Barker are published by Faber & Faber and printed by permission of Elspeth Barker. The poems of W.S. Graham are published by Faber & Faber and printed by permission of Nessie Graham. The poems of D.J. Enright are published by Oxford University Press in *Collected Poems 1987* and printed by permission of Watson Little Ltd. and the author. The poems of Michael Hamburger, published by Anvil Press Ltd., are printed by permission of the author. Charles Tomlinson's 'Swimming Chenango Lake', 'Assassin' and 'The Way In' from his *Collected Poems* (1985), 'A Rose for Janet' from *The Return* (1987) and 'The Door in the Wall' from *The Door in the Wall* (1992) are printed by permission of Oxford University Press. The poems of Thomas Kinsella, published by the Peppercanister Press (Dublin) and Oxford University Press, are printed by permission of the author. Thom Gunn's poems are published by Faber & Faber; those hitherto uncollected have appeared in *Threepenny Review*, *Agenda*, the *Times Literary Supplement* and *PN Review* and are printed by permission of the author. The poems of Judy Gahagan are printed by permission of the author. Peter Scupham's poems 'The Gatehouse' from *Summer Palaces* (1980), 'Young Ghost' from *Watching the Perseids* (1990), 'Under the Barrage' from *The Air Show* (1988), extracts from 'A Midsummer Night's Dream' from *Out Late* (1986) and extracts from 'A Habitat' from *The Ark* (1994) are printed by permission of Oxford University Press. Anne Stevenson's 'Minister' and 'Small Philosophical Poem' from her *Selected Poems 1956-1986* (1987) and 'When the Camel is Dust it Goes through the Needle's Eye' from *Four and a Half Dancing Men* (1993) are printed by permission of Oxford University Press. The poems of R.F. Langley are printed by permission of the author. The poems of Peter Bland are printed by permission of the author. The poems of Robert Nye are printed by permission of the author. The poems of Robert Pinsky are printed by permission of the author. The poems of Jeremy Hooker are published by Enitharmon Press and are printed by permission of the author. David Constantine's extracts from 'In Memoriam' from *A Brightness to Cast Shadows*, 'Mary Magdalene and the Sun' from *Watching for Dolphins*, 'Eldon Hole' from *Madder* and 'Local Histories' from *Selected Poems* are printed by permission of Bloodaxe Books Ltd., and 'Ground Elder' by permission of the author. The poems of Dick Davis are published by Anvil Press Ltd.; the hitherto uncollected poems included here are printed by permission of the author. The poems of Michael Haslam are printed by permission of the author. The poems of Michael Vince are published by Carcanet Press Ltd.; the hitherto uncollected poems included here are printed by permission of the author. The poems of Robert Wells are published by Carcanet Press Ltd.; the hitherto uncollected poems in this issue are printed by permission of the author. Denise Riley's poems, except for 'Milk Ink' and 'Problems of Horror' (hitherto uncollected), are from *Mop Mop Georgette* published by Reality Street Editions, London, in 1993, and are all printed by permission of the author. Marius Kociejowski's poem 'Coast' is from his collection *Doctor Honoris Causa* (1993), published by Anvil Press Ltd., by whose permission it is printed here. Frank Kuppner's poems are published by Carcanet Press Ltd.; the uncollected poem 'The Kuppneriad' is printed by permission of the author. Gregory Woods's poems are published by Carcanet Press Ltd.; the hitherto uncollected poems included here are printed by permission of the author. John Burnside's poem 'Signal Stop, near Horsley' from *Common Knowledge* and 'Septuagesima' and 'Aphasia in Childhood' from *Feast Days* are printed here by permission of Secker & Warburg; 'Halloween' and 'Avoirdupois' from *The Myth of the Irish* are printed by permission of Jonathan Cape Ltd. The poems of Carol Ann Duffy are printed by permission of Anvil Press Ltd. Michael Hulse's 'Raffles Hotel' and 'The Architecture of Air' from *Eating Strawberries in the Necropolis* (1991) are printed by permission of Collins Harvill; 'Burlem' (uncollected) and 'Knowing' (from *Knowing and Forgetting*, Secker & Warburg, 1981) are printed by permission of the author. Michael Hofmann's 'Kleist in Paris' and 'For Gert Hofmann' are printed by permission of the author; 'Nights in the Iron Hotel' from the book of that title, 'Author, Author' from *Acrimony* and 'Sally' and 'Postcard from Cuernavaca' from *Corona, Corona* are printed by permission of Faber & Faber Ltd. Stephen Romer's poems 'Higher Things' and 'Coming Back' from *Idols* (1986) and 'The Weight of It' and 'The Work' from *Plato's Ladder* (1992) are printed by permission of Oxford University Press; the uncollected poem 'Blocks and Scaffolds' is printed by permission of the author. The poems of Iain Bamforth are published by Carcanet Press Ltd.; the uncollected poems included here are printed by permission of the author. The poems of Vona Groarke, from her first collection, are printed by permission of the author and of Gallery Press. The poems of Miles Champion are printed by permission of the author. The poems of Sinéad Morrisey are printed by permission of the author. The poems of Edgell Rickword, Laura Riding, E.H. Scovell, Sorley Maclean, F.T. Prince, Anne Ridler, C.H. Sisson, John Heath-Stubbs, Edwin Morgan, David Wright, Donald Davie, Patricia Beer, Christopher Middleton, John Ashbery, Iain Crichton Smith, Elaine Feinstein, P.J. Kavanagh, Alistair Elliot, Jon Stallworthy, Gillian Clarke, Les Murray, Brian Jones, Andrew Waterman, John Peck, Roger Garfitt, Eavan Boland, Jeffrey Wainwright, Mimi Khalvati, Clive Wilmer, Bill Manhire, Norm Sibum, Neil Powell, Grevel Lindop, Vicki Raymond, John Gallas, Charles Boyle, Alison Brackenbury, Sujata Bhatt, Ian McMillan, Peter Sansom, Chris McCully, Justin Quinn, Sophie Hannah and Adam Schwartzman are printed by permission of the authors or their Estates and Carcanet Press Ltd.

CONTENTS

Edgell Rickword   5
The Soldier Addresses His Body
Winter Warfare
Rimbaud in Africa
The Encounter
Rhapsody on Red Admirals
Note by Beatrix Hammarling

Laura Riding   7
The Sweet Ascetic
No More Are Lovely Palaces
Back to the Mother Breast
As Well as Any Other
The Troubles of a Book
The Wind Suffers
Earth
The Way It Is
Nor Is It Written
Note by Robert Nye

E.J. Scovell   9
Reflecting on Old Age
A Portrait of a Boy
Bright Margins
The Paschal Moon
The Evening Garden
Note

Sorley Maclean   10
Calvary
A Highland Woman
The Cry of Europe
Dogs and Warfare
Heroes
Hallaig
Note

F.T. Prince   13
from The Old Age of Michelangelo
At Beaulieu
from Drypoints of the Hassidim
from The Yüan Chên Variations
from Walks in Rome
from Family Mottoes
The Other Cheek
Note

Anne Ridler   16
A Matter of Life and Death
The Freezing Rose
Snakeshead Fritillaries
Note

George Barker   18
Battersea Park
'Turn on your side'
Elegy on the Death of Michael Roberts
from At Thurgarton Church
from Anno Domini
'Never, my love and dearest'
A version of Animula Vagula Blandula
Note by Elspeth Barker

C.H. Sisson   22
On a Troopship
The Nature of Man
Cotignac
Taxila
Casualty
Note

Judith Wright   23
Note

John Heath-Stubbs   23
Mozart
Quatrains
Plato and the Waters of the Flood
from Artorius
Saint Francis Preaches to the Computers
Homage to Marianne Moore
Note

W.S. Graham   26
from The Dark Dialogues
Letter VI
The Beast in Space
from Clusters Travelling Out
Listen Put on Morning
Loch Thom
I Leave This At Your Ear
Note by Nessie Graham

Edwin Morgan   28
In the Snack Bar
At The Television Set
Cinquevalli
Gangs
Aunt Myra (1901-1989)
Note

David Wright   31
By the Effigy of St Cecilia
Kleomedes
from Grasmere Sonnets
E.P. at Westminster
Procession
from Five Songs
In Memoriam David Archer

D.J. Enright   34
from Paradise Illustrated
History of World Languages
Note

Donald Davie   36
Rain on South-East England
The Trip to Huntsville
Brilliance
But there!
Note

Patricia Beer   39
Pharaoh's Dream
Pilgrims' Crossing
The Night Marlowe Died
Beach Party
From the Coach

Michael Hamburger   40
Birthday
Mad Lover, Dead Lady
Mornings
Garden, Wilderness
The Street, December
Mr Littlejoy's Prayer
Endless
Return
Conversation with a Blackbird
Note

Christopher Middleton   43
Saloon with Birds
Vietnamese Harp
The Old Tour Guide – His Interpreter
Small Carvings at Arycanda
Note

John Ashbery   45
He
How Much Longer Will I Be Able to Inhabit the Divine Sepulchre
Rivers and Mountains
At North Farm

Charles Tomlinson   48
Swimming Chenango Lake
Assassin
The Way In
A Rose for Janet
The Door in the Wall
Note

Thomas Kinsella   51
Chrysalides
Westland Row
Artists' Letters
Talent and Friendship
from At the Head Table
Note

Contents

Iain Crichton Smith 53
A Note on Puritans
John Knox
Old Woman
Lenin
Two Girls Singing
The Bible
Dying Man
Dogmas
Note

Thom Gunn 55
Duncan
In the Post Office
Enough
In Trust
Eastern Europe
Note

Elaine Feinstein 58
At Seven, a Son
Song of Power
Dad
from The Feast of Eurydice
from New Lyrics for Dido and Aeneas
Urban Lyric
Izzy's Daughter
Insomnia
Note

P.J. Kavanagh 60
Nature Poet
Severn Aisling
Message
Note

Alistair Elliot 62
Turnstones on Lewis
Two Cats in New Hampshire
Wetting Yourself
Another Day
Facing South
Taste Enhancers
Note

Judy Gahagan 65
Winter Day Fasanenpark
Together with Crows
Siesta
Swifts and Boys
Festival of Dark
When the Whole Mood Changed
Snake on the Road
Up and Down in Man-a-hat-ta
Note

Peter Scupham 68
The Gatehouse
Young Ghost
Under the Barrage
from A Midsummer Night's Dream
from A Habitat
Note

Anne Stevenson 70
Minister
Small Philosophical Poem
When the Camel is Dust it Goes through
    the Needle's Eye
History
Going Back
Note

Peter Bland 72
The Happy Army
Lament for a Lost Generation
Two Family Snaps
Letters Home – New Zealand 1885
Note

Jon Stallworthy 76
The Poem Is
The Almond Tree
The Source
Breakfast in Bed
Pour Commencer
Note

Gillian Clarke 78
The Hare
Radio Engineer
Anorexic
Musician
from Blood
Note

Les Murray 80
Green Rose Tan
The Say-but-the-word Centurion
Rock Music
Like Wheeling Stacked Water
It Allows a Portrait in Line-scan
Note

Brian Jones 83
At Great Tew
Prospero to Miranda
The Children of Separation
At Lullingstone
Letter from Elsewhere
Note

R.F. Langley 86
Juan Fernandez
Mariana
Note

Robert Nye 88
Familiar Terms
Darker Ends
Henry James
Going to the Dogs
Riposte

Andrew Waterman 89
The Two Roads
A Butterfly
Growing Pains
Outside
Christmas 1989
Uncle Bob
Postcards from Norfolk
Note

Robert Pinsky 92
Shirt
From the Childhood of Jesus
The Day Dreamers
The Want Bone
Poem with Refrains
Note

John Peck 95
Ars Poetica
White Deer Running
from Frieze from the Gardens of
    Copenhagen
Western Palace Rhapsodies
from Poem on Divine Providence
Passage to the Islands
Note

Jeremy Hooker 98
Steps
Black on Gold
In Praise of Windmills
Walking to Capernaum
Westerbork
Note

Roger Garfitt 102
The Hooded Gods
Lower Lumb Mill
The Broken Road
Skara Brae
At Vanishing Point
Note

Eavan Boland 105
Domestic Interior 1: Night Feed
The Journey
Envoi
The Science of Cartography
What We Lost
Anna Liffey
Love

David Constantine 110
from In Memoriam
Mary Magdalene and the Sun
Eldon Hole
Local Historian
Ground Elder
Note

Contents

Tom Leonard   112
in the beginning
Moral Philosophy
from Situations Theoretical and Contemporary
from nora's place
Note

Jeffrey Wainwright   113
Transitive
from The Swimming Body
From The Madness of George III
from Free Rein
Note

Mimi Khalvati   115
Rubaiyat
Four Interiors
Coma
Note

Dick Davis   118
A Monorhyme for Miscegenation
Gossip
A Translator's Nightmare
Note

Clive Wilmer   120
Saxon Buckle
The Parable of the Sower
Post-War Childhoods
Charon's Bark
Psalm
Note

Bill Manhire   122
On Originality
Loss of the Forest
Zoetropes
Hirohito
My Sunshine
Note

Michael Haslam   125
A Lubrick Loosened
Ovidian Slips
Note

Michael Vince   127
Goddess
Exchange of Population
The Crosses
Drive
As a Foreign Language
Note

Norm Sibum   128
Shakespeare in Verona
Note

Robert Wells   130
The Iran-Iraq War
The Fawn
After the Fire
Six Emblems
Bather and Horseshoe
Note

Neil Powell   131
Afternoon Dawn
The Way Back
The Bridge
The Stones on Thorpeness Beach
Hundred River
Note

Denise Riley   133
Poem Beginning with a Line from Proverbs
Well all right
Lure, 1963
Dark Looks
Milk Ink
Problems of Horror
Note

Grevel Lindop   136
Recumbent Buddha at Polonnaruwa
The Welsh Poppy
Summer Pudding
Russet Apples
from Trojan Voices
Note

Vicki Raymond   137
The Legend of Julian
Ardent Spirits
Note

John Gallas   140
The Atatürk Factory
Cornelius Fidus
Two Thoughtful Poems
from Mustafa Orbaneja
from Tillo: The Arrest of Fatih Düz
Note

Marius Kociejowski   143
Coast
Note

Charles Boyle   144
Species
Alex in February
Timur the Lame
The Chess Player
I Didn't Mean to Kill my Husband
Note

Frank Kuppner   145
The Kuppneriad
Note

Alison Brackenbury   148
Rented Rooms
Constellations
Bookkeeping
The Queen's Funeral
After Beethoven
Note

Gregory Woods   149
Like a Shark's
Post Mortem
A Blind Man Looks at a Boy
Celibate
Warlord
Maker
'Sandpaper the sun'
'You can tell he wants'
'Offer him a drink'
'All the more tranquil for'
Note

John Burnside   151
Signal Stop, near Horsley
Halloween
Avoirdupois
Septuagesima
Aphasia in Childhood
Note

Carol Ann Duffy   153
Whoever she Was
Warming her Pearls
The Grammar of Light
Prayer
Mrs Midas

Michael Hulse   155
Burslem
Raffles Hotel
The Architecture of Air
Knowing
Note

Sujata Bhatt   157
Clara Westhoff to Rainer Maria Rilke
from Search for my Tongue
A Different History
Angels' Wings
The Stare
Note

Michael Hofmann   161
Kleist in Paris
Nights in the Iron Hotel
Author, Author
Sally
Postcard from Cuernavaca
For Gert Hofmann
Note

Stephen Romer   164
Higher Things
Coming Back
The Weight of it
The Work
Blocks & Scaffolds
Note

Ian McMillan   166
The Grimness: BBC Radio 4,
    Tuesday 8:30 pm
Halifax!
Mining Town
A Cliché Defines the Moment in a
    Poem about Language and
    Oppression
Postmodernist Summer Nights in the
    Dearne Valley
Note

Peter Sansom   168
The Folklore of Plants
Al & Clare Have Bought a Middle
    Terrace instead of being Married
I Opened the Door
January
To Leigh Hunt
Note

James Keery   171
Necessary Laziness
Distractions of March
How Many Streams Can You Rake
The Strength of a Rope
Grebe Lodge
Note

Chris McCully   172
Houses
Rain
Bede's Copyist
This
Some Say
Note

Iain Bamforth   175
Reluctance
The Water Tower
Lenz
Open Workings
Mountains and Valleys

Vona Groarke   176
Patronage
Rindown
Figures on a Cliff
Home
A Tree Called the Balm of Gilead
Note

Justin Quinn   178
To Jan Neruda
Two Political Poems
Note

Miles Champion   180
from Butterfly Knot
The Tenth Chaffinch
Note

Sophie Hannah   182
Early Bird Blues
Mad Queen Hospital
One-Track Mind
Ghazal
The Mystery of the Missing
A Fairly Universal Set
Hotels like Houses
Note

Sinéad Morrissey   184
Clothes
Awaiting Burial
Saturday
The Juggler
Belfast Storm
After the Hurricane
Among Communists

Adam Schwartzman   185
The Legitimizing World
Sunday School
Beach Drive
The Sanctuary
Bertrams Suburb
Note

Contents

EDGELL RICKWORD

The Soldier Addresses His Body
I shall be mad if you get smashed about;
we've had good times together, you and I;
although you groused a bit when luck was out,
and a girl turned us down, or we went dry.

Yet there's a world of things we haven't done,
countries not seen, where people do strange things;
eat fish alive, and mimic in the sun
the solemn gestures of their stone-grey kings.

I've heard of forests that are dim at noon
where snakes and creepers wrestle all day long;
where vivid beasts grow pale with the full moon,
gibber and cry, and wail a mad old song;

because at the full moon the Hippogriff
with crinkled ivory snout and agate feet,
with his green eye will glare them cold and stiff
for the coward Wyvern to come down and eat

Vodka and kvass, and bitter mountain wines
we've never drunk, nor snatched at bursting grapes
to pelt slim girls among Sicilian vines,
who'd flicker through the leaves, faint frolic shapes.

Yes, there's a thousand things we haven't done,
but it's a sweat to knock them into rhyme,
let's have a drink, and give the cards a run
and leave dull verse to the dull peaceful time.

Winter Warfare
Colonel Cold strode up the Line
(tabs of rime and spurs of ice);
stiffened all that met his glare:
horses, men, and lice.

Visited a forward post,
left them burning, ear to foot;
fingers stuck to biting steel,
toes to frozen boot.

Stalked on into No Man's Land,
turned the wire to fleecy wool,
iron stakes to sugar sticks
snapping at a pull.

Those who watched with hoary eyes
saw two figures gleaming there;
Hauptman Kalte, Colonel Cold,
gaunt in the grey air.

Stiffly, tinkling spurs, they moved,
glassy eyed, with glinting heel
stabbing those who lingered there
torn by screaming steel.

Rimbaud in Africa
In the character of the damned conjurer

Through my small town I roamed, a taunting ghost
out of a world like rock and wind to yours,
and counted friends and honour nothing lost
to feed the inner pride that burned my hours.

Faustus, whom your academy once crowned,
spent midnight oil on ill-spelt smutty books;
your approbation's dirty insult drowned
in comradeship with idiots and crooks.

Beauty is epicene, whipped slave to show,
yet Helen swan-like glided to his bed,
whom he put scornfully away as though
he sought no pleasure in the life he led.

Such hot disdain scorched desert solitude
around him, where he practised magic art;
from elemental soul sublimed a crude
companion who would share no human heart.

All the devotion of his spirit yearned
on this frail vessel and refined its clay
till with slow eyes it answered him and turned
his pride to wings and went its lonely way.

Now Faustus in the desert trades for gold,
nations acknowledge his peculiar spell;
an utter silence feeds the pride grown old;
respect is mockery and sharpens hell.

The Encounter
Twittingpan seized my arm, though I'd have gone
willingly. To be seen with him alone,
the choicest spirit of the present age,
flattered my vanity into quite a rage.
His was the presence always in dispute
by every cocktail hostess of repute;
and I'd long enjoyed seeing his drooping form
breast each successive, new-aesthetic storm.
He had championed Epstein, Gertrude, and *Parade*,
and even now was nothing of a die-hard;
(I had last heard him on some Red-film show-day
expounding *tonal montage* in the foyer);
being two days nimbler than the smartest clique
he gave the cachet to the safest chic.

We turned from Regent Street to Conduit Street.
He thought my overcoat was far from neat,
offered his tailor's name and then forgot.
His mind was in a turmoil and overshot
immediate objects in transcendent aims.
Juggling voluptuously with Christian names
he listed for me each new partnership
contracted since I'd given Town the slip
for ten days in the wilds near Sevenoaks;
and Lord! I thought, no wonder Douglas[1] croaks
imminent fire and brimstone; though no Prudhomme,
I could never quite regret the fate of Sodom.

This intellectual athlete next began
praising the freedom of the modern man
from dogma, morals, and the plagues of nature –
a scientific, half-angelic creature,
immune from all – my hero almost winces –
Tokyo is down, but dancing's on at Prince's.
He summed up briefly all religion means
and then explained the universe by Jeans.
Burly Jack Haldane next supplied his text
(and as the Sacred Writ is always vext
into queer meanings for sectarian ends),
Twittingpan preached the marriage of true friends
when blessed parthenogenesis arrives
and he-uranians can turn honest wives.

'Consider Bond Street,' as we reached it, cried
falsetto Twittingpan our period's pride,
'Does it not realise in microcosm
the whole ideal Time nurses in its bosom?
Luxury, cleanliness and objets d'art,
the modern Trinity for us all who are
freed from the burden of the sense of sin.
Lord Russell says…' I feared he would begin
an exposition of the free man's worship,
that neo-anabaptist, compelled to dip
not now from mystic but hygienic motives.
'But look, in Shank's shop the Past still lives;
those gross utensils symbolically bind us
to the brute part we soon shall leave behind us,
for Haldane promises in the world-to-come
excretion's inoffensive minimum.'
He gestured freely and grew inquiring stares
from elegant shoppers wrapped like dainty bears,
whilst I blushed like a country cousin come
to the Time-metropolis from an archaic home.
He saw my red cheeks, and with a kindly air
proclaimed sophistication everywhere.
'You must meet Iris, she who lives serene
in the intense confession of the obscene
and drags her tea-time sex-affair all fresh
to the dinner-table, like a cat with flesh.
Her new book is, I hear, just too, *too* topical,
though Janet's peeved not to be in it at all.
But Basil's poems are far more utter than
you can imagine, as you don't know the man.'

With that he handed me a deckled sheet
where these lines staggered on uncertain feet:
    you the one onely
    not more but one than
    two is superfluous two is
    i reminds you of me
    me reminds i of you
    i is another
    identity unidentifiable
    then say is love not
    the word
    all love is perhaps no love
    or is perhaps luck
    or no luck is no love rather.

'Chaste, isn't it? And yes, I must explain
that I inspired it, at risk of seeming vain;
otherwise you might miss its fine notations
which do convey so subtly my relations
with the dear fellow. You two must really meet;
he would impress you even in the street.'
I fixed my look at 'silent admiration'
and paced along all tense with expectation,
though bashful at my Siamese-like linking
with the lank oracle of modern thinking.
'Lewis and Middleton Murry are, I'm sure,
the only moderns likely to endure
of the older crowd; for Eliot's later works
are merely sanctimonious quips and quirks;
and Huxley is portentously obsessed
with the problems that make City clerks depressed.
Don't you think Wyndham Lewis too divine?
That brute male strength he shows in every line!
I swear if he'd flogged me in his last book but one,
as some kind person informed me he has done,
I'd have forgiven him for the love of art.
And you, too, ought to take his works to heart
as I have done, for torn by inner strife,
I've made him mentor of my mental life.
You cannot imagine what a change that worked.
I who was all emotion, and always shirked
the cold chaste isolation of male mind,
now thrust in front all I had kept behind.
I'd lived in Time and Motion and Sensation.
then smashed my watch and burnt the
                      Bloomsbury *Nation*…

But here comes Clarence, – Clarence with Basil!.' So
like a hot poker then he let my arm go;
and, stifling jealousy, hailed them with 'How nice!'
They flaunted gay shirts and a grand old vice.
Poor Twittingpan had no novelty to produce;
I was not shabby enough to be of use
as a quaint genius, nor smart enough for friend.
Poor wretch! To put his agony at an end
I touched my hat, *good-day, sir*-ed, like a tout,
and left my Twittingpan to lie it out.

1 James, not Norman. A vice-hound and high-brow baiter employed by the *Sunday Express*.

Rhapsody on Red Admirals
That March the cottage was alive with wings.
They yearned for the garden, fluttered on the panes.
'Cannot you see there are no leaves yet,
    and rime whitens the twigs?
Stay in here where the convector heater
makes mimic Eden as the walls' bogus blooms
shed velvety petals down till ankle high.
Let your tawny images float in her deep eyes
till we've forgotten autumnal storms must rage.
Only each busy heart, tapping the breast,
links us with time and travail, seasons, grief –
when your shrivelled husks shall litter dusty sills.'

Edgell Rickword

Note *by Beatrix Hammarling*
In selecting five poems by Edgell Rickword, I have tried to choose something that represents each of his main collections.

'The Soldier Addresses His Body' and 'Winter Warfare' are both war poems from the collection *Behind the Eyes*, which was published in 1921. 'Rimbaud in Africa' is from *Invocation to Angels* published in 1928 and perhaps his best collection. (Edgell had earlier written a biography and critical study of Rimbaud.) 'The Encounter' is from his last main collection, *Twittingpan*, published in 1931, a collection of satirical poems. Finally, mainly for sentimental reasons, I have included an example of his later poems, 'Rhapsody on Red Admirals' which was published in 1976 with the dedication 'The Butterflies are for Beatrix.'

LAURA RIDING

The Sweet Ascetic
Find me the thing to make me less
Delivered to my earthliness,
Some rarer love to live upon,
A berry grown in Avalon,
Something that will, in this emprise,
Suffice me to etherealize
The coarser strain and purify
The flesh that had preferred to die.

Find me this thing and plant it near
My garden gate so that some day,
When I am going out of it,
I'll stoop to pick the ripest bit
And, humming as I walk away,
Smile just a little and disappear.

No More Are Lovely Palaces
No more are lovely palaces
And Taj-Mahal is old.
The listening tenements,
The wakeful entertainments,
Waited wide and many ages
For the spirits of the promises
That more than men would come,
Would come the visitants evoked
By lovely palaces
And such emblazoned places
Men would never light for men.

A little surer now you know
They do not come the way you go.
And better build you and more soberly –
Houses fitter for you to leave
Than to receive
The more than haughty hosts
Of the imperishable ghosts,
That swing death's doors
And suck you into topless palaces,
Untrembling on the blowing bluish spaces,
Where you gasp out your gratitude
And say breathless;
Heaven's hand is not gentle,
The lovely palaces were too lovely,
True lavish is the terrible.

Back to the Mother Breast
Back to the mother breast
In another place –
Not for milk, not for rest,
But the embrace
Clean bone
Can give alone.

The cushioning years
Afraid of closer kiss
Put cure of tears
Before analysis;
And the vague infant cheek
Turned away to speak.

Now back to the mother breast,
The later lullaby exploring,
The deep bequest
And franker singing
Out of the part
Where there is no heart.

As Well as Any Other
As well as any other, Erato,
I can dwell separately on what we know
In common secrecy,
And celebrate the old, adoréd rose,
Retell – oh why – how similarly grows
The last leaf of the tree.

But for familiar sense what need can be
Of my most singular device or me,
If homage may be done
(Unless it is agreed we shall not break
The patent silence for mere singing's sake)
As well by anyone?

Mistrust me not, then, if I have begun
Unwontedly and if I seem to shun
Unstrange and much-told ground:
For in peculiar earth alone can I
Construe the word and let the meaning lie
That rarely may be found.

The Troubles of a Book
The trouble of a book is first to be
No thoughts to nobody,
Then to lie as long unwritten
As it will lie unread,
Then to build word for word an author
And occupy his head
Until the head declares vacancy
To make full publication
Of running empty.

The trouble of a book is secondly
To keep awake and ready
And listening like an innkeeper,
Wishing, not wishing for a guest,
Torn between hope of no rest
And hope of rest.
Uncertainly the pages doze
And blink open to passing fingers
With landlord smile, then close.

The trouble of a book is thirdly
To speak its sermon, then look the other way,
Arouse commotion in the margin,
Where tongue meets the eye,
But claim no experience of panic,
No complicity in the outcry.
The ordeal of a book is to give no hint
Of ordeal, to be flat and witless
Of the upright sense of print.

The trouble of a book is chiefly
To be nothing but book outwardly;
To wear binding like binding,
Bury itself in book-death,
Yet to feel all but book;
To breathe live words, yet with the breath
Of letters; to address liveliness
In reading eyes, be answered with
Letters and bookishness.

The Wind Suffers
The wind suffers of blowing,
The sea suffers of water,
And fire suffers of burning,
And I of a living name.

As stone suffers of stoniness,
As light of its shiningness,
As birds of their wingedness,
So I of my whoness.

And what the cure of all this?
What the not and not suffering?
What the better and later of this?
What the more me of me?

How for the pain-world to be
More world and no pain?
How for the old rain to fall
More wet and more dry?

How for the wilful blood to run
More salt-red and sweet-white?
And how for me in my actualness
To more shriek and more smile?

By no other miracles,
By the same knowing poison,
By an improved anguish,
By my further dying.

Earth
Have no wide fears for Earth:
Its universal name is 'Nowhere'.
If it is Earth to you, that is your secret.
The outer records leave off there,
And you may write it as it seems,
And as it seems, it is,
A seeming stillness
Amidst seeming speed.

Heavens unseen, or only seen,
Dark or bright space, unearthly space,
Is a time before Earth was
From which you inward move
Toward perfect now.

Almost the place it is not yet,
Potential here of everywhere –
Have no wide fears for it:
Its destiny is simple,
To be further what it will be.

Earth is your heart
Which has become your mind
But still beats ignorance
Of all it knows –
As miles deny the compact present
Whose self-mistrusting past they are.
Have no wide fears for Earth:
Destruction only on wide fears shall fall.

The Way It Is
It falls to an idiot to talk wisely.
It falls to a sot to wear beauty.
It falls to many to be blessed
In their shortcomings,
As to the common brute it falls
To see real miracles
And howl with irksome joy.

Many are the confusions that fall,
Many are the inspired ones.
Much is there indeed contrary,
Much is there indeed wonderful.
A most improbable one it takes
To tell what is so,
And the strangest creature of all
To be natural.

Nor Is It Written
Nor is it written that you may not grieve.
There is no rule of joy, long may you dwell
Not smiling yet in that last pain,
On that last supper of the heart.
It is not written that you must take joy
Because not thus again shall you sit down
To ply the mingled banquet
Which the deep larder of illusion shed
Like myth in time grown not astonishing.
Lean to the cloth awhile, and yet awhile,
And even may your eyes caress
Proudly the used abundance.

Laura Riding

It is not written in what heart
You may not pass from magic plenty
Into the straitened nowadays.
To each is given secrecy of heart,
To make himself what heart he please
In stirring up from that fond table
To sit him down at this sharp meal.
It shall not here be asked of him
'What thinks your heart?'

Long may you sorely to yourself upbraid
This truth unwild, this only-bread.
It is not counted what large passions
Your heart in ancient private keeps alive.
To each is given what defeat he will.

Note *by Robert Nye*
During the twenty years or so of her active poethood, Laura Riding said several things about the nature of poetry which illuminate not just poetry itself but her own practice of it. One of the most memorable and arresting comes at the beginning of her book of essays entitled *Contemporaries and Snobs* (Cape, 1928), where she declares: 'There is a sense of life so real that it becomes the sense of something more real than life... It is the meaning at work in what has no meaning; it is, at its clearest, poetry.' A decade later, introducing her *Collected Poems* (Cassell, 1938), she referred to a poem as 'an uncovering of truth of so fundamental and general a kind that no other name besides poetry is adequate except truth.' Both definitions bespeak a seriousness regarding the poetic vocation which might be rated rare in any century. Both definitions also bespeak a faith in poetry so high, intense and whole-hearted that Laura Riding's silence as a poet after a certain point could be imagined to betoken a mystery... Respecting this decision as one must, I would still remark that Laura Riding's poems seem to me to express what would be otherwise inexpressible, saying that which could not be said were it not for the moment of the poem and the medium of poetry. Her finest poems, moreover, seem to me those in which she makes discovery as she writes, poems in which the heart's and mind's truth comes more as something learned than something taught. Prose may be the medium for those who know what they mean before they say it, whereas in poetry there is never quite that degree of intention, the meaning being what the poet finds in the act of writing. Laura (Riding) Jackson's published post-poetic explanations of her own poems and her reasons for not writing more of them after 1939 leave out of account the involuntary nature of the poetic genius which she undoubtedly possessed.

E.J. SCOVELL

Reflecting on Old Age
We are as light as wood ash, dense as stone.
Our muscles come to know the weight of bone,
The sensual happiness of lying down.
A little milk the gradual years have pressed
Into our eyes that easily over-run.
Our vague hair is as volatile as dust.

Waking and sleep are mutual, so far on
In marriage that we speak of one alone,
Sleep without waking, as in a foreign tongue
Stumbling on consonants. Against the dark,
Coeval kindness, beneficence of the young
With our time's cares cross in a lattice-work.

Honey of small events, of passing states
We take – as when a light flame oscillates
In the smokeless coal, in the winter grate's
Rock garden it blows, translucent as a wild
Flower, as woodsorrel; or a bird's heart, it beats;
And gives peace, as if worlds were reconciled.

On the railway bank not only bracken, once,
I remember, but the dying grass was bronze
In transverse light; and beyond the journey, friends.
Happiness even passing imagination,
Foretold by straws of grass and bracken fronds,
Late in the day, their welcome at the station.

Too hard in age to trawl the heavy seas.
I settle for summations, instances,
Remembering (in time's interstices)
Time taken to sit in the tropic after-sun
In an open gallery, in hands cup or glass,
With two or three; here now, by a fire, with one.

A Portrait of a Boy
He frowns a little, facing the light.
The large leaves' shadows blot and camouflage
Him, laurel-shaped leaves and broad wings of poinsettia.

He has folded his arms, being eleven,
A proud age, and looks forward wholly directly
Out of the shadows, though he frowns a little

As if the light and the open prospect
Were adulthood, and he considering it
With all his attention, mustering all he can

Out of his leaf-pied childhood; and further
As if he were Man emergent from the forest
Of animal nature, Adam confronting his fate –

Knowledge, the shelterless light-washed spaces
Spread for him on and on – and bringing to bear
Consciousness: his integrity, all that he has.

Bright Margins
I thought of decoration, such as once was done
To frame a manuscript – how the finished work is one,
Cornflowers and gold are one with the marmoreal
Script, with the firm and sounding Latin words as well
And the meaning of the words – no meaning but a bell

Whose overtones dissolve its note that would be clear;
And thought again – in the wide borders of the year
Walking by blue and golden flowers and like the moon
Self-shadowed white, short-lived, in autumn garden beds
That are bright margins too – how they seem the silk of
    threads
Not woven in the cloth, embroideries, not the words
Nor the meaning of the words; and still the work is one.

The Paschal Moon
At four this April morning the Easter moon –
Some days to full, awkwardly made, yet of brazen
Beauty and power, near the north-west horizon
Among our death-white street lamps going down –
I wondered to see it from a lower storey
Netted in airy twigs; and thought, a fire
A mile off, or what or who? But going higher
I freed it (to my eyes) into its full glory,
Dominant, untouched by roofs, from this height seen
Unmeshed from budding trees; not silver-white
But brazed or golden. Our fluorescent light,
That can change to snow a moment of young green
In the maple tree, showed ashen, null and dead
Beside such strength, such presence as it had.

The Evening Garden
Not dark nor light but clear,
But lucid with no source of light,
But breathing with no flow of air
The garden journeys into night.

Late gangling flowers lean –
Anemones, tobacco flowers –
Over the gravel, over the brown
And silken leaves that mulch the grass.

More than I did, I now
Leave in this lighted room undrawn
The curtains. More than it used to do
The garden presses on the pane,

Or seems it does, in this
One hour when all is seeming, when
It wars with shadowy lights in the glass,
And losing, is most potent then –

Only in this one hour,
Tidal, returns – day's utmost edge –
Pressing with eyes of question or power,
Gold wild-cat eyes on the window-ledge.

Walled plot of fruit-trees, flowers,
What strength it wields, how hard it bears!
Why should it not bear hard? It has
Behind it all the universe.

The lighted room is small.
Now we exist; and now we fashion
A garden and a girdling wall,
Our salient into wild creation.

Note
These poems are chosen from the later years of my life, because they seem to illustrate best what I think is a central theme of much lyric poetry, including mine. This is the kind of poetry that arises when something seen or felt or imagined, some item of existence, is apprehended as completely itself and at the same time as embodying a reality beyond and far wider than itself – as speaking for some large generality; yet this can often only be expressed through faithfulness to the particular. So I keep a distant ideal of objectivity even when the 'object' may be a subjective feeling or thought, and at times I envy representational painters their necessary commitment to the concrete and visible.

   I have also all my life loved metre and rhyme and the attempt to use them, and have sometimes thought of the two activities of expressing and making as the two axes of a graph between which, responding to both, the poem must find its way. Of course the analogy is a very limited one; in the happiest poetry expressing and making are not distinguishable.

SORLEY MACLEAN

Calvary
My eye is not on Calvary
nor on Bethlehem the Blessed,
but on a foul-smelling backland in Glasgow,
where life rots as it grows;
and on a room in Edinburgh,
a room of poverty and pain,
where the diseased infant
writhes and wallows till death.

A Highland Woman
Hast Thou seen her, great Jew,
who are called the One Son of God?
Hast Thou seen on Thy way the like of her
labouring in the distant vineyard?

The load of fruits on her back,
a bitter sweat on brow and cheek,
and the clay basin heavy on the back
of her bent poor wretched head.

Thou hast not seen her, Son of the carpenter,
who art called the King of Glory,
among the rugged western shores
in the sweat of her food's creel.

This Spring and last Spring
and every twenty Springs from the beginning,
she has carried the cold seaweed
for her children's food and the castle's reward.

And every twenty Autumns gone
she has lost the golden summer of her bloom,
and the Black Labour has ploughed the furrow
across the white smoothness of her forehead.

And Thy gentle church has spoken
about the lost state of her miserable soul,
and the unremitting toil has lowered
her body to a black peace in a grave.

And her time has gone like a black sludge
seeping through the thatch of a poor dwelling:
the hard Black Labour was her inheritance;
grey is her sleep tonight.

The Cry of Europe
Girl of the yellow, heavy-yellow, gold-yellow hair,
the song of your mouth and Europe's shivering cry,
fair, heavy-haired, spirited, beautiful girl,
the disgrace of our day would not be bitter in your kiss.

Would your song and splendid beauty take
from me the dead loathsomeness of these ways,
the brute and the brigand at the head of Europe
and your mouth red and proud with the old song?

Would white body and forehead's sun take
from me the foul black treachery,
spite of the bourgeois and poison of their creed
and the feebleness of our dismal Scotland?

Would beauty and serene music put
from me the sore frailty of this lasting cause,
the Spanish miner leaping in the face of horror
and his great spirit going down untroubled?

What would the kiss of your proud mouth be
compared with each drop of the precious blood
that fell on the cold frozen uplands
of Spanish mountains from a column of steel?

What every lock of your gold-yellow head
to all the poverty, anguish and grief
that will come and have come on Europe's people
from the Slave Ship to the slavery of the whole people?

Dogs and Wolves
Across eternity, across its snows
I see my unwritten poems,
I see the spoor of their paws dappling
the untroubled whiteness of the snow:
bristles raging, bloody-tongued,
lean greyhounds and wolves
leaping over the tops of the dykes,
running under the shade of the trees of the wilderness,
taking the defile of narrow glens,
making for the steepness of windy mountains;
their baying yell shrieking
across the hard barenesses of the terrible times,
their everlasting barking in my ears,
their onrush seizing my mind:
career of wolves and eerie dogs
swift in pursuit of the quarry,
through the forests without veering,
over the mountain tops without sheering;
the mild mad dogs of poetry,
wolves in chase of beauty,
beauty of soul and face,
a white deer over hills and plains,
the deer of your gentle beloved beauty,
a hunt without halt, without respite.

Heroes
I did not see Lannes at Ratisbon
nor MacLennan at Auldearn
nor Gillies MacBain at Culloden,
but I saw an Englishman in Egypt.

A poor little chap with chubby cheeks
and knees grinding each other,
pimply unattractive face –
garment of the bravest spirit.

He was not a hit 'in the pub
in the time of the fists being closed,'
but a lion against the breast of battle,
in the morose wounding showers.

His hour came with the shells,
with the notched iron splinters,
in the smoke and flame,
in the shaking and terror of the battlefield.

Word came to him in the bullet shower
that he should be a hero briskly,
and he was that while he lasted
but it wasn't much time he got.

He kept his guns to the tanks,
bucking with tearing crashing screech,
until he himself got, about the stomach,
that biff that put him to the ground,
mouth down in sand and gravel,
without a chirp from his ugly high-pitched voice.

No cross or medal was put on his
chest or to his name or to his family;
there were not many of his troops alive,
and if there were their word would not be strong.
And at any rate, if a battle post stands
many are knocked down because of him,
not expecting fame, not wanting a medal
or any froth from the mouth of the field of slaughter.

I saw a great warrior of England,
a poor manikin on whom no eye would rest;
no Alasdair of Glen Garry;
and he took a little weeping to my eyes.

Hallaig
'Time, the deer, is in the wood of Hallaig'

The window is nailed and boarded
through which I saw the West
and my love is at the Burn of Hallaig,
a birch tree, and she has always been

between Inver and Milk Hollow,
here and there about Baile-chuirn:
she is a birch, a hazel,
a straight, slender young rowan.

In Screapadal of my people
where Norman and Big Hector were,
their daughters and their sons are a wood
going up beside the stream.

Proud tonight the pine cocks
crowing on the top of Cnoc an Ra,
straight their backs in the moonlight –
they are not the wood I love.

I will wait for the birch wood
until it comes up by the cairn,
until the whole ridge from Beinn na Lice
will be under its shade.

If it does not, I will go down to Hallaig,
to the Sabbath of the dead,
where the people are frequenting,
every single generation gone.

They are still in Hallaig,
MacLeans and MacLeods,
all who were there in the time of Mac Gille Chaluim
the dead have been seen alive.

The men lying on the green
at the end of every house that was,
the girls a wood of birches,
straight their backs, bent their heads.

Between the Leac and Fearns
the road is under mild moss
and the girls in silent bands
go to Clachan as in the beginning,

and return from Clachan
from Suisnish and the land of the living;
each one young and light-stepping,
without the heartbreak of the tale.

From the Burn of Fearns to the raised beach
that is clear in the mystery of the hills,
there is only the congregation of the girls
keeping up the endless walk,

coming back to Hallaig in the evening,
in the dumb living twilight,
filling the steep slopes,
their laughter a mist in my ears,

and their beauty a film on my heart
before the dimness comes on the kyles,
and when the sun goes down behind Dun Cana
a vehement bullet will come from the gun of Love;

and will strike the deer that goes dizzily,
sniffing at the grass-grown ruined homes;
his eye will freeze in the wood,
his blood will not be traced while I live.

Note
Excessive reading of history in my early teens and the strictest of Calvinist Fundamentalism in my environment in my childhood made me expect the worse to happen for the great masses of people in this life and in eternity, and out of this came, in 1938, 'A Highland Woman'. It was still the Great Depression and I had seen the very worst days of it from 1929 to 1934, in Edinburgh and in Glasgow, as the little poem 'Calvary' indicates. Besides I had seen from my earliest childhood so many Highland and Island women prematurely aged by hard work in the fields because their men folk had to be away at fishing or seasonal occupations for much of the year. The poem was written in Mull, an island pitifully devastated in the seventeenth century by its Jacobite Royalism and in the nineteenth century by Clearances, but it was very beautiful and had been the land of the people whom Neil Munro called 'the proud MacLeans'.

'The Cry of Europe' was written after 'A Highland Woman', late in 1938 or early in 1939, at any rate after Munich, which made me expect that Fascism was to take over Europe even without a great war. In 1936 I had told my noble-minded friend Jack Stuart that because of family circumstances I could not go to Spain with him, but in August 1937 I was introduced to an Irish Catholic girl by one of my greatest friends. I understood from him that he wanted to marry her himself and I held off, but realised that if it were only a question of Spain or that girl, it would be the girl. She was a Gael, a fine singer and a player on the Clarsach, and from what my friend told me there was a nobleness about her. I was disturbed by my own lack of single-mindedness. The rhythm of the poem is, as far as I know, original and spontaneous. That itself is important to me.

'Dogs and Wolves' is a tragic poem, but the tragedy of it is not primarily mine. In December 1939 a girl told me that she had been terribly unfortunate three years before that time. Less than a week later I got out of bed about three in the morning and wrote down two poems as fast as I could. The first is a bad poem, the second is 'Dogs and Wolves'. I am still convinced I composed both in a dream, or between sleeping and waking, as the conclusion of my long poem 'The Cuillin' was. It came a night or two later than 'Dogs and Wolves'. They both have a kind of surrealist spontaneity, a welling from the subconscious, and partly because of that I think them important.

'Heroes' was not published until long after it was written because I did not like something in it, which I suppressed. I think some war poems benefit from pre-war matter. The poem is allusive. Alasdair of Glengarry was not Scott's friend or of

Raeburn's portrait, but one who died about 1720 and had a spate of elegies, the finest of which is by a relative, Julia of Keppoch, It begins and ends, 'Alasdair of Glengarry, today you brought weeping to my eyes.' Lannes was Napoleon's Marshal, one of those noted for his courage. Gillies MacBain was second-in-command of the Clan Chattan at Culloden. His feats were prodigious. MacLennan was Seaforth's banner-man at Auldearn. He refused when ordered to retreat, saying that the banner had never gone back in the hands of one of his family. The poem has much of my feeling of the cruelties of Nature and of circumstances. Of course it is not anti-English. I saw many Englishmen in Libya who were as splendid in physique as they were in courage.

'Hallaig' was written in 1952 or 1953. The place is in Rassay and is very beautiful. It was cleared of crofters about 1852 to make way for one sheep-farmer. Where there were people and cattle there are now resurgent native woods and bracken. Hallaig, the place, evokes feelings of permanence, what was is always, and there is the dichotomy symbolised by the deer of transience. The poem is doubly, and sometimes trebly symbolist, and I think it is full of the sadness of all human existence.

[The poems are printed here in English translations which Sorley Maclean himself has made from the Scots Gaelic originals.]

F.T. PRINCE

from **The Old Age of Michelangelo** *(1954)*
… For you must know I am of all men ever born
Most inclined to love persons, and whenever I see someone
Who has gifts of mind and body, and can say or show me
                                          something
Better than the rest,
Straightway I am compelled
To fall in love with him, and then I give myself
Up to him so completely, I belong no longer to myself,
He wresting from me
So great part of my being, I am utterly
Bewildered and distraught, and for many days know nothing
Of what I am doing or where I am…

                    *

– I am always alone, I speak to no one
But that shabby Bernardo, nor do I wish to:
Trudging up and down Italy, wearing out my shoes and life,
Toiling still to grow poorer, ugly, sad,
Proud, narrow, full of unfulfilled desires!

Yet I have come to Rome, rich in its ruins, and for the last
                                          time,
As if I made to cross a little stream dry-foot
That had divided us, and yet again for the last time
My dream grows drunk within me,
And opens its great wings and like an eagle
Wild naked perfect pure, soars from its nest.
Almost I am persuaded, almost, that it is possible,
My love, like anybody's love, is possible.
My eye stares on your face, and my old mind
Soars naked from its cliff, and thinks to find
– Drunk with illumination as the sky itself is drunken
Or a dry river-bed with light –
The wild path to its thought…

At Beaulieu
Tall oaks are
Speckled yellow
At the edges,
By that grey wreck
De Bello
Loco Regis

And there on view
Is what they
Call a heart-
coffin for two:
Crumbled away
In part,

Two cells or
Cavities
In a stone block,
Are as for
Heart's ease
Cut to interlock;

And still insconce
One green-
glazed broken cup,
Where a heart once
Had been
Closed and laid up.

from **Drypoints of the Hasidim** *(1975)*
To believe is above all to be in love,
And suffer as men do who are in love…

                    *

But they are telling stories,
    Stories of kings and sons of kings

Of hidden just men who could be Messiahs
    Had they not put away the thought;
Rays, glimpses in shadow
                    and that sweetness –
    Love justice sonship brotherhood –
Which makes the longing of the world:
                    Messiah son of Joseph,
Who could be anywhere

    a youth half-grown
  Born anywhere in Hungary or Poland
 – Perhaps the boy of seventeen
Who had undoubtedly been seen
 In Buda, with a threadbare coat

And face of an amazing starlike purity

       *

  Hayyim of Zans who liked to talk
To market-people, would tell of one who said:

'Good sir, I have got nothing of life.
  I spend my time day after day
Jogging and shuttling to and fro from Hanipol
  To Brod
    and climbing in and out of carts,
And being thought a cheat.
  But what is this when one considers

'How beyond boredom and disgust, how sweet it is
  To be able to know and say
I can enter any night or day
     myself
  In my nakedness before the Holy One:

'To bathe in God, to pray'

from **The Yüan Chên Variations** *(1981)*
Po Chü-i (772-846) looks back over the beginnings of his life-long friendship with Yüan Chên. After some years of study in the capital, Chinese scholar-poets would be sent to administer remote provinces.

A cheerless kingdom lay spread
for our latter days –
plains, mountain chains,
highroads, river-ways.
Bored by the rough and ill-bred,
we should take pains

and must face as commonplace
that we would lose
friends, all that mattered.
No one could choose,
when failure and good grace
equally scattered.

Yet our short time was cut.
You were insolent
they said, and should be sent
to cool, in Lan-t'ien –
make yourself useful, but
off there, unseen

After you left, a few tears.
Then, when you were, day
by day, further away,
I dreamt one night
you came, sad and in fears
that you could not write

A knocking woke me – 'Doo-n
doo-ng' – and there came
a letter in your name!
There you were thinking
and writing, the mountain moon
of Yang-Ch'êng sinking

You wrote by candle-light,
an exile's heartaches –

worst, that the road he takes
lacks friends: and ten
verses with moon, flower, midnight
said it again…

from **Walks in Rome** *(1987)*
A week in Rome breaking a journey from the Middle East combines memories of fifty years before with looking again at some familiar places.

Nahman of Bratslav says 'True
faith has no need to grapple
with evidence or research.
Faith comes through silence.'
I see that too,
and enter the French Church

We come here now for the chapel
by Caravaggio.
Christ on the left wall
points a finger to call
Matthew the money-changer –
sitting well-dressed, in no danger

On the right there is rage,
blood, death: in his old age
a naked killer bawling
has cut him down.
A boy wails, and an angel
dives with the martyr's crown

Another angel, behind
the altar between Calling
and Death, indites
the Gospel, and he writes,
looking up as in doubt
of his own mind

At both beginning and end,
grouped as bystanders,
gaudily-dressed idle young
cronies, well-fed parasites
and older panders,
lazily attend

Christ's face is mysterious,
oblique in the strong lights
and shadows. The dense
wild canvases
bully and in the end weary us
with ambiguities

So, feeling himself like us,
back of the murder-scene
Michelangelo Merisi
da Caravaggio
turning, about to go,
looks pale and queasy…

from **Family Mottoes** *(1990)*
(i)
Splendeo tritus
'I shine from use':

The name being Ferrers,
A horse-shoe
In the blazon
Plays on
That, as 'farriers'.

So, to pursue
Virtue in service
Wears the dull surface,
To reveal
The shine of steel.

(ii)
Lesses dire
'Let them talk':

The French alone
(And in that spelling)
Would have us know
That someone like a hawk
Up there, is free
To do and be,
And drop here
Like a stone
To kill;

While others dwelling
In the barnyard below
Will
Undoubtedly
Squawk.

The Other Cheek
Jamie, who is ten or so,
Says 'Gaffer, do you know
I've grown,
And now it's clear
That I'm a freak.
You see, I have five
Cheeks. I've
Two up here,
And two below
Which I can show:
And then I have a cheek
All of my own.'

Note
Some of my best poems are long by the standards of twentieth-century readers, running to 100 lines in earlier books and 300 or more later. These are symphonic pieces, and need to be read or heard in full, not in excerpts.

It is not easy, in any case, to choose from a collected volume covering sixty years. I have found myself feeling cool towards the young and middle-aged poet, and chosen from the vantage-point of what I have written over the last twenty-five years. (Since 1988 I have been able to write only short poems.)

For me, poetry has to aim at continuous sound, and continuous sense. Continuous sound implies verse, however 'free' or unconventional. Continuous sense can hardly nowadays be limited to the rational mode of the Augustans; but if we define it as sustained or coherent *intention*, it has been vital to the ordering and structure of my longer poems.

These longer poems began by being dramatic monologues, following the Pound/Eliot revival and liberation of the Victorian 'realistic' monologue established by Browning. 'My Last Duchess' or 'Andrea del Sarto', for example, are compressed costume dramas, in which a realistic speaker in a precise setting reveals himself and the 'story', often to a silent listener. Eliot's 'Gerontion' has a realistic speaker in a sordid realistic setting, the old man in a rented house, but he reveals himself and the 'story' in discontinuous thoughts, memories, comments and flashes of vision. There is a musical unity, but the verse is as broken as the 'story', combining Poundian rhythms (as in *Cathay*) with Jacobean dramatic eloquence.

The liberated dramatic monologue led me to poems containing elements of narrative, comment and quoted speech. So in *Drypoints of the Hasidim*, sayings and anecdotes from Martin Buber's collections are built into a picture and interpretation of the original Hasidic movement (an interpretation which had to be constructed from the outside, and could only be personal).

One of my qualifications as a poet is, I believe, a feeling for the sound and movement of words. But I find this is not in itself a source of inspiration; it has to be mobilised by 'subject-matter' – emotions, ideas, experiences. And my subject-matter is obviously merely human, not cerebral – everything that I have heard dismissed by tough-minded Americans as 'Love and Death' and 'Italian Opera', and that is regarded with distaste by many of our own *literati*.

I have always been wary of the generally accepted prosody of English verse from Surrey to Bridges, and tried in various ways to escape from it or stretch it. After experimenting with Bridges' syllabics, I invented a new metre in 1981 (in 'The Yüan Chên Variations'): this combines a syllabic discipline (lines from four syllables to seven) with rhyme. Both elements are essential. *Walks in Rome* uses the same metre more flexibly, and its influence appears in other later poems.

ANNE RIDLER

A Matter of Life and Death
I did not see the iris move,
I did not feel the unfurling of my love.

This was the sequence of the flower:
First the leaf from which the bud would swell,
No prison, but a cell,
A rolled rainbow;
Then the sheath that enclosed the blow
Pale and close
Giving no hint of the blaze within,
A tender skin with violet vein.
Then the first unfurling petal
As if a hand that held a jewel
Curled back a finger, let the light wink
Narrowly through the chink,
Or like the rays before the sunrise
Promising glory.

And while my back is turned, the flower has blown.
Impossible to tell
How this opulent blossom from that spick bud has grown.
The chrysalis curled tight,
The flower poised for flight –
Corolla with lolling porphyry wings
And yellow tiger markings
A chasing-place for shade and light:
Between these two, the explosion
Soundless, with no duration.
   (I did not see the iris move,
   I did not feel my love unfurl.)
The most tremendous change takes place in silence,
Unseen, however you mark the sequence,
Unheard, whatever the din of exploding stars.

Down the porphyry stair
Headlong into the air
The boy has come: he crouches there
A tender startled creature
With a fawn's ears and hair-spring poise
Alert to every danger
Aghast at every noise.
A blue blink
From under squeezed-up lids
As mauve as iris buds
Is gone as quickly as a bird's bright wink.
Gone – but as if his soul had looked an instant
   through the chink.
And perfect as his shell-like nails,
Close as are to the flower its petals,
My love unfolded with him.
Yet till this moment what was he to me?
Conjecture and analogy;
Conceived, and yet unknown;
Behind this narrow barrier of bone
Distant as any foreign land could be.

I have seen the light of day,
Was it sight or taste or smell?
What I have been, who can tell?
What I shall be, who can say?

He floats in life as a lily in the pool
Free and yet rooted;
And strong though seeming frail,
Like the ghost fritillary
That trails its first-appearing bud
As though too weak to raise it from the mud,
But is stronger than you dream,
And soon will lift its paper lantern
High upon an arched and sinewy stem.

His smiles are all largesse,
Need ask for no return,
Since give and take are meaningless
To one who gives by needing
And takes our love for granted
And grants a favour even by his greed.
The ballet of his twirling hands
His chirping and his loving sounds,
Perpetual expectation
Perpetual surprise –
Not a lifetime satisfies
For watching, every thing he does
We wish him to do always.

   Only in a lover's eyes
   Shall I be so approved again;
   Only the other side of pain
   Can truth again be all I speak,
   Or I again possess
   A saint's hilarious carelessness.

He rows about his ocean
With its leaning cliffs and towers,
A horizontal being,
Straddled by walking people
By table-legs and chairs;
And sees the world as you can see
Upside-down in water
The wavering heights of trees
Whose roots hang from your eyes.
Then Time begins to trail
In vanishing smoke behind him,
A vertical creature now
With a pocket full of nails,
One of a gang of urchin boys
Who proves his sex by robber noise –
Roar of the sucking dove
And thunder of the wren.
Terror waits in the woods
But in the sun he is brazen
Because our love is his
No matter what he does;
His very weakness claims a share
In the larger strength of others,
And perfect in our eyes
He is only vulnerable there.

But not immortal there, alas.
We cannot keep, and see. The shapes of clouds
Which alter as we gaze
Are not more transient than these living forms
Which we so long to hold
For ever in the moment's mould.
The figures frozen in the camera's record
And carried with us from the past
Are like those objects buried with the dead –
Temporal treasures irrelevant to their need.
Yes, this is the worst:
The living truth is lost,
And is supplanted by these album smiles.

> *What you desire to keep, you slay:*
> *While you watch me, I am going.*
> *Wiser than you, I would not stay*
> *Even if I could: my hope's in growing.*
> *My form as a dapple of sun that flies*
> *On the brook, is changed; my earliest word*
> *Is the call you learnt to recognize*
> *And now forget, of a strange bird.*

Yet, as the calyx contains the life of the bud
So the bud is contained within the flower
Though past in time:
The end is not more true than the beginning,
Nor is the promise cancelled by the prime.
Not only what he was, and is, but what he might have been,
In each is rolled within.
Our life depends on that:
What other claim have we to resurrection?
For now that we can contemplate perfection
We have lost the knack of being it. What should be saved
Of these distorted lives?

All we can pray is
               Save us from Nothingness.
Nothingness, which all men dread;
Which makes us feel an irrational pity for the dead,
And fight the anodyne
Even while we long for deliverance from pain.

So, I have read,
When a man gave his darling in grief to the grave
About her neck in a locket tied
He set this urgent word –
Not to drink Lethe, at all costs not to forget.
And this is truth to us, even yet.
For if life is eternal
All must be held, though all must be redeemed.
But what can ever restore
To these sad and short-coming lives of ours
The lovely jocund creatures that we were
And did not know we were?
What can give us at once
The being and the sense?

Why, each within
Has kept his secret for some Resurrection:
The wonder that he was
And can be, which is his
Not by merit, only by grace.
It comes to light, as love is born with a child,
Neither with help nor herald
(I did not see the iris move);
Neither by sight nor sound –
I did not feel the unfurling of my love.

The Freezing Rose

All wear the freezing rose
This winter season,
Like the flesh we carry
A common agony
The ground of joys and sorrows.

When all are covered so in glory
Who is to be proud
Who is to be bowed in shame?
Snow upon the roof-tree
Snow upon the leafing tree.

The shade covered with sapphire;
With white sleep the nursling:
His sappy fingers,
And withered kex of working hands,
As the sun descends,
With the same reflected fire.

'With my body I thee worship.'
This is to dispense with
Distrust of the sense
And of one's own ugliness:
The new-born, the warped and worn,
Beauty, suffering, splendour,
Bear this common shape.

And to love those
Is love without longing.
I make offering
Of what each one possesses –
The common, fallen rose.

Snakeshead Fritillaries

Some seedlings shoulder the earth away
Like Milton's lion plunging to get free,
Demanding notice. Delicate rare fritillary,
You enter creeping, like the snake
You're named for, and lay your ear to the ground.
The soundless signal comes, to arch the neck,
Losing the trampled look,
Follow the code for colour, whether
White or freckled with purple and pale –
A chequered dice-box, tilted over the soil,
The yellow dice held at the base.

When light slants before the sunset, this is
The proper time to watch fritillaries.
They enter creeping; you go on your knees,
The flowers level with your eyes,
And catch the dapple of sunlight through the petals.

Note

I have chosen 'A Matter of Life and Death' as offering 'the clearest introduction to my work', because I think that here my technique was most nearly adequate to cope with the ideas I wanted to express. I had been thinking about Eliot's views on the relation of poetry to music, and wondering whether such a construction as Sonata Form, with its subject, counter-subject, development, modulation, re-capitulation, could be applied to poetry. Deciding that the difference in the medium made this impossible, I nevertheless found that the ideas for the poem I wanted to write did present themselves in a way that was related to musical form, having a main theme developed, repeated and fragmented, and a counter-subject represented by the child's voice.

Stephen Spender saw this poem as the culmination of my long effort to write about children and infancy; I am grateful to him for saying so (in a letter), but I should be sorry if, by choosing to print it here, I may have reinforced the impression that I am just a poet of domesticity. I have chosen my second poem, 'The Freezing Rose' although there is a child in it also, because I hope that it belongs to a tradition of English verse which 'links common family joy and the high traditions of Neo-Platonic mysticism and Courtly Love', as Lesley Chamberlain describes it. Writing in the *Independent* one Christmas, she quoted my poem in this context, calling it 'a dual celebration of life and death, of the satisfaction of sensual love and its passing' – which was what I meant in writing of the snow as a symbol of our physical being and its transitoriness.

It was Geoffrey Grigson who said that everyone before he died should walk once in a fritillary field. I have planted the corms in my garden, and observed the disconcerting way the flowers have of looking on a first appearance as though someone had trodden on them. In this, as in other of my more recent, shorter poems, I have been less obsessed with musical effect, and more with the effort to convey the essence of a subject by minute observation.

GEORGE BARKER

Battersea Park
To Anne Ridler

Now it is November and mist wreathes the trees,
The horses cough their white blooms in the street,
Dogs shiver and boys run; the barges on the Thames
Lie like leviathans in the fog; and I meet
A world of lost wonders as I loiter in the haze
Where fog and sorrow cross my April days.

I recollect it was so often thus; with
Diamonds and pearls like mineral water pointing
The Park railings and the gardens' evergreens:
I spent my winters in summer's disappointments.
The things that burned so bright in my Augusts
Scattering me with their November dusts.

Now I marvel that I am again investigating
The fringes of the bare gardens in the winter.
I had expected to be otherwise now,
Where the worm coils about the bone's splinter.
Now what good is the great world where I walk
That only revives desire to live once more?

How in the fog of failure and distress
Glitter of things seen in a flicker can
Paralyse will and deter determination,
Make a man afraid of the ghost of a man.
It is the wile of the world of crystal things
That catch the eye and keep me in their rings.

What I saw was Sorrow loitering along by
The Thames near the tall bridge by Battersea Park;
He had in his hand Pavlova or a swan,
And I heard him singing softly in the dark:
My twin, he sang to me, whatever of thine
Is sad and sorry, shall be glad of mine.

And he went on, singing a gay tune.
And now I know that the sorrow is this,
Not that the world a space of sorrow is
But that it's glad. O so gay a grief!
How can I ever be at home here
Where Sorrow sings of Joy in my ear?

How can I ever be happy here, where
Cock robin whistles with a gun at his breast;
Here where the flower has for bud a tear,
Here where Beauty breeds fodder for the Beast?
How can I here be happy, when I know
I can be happy only here and now?

'Turn on your side and bear the day to me'
Turn on your side and bear the day to me
Beloved, sceptre-struck, immured
In the glass wall of sleep. Slowly
Uncloud the borealis of your eye
And show your iceberg secrets, your midnight prizes
To the green-eyed world and to me. Sin
Coils upward into thin air when you awaken
And again morning announces amnesty over
The serpent-kingdomed bed. Your mother
Watched with as dove an eye the unforgivable night
Sigh backward into innocence when you
Set a bright monument in her amorous sea.
Look down, Undine, on the trident that struck
Sons from the rock of vanity. Turn in the world
Sceptre-struck, spellbound, beloved,
Turn in the world and bear the day to me.

Elegy on the Death of Michael Roberts

How dare the greatest die? For whom else daily
    Will water and wilderness come down to us with bread?
Where is the hole in the world proud enough to keep
    Him deep in the grave of the gravelled dead:
While about his skull, coiling, the unsaid poems vainly
    Mourn, and in his schoolroom the fooling
Truth ogles a mirror and forgets that eagled head?

So wasteful the world is with her few of best.
    O pinnacles where the elected princes die
With their dogstar boots on and a truth in hand,
    O tabernacles glittering to attest
So few have ever ascended so far or so high,
    O Michael's bone enshrined in altitude,
Truth is meridian to tempt kings to try.

The proud ride past us on their hippogryphs
    To lazy empires opulent with trophies
Others caught up from the holocaust and the hazards
    At what a price. I saw you stride across
A Fitzroy room and leave, stamped on the boards,
    In the nailed image heroes and poems possess,
A symbol of spirit that did not call for words,

And skulled as aquiline as the two-headed Maximus
    You, Michael, also. Gazing towards the left
You leaned a shoulder against the ideal azimuth
    And theories shook their seven veils and laughed.
You turned your head to the principle of right
    And a principle came down to earth, and performed:
So you were active a man and a teacher, formed
    Together, and the poem walked upright.

But can the harp shoot through its propellers? At heart
    There was an Orphic unicorn in his chest
Who, dying, drove the spindle through his breast
    And both of them died. O he unsung apart
The Siamese master who could daydream and act:
    He would not let his harpstrung fellow sing
And so the poet choked him with a fact.

He lolled against a mantelpiece, and a tree
    Of loving kindness sprouted in the grate,
Catching all friends up in its talkative branches
    As the bright bird's-eye glittered behind glass.
Too seldom, I know now, I watched this face
    Talk through the truth like a ship through the sea,
With the noumena tying roses on the anchors
    And the anchors conquering the great sea.

How dare the greatest die? They do not die.
    Over my writing shoulder, now, guiding
As many before he guided, head and master, with all
    The teaching fathers fit for such presiding,
He returns when the poem comes down from the sky
    With the truth in its claws. The best of all
Teach us that death is no easy place of hiding.
But an everest where, higher, the greater fall.

from **At Thurgarton Church**
To the memory of my father

At Thurgarton Church the sun
burns the winter clouds over
the gaunt Danish stone
and thatched reeds that cover
the barest chapel I know.

I could compare it with
the Norse longboats that bore
burning the body forth
in honour from the shore
of great fjords long ago.

The sky is red and cold
overhead, and three small
sturdy trees keep a hold
on the world and the stone wall
that encloses the dead below.

I enter and find I stand
in a great barn, bleak and bare.
Like ice the winter ghosts and
the white walls gleam and flare
and flame as the sun drops low.

And I see, then, that slowly
the December day has gone.
I stand in the silence, not wholly
believing I am alone.
Somehow I cannot go.

Then a small wind rose, and the trees
began to crackle and stir
and I watched the moon by degrees
ascend in the window till her
light cut a wing in the shadow.

I thought: the House of the Dead.
The dead moon inherits it.
And I seem in a sense to have died
as I rise from where I sit
and out into darkness go.

I know as I leave I shall pass
where Thurgarton's dead lie
at those old stones in the grass
under the cold moon's eye.
I see the old bones glow.

No, they do not sleep here
in the long holy night of
the serene soul, but keep here
a dark tenancy and the right of
rising up to go.

Here the owl and soul shriek with
the voice of the dead as they turn
on the polar spit and burn
without hope and seek with
out hope the holy home below.

Yet to them the mole and
mouse bring a wreath and a breath
of the flowering leaves of the soul, and
it is from the Tree of Death
the leaves of life grow.

The rain, the sometime summer
rain on a memory of roses
will fall lightly and come a-
mong them as it erases
summers so long ago.

And the voices of those
once so much loved will flitter
over the nettled rows
of graves, and the holly tree twitter
like friends they used to know.

And not far away the
icy and paralysed stream
has found it also, that day the
flesh became glass and a dream
with no where to go.

Haunting the December
fields their bitter lives
entreat us to remember
the lost spirit that grieves
over these fields like a scarecrow.

from **Anno Domini**

– at a time of bankers
    to exercise a little charity;
at a time of soldiers
    to cultivate small gardens;
at a time of categorical imperatives
    to guess about clouds;
at a time of politicians
    to trust only to children and demigods.
And from those who occupy seats of power
    to turn, today, away
without incurring permanent reprisals.
    When the instruments of torture
are paraded in public places
    permit us to transmute them,
somehow, into ploughshares.
    When the tribulations of some tribes, or persons,
seem, as so often, to exceed a reasonable allotment,
    condescend, superior, to examine fate
and make sure that its machinery has not gone wrong.
    When those who deserve little more than
a severe whipping, wake up to a morning of pink
    champagne and strawberries,
visit them, surely, with one moment of retribution
    and slight indigestion. Expunge
from the punishment book of the frivolous
    those impositions incurred for singing at funerals;
and to the hopelessly optimistic
    award, if you will, a few kisses.

Never, my love and dearest

Never, my love and dearest,
    we'll hear the lilies grow
or, silent and dancing,
    the fall of the winter snow,
or the great clouds of Summer
    as on their way they go.

Never, my love and dearest
    we'll hear the bluebells chime
or the whole world turn over
    after the harvest time.
O not everything, my dearest,
    needs to be said in rhyme!

A Version of Animula Vagula Blandula

I know where you are now. But do you know?
Are you here in this word? I have not heard
you whistling in the dark. Do not allow
the noun or pronoun or the verb to disturb you.
Sometimes, I think that death is really no joke
but then I have died only two or three such times.
Perhaps there is always someone to attend the
absconding mountebank. But you, farewelling ghost, poor
imperial little thing, go you alone?
Go you alone to the altering? Or am I with you?

Note *by Elspeth Barker*

I chose these poems with difficulty. George's range is so wide that even the generous space offered by *PN Review* must exclude some characteristic work. Most notably, there is nothing here of his scurrilous verse, his gleeful jokes and gibes and enraging puns. I have also been unable to include anything from *Dreams of a Summer Night*, with its overwhelmingly rich orchestral rhythms, although there is a hint of them in the much earlier 'Elegy for Michael Roberts'. So there we go, and I hope that these poems may provide some suggestion of his many voices.

'Battersea Park' belongs to his youth and its taut metric, word play, echoing rhymes and half-rhymes, and its lyric melancholy are characteristics which appear in intensified form in later work. 'Turn on your Side' speaks for itself. George wrote a number of powerful elegies, any one of which I might have chosen. Michael Roberts was his friend and mentor. I envy him those talkative branches. 'At Thurgarton Church' reflects GB's feeling for North Norfolk's bleak winter landscape; it is also a profound religious meditation. Love, death, hell, guilt and innocence were intense preoccupations, as were car engines and Saturday TV wrestling. The sonorous rhythms, wit and anger of *Anno Domini* are vibrant with George's personality. In his three books of verse for children there is a luminous purity. 'Never Again' is to be found in *Runes and Rhymes* (Faber). They do say that they will issue a single volume in a year or two. 'Animula Vagula Blandula' was published posthumously in *Street Ballads* (Faber). I have included it for obvious reasons. In the Spring of 1995 Faber, who published the monumental *Collected Poems* in 1987, are bringing out a *Selected Poems*.

OXFORD POETS

FIRST IN LINE

D. J. Enright

'He is wise and intelligently innocent and observant' **A.S. Byatt**, *Independent*

Old Men and Comets	£6.99
Collected Poems	£7.95
Selected Poems 1990	£6.95
Under the Circumstances	£5.99

'You with your bedtime mug of disappointment' (Thomas Kinsella)

Thomas Kinsella

'the best Irish poet since Yeats' Robert Nye, ***The Scotsman***

From Centre City	£7.99
Blood and Family	£6.95

Peter Scupham

'Scupham ranks among the most arresting of newer English poets.' ***Spectator***

The Ark	£6.99
Selected Poems 1972-1990	£7.95
Out Late	£5.99
Watching the Perseids	£5.99

Stephen Romer

'His apparent mix of influences is fascinating.' **Thom Gunn**

Plato's Ladder	£6.99
Idols	£5.99

'No roofs this morning, alps, ominous message...' (Anne Stevenson)

Anne Stevenson

'A sturdy backbone of intellectual vigour strengthens the most intuitive work.' *Independent*

Four and a Half Dancing Men	£6.99
The Other House	£5.95
Selected Poems 1956-1990	£6.95

Charles Tomlinson

'one of his generation's outstanding English Poets' ***Poetry Review***

Jubilation	£6.99 (March 1995)
Annunciations	£5.95
Collected Poems	£6.95
The Door in the Wall	£6.99
The Return	£5.99

Oxford University Press

C.H. SISSON

On a Troopship
They are already made
Why should they go
Into boring society
Among the soldiery?
But I, whose imperfection
Is evident and admitted
Needing further assurance
Must year-long be pitted
Against fool and trooper
Practising my integrity
In awkward places,
Walking till I walk easily
Among uncomprehended faces
Extracting the root
Of the matter from the diverse engines
That in an oath, a gesture or a song
Inadequately approximate to the human norm.

The Nature of Man
It is the nature of man that puzzles me
As I walk from Saint James's Square to Charing Cross;
The polite mechanicals are going home,
I understand their condition and their loss.

Ape-like in that their box of wires
Is shut behind a face of human resemblance
They favour a comic hat between their ears
And their monkey's tube is tucked inside their pants.

Language which is all our lives has us on a skewer,
Inept, weak, the grinning devil of comprehension; but sleep
Knows us for plants or undiscovered worlds;
If we have reasons, they lie deep.

Cotignac
River, deep as death, deeper, Avernus,
Red water of ox-hide, ox-blood, clouded,
Drawn across these caverns like a taut sheet,
What is down there, under the cliff edge,
Deeper than hell? Village
Lost to all time, under the sick archway,
The lost steps lead there, the life
Stirs like a movement of moss.

If I were to awake in that underworld, whom should I see?
Not Nestor, nor Paris,
Not any heroic shadow, long putrescent,
Blown into dust: no woman
Caught my wandering eye last summer
Or any summer gone. The friends of shadows,
The commonplace merchants of ambition,
These are the ones, bragging in the market-place
So vain is all philosophy
My teeth were set on edge by such merchants
Half a caravan back: and when they came
To the high street where the palms set the form
It was eating and drinking who must,
Who laughed loudest, who spat,
While I stood by discreetly.
Worn hours! bitter heart! petty mind below all
No kiss of sun can cure, autumn eyes
Seeking rather between shadows the hurt.

There are gigantic shadows upon the cliff-face
I have seen them scowl and lour over the village.
All villages have them: they are the governors
Living among themselves without passions
Touching our parts. I had lived among them as evil
No man knew better their vain twists,
Admired what he hated most
Or so fell to dreaming of impossibles
Which are only eaten ambition
Knives in the heart, or pure reason.

A handful of almonds, a few grapes
All that the fine fingers could pick
Out of the residue of the world
Was not enough for this termagant.
The fine surface of bodies touched
By the sun and rendered potable
Was not enough for the eye-palimpsest;
The half-eaten moaner must moan.
What cages for tigers, whips for scorpions or other
Replicas of effete damnation
Had been prepared, must find a place
Within the cataclysm of each mind.
Mine was none of the stablest, I felt,
Looking over the impeccable scene,
The cicada chipping the hillside.

Taxila
There is a rail-head at Havelian
– Or was, for I was there long ago –
Around it a sweet plain circled by hills:
This was my Greece, the only one I know.

It was a ghost of olives that I saw:
I had not seen the Mediterranean light
Where it falls, but I had dreamed of it.
I who had not been born woke to the sight.

Rus in urbe, urbs in the dazzling grey
– Or was it green? – green, but so grey and brown,
A spot of light in the surrounding darkness:
Taxila was the name of the town,

The heart of all I loved and could not have;
And in that limy track, as I approached,
A child with bright eyes offered a coin.
It was a bargain that was proposed.

Would I, the soldier of an alien army,
Neither the first nor last to come that way,
Purchase for rupees certain disused drachmas
Left by the army of an earlier day?

Alexander himself came down from those hills,
Over the mountains beyond them to the north
– Far lands, the boy said, but mine was farther
And longer ago still my setting forth

For my exile burned me like the sun.
I should have bought that coin, I often thought of it
After that time, and in far different places:
It would have carried me over the Styx.

I would have returned, but there is no returning.
Yet you may rise, ghosts, or I sink to you.
The world is in my hand, breathing at last
For now I know, only the past is true.

Casualty
It is not the spoken word but the word spoken
In silence, not directed at anyone,
But holding meaning till it spills over,
Which finds its way into the casual mind.
Poetry, ha? The bed-rock of that art
On which those few can build who lose themselves.

Note
I did not know, when I first selected these poems, that I was to be invited to explain my reasons for choosing them. Certainly I was not trying to select what I thought were my five best poems – a task I would frankly decline. The choice of the first poem was easy: it was the first poem of my adult life, and was preceded by eight or nine years during which I abstained from writing poems, after having committed that folly in childhood and adolescence, until enlightenment overtook me in Berlin in 1934 – a time when that city was not famous for enlightenment. The relapse on a troopship may perhaps be excused in one who had been tossing about for weeks in the wintry Atlantic and had moved into tropical waters.

The second poem was written some years after the war, when – as the poem indeed makes clear – I was an office-worker and a commuter, a dual role which continued for most of my working life. It does not take all day to be a poet and I have never understood the contentions of those eccentrics who think that a poet should not have to earn his living like the next man. Human nature is certainly not less noticeable in the ordinary world of work than it is to the genius who fancies solitude.

The third poem, 'Cotignac', comes from a much later period, when I had leisure, and we used sometimes to borrow a house in Provence. Not all my Provençal poems were written during my stays in Cotignac, but this one was, and there are confused references in it to my already remote career in St James's Square and such places. The only other justification I would give is that the house we lived in – and indeed the whole of the little town – was overhung by a cliff-face.

The fourth poem, 'Taxila' – a place on the North-West Frontier Province of what was then India where one might see Buddhas with classical Greek draperies – is, as will be evident, a throw-back to my army days.

The fifth poem is perhaps the only one for the presence of which I might allege something like a reason. It is a declaration that the poet has to escape from his – or even her – personality, however charming that may be.

JUDITH WRIGHT

Note
I have really already chosen the poems in *PN Review* 87. They were 'Woman to Man', 'The Two Fires', 'Eve to her Daughters', 'Two Dreamtimes', 'Lament for Passenger Pigeons' and 'The Shadow of Fire: Ghazals'.

JOHN HEATH-STUBBS

Mozart
Mozart walking in the garden,
Tormented beside cool waters,
Remembered the empty-headed girl,
And the surly porters,

The singing-bird in the snuff-box,
And the clown's comic nose;
And scattered the thin blue petals
Of a steel rose.

Quatrains
The Dog Star now, negating all desires,
Hurls through the atmosphere destructive fires;
    In mute indifference heart and pen must lie,
Though Fame still tarries, and though Love expires.

For we have seen the rage of Time consume
Those temples which the Muses' lamps illume;
    If their resplendent torches gutter down,
To smoulder on shall burnt-out stubs presume?

Some verses still unpublished I avow…
A sausage-roll, a pint of beer – but Thou?
    The Thou whose image prompts my midnight tears
Is ash at Mortlake Crematorium now.

The leaves made languid under August skies
In Bloomsbury Square reproach my life; and cries
   The voice Verlaine within his prison heard,
And '*Qu'as-tu fait de ta jeunesse?*' it sighs.

Sweet-scented, possibly, the manuscript
Of half my span is closed, and better skipped;
   We slumber in Hope's lap an hour or two
An unquiet sleep – and wake to find we're gypped.

There was a time when the enchanting bird
Of poetry was in my orchards heard –
   The green boughs whitened with ideas in bloom,
And easy on my lips lighted the word.

Fate's discords have unharmonized those tunes,
And blank abstractions blotted out the runes;
   Each finds his loneliness: FitzGerald knew
Like impotence among the Suffolk dunes.

Time with unpitying and iron feet
Bears down upon us all; we learn to greet,
   Without despair, the inevitable void,
Whether in Nishapur or Russell Street.

Little Russell Street, Bloomsbury
August 1953

Plato and the Waters of the Flood

In one of the remoter parts of Asia Minor, near what was once the southern boundary of the Phrygians, there is a warm spring flanked by a Hittite monument, and known to the Turks as Plato's Spring. The reason for the name is that it was at this spot, according to Arab legend, that Plato succeeded in stopping the Flood by making the waters run underground.
                      W.K.C. GUTHRIE, *Orpheus and Greek Religion*

When on Armenian Ararat
   Or Parnassus ridge
Scrunched the overloaded keel,
   Pelican, ostrich,
Toad, rabbit, and pangolin –
   All the beasts of the field –
Scrambled out to possess once more
   Their cleansed and desolate world.
        Plato, by that fountain,
           Spoke to the swirling deep:
     'Retire, you waters of Chaos,
       Flow retrograde, and sleep;
     Above the swift revolving heavens
       Rule the intelligible,
     Chaste and undecaying ideas;
       Brackish waters, fall!'

Plato, in the academic grove,
   Among the nightingales,
Expounded to wide-eyed ephebes
   His geometric rules;
Reared a republic in the mind
   Where only noble lies
Reign; he expelled the poets
   (With courtesy, with praise).
Loaded with useless garlands,
   Down to that fountain
The exiled poets proceeded:
   'When will you rise again,
Ten-horned, seven-headed seraphim,
   Out of your abyss,
Against the beautiful Republic –
   Nor tamed by Plato's kiss?'

from Artorius

'We send you, body of a notable man,
By the waste paths of the sea,
The salt, unharvested element,

'To the polity of the fish,
To the furtiveness of the crab,
To the tentacle of the squid,

'To the red ruler of the tornado,
To the green ruler of the undersea,
To the black ruler of the dead,

'To the three-headed dog,
To the sharp-toothed Scylla –
Cuttle fish, and sea-bitch.

'O Lord, who said to the deep:
"So far, and no further!"
Deliver Thy darling from the tooth of the shark.

'O Christ descending
To the profound, redeem him
From the belly of the fish.

'O Spirit, brooding on tohu-bohu, save
From the embrace of the sea-morgan,
From Tiamat, the formless

'Dove, bearing your olive leaf
Through the rains of the new year,
Breathe into the nostrils of the drowned.

'Star of the Sea,
In intercession gleam
Over the black waters.

'And our vows follow him,
Like petrels flittering
Over the crests and troughs of the waves.

'To the verdict and oblivion of the sea,
Artorius, we consign
Your actions, your defeat.'

Saint Francis Preaches to the Computers
Saint Francis found his way (saints, in a dream,
An ecstasy, slip in and out of time)
Into the computer shop. The chipper little chaps
All chrome and plastic, stainless steel,
Gleaming and winking, chirped and buzzed and whirred
And pipped and peeped, much like the congregation
The saint had just been preaching to – of Ruddocks, Dunnocks,
Citrils, Serins, Siskins, Spinks,
Orphean warblers, Ortolans, Golden Orioles.
So he began to do his stuff again –
You know the kind of thing that he would say: – he told them
To praise the Lord who had created them,
Had made them bright and new, had programmed them,
Had plugged them in, and kept them serviceable.
But somehow they looked glum; hint of a minor key
Seemed to infect their electronic singing:
'Alas,' they said, 'for we were not created
By God, Whoever He or She may be,
But by the shaved ape, the six-foot Siamang
The pregnant mandrake root, cumulus in pants,
Glassily-essenced Man. We are no more clever
Than he who made us, though we think faster. Nor were we
   programmed
With thoughts that take off into timelessness,
Nor trans-death longings. But we have one fear,
And it is rust, is rust, is rust, is rust,
The eternal rubbish tip and the compressor.'
'My little mechanical brothers,' rejoined the saint,
'I'll tell you something that a Mullah said,
One that was in the Soldan's entourage,
That time I visited his camp. They postulate
A moderate-sized menagerie in heaven.
I'll only mention Balaam's percipient ass,
Tobias's toby dog, that other faithful fido
Who hunted in his dreams in that Ephesian den
The seven sleepers snorted in, and snarled
At Roman persecutors, and, golden-crested,
Cinnamon-breasted, with broad dappled wings
The hoopoe, which was the wise King Solomon's
Special envoy to the queen of Sheba –
That sweet blue-stocking with the donkey's toes.'
'If these could pass into eternity,
It was for love and service. And Eternity,
Loving through mankind, loved them,
And lifted them into a resurrection, as shall be lifted
The whole creation, groan though it does and travail.
And if these brute beasts were loved, then so may you be,
Along with the Puffing Billies, Chitty Chitty Bang Bangs,
Barnacled Old Superbs, Ezekiel's wheels,
Elijah's fiery space-ship. You shall be built as stones
That gleam in the High-priestly breastplate
Which is the wall of that bright golden city –
Itself the human body glorified.'

Homage to Marianne Moore
'Imaginary gardens with real toads in them' –
Your prescription for a poem;
But for me, perhaps,
Three wise frogs
Who see no evil, hear no evil, croak no evil.

Note
I have been seriously engaged in trying to write poetry since the age of eleven or twelve. Juvenilia aside, I have decided to represent my work by taking one poem from each decade of my adult life. 'Mozart' was written while I was still an undergraduate. It was printed in Tambimuttu's *Poetry London*, and was, I think, the first poem of mine to appear in print, outside school and student publications. I had an early musical education, and music especially that of Mozart, has always been important to me. N.B. I would not now tolerate the cockney rhyme 'waters' and 'porters'.

The next poem was written not long after my thirty-fifth birthday. I had recently lost, in tragic circumstances, a passionately loved friend, and I was entering upon the middle years. These years were to be difficult for me in many ways. The poem is, of course, a parody/pastiche of Edward Fitzgerald's *Rubaiyyat of Omar Khayyam*, a poem which has always meant a lot to me.

'Plato and the Waters of the Flood', written in my early forties shortly after I had returned from three years in Egypt, is about the conflict, within each one of us, and in the cultures all about us, between the impulse to order and abstraction (represented by Plato) and the chaotic forces of the Flood from which, however, fresh life must spring.

It was in my fifties that I embarked on my most ambitious project, my long poem 'Artorius'. I had thought of composing such a poem as early as my twenties, and some twenty five years of research preceded my actual embarking on its composition. The extract I include here is from the final section of the poem, and is a lyrical lament over the sea-burial of the hero.

One of the challenges a twentieth century poet has to meet is the coming to terms with modern science and technology. I have therefore included 'St Francis preaches to the Computers' to represent my sixties. It can also stand for my lifelong passionate interest in ornithology.

I conclude with a brief poem written this year, and not previously printed. I like to end on a slightly enigmatic note.

W.S. GRAHAM

from **The Dark Dialogues**

        I

I always meant to only
Language swings away
Further before me.

Language swings away
Before me as I go
With again the night rising
Up to accompany me
And that other fond
Metaphor, the sea.
Images of night
And the sea changing
Should know me well enough.

Wanton with riding lights
And staring eyes, Europa
And her high meadow bull
Fall slowly their way
Behind the blindfold and
Across this more or less
Uncommon place.

And who are you and by
What right do I waylay
You where you go there
Happy enough striking
Your hobnail in the dark?
Believe me I would ask
Forgiveness but who
Would I ask forgiveness from?

I speak across the vast
Dialogues in which we go
To clench my words against
Time or the lack of time
Hoping that for a moment
They will become for me
A place I can think in
And think anything in,
An aside from the monstrous.

And this is no other
Place than where I am,
Here turning between
This word and the next.
Yet somewhere the stones
Are wagging in the dark
And you, whoever you are,
That I am other to,
Stand still by the glint
Of the dyke's sparstone,
Because always language
Is where the people are.

Letter VI

A day the wind was hardly
Shaking the youngest frond
Of April I went on
The high moor we know.
I put my childhood out
Into a cocked hat
And you moving the myrtle
Walked slowly over.
A sweet clearness became.
The Clyde sleeved in its firth
Reached and dazzled me.
I moved and caught the sweet
Courtesy of your mouth.
My breath to your breath.
And as you lay fondly
In the crushed smell of the moor
The courageous and just sun
Opened its door.
And there we lay halfway
Your body and my body
Oh the high moor. Without
A word then we went
Our ways. I heard the moor
Curling its cries far
Across the still loch.

The great verbs of the sea
Come down on us in a roar.
What shall I answer for?

The Beast in the Space

Shut up. Shut up. There's nobody here.
If you think you hear somebody knocking
On the other side of the words, pay
No attention. It will be only
The great creature that thumps its tail
On silence on the other side.
If you do not even hear that
I'll give the beast a quick skelp
And through Art you'll hear it yelp.

The beast that lives on silence takes
Its bite out of either side.
It pads and sniffs between us. Now
It comes and laps my meaning up.
Call it over. Call it across
This curious necessary space.
Get off, you terrible inhabiter
Of silence. I'll not have it. Get
Away to whoever it is will have you.

He's gone and if he's gone to you
That's fair enough. For on this side
Of the words it's late. The heavy moth
Bangs on the pane. The whole house
Is sleeping and I remember
I am not here, only the space
I sent the terrible beast across.
Watch. He bites. Listen gently
To any song he snorts or growls
And give him food. He means neither
Well or ill towards you. Above
All, shut up. Give him your love.

from **Clusters Travelling Out**
Clearly I tap to you clearly
Along the plumbing of the world
I do not know enough, not
Knowing where it ends. I tap
And tap to interrupt silence into
Manmade durations making for this
Moment a dialect for our purpose.
TAPTAP. Are you reading that taptap
I send out to you along
My element? O watch. Here they come
Opening and shutting Communication's
Gates as they approach, History's
Princes with canisters of gas
Crystals to tip and snuff me out
Strangled and knotted with my kind
Under the terrible benevolent roof.
Clearly they try to frighten me
To almost death. I am presuming
You know who I am. To answer please
Tap tap quickly along the nearest
Metal. When you hear from me
Again I will not know you. Whoever
Speaks to you will not be me.
I wonder what I will say.

Listen. Put on Morning
Listen. Put on morning.
Waken into falling light.
A man's imagining
Suddenly may inherit
The handclapping centuries
Of his one minute on earth.
And hear the virgin juries
Talk with his own breath
To the corner boys of his street.
And hear the Black Maria
Searching the town at night.
And hear the playropes caa
The sister Mary in.
And hear Willie and Davie
Among bracken of Narnain
Sing in a mist heavy
With myrtle and listeners.
And hear the higher town
Weep a petition of fears
At the poorhouse close upon
The public heartbeat.
And hear the children tig
And run with my own feet
Into the netting drag
Of a suiciding principle.
Listen. Put on lightbreak.
Waken into miracle.
The audience lies awake
Under the tenements
Under the sugar docks
Under the printed moments.
The centuries turn their locks
And open under the hill
Their inherited books and doors
All gathered to distil

Like happy berry pickers
One voice to talk to us.
Yes listen. It carries away
The second and the years
Till the heart's in a jacket of snow
And the head's in a helmet white
And the song sleeps to be wakened
By the morning ear bright.
Listen. Put on morning.
Waken into falling light.

Loch Thom

1

Just for the sake of recovering
I walked backward from fifty-six
Quick years of age wanting to see,
And managed not to trip or stumble
To find Loch Thom and turned round
To see the stretch of my childhood
Before me. Here is the loch. The same
Long-beaked cry curls across
The heather-edges of the water held
Between the hills a boyhood's walk
Up from Greenock. It is the morning.

And I am here with my mammy's
Bramble jam scones in my pocket.
The Firth is miles and I have come
Back to find Loch Thom maybe
In this light does not recognise me.

This is a lonely freshwater loch.
No farms on the edge. Only
Heather grouse-moor stretching
Down to Greenock and One Hope
Street or stretching away across
Into the blue moors of Ayrshire.

2

And almost I am back again
Wading the heather down to the edge
To sit. The minnows go by in shoals
Like iron-filings in the shallows.

My mother is dead. My father is dead
And all the trout I used to know
Leaping from their sad rings are dead.

3

I drop my crumbs into the shallow
Weed for the minnows and pinheads.
You see that I will have to rise
And turn round and get back where
My running age will slow for a moment
To let me on. It is a colder
Stretch of water than I remember.

The curlew's cry travelling still
Kills me fairly. In front of me
The grouse flurry and settle. GOBACK
GOBACK GOBACK FAREWELL LOCH THOM.

I Leave This at Your Ear
for Nessie Dunsmuir

I leave this at your ear for when you wake,
A creature in its abstract cage asleep.
Your dreams blindfold you by the light they make.

The owl called from the naked-woman tree
As I came down by the Kyle farm to hear
Your house silent by the speaking sea.

I have come late but I have come before
Later with slaked steps from stone to stone
To hope to find you listening for the door.

I stand in the ticking room. My dear, I take
A moth kiss from your breath. The shore gulls cry.
I leave this at your ear for when you wake.

Note *by Nessie Graham*

'The Dark Dialogues' Part One: On more than one occasion Sydney said that this was his best poem.

'Letter VI': A completely lyrical poem – 'moving the myrtle' refers to the aromatic bog myrtle, a plant, not the tree.

'… the Clyde sleeved in its firth
reached and dazzled me…'
'… the sweet courtesy of your mouth…'
– then the strong, unexpected, dramatic statement at the end in the last three lines.

'The Beast in the Space': A poem that is quintessential Sydney and less well-known than the 'Constructed Space'. One of the best examples of talking about the nature of a poem and being a poet. He was a poet of language and love.

'Clusters Travelling Out' Part One: The image of the nearby workhouse, which had later been converted into a slaughterhouse, informed this poem and demonstrates Sydney's fusion of human feelings with the examination of communication and language. He was acutely aware of human suffering, misery, cruelty (see 'Ten Shots of Mr Simpson').

'Listen. Put on Morning': Speaks of Continuity, Resurrection and Renewal – philosophical elements – as in

'Loch Thom': Trout ringed. The Nature of Time and Identity (Heidegger).

'I Leave This At Your Ear *for Nessie Dunsmuir*': This poem shows elegance and economy of form and statement.'

EDWIN MORGAN

In the Snack-bar

A cup capsizes along the formica,
slithering with a dull clatter.
A few heads turn in the crowded evening snack-bar.
An old man is trying to get to his feet
from the low round stool fixed to the floor.
Slowly he levers himself up, his hands have no power.
He is up as far as he can get. The dismal hump
looming over him forces his head down.
He stands in his stained beltless gaberdine
like a monstrous animal caught in a tent
in some story. He sways slightly,
the face not seen, bent down
in shadow under his cap.
Even on his feet he is staring at the floor
or would be, if he could see.
I notice now his stick, once painted white
but scuffed and muddy, hanging from his right arm.
Long blind, hunchback born, half paralysed
he stands
fumbling with the stick
and speaks:
'I want – to go to the – toilet.'

It is down two flights of stairs, but we go.
I take his arm. 'Give me – your arm – it's better,' he says.
Inch by inch we drift towards the stairs.
A few yards of floor are like a landscape
to be negotiated, in the slow setting out
time has almost stopped. I concentrate
my life to his: crunch of spilt sugar,
slidy puddle from the night's umbrellas,
table edges, people's feet,
hiss of the coffee-machine, voices and laughter,
smell of a cigar, hamburgers, wet coats steaming,
and the slow dangerous inches to the stairs.
I put his right hand on the rail
and take his stick. He clings to me. The stick
is in his left hand, probing the treads.
I guide his arm and tell him the steps.
And slowly we go down. And slowly we go down.
White tiles and mirrors at last. He shambles
uncouth into the clinical gleam.
I set him in position, stand behind him
and wait with his stick.
His brooding reflection darkens the mirror
but the trickle of his water is thin and slow,
an old man's apology for living.
Painful ages to close his trousers and coat –
I do up the last buttons for him.
He asks doubtfully, 'Can I – wash my hands?'
I fill the basin, clasp his soft fingers round the soap.
He washes, feebly, patiently. There is no towel.
I press the pedal of the drier, draw his hands
gently into the roar of the hot air.
But he cannot rub them together,
drags out a handkerchief to finish.
He is glad to leave the contraption, and face the stairs.
He climbs, and steadily enough.
He climbs, we climb. He climbs
with many pauses but with that one
persisting patience of the undefeated
which is the nature of man when all is said.

And slowly we go up. And slowly we go up.
The faltering, unfaltering steps
take him at last to the door
across that endless, yet not endless waste of floor.
I watch him helped on a bus. It shudders off in the rain.
The conductor bends to hear where he wants to go.

Wherever he could go it would be dark
and yet he must trust men.
Without embarrassment or shame
he must announce his most pitiful needs
in a public place. No one sees his face.
Does he know how frightening he is in his strangeness
under his mountainous coat, his hands like wet leaves
stuck to the half-white stick?
His life depends on many who would evade him.
But he cannot reckon up the chances,
having one thing to do,
to haul his blind hump through these rains of August.
Dear Christ, to be born for this!

At the Television Set
Take care if you kiss me,
you know it doesn't die.
The lamplight reaches out, draws it
blandly – all of it – into fixity,
troops of blue shadows like the soundless gunfight,
yellow shadows like your cheek by the lamp
where you lie watching, half watching
between the yellow and the blue.
I half see you, half know you.
Take care if you turn now to face me.
For even in this room we are moving out through stars
and forms that never let us back, your hand
lying lightly on my thigh and my hand on your shoulder
are transfixed only there, not here.

What can you bear that would last
like a rock through cancer and white hair?

Yet it is not easy
to take stock of miseries
when the soft light flickers
along our arms in the stillness
where decisions are made.
You have to look at me,
and then it's time that falls
talking slowly to sleep.

Cinquevalli
Cinquevalli is falling, falling,
The shining trapeze kicks and flirts free,
solo performer at last.
The sawdust puffs up with a thump,
settles on a tangle of broken limbs.
St Petersburg screams and leans.
His pulse flickers with the gas-jets. He lives.

Cinquevalli has a therapy.
In his hospital bed, in his hospital chair
he holds a ball, lightly, lets it roll round his hand,
or grips it tight, gauging its weight and resistance,
begins to balance it, to feel its life attached to his
by will and knowledge, invisible strings
that only he can see. He throws it
from hand to hand, always different,
always the same, always
different, always the
same.
His muscles learn to think, his arms grow very strong.

Cinquevalli in sepia
looks at me from an old postcard: bundle of enigmas.
Half faun, half military man; almond eyes, curly hair,
conventional moustache; tights, and a tunic loaded
with embroideries, tassels, chains, fringes; hand on hip
with a large signet-ring winking at the camera
but a bull neck and shoulders and a cannon-ball
at his elbow as he stands by the posing pedestal;
half reluctant, half truculent,
half handsome, half absurd,
but let me see you forget him: not to be done.

Cinquevalli is a juggler.
In a thousand theatres, in every continent,
he is the best, the greatest. After eight years perfecting
he can balance one billiard ball on another billiard ball
on top of a cue on top of a third billiard ball
in a wine-glass held in his mouth. To those
who say the balls are waxed, or flattened,
he patiently explains the trick will only work
because the spheres are absolutely true.
There is no deception in him. He is true.

Cinquevalli is juggling with a bowler,
a walking-stick, a cigar, and a coin.
Who foresees? How to please.
The last time round, the bowler
flies to his head, the stick sticks in his hand,
the cigar jumps into his mouth, the coin
lands on his foot – ah, but
is kicked into his eye
and held there as the miraculous monocle
without which the portrait would be incomplete.

Cinquevalli is practising.
He sits in his dressing-room talking to some friends,
at the same time writing a letter with one hand
and with the other juggling four balls.
His friends think of demons, but
'You could all do this,' he says,
sealing the letter with a billiard ball.

Cinquevalli is on the high wire in Odessa.
The roof cracks, he is falling, falling
into the audience, a woman breaks his fall,
he cracks her like a flea, but lives.

Cinquevalli broods in his armchair in Brixton Road.
He reads in the paper about the shells whining
at Passchendaele, imagines the mud and the dead.
He goes to the window and wonders through that dark
   evening
what is happening in Poland where he was born.
His neighbours call him a German spy.
'Kestner, Paul Kestner, that's his name!'
'Keep Kestner out of the British music-hall!'
He frowns; it is cold; his fingers seem stiff and old.

Cinquevalli tosses up a plate of soup
and twirls it on his forefinger; not a drop spills.
He laughs, and well may he laugh
who can do that. The astonished table
breathe again, laugh too, think the world
a spinning thing that spills, for a moment, no drop.

Cinquevalli's coffin sways through Brixton
only a few months before the Armistice.
Like some trick they cannot get off the ground
it seems to burden the shuffling bearers, all their arms
cross-juggle that displaced person, that man
of balance, of strength, of delights and marvels,
in his unsteady box at last into the earth.

Gangs

Naw naw, there's nae big wurds here, there ye go.
Christ man ye're in a bad wey, kin ye staun?
See here noo, wance we know jist where we're gaun,
we'll jump thon auld – stoap that, will ye – *Quango*.
Thaim that squealt *Lower Inflation*, aye, thaim,
plus thae *YY Zero Wage Increase* wans,
they'll no know what hit thim. See yours, and Dan's,
and mine's, that's three chibs. We'll soon hiv a team.
Whit's that? *Non-Index-Linked!* Did ye hear it?
Look! *Tiny Global Recession!* C'moan then,
ya bams, Ah'll take ye. *Market Power fae Drum!*
Dave, man, get up. Dave! Ach, ye're no near it.
Ah'm oan ma tod. But they'll no take a len
a me, Ah'm no deid yet, or deif, or dumb!

Aunt Myra (1901–1989)

A horse in a field in a picture is easy.
A man in a room with a fan, we wonder.
It might be whirring blades in steamy downtown –
but no, it's what she's left beside her dance-cards.
How she sat out a foxtrot at the Plaza
and fanned her brow, those far-off flirty Twenties
he opens and shuts with an unpractised gesture
that leaves the years half-laughing at the pathos
of the clumsy, until rising strings have swept them
dancing again into silence. The room darkens
with a blue lingering glow above the roof-tops
but the man still stands there, holding up the dangling
dance-cards by their tiny attached pencils.
The cords which are so light seem to him heavy
as if they were about to take the strain of
tender evenings descending into memory.
Something is hard, not easy, though it's clearly
a man, a fan, a woman, a room, a picture.

JOHN BURNSIDE
The Myth of the Twin

ONE OF THE TWENTY NEW GENERATION POETS
AND WINNER OF THE GEOFFREY FABER MEMORIAL PRIZE

'John Burnside has dazzled his readers as a poet of time and place, for whom language, with breathtaking precision, can describe the relation of the mystical to the ordinary. His new collection, *The Myth of the Twin*, shows him sharpening his focus, honing his language to razor-sharp effectiveness, and presenting a pattern of poems which have a symphonic sweep that carries the reader through the very landscape of a myth, while never expecting them to lose sight of reality.'
MICHAEL BRACEWELL, *GUARDIAN*

'Burnside's vision is of an other, sacred, fragile world that co-exists with our own dailiness: his gift is the ability, through poems of a rare and exquisite precision of language, to let his reader glimpse it.'
ELIZABETH BURNS, *SCOTSMAN*

'The prolific and amazing Burnside has, in three collections, moved to the very front rank of contemporary poetry.'
ADAM THORPE, *OBSERVER*

CAPE POETRY

Note

'In the Snack-bar': Today there is much concern about how we treat handicapped people, but this poem was written in 1964, when there was little evidence of that concern, and indeed it is not a 'theme' poem but a response to an actual experience which roused a strong mix of feelings.

'At the Television Set': Written in 1967.

'Cinquevalli': Written in 1980. I like poetry that projects characters, real, legendary, or imaginary. A peculiar interest, and a pathos which is not weak or sentimental, attaches to genuine talents once famous and later forgotten. Cinquevalli was, and is, something of an enigma.

'Gangs': Written in 1984, and one of a sequence of 51 *Sonnets from Scotland* published as a book in that year. A collection concentrating on 'the matter of Scotland' came as a response to the failure of the 1979 Referendum to deliver a Scottish assembly or parliament.

'Aunt Myra (1901–1989)': Written in the year of my aunt's death. She was a widow with no family, and I as her nearest relative had to look after her and her affairs. Sorting out her effects, I was moved by the things she had kept from such a long time ago.

DAVID WRIGHT

By the Effigy of St Cecilia

Having peculiar reverence for this creature
Of the numinous imagination, I am come
To visit her church and stand before the altar
Where her image, hewn in pathetic stone,
Exhibits the handiwork of her executioner.

There are the axemarks. Outside, in the courtyard,
In shabby habit, an Italian nun
Came up and spoke: I had to answer, 'Sordo.'
She said she was a teacher of deaf children
And had experience of my disorder.

And I have had experience of her order,
Interpenetrating chords and marshalled sound;
Often I loved to listen to the organ's
Harmonious and concordant interpretation
Of what is due from us to the creation.
But it was taken from me in my childhood
And those graduated pipes turned into stone.
Now, having travelled a long way through silence,
Within the church in Trastevere I stand
A pilgrim to the patron saint of music

And am abashed by the presence of this nun
Beside the embodiment of that legendary
Virgin whose music and whose martyrdom
Is special to this place: by her reality.
She is a reminder of practical kindness,

The care it takes to draw speech from the dumb
Or pierce with sense the carapace of deafness;
And so, of the plain humility of the ethos
That constructed, also, this elaborate room
To pray for bread in; they are not contradictory.

Kleomedes

Both Plutarch and Pausanias tell a story
That is a worry to imagination.
It's of the athlete Kleomedes, a moody
Instrument for a theophanic anger
And for an outrageous justice not our own.

Plutarch reports the tale in the barest outline,
Evidently having no comment to offer,
And certainly no word of explanation
To throw light upon what happened to Kleomedes
Or the subsequent oracular non sequitur.

As for Kleomedes: at the Olympic Games he
Killed his opponent in the boxing-contest.
The ox-felling blow was not his, he claimed; the
Fury struck through him, it was not his own strength.
He'd won, but they withheld the palm nevertheless.

The injustice of it. Nursing rage like a pot-plant,
Watering it with his thoughts, which were few and stupid,
When he drank with others he drank with his back turned
To cherish that shrub till one more bud had sprouted.
It was growing to be a beauty and he loved it.

The palm of victory, his by rights, denied him.
Well, he would go home to Astypalaea.
There they would understand; were they not his own kin?
Anger. His heart fed an ulcer. Would it disappear
At sight of the headland of his own dear island?

So Kleomedes went away; his rage didn't.
It's hard being done by foreigners, but far worse
When the people one grew up with see no harm in it.
Even the light of the noonday sun seemed altered
In the familiar market-place where fools chaffered.

Wrath. Wrath. In an access of it he stood up.
May God damn the lot of you, he said, seizing the first
Thing his eye fell on: it was a marble column.
Ah, and he tugged. Tugged. And his brow pimpled with sweat.
Possessed, he exerted more than his might. It tumbled.

Slowly a coping-stone slid. Then the whole roof
Collapsed with a roar. Thunder. A pall of dust
Stood like a rose where had been a schoolroom of children.
Kleomedes saw their blood lapped up by the earth.
There was silence and grief. Then a cry, Murderer!

Murderer! Murderer! He was among strangers.
Hatred and anger in that man's, that woman's eye.
And now they were one eye. The eye of an animal,
Hackles up, about to rend. Its name Mob, hairy
Gorgon. Brute, it is a beast made up of us all;

May none of us ever be or see it! He saw,
Miserable quarry, lust ripple its muscles.
Act now or die! He acted. Ran for sanctuary
To the holy temple, the temple of Pallas Athena:
Mob may respect the precinct of the armed goddess.

But what does a beast know of gods? He heard baying
Hard at his heels. Saw a chest there in the forecourt.
Prayed it be empty. He lifted the lid. Stepped in
Pulling the lid behind him, and held it fast shut.
More strength that his own held it against all efforts.

I don't understand the story from this point on.
Here enters mystery. Levering a crowbar
They heaved at hinges; the wood groaned and a hasp cracked.
Now for the fellow. Kleomedes did not appear.
They looked; but the chest was empty; the man was gone.

It was anticlimax. Fear fluttered from dismay.
They were people again. The sun continued to shine
As it had done. There were the children to bury.
Catastrophe and the violated shrine
Remained; and, before them, a vacant box grinning.
Astypalaea sent to Delphi embassies
To ask the pythoness what these events forebode;
What might be their significance; where the guilt lay.
The oracle kept silence. Then vouchsafed its word.
'The last of the heroes was Kleomedes.'

from Grasmere Sonnets

There is a cragbound solitary quarter
Hawk's kingdom once, a pass with a tarn
High on its shoulder. Inscribed on a stone
With graveyard letters, a verse to his brother
Says it was here they parted from each other
Where the long difficult track winding down
A bald blank bowl of the hills may be seen
Leading the eye to a distant gleam of water.
After that last goodbye and shake of the hand
A bright imagination flashed and ended;
The one would live on, for forty years becalmed
Among the presences he had commanded –
Those energies in which the other foundered,
Devoured by wind and sea in sight of land.

E.P. at Westminster

Old whitebearded figure outside the abbey,
Erect, creating his own solitude,
Regards, tremulously, an undistinguished crowd,
Literati of the twentieth century.
They have come to pay homage to his contemporary;
He, to a confederate poet who is dead.
The service is over. Fierce and gentle in his pride,
A lume spento, senex from America,

He can only remember, stand, and wonder.
His justice is not for us. The solitary
Old man has made his gesture. Question now
Whom did the demoded Muse most honour
When she assigned with eternal irony
An order of merit and a cage at Pisa?

Procession

Sober the overhead trees, and fields tilted
And framed by laborious walls on the framing hills,
No colour but a heavy green of August
Till the sun steps over a cloud, and light falls bare
On a pastoral lake and valley, where tourists
In their bright anoraks have come to stare.

Beyond the rectory, over the stone bridge,
The band assembles, cardigans and gleaming brass,
Waits by the teashop and nursery gardens;
A trombone has gone to the gents in the coach park.
Under the church tower, among those gaily
Shirted, I take my place, a sight-seer.

From its due angle the afternoon sunlight
Glances on us, the children in white and green,
The boys with rushes and the girls garlanded,
And on the gravemounds lies, autumnal almost.
The parishioners, in Sunday best, are ready
To move in procession. The Rush-bearing at Grasmere

Begins to parade toward the Rothay Hotel
Slowly; band, vicar, sidesmen, and choir,
With hesitant banners, the living, and the new-born
In perambulators gaudy with flowers.
Out of sight now, turning the corner, they'll return
A moment later, as they did last year.

What hymn is the band playing? They reappear,
The local dwellers followed by children,
Here and now, past and to be contained together;
Like the plain water that stumbles below
The bridge I stand on, keeping the bed of the stream,
So altering that it seems never to alter.

from Five Songs

Stream
This young water
In my young day
Nosed like a hound
Through the meadow.

Changing, scarcely
Changed, it winds
Through Gloucestershire,
The Windrush stream.

Winds in a changeless
Image a
Recalling eye
Throws to the mind.

Mine is what's gone,
Not what's to come;
Then, I lived now,
Now, I live then.

David Wright

Moon
O up there, zero
Shape illumining
These hills, and that lake –
Puller of water,

Puller of blood, blind
Eye not looking, but
There, opaque, a ball:
Have seen you over

A dead roofscape of
Human sleep; wondered
Why you beat so still.
Even the mobile

Windy surface of
Ocean seems, under
The quiet metal
Of that refracted

Lambency, gorgon
Struck.
    Now have seen how,
Soft as a fruit,

Our blueveined mother
The warm, appalling
Earth rises, vapoury,
Over your shoulder.

Mountain
An outjutment
Where a slow bald
Swell of moorland
Declines. Old bone,

Old stone bone, wind
Beater still, still
There, in cloud or
Under snow, a

Waterbitten
Old mountain, stone
Obstruct. Cohere
Old rock, black slate!

Water can break
Granite: softest
Beat hardest, but
Not this mountain.

The mountain is
Rooted in bog, and
Glittering water.

Here below, bogrush,
Ragged robin, streams
Quick with fish. Heavy
Winged herons flap off

And a thumping hare
Tacks through white grass. What
Antithetical
Short stir, softness.

Cold now, cloudshrouded
Helmet of wind, a
Congealed mud, oldest
Rock, almost deaf as

Starlight. The light turf,
Scabbed lichen, cracked stone,
Holding a sky up.

Juxtapositions
Six decades gone and one to come,
In summer leaves I read, autumn.

July foliage, winter form:
Beech in leaf and barebones elm.

I saw a salmon leap and fail,
Fail and leap where water fell.

A wake of wild geese flying by
A river mirroring their sky.

Low river, slow river, heron
Slow also, loth to go, going.

In Memoriam David Archer
At the corner of a bar, lit by opaque windows,
Times and *New Statesman* still in their newsagent's fold,
    tucked
Under a withered arm shut like the wing of a bird,
Worried, inarticulate, dressed like a chief clerk,

David Archer that was, in the Wheatsheaf or Black Horse
– On Sundays at Notting Hill, the Old Swan or Windsor
    Castle,
A folder of plans toward some communal service
Clipped under the defeated arm as often as not.

A diffident but fanatic man; courteous;
Easily frightened; recovering courage, he'd look
Sidelong through spectacles, again like a bird, sharp and
    scared:
'I'm shaking like an aspirin tree. What'll you have?'

Neutral in a dark suit, holding a glass of Guinness,
That was his role and how he stood when the myths were
    made,
As necessary as a background and as modest,
Where they talked, struck light and took fire over his head.

Poured away and wasted like all valid sacrifice,
Libation of a subsistence. Died at Rowton House.
Impractical. Gone to immaterial reward
Along with Colquhoun and MacBryde, and Dylan Thomas.

D.J. ENRIGHT

from **Paradise Illustrated** (1978)

I
'Come!' spoke the Almighty to Adam.
'There's work to do, even in Eden.'

'I want to see what you'll call them,'
The Lord said. 'It's a good day for it.'
'And take your thumb out of your mouth,'
He added. (Adam was missing his mother.)

So they shuffled past, or they hopped,
Or they waddled. The beasts of the field
And the fowls of the air,
Pretending not to notice him.

'Speak up now,' said the Lord God briskly.
'Give each and every one the name thereof.'

'Fido,' said Adam, thinking hard,
As the animals went past him one by one,
'Bambi', 'Harpy', 'Pooh',
'Incitatus', 'Acidosis', 'Apparat',
'Krafft-Ebing', 'Indo-China', 'Schnorkel',
'Buggins', 'Bollock' –

'Bullock will do,' said the Lord God, 'I like it.
The rest are rubbish. You must try again tomorrow.'

V
 'About them frisking played
 All beasts of th'earth…'

'If we have a baby,
That elephant will have to go –
He's too unwieldy.'

'What's a baby?'
'A word I've just made up,'
Said Adam smugly.

'If we have a child,
That bear will have to go –
He's wild.'

'What's a child?'
'A word I've just made up,'
He smiled.

'If we have a brood,
That ape will have to go –
He's very rude.'

'What's a brood?'
'A word I've just made up,'
He cooed.

She said:
'But won't the wolf lie down with the lamb?'
He said:
'I think of words, therefore I am.'

IX
Satan considered the creatures.
Satan selected the serpent.

'The subtle snake, the fittest imp of fraud,'
So spoke the Fallen Angel, fond of artful sound,
So spoke the Fiend, alliteration's friend.

Unfeared and unafraid,
The silken snake lay sleeping…

In at his mouth the Enemy entered,
Thorough his throat commodious
Filtered our fatal Foe.

Then up he rose –
As yet the snake stood upright on his tail,
This sleek unfallen fellow,
He surged, not slithered –

And off the Tempter tripped,
And off swept Satan Snakeskin,
In search of silly She.

XIX
So the Archangel, out of pity,
Now disclosed the liberal arts
That should relieve man's fallen lot.
'Like music, painting, plays and books.'

'Long books?' asked doleful Adam,
Whom the stern Angel had apprised
Of death and rape and guns and hunger.

'A book there'll be,' the Angel said,
'About this very business –
A poem of ten thousand lines, which one
Called Milton shall compose in time to come.'

'Oh dear!' Then Adam brightened.
'Am I the hero of this book perchance?'
'Not quite the hero,' Michael mildly said,
'And yet you feature largely in it –
God, not unnaturally, is the hero.'
'Should have known,' groaned Adam.

'Although there are – or will be – those
Who claim the hero really is – or will be –
Satan. As I of late foretold,
Henceforth the human race is fallible.'

'That circus snake?' hissed Adam scornfully.
Eve hid her blushes in her work,
A garment she was knitting, made with
Real lamb's wool, tight-fitting.

'In my opinion, which I trust
You won't repeat,' the Angel whispered,
'The hero really is the Son,
Called Jesus, even though his lines
Are fewer in the poem than are mine.'

'And me?' Eve raised her eyes. 'Am I in this –
This book of yours? Or, as I well suppose,
Are all the characters men?'

'Indeed you are!' the genial Angel cried,
'Without an Eve there'd be no tale.
While Mr Milton's not a woman's man,
He does your beauty justice, and your brains.'

'A female intellectual?' Eve grew vexed,
Old-fashioned in her ways as yet.
'No,' spoke the nervous Angel, blushing more,
'I only meant, not just a pretty face.'

Eve held the knitting to her breast.
'By me the Promised Seed shall all restore.'
And Michael knew the time was ripe to leave.
'All – or some,' he murmured at the door.

XXI
'I had no voice,'
Sighed Adam. 'No real choice.'

Eve wiped a tear and said,
'I wanted you, alive or dead.'

'Whether boon or curse.'
'For better or for worse.'

'Come fair or foul, we have to eat' –
She watched for herbs beneath their feet.

The world lay there, and they could choose.
He said, 'I'll learn to make you shoes.'

XXII
'Why didn't we think of clothes before?'
Asked Adam,
Removing Eve's.

'Why did we ever think of clothes?'
Asked Eve,
Laundering Adam's.

History of World Languages
They spoke the loveliest of languages.
Their tongues entwined in Persian, ran
And fused. Words kissed, a phrase embraced,
Verbs conjugated sweetly. Verse began.
So Eve and Adam lapped each other up
The livelong day, the lyric night.

Of all known tongues most suasive
Was the Snake's. His oratory was Arabic,
Whose simile and rhetoric seduced her
('Sovran of creatures, universal dame'),
So potent its appeal –
The apple asked for eating,
To eat it she was game.

Now Gabriel turned up, the scholars say,
Shouting in Turkish. Harsh and menacing,
But late. And sounds like swords were swung.
Fault was underlined, and crime defined.
The gate slammed with the clangour of his tongue.

Eden was gone. A lot of other things
Were won. Or done. Or suffered.
Thorns and thistles, dust and dearth.
The words were all before them, which to choose.
Their tongues now turned to English,
With its colonies of twangs.
And they were down to earth.

Note
For me, a sequence of poems on the theme of Eden and its loss seemed to offer an opportunity to consider (a) the sense of newness, the starting from scratch; (b) the possible advantages, at least the greater liveliness or 'interest', inevitably as this might occur to a postlapsarian mentality, of the fallen state over the (barely imaginable) unfallen; (c) the birth and growth of language; and (d) the anticipation, muddled and fragmentary, of future conditions and events mooted anachronistically, through wordplay, in the language I was using. Matters of some moment, one might think, indeed primal; even if treated in a fashion decidedly unMiltonic, not to say (as somebody unkindly said) an approximation to the strip cartoon. I have never felt that humour was necessarily out of place, however serious the circumstances or subject in question.

'History of World Languages', putting in a good word for a specific tongue, was the first of what would be many afterthoughts and returns.

DONALD DAVIE

Rain on South-East England
This place is so much
Mauled, I have to think
Others beside these Dutch
And low green counties drink
The summer rains, before
I hold it in my mind
What a soft rain is for:
To ease, flush through, unbind.

Tightly starred, on the flat
Marred ground once, with a thin
Unambitious mat
I mended England's ruin.
Growth these last years works
My roots into the air;
Aspiring on long stalks,
My blooms digest no fare
Coarser than light. The strain
Of self-enhancement frees:
I take no care for the rain,
Soured soil, and shattered trees.

The Trip to Huntsville
To be constant through a lifetime
does every one some harm
more than conceivably in
a stiffening self-esteem.

A curious freedom that
feels like incarceration
is to recognize, at sixty,
one has become an *exemplum*.

It is long past midnight now.
Birds begin to squeal their
too little experienced chirpings
the other side of my drawn
curtains in Tennessee.

Chirp, chirp, my little tyros. A
    bird's life is a short one.
Practise your amorous changes.

Chirp, loyal turtles, and
   cheep, libidinous sparrows,
each according to nature and
    I too have no choice in the matter.

Eos and Hesperus have
waxed and waned unnoticed.
No thanks to me, on no
grounds of my beseeching
whether for eyes, for ears
to hear, or a nose for the new,
the sun all the same has risen;
ball of fire, no less.
Charioteer would be more.

Challenger is the latest
space vehicle, named not christened
in Huntsville, Alabama,
the Werner von Braun motel
in and against the sunrise.

The great sun rises;
flashes; it
cuts no ice
with or within me, approaching
in terror the cigar-shaped
bounties of Peenemunde.

Was at the receiving end
of those, my bride was, in
a long-ago war in London.

Pulaski, Tennessee
I pass by, where
Nathan Bedford Forrest,
a Christian gentleman,
created the Ku Klux Klan.

Defeated but unvanquished
after a hundred years,
a Christian gentleman
blasts off against Mugabe.
He wanted Ian Smith
to go down fighting.

Avenues of perception
are choked with those to action,
my Christian gentleman says,
and with some show of reason:
numbness is no sort of
response to shining-eyed
grandsons already recruited

seeing a loud moon-buggy
and a tinted visor are
the gods they carry from Huntsville.

Constancy? To be sure.
See, the exemplary sunset!

Shadows begin to lengthen;
small boys start to be fractious.
Equinoctial storms had
in autumn flurried the Gulf of
Corinth, so we drove to
Olympia's weeping twilight.

Night comes down on the Cumberland
River some hours after
night comes down on the Thames.

Night comes, however; night
    has fallen on Corinth also.

Brilliance
Some virtue in
      the ultimate
lack of emphasis: 'Gods
      or it may be one God moves
about us in bright air.'

Not for you. You were brilliant. You always meant to be that.
You were, and still are at times.

Brilliance, still you want it
impenitently. Truth, oh as for…

You were never in love with the world
or never for long, and only with bits of it:
the usual bits. Trees in a forest? Not often.

Better in a vicarage garden
in the fens, a shelf of cedar
above two deck-chairs, untenanted then and for ever
at four o'clock of a summer afternoon.

But that was not brilliant enough, or not for long.

      Diamonds, and still the blonde deserves them,
      a whole tiara, festoons on the sky at night

      or on the white page, black facets;
      impenitence, a diamond in itself,
      unbreakable, breaking others.

The sinne of Judah is written
with a pen of yron,
and with the point of a diamond it is graven
on the tables of their hearts.

Constant, but only in
the impenitent pursuit
of self-destruction – has
that little earned the garlands
of cadence and clear colour?

The alcoholic's delusion
that he controls his habit,
the warrior, his –
is this to be esteemed and
heroically lamented

      in Dylan Thomas, in
      a broken Coriolanus?

If to be free of delusion
is the worst delusion of all,
are we to save our applause
for those whose delusions are noblest;
for instance, loving the world?

Granted, the noble is
unarguable, known as
soon as apprehended;
still, Delusion limes his
limp nets also for eagles.

Brilliance is known in
what the tired wing, though
it never so crookedly towers,
wins at last into: air
diamond-clear, unemphatic.

Brilliance, then, is noble;
not in the subject but
in what the subject attains to:
a metaphysical, not
in the first place human, property.

'Can you tell the down from the up?'
The unthinkable answer: No.
God moves about us, and
brilliance is His preferred
supernal way of moving.

But there!
I was there, I was walking on air
And all the brightness of air.
But there! I was either not
In earnest, or wasn't aware.

A self-transcendence I had
(I am reminded) hoped for
Twenty years before
Happened, and I wasn't there.

Because in the interim
The terms had changed in my sense
Of what concerned me, I missed
The aerier range I had promised.

Instead, the decrepitude
Of England and Alabama
Fell in with a practised mood,
So I fell in with that.

Though schooled to a manlier carriage,
The ebbing of the waters
Of history I could manage
To a respectable pathos.

And brilliance seemed to arise
In 1989
As a top-dressing to pathos;
Whereas it filled the skies.

But there! I never heeded:
The heavens pursued me and
The only escape I needed
Was failing to attend.

Note

The first poem was written some thirty years ago from Essex, where I was living at that time. It appears to announce a new departure that I'm to follow in my writing: no more meditations on history, soaked in elegiac despondency – instead I'm to abjure images of earth and water, in favour of the ahistorical element, air. This programme was never implemented, partly because Essex proved impossible and in 1968 I departed for the US, where I'd spend most of the next twenty years. This move opened up for me new vistas in both geography and history, and these provoked me, happily enough, into writing once again poems that were *earthy*, anchored in specific places and recorded events. 'The Trip to Huntsville' is such a poem; entirely straightforward, I thought, until I discovered with dismay that some readers' minds are not more blank about Eos and Hesperus than about momentous names from my own lifetime: Werner von Braun and Peenemunde, Mugabe and Ian Smith. It was my friend John Peck who made me see that in 'Brilliance', the third poem here, I had after all achieved what my long-ago poem from Essex had promised: a poem of *air*, ahistorical, metaphysical, also impersonal. But I had sleepwalked into this, which is why John Peck had to awaken me. Moreover, 'Brilliance' and 'The Trip to Huntsville' were both originally parts of one poem, called 'The Gardens of the Savoy', which I had published in the New York magazine *Parnassus* (Spring/Summer 1986). I should like to reprint this here, but it is much too long. For that reason, or for others that I can't now recover with certainty, I rejected 'The Gardens of the Savoy' when I put together *Collected Poems*, and represented it only by the two poems that I then and there quarried from it. There would be nothing odd or interesting about this if I could dispense with the rest of 'The Gardens of the Savoy'. But I can't, if only because another of my friends, Helen Vendler, has responded to it very warmly and sympathetically. And even without Helen I always knew that 'The Gardens of the Savoy' was more than a rambling botch, a self-indulgent and premature draft from which 'A Trip to Huntsville' and 'Brilliance' are the only parts worth saving. Not so; I have three poems on my hands, of which two are made up of verses filched from the third. What is the meaning of this, and what can I do about it? What I *have* done isn't anything I regret, but it leaves me with much unfinished business. What is involved, I think, is a recognition that poems come in different shapes; and that one sort of shapeliness precludes others. The name that hovers, and must now be invoked, is Ezra Pound. Pound is a presence in all three of these poems, but in 'The Gardens of the Savoy' his presence is overt and pervasive: that poem has, as I think I knew when I wrote it, the shape of a Pound 'canto'. To many or most readers a Pound Canto is shapeless, by definition. But I discovered, in the course of writing 'The Gardens of the Savoy', that that isn't so. And I feel guiltily that by excluding that piece from *Collected Poems* I helped to perpetuate false notions about that one of my (and every one's) masters. In the best of the Cantos earth and water *and* air are equally present, equally honoured; history is there, along with what transcends history.

The poem that brings up the rear, 'But there!', is something I wrote the other day, in the unambitious verse that nowadays is all I can manage. Without naming titles, it looks back over 'The Trip to Huntsville' and 'Brilliance' to 'Rain on South-East England'.

 INTERNATIONAL POETRY AND LITERATURE FROM

Harvill

Publishers of books by or about: Ingmar Bergman, Mikhail Bulgakov, Raymond Carver, Richard Ford, Lidiya Ginzburg, Dermot Healy, Peter Høeg, Josephine Humphreys, Robert Hughes, Ismail Kadare, Aleksandr Kushner, Giuseppe Tomasi di Lampedusa, Claudio Magris, Nadezhda Mandelstam, Osip Mandelstam, Peter Matthiessen, Jesús Moncada, Cees Nooteboom, Boris Pasternak, Georges Perec, Jonathan Raban, José Saramago, Leonardo Sciascia, Alexander Solzhenitsyn, Marina Tsvetaeva, Marguerite Yourcenar

THE AKHMATOVA JOURNALS
Volume 1: 1938–41
Lydia Chukovskaya
*Translated from the Russian
by Milena Michalski and Sylva Rubashova
Akhmatova's poetry translated by Peter Norman*
"In plain but sparkling prose, Chukovskaya celebrates Akhmatova's inner strength and nobility"
CATHY PORTER, *Independent on Sunday*

A SNAIL IN MY PRIME
New and Selected Poems
Paul Durcan
"The vision of the transfigured real finds its best expression in these new poems, together with a new gravity and grace. Truly Durcan is in his prime"   DEREK MAHON, *Irish Times*

EATING STRAWBERRIES IN THE NECROPOLIS
Michael Hulse
"He is an elegant, occasionally an opulent poet: clever, various and engaging"
C.K.STEAD, *London Review of Books*

THE WANDERING BORDER
Jaan Kaplinski
*Translated from the Estonian
by the author with Sam Hamill and Riina Tamm*
"He is a rare mixture of intellect and real simplicity"
PHILIP GROSS, *Poetry Review*

Forthcoming:
A GILDED LAPSE OF TIME
Gjertrud Schnackenberg

PATRICIA BEER

Pharaoh's Dream
In childhood I thought of cows and dreams together
Starting from Pharaoh's dream of seven well-favoured kine
Followed by seven other kine, lean-fleshed
That did eat them up.

Joseph the farmer, dressy as Pharaoh, told him
At once that throughout his many-coloured land
Famine would succeed plenty, seven years of each.
Pharaoh wrung his smooth

Hands, not having considered such a meaning.
Literal in eastern daylight he could not see
Cows eating each other or being real danger.
I thought he was stupid.

I knew the red cows of East Devon.
Our branch-line ran through water-meadows and they
Were always getting on the track. We knew
The times of the trains

And shooed them off. Even a child could do it.
But they did not go far. Making red footprints
In the frail grass, they mooched a few yards then turned
To face the track again.

Pharaoh only dreamed of cows. In my case
They were the dreams themselves, bad dreams
That never quitted the field though you could scatter them
Simply by waking up.

Most of them left gently but one always looked round
With the death-rattle of a moo,
Swinging a bright chain of spittle, a torturer
Who planned to be back.

Pilgrims Crossing
Watch out for pilgrims crossing. Their
Good hour strikes. The messenger
From the eternal city has come
Back into time to summon them.

A dreadful master they have found
Time to be. They never owned
Much, and now these common waves
Deny them even their own graves.

All the misfortunes they have met
Were on some other man's estate.
Christian saw Apollyon
Coming across his fields at noon

Calling him in a dragon's voice
A servant. Waiting now to cross
The river, confident, they stand
On the coast of Beulah Land.

Beulah is a deathbed dream
Of what will be the heavenly home
And never was on earth: the arts,
Help in the house and beds with sheets,

No need to walk, no need to sleep,
A piece of land that they can keep.
At the riverside they glimpse these things
In the city of the King of Kings.

Ready-to-Halt has given away
His crutches. He will always be
A cripple but now very rich,
A lame man in a golden coach.

The village idiot, Feeble-mind,
Has left his moonstruck brain behind
With his protective mops and mows.
He will be needed where he goes.

They do not look for other change.
The celestial kingdom is not strange,
Simply a better-governed one,
A kindly version of their own.

They crossed the river long ago.
What happened there we cannot know.
The only man who might have said,
The man who made them up, is dead.

The trumpet and the chariot
Meant nothing much to him. He put
More value on the pilgrims' pains
And progress in this world. Grace reigns.

The Night Marlowe Died
Christopher Marlowe was a spy, it seems.
His day of pleasure by the River Thames
Should have brought him a handshake and a watch
For faithful service. He had done as much
For anyone who paid him and so had
His three companions. They were really good.

In those days spying was expertly done.
Informers took each other's washing in.
Double agents cancelled themselves out.
Spying had paid for all the wine and meat
Which filled the little room that day in spring
When Marlowe met a different reckoning.

He had been his usual snorting, railing
Blasphemous self, but loyal to his calling,
As they all had to be, to live so well.
He sang a noisy song before he fell,
A dagger stuck in his eye after the feast
As though the Cross had got to him at last.

They saw each other home after his death.
The rats had tired, the streets were out of breath.
Somewhere asleep, the top spymasters lay
Unpicking webs that they had spun by day.
Somewhere, across a park, a peacock's cries
Bewailed the pointlessness of murdering spies.

Beach Party
One week after the death exactly
Friends took us out
To the shadowless beach of childhood
Where every summer Saturday,
A blue flower filling the sky,
We had gone with my mother.

We found we could still play.
We yelled at the hot sand,
Screamed at the cold water.

Then a wind got up.
The corn on the cliff top
Became a whispering gallery
That boomed around the bay,
And a cloud, fat and foreign as a zeppelin,
Trundled out of some strange place.

Over the sand its shadow crept towards us
Welcome at first. I had never minded
The heat of the sun before.

As it came nearer I curled up like prey.
At my right temple it narrowed and streamed in,
The comic strip of a ghost.

All afternoon,
Pretending to be sad which they understood,
I watched the empty sand
On the other side of me.

And when the beach party got up to go,
As at all picnics everybody carried something.

MICHAEL HAMBURGER

Birthday
A shovel scrapes over stone or concrete.
Cars drone. A child's voice rises
Above the hubbub of nameless play.

An afternoon in August. I lie drowsing
On the garden bench. Fifty years melt
In the hot air that transmits
The sounds of happenings whose place and nature
Hang there, hover. That's how it was
For the baby laid down on a balcony
At siesta time in a distant city;
And is here, now. The known and the seen
Fall away. A space opens,
Fills with the hum, the thrumming of what
I am not; the screams, too, the screeching;
Becomes the sum of my life, a home
I cannot inhabit – with the sparrows even
Mute this month, all commotion human.

From the Coach
Wenceslas is the driver's name. Under woods
That steam all day and past goose farms
Livelier than zoos, he takes to the hills
Where castles congregate in his driving mirror.
In town squares, hanging baskets of marigolds
Spin as wheels and a high wind bowl by.
Swans rise from the river more suddenly
Than a blown newspaper and crackle towards the frontier.

Beneath them, out of sight sooner, a train
Slithers into the next country, whichever
That might be. We are surrounded
By other countries. They could close in.
The guide moves youthfully but with wary eyes.
She describes the morning of her own land:
'This race was an independent people' she says.
'They were not slaving for anybody.'

Every night in the small hours
A station announcer blares about a phantom train.
Every morning is a new turning of the back.
Our coach leaves early while people are going to work.
We shall not see them coming home or hear
How they got on. The castles we clamber over
From time to time are neither theirs nor ours.
We belong to the inside of the coach.

Middle-aged husbands and wives sit together,
Bookends with no books in between.
We used to go to work, once upon a time,
In our own way announced trains, fed geese.
Long ago we fought in a world war.
Now from our capsule we look out on the earth,
Its dwellers gone into the afternoon
Its disused castles swinging around the sun.

Elsewhere, my mother at eighty-eight
Lies on a deck chair, drowning
In that same space. Were my father alive
Today he'd be ninety, the tissue
Undone in him larger by thirty-five years;
But the sounds and the silence round him
The same; here, to receive him, the space.

A train rattles by. A drill, far off,
Throbs. A cup falls, shatters.

Mad Lover, Dead Lady
Oh, my Diotima.
Is it not my Diotima you are speaking of?
Thirteen sons she bore me, one of them is Pope,
Sultan the next, the third is the Czar of Russia.
And do you know how it went with her?
Crazy, that's what she went, crazy, crazy, crazy.

Thirteen funerals they gave me when I died.
But she was not there. Locked up in a tower.
That's how it goes: round the bend
Out of the garden where lovers meet,

Walking, talking together. Over the wall.
No one there. Till you visitors come:
Will the corpse write a poem today
About his mad lady?

But I'll tell you a secret: we meet.
Round the bend, on the other side of the wall
Our garden is always there,
Easy, with every season's flowers.
Each from a dark street we come
And the sun shines.
She laughs when I tell her
What's it's like to be dead.
I laugh when she gives me
News of our crazy children
Who've made their way in the world.

No poem today, sir.
Go home. In a dream you'll see
How they remove themselves, your dead
Into madness. And seem to forget
Their loved ones, each in his own dark street.
How your made loved ones
Seem to forget their dead.
That's how it goes. No one there.
Oh, my Diotima.
Waiting for me in the garden.

Mornings

String of beginnings, a lifetime long,
So thin, so strong, it's outlasted the bulk it bound,
Whenever light out of haze lifted
Scarred masonry, marred wood
As a mother her child from the cot,
To strip, to wash, to dress again,
And the cities even were innocent.
In winter too, if the sun glinted
On ice, on snow,
Early air was the more unbreathed
For being cold, the factory smoke
Straighter, compact, not lingering, mingling.

I look at the river. It shines, it shines
As though the banks were not littered
With bottles, cans, rags
Nor lapped by detergents, by sewage,
Only the light were true.
I look at light: but for them, mornings,
Every rising's not-yet,
Little remains now to wait for, wish for,
To praise, once the shapes have set;
And whatever the end of my days, to the last
It will hold, the string of beginnings,
Light that was, that will be, that is new.

Garden, Wilderness

Green fingers, green hand, by now green man
All through, with sap for blood,
Menial to it, gross nature,
And governor of a green tribe
No law can tame, no equity can bend
From the sole need of each, to feed and seed,
Unless, refined beyond resistance to a blight
More grasping than their greed,
Rare shoots evade the keeper's pampering.

He goes to referee
A clinch of lupin, bindweed, common cleavers
And stinging nettle – each with a right to be
Where if one thrives the other three must weaken;
And with his green hand, kin to tendril, root,
Tugs at the wrestlers, to save, to separate
Although his green heart knows:
While sun and rain connive,
Such will the game remain, such his and their estate.

More rain than sunshine: his green lungs inhale
Air thick with marestail spore,
Grass pollen; his legs trail
Trains of torn herbage, dragging through swollen growth
Twined, tangled with decay.
For his green food he gropes,
To taste his share, bonus of fruit and berry,
Tribute for regency,
Sweet compensation for defeated hopes
Or dole despite the drudgery, the waste.

A garden of the mind,
Pure order, equipoise and paradigm
His lord, long far away and silent, had designed,
With bodies, never his, indifferent machines
To impose it and maintain
Against the clinging strand, the clogging slime;
And best invisible, as now that lord's become
Whose ghost the green man serves; that contemplated flower
Whose day of stillness filled all space, all time.

The Street, December
For Charles Causley

By inane innuendo he and she converse,
She and she, he and he, run into each other,
Exchanging as ever the message already familiar,
Safe in littleness, tucked away in discretions
And devious, devious, lest two raw wounds touch;
By local cryptograms of health, prices and weather
Conveying the constants, the universals of care.

May the Goodness that knows, the Lord that loves a duck
Keep it so, keep them so, never let them bumble
Into extinction, as bustard will, dodo did
In gun weather, knife weather, and worse to come
With prices too cruel for health.
May the drabbest, dumbest of birds and their words get
    through,
Zigzagging clear of on-target missiles.

Mr Littlejoy's Prayer
Logos, one Word before the world was peopled,
Take back your progeny of words, words, words
Whose babbling intercourse, proliferation
Makes counterworlds, more packed than tube trains are
When offices close, with some not even sure
Of a mere dosshouse bed; and with no Malthus
To warn, far less to legislate, against
Their polymorphous promiscuity.
Oh, and immortal, thanks to tablet, paper,
Translator, necromancer, necrophile
For whom the living are not good enough,
Too mixed, too lax, too ugly or too blank.
In ever-growing graveyards, libraries,
Once more they copulate and grossly breed,
Dead with the dead or living with the dead.
Contain them, Logos, curb the lexic mob.

If now I speak, it is to clear a space
Where things are things, grow nameless in your name.

Be in that narrow silence, Word, and fill it.

Endless
It began as a couch-grass root,
Stringy and white,
Straggling, to no end,
Branching out, breaking
For procreation.

Traced and pulled, it became
A bramble shoot that climbed
Through leafage of shrub, tree
With a root at its tip, for plunging.

I pulled at it, pulled,
Miles of the thing came away,
More and more.

I pulled and pulled until
I saw that now
Straight up it had risen
With its end in space,
With a root in heaven.

Return
Making today for the hill track,
The rock-riven slopes, the grottoes,
Water's hard course to the sea,
Tree-root's to water, light's
Through the trees, and the light broken
By brushstrokes of wind and cloud
Over contours, colours themselves mutated
By growth, erosion, decay,
I was halted: to the horizon sprawled
A flat surface, fenced off.
And in garish letters on boards I read:
Memorial Park. Through the palings
Glimpsed a single sheep penned,
One cow, one goat farther off,

Last, a pinkness that could be one pig –
Exhibits, I took it, memorials
Indeed to forgotten breeds
Never seen here, homestead for herons,
Pasture for wild geese in passage,
And both for wandering senses,
Minds that in motion found rest.

At a roped gap in the fence
A Minister loitered, chatting
With local officials dressed up
For the Park's inauguration.
'Welcome!' he called to me, smiling,
'In your keenness you've come a bit early,
The cashbox is not yet in place.'

Late, I thought, much too late –
But early if I could return,
Man, woman, child could be here
For the land's reopening,
For the resurrection of hills.

Conversation with a Blackbird
'Will you please, will you please, will you please'
He begins, and I wait for more
Which comes, indistinct, unemphatic.
'Keep away' I think I make out
Or 'let things be'
May or may not have heard:
The vowels are blurred,
The consonants missing.
Oh, and the rhythm is free
After that courteous request.

Translated, my answering whistle says:
'Be more explicit. Our kind can't endure
Things unsure, songs open-ended.
To be kept guessing is more
Than we can bear for long.'

Does he laugh? 'Please, please, please, please, please'
Is the reply. Then coloratura, among it these phrases:
'We repeat, don't complete.
Mysteries, mysteries.
Improvise, weather-wise.
Now I dip, now I rise.
Vary it. Don't care a bit
If it's indefinite.
Now I sit, twitter. Now I flit.'

Michael Hamburger

Note
When asked to select one of my poems for the anthology *Poet's Choice* (The Dial Press, New York, 1962), I chose one of three poems recently written, because I was excited about the belated breakthrough into what I felt to be a new freedom in the writing of those poems. For the same anthology Philip Larkin chose his 'Absences' 'because I fancy it sounds like a different, better poet than myself. The last line, for instance, sounds like a slightly-unconvincing translation from a French symbolist. I wish I could write like this more often.' That was before the persona Larkin adopted became a permanent fixture. I find the –slightly-tongue-in-cheek – statement interesting because he chose what he thought his least characteristic poem; and because I'm incapable of recognizing any single persona, let alone 'image', of myself as poet, in my work as a whole.

Even when asked to put together a *Selected Poems* for Carcanet six years ago, I came up against this difficulty and had to ask four friends and relatives to do the choosing, decided by proportional representation. Here, too, I've been guided in part by the choice of Anne Beresford, my wife, and Michael Schmidt, to both of whom I'm most grateful for helping me out.

For reasons of space I had to discard several of their choices; and an extract from my two sequences, which many regard as my best work, was out of the question for me. Being 'variations', as I called them, they must stand or fall as longer poems.

After more than fifty years of writing and publication I know only that I've tried to do very many different things in verse – something that would be taken for granted if we still had the notion of kind or 'genre' in poetry, instead of the notion of a 'voice', a 'personality' or, most recently, a brand name. Because I care most about the people, things or phenomena I write about, and these are necessarily various, every poem I write is an attempt to do justice in the appropriate words and shape to a particular experience of one of these. The dreams I include among the phenomena demands an ordering quite different from that demanded by the phenomena of waking life, which may also be as single and clear-cut as a specific animal or tree or composite and complex.

The few poems picked out here cannot possibly represent the diversity or range of which I'm much more aware than of the unity that critics have found – or failed to find – in my work.

It has to be said, too, that I am not a reader or critic of my own work, except that becomes unavoidable for purposes of selection. Such critical faculties as one has ought to be operative in the process of writing itself. But it's for others to decide whether the product was well or badly finished – and whether the choice I have made leaves them more or less inclined than before to grapple with the heterogeneous whole.

CHRISTOPHER MIDDLETON

Saloon with Birds
If someone barefoot stood in a saloon,
His dromedary might be chomping, outside,
That majestic meal. High olive notes
Plucked from a mandolin. Fumes. Leafgreen.

A dark descends. There, with banana palm,
Consorts forbidden music. Ugly. Ocean.
Delay it. First a clatter, from the birds.
They wax decrepit. Vocal signatures:

Who could ever have so illuminated them
That the letters, cut from stark air,
Assume no solitary monumental pose,
But wavily ache with the boat hulls?

Certain or not, an urgent finger prodded
Epsilons and wagtailed gammas free
From habit, a peculiar glue. No help. No
Waste. In the saloon each dust spake.

In the saloon the spokes of another
Sunlight, still this ocular companion though,
Rolled afternoons around, like meatballs,
Bubbles of corn sizzling in a crystal pan.

Throaty owls also, they could entertain
Quick, tensile teeth. A joy. Pelican moonlit.
Look at a pine nut. It exists, you know.
Little furred insects inhabit vast smells.

For this the saloon is open. A waft.
A waft is all it takes. A venetian blind
Has wrinkled the wash basin. A cool expounds
Blood orange, air in China, appalling beliefs.

Air wraps the mast. Air singing. Air,
The solo invader who timed anew
Our free objects. The saloon twangs,
Dust swims, a gong letting its hum fly.

Closing never. Least of all on syllables.
A split lemon has released from evil
Any soul what's willing. Get that. Now
Never you move like you were shrunk to be.

Or else forgo the little sorrow. Treasure
The big one. Tell, in the saloon,
Nothing of it. Look up. Long enough
The ocean has delayed. You can breathe again.

Vietnamese Harp
Before first light awake
   At a touch on a button
One taut steel string plucked I heard
   And another, another

Penetrating the dark a music
   Of spine and thighbone
Clear as the contour of a waterlily
   Ghostly as the snow it cups

Floated from its peak
   To ground, a shimmering pagoda
Spreads and folds its wings
   Stands where I lay

Amazingly nowhere, almost
    Too much trance for a body
So soon in the day, cut loose
    From the singing zigzags

I walked outside, by the open window
    Taking the same sounds in
But curious who in spirit
    Now might weep to be listening

The Old Tour Guide – His Interpreter

He says there is a Greek house in Mustafapasha,
He says you go down a winding stone staircase
Into a crypt. On more stairs down to a crypt
Beneath it, a secret door opens. Now
There is more to be said, it seems.

I think he is saying that a blue sun
And utter stillness enfold the numen:
He says that in a third crypt under the second
A Christ of Sorrows stands alone, his face
Preserved in the original paint. That the face,
He says, illuminates all memory of the house,
Once you have been there, for your lifetime,
Is not certain.

What was he saying next? He says they found
A lost valley, by chance, two summers gone.
Conical churches there contain sealed tombs,
Full of treasure. Present, for anyone to touch,
A desiccated loaf, on an altar, a curled up
Sandal, each of a substance
Evidently shunned by mice.

Now he says there are many places
Not to be gone to. Memory has no desire
To be disappointed. But, he says, nothing,
Nothing stops you wanting to go there.

He is describing the valley, how across
Its clear stream, from one willow bush
To the next, singing warblers flit: the bird
Called popularly heaven bird can be seen there,
Crested, with blue wings, throat of rose,
Best heard at noontime when it flutes alone.

That is what I think he said. In his thick
Local accent now he is saying this:
You must not cut loose from here and now,
Both hands taking hold have to pull, he says:
Let the crypt call to you, as the long road did,
Let the valley track the turning of your eyes
And always haunt the here and now you see.

That is the gist. Wait, what wild talk is this
Of war striking a far country…
              Stored at home his great bow?
Seven times I heard the suffix
Which in his language indicates hearsay,
The saying a matter of doubt to the sayer,
Critical things might happen to have been
Otherwise.

Ah yes, he says,
Ah yes, this is the country of people after midnight;
Few have spelled out into the pleasure of a heartbeat,
Into a knot of mind, once and for all,
The loops of light they see spreading at sunrise,
The braid that snakes down a girl's bare back.
When we go to see what is there to be seen,
The knots and braids easily slip;
We learn to know how little we understand.

But as we go I believe he is saying
May Allah lift the griefs from all of us.

Small Carvings at Arycanda

Not much is left:
Like a bubble with a cleft
At twelve o'clock, a flying heart
Floats from a stem, which stoops
As the stem of a bluebell does.

Somewhere else, an inch or two
Above the ground,
A cluster of grapes, diminutive, hangs
Bursting from its marble slab,
Halfway liquid in your mouth.

All this, equally for the poor:
On several tombstones flying
The bluebell heart, lightly weighted,
And on a sunken slab
Clustering grapes that call

To be caught in the cup of a hand,
To be fondled, every one,
By the flesh of a fingertip,
Till bud can bud no more
And spurts its grapeness out.

Hyperbole, no doubt. How else
To feel the flash and throb afresh
Two hands, a little hammer,
And a blade of bronze
Divined in the dead stone?

How else to breathe again the life
Of carnal imagination working as a hinge:
The door the dead saunter through
And the living rush at, opens:
Here heart and grape mark

The narrow rapids where they meet
And spirit streams, making faces;
Gently now, nervous as the nostrils
Of a unicorn, or, come to that,
Of a gundog, the signs explode

Our electric shellac myths
Of Madonna and all that rot:
For a minute the bilge of our kitsch
Ebbs, heart beats
And the grapes come out on top.

Note
Fresh from the Turkish-Georgian border mountains, and with a vivid memory of the low-relief carvings still embedded in the façades of ancient Georgian churches (ninth–eleventh centuries), I made my choice of poems for *PNR* 100 bearing in mind the braidings and knots which dominate those carvings and constitute a magic symbolism: the carver adhered, at least, to a value-system in which, from all directions, earthly and heavenly fields of force are fruitfully connected. – I have wondered why poems can lapse into a diluted, univocal, and narrow discourse nowadays, to project a 'view', the phrasing tinged and smart, not stained and ragged, with emotion. My aspiration, the poem in mind, is otherwise: a re-threading of language strands which common (and 'massive') use has frazzled; a dense text and a wiry one; a braiding and knotting of threads which do voice emotion intelligently on the hop, in action or suspense; strong colours; the wording pungent and many-layered (though not exactly 'choral'); not patchworks but networks – matter or mind as 'strings' orchestrally braided, or knotted, and then slipping, too, as the dialectic thickens. – 'The Old Tour Guide – His Interpreter' is at least a gesture in that direction: it leaves open the question of what the informant might have meant; the interpreter only mediates, perhaps he is not aware that the tour is to start from the threshold of an underworld. Blood for ghosts. Also a transfusion which does not bar the Gorgon's approach (at which moment even Odysseus fled). – I would like a reader to speak the poems in a kind of crystalline murmur (is that thinkable?), as if they were breaks in settled language, or peep holes. Dethroned, dizzy, the speaker gazes down through the layers of the shaft on which, as ego, he or she was mounted. There must be a poetry which enacts utter consternation – the tremors, short or long, sickening or delightful the vibrancy, of the imagined world, and which enacts, no less, as nearly as possible in time, the movements of life-signs as they are being instantaneously perceived and, from now to now, deciphered.

The Arycanda carvings are Hellenistic, not Georgian.

JOHN ASHBERY

He

He cuts down the lakes so they appear straight
He smiles at his feet in their tired mules.
He turns up the music much louder.
He takes down the vaseline from the pantry shelf.

He is the capricious smile behind the colored bottles.
He eats not lest the poor want some.
He breathes of attitudes the piney altitudes.
He indeed is the White Cliffs of Dover.

He knows that his neck is frozen.
He snorts in the vale of dim wolves.
He writes to say, 'If ever you visit this island,
He'll grow you back to your childhood.

'He is the liar behind the hedge
He grew one morning out of candor.
He is his own consolation prize.
He has had his eye on you from the beginning.'

He hears the weak cut down with a smile.
He waltzes tragically on the spitting housetops.
He is never near. What you need
He cancels with the air of one making a salad.

He is always the last to know.
He is strength you once said was your bonnet.
He has appeared in 'Carmen'.
He is after us. If you decide

He is important, it will get you nowhere.
He is the source of much bitter reflection.
He used to be pretty for a rat.
He is now over-proud of his Etruscan appearance.

He walks in his sleep into your life.
He is worth knowing only for the children
He has reared as savages in Utah.
He helps his mother take in the clothes-line.

He is unforgettable as a shooting star.
He is known as 'Liverlips'.
He will tell you he has had a bad time of it.
He will try to pretend his pressagent is a temptress.

He looks terrible on the stairs.
He cuts himself on what he eats.
He was last seen flying to New York.
He was handing out cards which read:

'He wears a question in his left eye.
He dislikes the police but will associate with them.
He will demand something not on the menu.
He is invisible to the eyes of beauty and culture.

'He prevented the murder of Mistinguett in Mexico.
He has a knack for abortions. If you see
He is following you, forget him immediately:
He is dangerous even though asleep and unarmed.'

**'How Much Longer Will I Be Able
to Inhabit the Divine Sepulcher…'**
How much longer will I be able to inhabit the divine sepulcher
Of life, my great love? Do dolphins plunge bottomward
To find the light? Or is it rock
That is searched? Unrelentingly? Huh. And if some day

Men with orange shovels come to break open the rock
Which encases me, what about the light that comes in then?
What about the smell of the light?
What about the moss?

In pilgrim times he wounded me
Since then I only lie
My bed of light is a furnace choking me
With hell (and sometimes I hear salt water dripping).

I mean it – because I'm one of the few
To have held my breath under the house. I'll trade
One red sucker for two blue ones. I'm
Named Tom. The

Light bounces off mossy rocks down to me
In this glen (the neat villa! which
When he'd had he would not had he of
And jests under the smarting of privet

Which on hot spring nights perfumes the empty rooms
With the smell of sperm flushed down toilets
On hot summer afternoons within sight of the sea.
If you knew why then professor) reads

To his friends: Drink to me only with
And the reader is carried away
By a great shadow under the sea.
Behind the steering wheel

The boy took out his own forehead.
His girlfriend's head was a green bag
Of narcissus stems. 'OK you win
But meet me anyway at Cohen's Drug Store

In 22 minutes'. What a marvel is ancient man!
Under the tulip roots he has figured out a way to be a religious
    animal
And would be a mathematician. But where in unsuitable
    heaven
Can he get the heat that will make him grow?

For he needs something or will forever remain a dwarf,
Though a perfect one, and possessing a normal-sized brain
But he has got to be released by giants from things.
And as the plant grows older it realizes it will never be a tree,

Will probably always be haunted by a bee
And cultivates stupid impressions
So as not to become part of the dirt. The dirt
Is mounting like a sea. And we say goodbye

Shaking hands in front of the crashing of the waves
That give our words lonesomeness, and make these flabby
    hands seem ours –
Hands that are always writing things
On mirrors for people to see later –

Do you want them to water
Plant, tear listlessly among the exchangeable ivy –
Carrying food to mouth, touching genitals –
But no doubt you have understood

It all now and I am a fool. It remains
For me to get better, and to understand you so
Like a chair-sized man. Boots
Were heard on the floor above. In the garden the sunlight was
    still purple

But what buzzed in it had changed slightly
But not forever… but casting its shadow
On sticks, and looking around for an opening in the air, was

quite as if it had never refused to exist differently. Guys
In the yard handled the belt he had made

Stars
Painted the garage roof crimson and black
He is not a man
Who can read these signs… his bones were stays…

And even refused to live
In a world and refunded the hiss
Of all that exists terribly near us
Like you, my love, and light.

For what is obedience but the air around us
To the house? For which the federal men came
In a minute after the sidewalk
Had taken you home? ('Latin… blossom…')

After which you led me to water
And bade me to drink, which I did, owing to your kindness.
You would not let me out for two days and three nights,
Bringing me books bound in wild thyme and scented wild
    grasses

As if reading had any interest for me, you…
Now you are laughing.
Darkness interrupts my story.
Turn on the light.

Meanwhile what am I going to do?
I am growing up again, in school, the crisis will be very soon.
And you twist the darkness in your fingers, you
Who are slightly older…

Who are you, anyway?
And is it the color of sand,
The darkness, as it sifts through your hand
Because what does anything mean,

The ivy and the sand? That boat
Pulled up on the shore? Am I wonder,
Strategically, and in the light
Of the long sepulcher that hid death and hides me?

Rivers and Mountains
On the secret map the assassins
Cloistered, the Moon River was marked
Near the eighteen peaks and the city
Of humiliation and defeat – wan ending
Of the trail among dry, papery leaves
Gray-brown quills like thoughts
In the melodious but vast mass of today's
Writing through fields and swamps
Marked, on the map, with little bunches of weeds.
Certainly squirrels lived in the woods
But devastation and dull sleep still
Hung over the land, quelled
The rioters turned out of sleep in the peace of prisons
Singing on marble factory walls
Deaf consolation of minor tunes that pack
The air with heavy invisible rods
Pent in some sand valley from

John Ashbery

Which only quiet walking ever instructs.
The bird flew over and
Sat – there was nothing else to do.
Do not mistake its silence for pride or strength
Or the waterfall for a harbor
Full of light boats that is there
Performing for thousands of people
In clothes some with places to go
Or games. Sometimes over the pillar
Of square stones its impact
Makes a light print.

So going around cities
To get to other places you found
It all on paper but the land
Was made of paper processed
To look like ferns, mud or other
Whose sea unrolled its magic
Distances and then rolled them up
Its secret was only a pocket
After all but some corners are darker
Than these moonless nights spent as on a raft
In the seclusion of a melody heard
As though through trees
And you can never ignite their touch
Long but there were homes
Flung far out near the asperities
Of a sharp, rocky pinnacle
And other collective places
Shadows of vineyards whose wine
Tasted of the forest floor
Fisheries and oyster beds
Tides under the pole
Seminaries of instruction, public
Places for electric light
And the major tax assessment area
Wrinkled on the plan
Of election to public office
Sixty-two years old bath and breakfast
The formal traffic, shadows
To make it not worth joining
After the ox had pulled away the cart.

Your plan was to separate the enemy into two groups
With the razor-edged mountains between.

It worked well on paper
But their camp had grown
To be the mountains and the map
Carefully peeled away and not torn
Was the light, a tender but tough bark
On everything. Fortunately the war was solved
In another way by isolating the two sections
Of the enemy's navy so that the mainland
Warded away the big floating ships.
Light bounced off the ends
Of the small gray waves to tell
Them in the observatory
About the great drama that was being won
To turn off the machinery
And quietly move among the rustic landscape
Scooping snow off the mountains rinsing
The coarser ones that love had
Slowly risen in the night to overflow
Wetting pillow and petal
Determined to place the letter
On the unassassinated president's desk
So that a stamp could reproduce all this
In detail, down to the last autumn leaf
And the affliction of June ride
Slowly out into the sun-blackened landscape.

At North Farm
Somewhere someone is traveling furiously toward you,
At incredible speed, traveling day and night,
Through blizzards and desert heat, across torrents, through
    narrow passes.
But will he know where to find you,
Recognize you when he sees you,
Give you the thing he has for you?

Hardly anything grows here,
Yet the granaries are bursting with meal,
The sacks of meal piled to the rafters.
The streams run with sweetness, fattening fish;
Birds darken the sky. Is it enough
That the dish of milk is set out at night,
That we think of him sometimes,
Sometimes and always, with mixed feelings?

Note
The poems I wrote, say between the ages of eighteen and twenty eight, which were collected in *Some Trees*, seem to have a (for me) pleasingly surrealist shimmer, but even before that book appeared in America I had gone to live in France where I would end up spending the next ten years. I wanted to write in a different way, but in a way which would satisfy me in the way that the earlier poems had. This resulted in a book of odd experiments, many of them very disjointed, called *The Tennis Court Oath*. '… Sepulchre' is perhaps a typical example from that period. I intended to put the pieces back together, so to speak, when I could figure out a way to do so. I felt that I had begun to do that in the poem 'Rivers and Mountains', which at that time seemed to me a kind of turning point. It was then a question of easing back into a continuation of my first period – work I hoped would be 'the same only different'. I think I may have done something like that and 'At North Farm' may be an illustration of this.

CHARLES TOMLINSON

Swimming Chenango Lake
Winter will bar the swimmer soon.
   He reads the water's autumnal hesitations
A wealth of ways: it is jarred,
   It is astir already despite its steadiness,
Where the first leaves at the first
   Tremor of the morning air have dropped
Anticipating him, launching their imprints
   Outwards in eccentric, overlapping circles.
There is a geometry of water, for this
   Squares off the clouds' redundances
And sets them floating in a nether atmosphere
   All angles and elongations: every tree
Appears a cypress as it stretches there
   And every bush that shows the season,
A shaft of fire. It is a geometry and not
   A fantasia of distorting forms, but each
Liquid variation answerable to the theme
   It makes away from, plays before:
It is a consistency, the grain of the pulsating flow.
   But he has looked long enough, and now
Body must recall the eye to its dependence
   As he scissors the waterscape apart
And sways it to tatters. Its coldness
   Holding him to itself, he grants the grasp,
For to swim is also to take hold
   On water's meaning, to move in its embrace
And to be, between grasp and grasping, free.
   He reaches in-and-through to that space
The body is heir to, making a where
   In water, a possession to be relinquished
Willingly at each stroke. The image he has torn
   Flows-to behind him, healing itself,
Lifting and lengthening, splayed like the feathers
   Down an immense wing whose darkening spread
Shadows his solitariness: alone, he is unnamed
   By this baptism, where only Chenango bears a name
In a lost language he begins to construe –
   A speech of densities and derisions, of half-
Replies to the questions his body must frame
   Frogwise across the all but penetrable element.
Human, he fronts it and, human, he draws back
   From the interior cold, the mercilessness
That yet shows a kind of mercy sustaining him.
   The last sun of the year is drying his skin
Above a surface a mere mosaic of tiny shatterings,
   Where a wind is unscaping all images in the flowing obsidian,
The going-elsewhere of ripples incessantly shaping.

Assassin
The rattle in Trotsky's throat and his wild boar's moans
                             Piedra de Sol (Octavio Paz)

Blood I foresaw. I had put by
   The distractions of the retina, the eye
That like a child must be fed and comforted
   With patterns, recognitions. The room
Had shrunk to a paperweight of glass and he
   To the centre and prisoner of its transparency.

He rasped pages. I knew too well
   The details of that head. I wiped
Clean the glance and saw
   Only his vulnerableness. Under my quivering
There was an ease, save for that starched insistence
   While paper snapped and crackled as in October air.

Sound drove out sight. We inhabited together
   One placeless cell. I must put down
This rage of the ear for discrimination, its absurd
   Dwelling on ripples, liquidities, fact
Fastening on the nerve gigantic paper burs.
   The gate of history is straiter than eye's or ear's.

In imagination, I had driven the spike
   Down and through. The skull had sagged in its blood.
The grip, the glance – stained but firm –
   Held all at its proper distance and now hold
This autumnal hallucination of white leaves
   From burying purpose in a storm of sibilance.

I strike. I am the future and my blow
   Will have it now. If lightning froze
It would hover as here, the room
   Riding in the crest of the moment's wave,
In the deed's time, the deed's transfiguration
   And as if that wave would never again recede.

The blood wells. Prepared for this
   This I can bear. But papers
Snow to the ground with a whispered roar:
   The voice, cleaving their crescendo, is his
Voice, and his the animal cry
   That has me then by the roots of the hair.

Fleshed in that sound, objects betray me,
   Objects are my judge: the table and its shadow,
Desk and chair, the ground a pressure
   Telling me where it is that I stand
Before wall and window-light:
   Mesh of the curtain, wood, metal, flesh:

A dying body that refuses death,
   He lurches against me in his warmth and weight,
As if my arm's length blow
   Had transmitted and spent its strength
Through blood and bone; and I, spectred,
   The body that rose against me were my own.

Woven from the hair of that bent head,
   The thread that I had grasped unlabyrinthed all –
Tightrope of history and necessity –
   But the weight of a world unsteadies my feet
And I fall into the lime and contaminations
   Of contingency; into hands, looks, time.

The Way In

The needle-point's swaying reminder
    Teeters at thirty, and the flexed foot
Keeps it there. Kerb-side signs
    For demolitions and new detours,
A propped pub, a corner lopped, all
    Bridle the pressures that guide the needle.

I thought I knew this place, this face
    A little worn, a little homely.
But the look that shadows softened
    And the light could grace, keeps flowing away from me
In daily change; its features, rendered down,
    Collapse expressionless, and the entire town

Sways in the fume of the pyre. Even the new
    And mannerless high risers tilt and wobble
Behind the deformations of acrid heat –
    A century's lath and rafters. Bulldozers
Gobble a street up, but already a future seethes
    As if it had waited in the crevices:

A race in transit, a nomad hierarchy;
    Cargoes of debris out of these ruins fill
Their buckled prams: their trucks and hand-carts wait
    To claim the dismantlings of a neighbourhood –
All that a grimy care from wastage gleans,
    From scrap-iron down to heaps of magazines.

Slowing, I see the faces of a pair
    Behind their load: he shoves and she
Trails after him, a sexagenarian Eve,
    Their punishment to number every hair
Of what remains. Their clothes come of their trade –
    They wear the cast-offs of a lost decade.

The place had failed them anyhow, and their pale
    Absorption staring past this time
And dusty space we occupy together,
    Gazes the new blocks down – not built for them;
But what they are looking at they do not see.
    No Eve, but mindless Mnemosyne,

She is our lady of the nameless metals, of things
    No hand has made, and no machine
Has cut to a nicety that takes the mark
    Of clean intention – at best, the guardian
Of all that our daily contact stales and fades,
    Rusty cages and lampless lampshades.

Perhaps those who have climbed into their towers
    Will eye it all differently, the city spread
In unforeseen configurations, and living with this,
    Will find that civility I can only miss – and yet
It will need more than talk and trees
    To coax a style from these disparities.

The needle-point's swaying reminder
    Teeters: I go with uncongealing traffic now
Out onto the cantilevered road, window on window
    Sucked backwards at the level of my wheels.
Is it patience or anger most renders the will keen?
    This is a daily discontent. This is the way in.

A Rose For Janet

I know
this rose is only
an ink-and-paper rose
but see how it grows and goes
on growing
beneath your eyes:
a rose in flower
has had (almost) its vegetable hour
whilst my
rose of spaces and typography
can reappear at will
(your will)
whenever you repeat
this ceremony of the eye
from the beginning
and thus
learn how
to resurrect a rose
that's instantaneous
perennial
and perfect now

The Door in the Wall
i.m. Jorge Guillén

Under the door in the wall
the slit of sun
pours out at the threshold
such an illumination,

one begins to picture
the garden in there,
making the wrinkled step
seem shadowy, bare;

but within the shadows
an underfoot world puts forth
in points of light
its facets of worth –

surfaces of such depth
you have only to eye them,
to find you are travelling
a constellation by them;

and the sun that whitens
every lightward plane
leaks up the stone jamb,
reappears again

where the flickering tangle
of thick leaves cover
the top of the wall and
ivy piles over.

So the garden in there
cannot mean merely
an ornamental perfection
when the gardener lets be

this climbing parasite
within whose folds
birds find a shelter
against rain and cold.

But let be the garden, too,
as you tread and travel
this broken pathway
where the sun does not dazzle

but claims company with
all these half-hidden things

and raising their gaze
does not ask of them wings –

fissures and grained dirt,
shucked shells and pebble,
a sprinkle of shatterings,
a grist of gravel

where the print and seal
the travelling foot has set
declares, Jorge Guillén,
the integrity of the planet.

Note

'Swimming Chenango Lake' and 'Assassin' both come from the same volume, *The Way of a World* (1969). These two contrasting poems belong to a book where I seemed to feel a certain growth in my work, an ability to write of the natural scene together with a sense of the political torments of our era. These antithetical realities appear in these two poems. To take the positive aspect first. I think that by the time of *The Way of a World*, I had begun to experience a confirmation of attitudes towards the sensory world that were already finding their way to consciousness in my earliest full-length book, *Seeing is Believing*. This confirmation came about from having lived a little longer – a decade or so – and having travelled in America and Mexico, and also from discovering quite unexpectedly in 1965 an ally in the poet from whom the epigraph to *The Way of a World* derived, the Spaniard Jorge Guillén:

> Y tanto se da el presente
> Que el pie caminante siente
> La integridad del planeta.

(And so much does the present give / That the travelling foot can feel / The integrity of the planet.) There were times in reading Guillén that I seemed to hear a familiar voice and when I read his introduction to the English edition of *Cántico*, I felt I was not alone in my approach, especially when he urges, 'One must cherish and advance this privilege of being among all things that have been, of sharing in their fulness… There is no mysticism here, no experience is more ordinary.' When he went on to speak of the physiological factor in this attitude, here was home territory indeed:

> Up to a point the human animal succeeds in fitting into his environment, and this adjustment between his eyes and the light of day, between his lungs and the air, between his feet and the ground involves a coordination so obvious that even the most observant persons are barely aware of it.

Coordination is one of the themes of 'Swimming Chenango Lake', a coordination which, by implication, extends from the particular physical act of swimming to the way we take hold on our world yet can never possess it, and the way it takes hold on us, confirming our human identity. This is to go with the grain of time, space and physicality. 'Assassin' moves against the grain, refusing relationship and refusing time, substituting for the latter what Octavio Paz in an account of this poem calls 'a philosophical eternity', a dizzying stasis out of and above time. At the end of the poem, the assassin falls back into real time and history. He is, by the very fact of human coordination, forced to return to the world of contingency – 'hands, looks, time'. If 'Swimming Chenango Lake' posits some ideal of relationship with the natural world, 'Assassin' tries to expose the kind of abstraction fanatics have continually offered us in this century, convinced that only they possessed the key to history. I wrote the poem at a time when Che Guevara was a popular hero, having read his book on guerilla warfare and been horrified by his phrase, 'We must transform ourselves into cold and efficient killing machines'. For this is what Trotsky's assassin tried to achieve.

These poems (a third, 'Prometheus', is 'Assassin' writ large across the vista of the Russian revolution) are two of the imaginative poles of my work. 'The Way In' stands beside them as an illustration of how other plausible, economic abstractions have seen the wreckage of our cities – those daily symbols of a possible coordination – during the post-war years. I have included 'A Rose for Janet' as an example of the lighter, more intimate poem-between-friends that I frequently write. 'The Door in the Wall' is here because, almost thirty years after first reading Guillén, 'the integrity (or completeness) of the planet' (quoted at the close) still stays anchored at the back of my mind. I first read that poem aloud in Spain beside Fernando Galván's lucid translation at that remarkable institution the Residencia de Estudiantes, Madrid. The Residencia stands very much for the ideal of Guillén and his friends of the generation of '98, 'a more open Spain', as he says. My poem thus signals a renewed interest on my part in Iberian culture, both Spanish and Portuguese. This interest first began long ago with my translations of Machado, and has recently resurfaced in many new poems which are the result of both travels and of contact with that brilliant younger generation who are the heirs of Guillén.

THOMAS KINSELLA

Chrysalides

Our last free summer we mooned about at odd hours
Pedalling slowly through country towns, stopping to eat
Chocolate and fruit, tracing our vagaries on the map.

At night we watched in the barn, to the lurch of melodeon
        music,
The crunching boots of countrymen – huge and weightless
As their shadows – twirling and leaping over the yellow
        concrete.

Sleeping too little or too much, we awoke at noon
And were received with womanly mockery into the kitchen,
Like calves poking our faces in with enormous hunger.

Daily we strapped our saddlebags and went to experience
A tolerance we shall never know again, confusing
For the last time, for example, the licit and the familiar.

Our instincts blurred with change; a strange wakefulness
Sapped our energies and dulled our slow-beating hearts
To the extremes of feeling – insensitive alike

To the unique succession of our youthful midnights,
When by a window ablaze softly with the virgin moon
Dry scones and jugs of milk awaited us in the dark,

Or to lasting horror: a wedding flight of ants
Spawning to its death, a mute perspiration
Glistening like drops of copper in our path.

Westland Row

We came to the outer light down a ramp in the dark
Through eddying cold gusts and grit, our ears
Stopped with noise. The hands of the station clock
Stopped, or another day vanished exactly.
The engine departing hammered slowly overhead.
Dust blowing under the bridge, we stooped slightly
With briefcases and books and entered the wind.

The savour of our days restored, dead
On nostril and tongue. Drowned in air,
We stepped on our own traces, not on stone,
Nodded and smiled distantly and followed
Our scattering paths, not stumbling, not touching.

Until, in a breath of benzine from a garage-mouth,
By the Academy of Music coming against us,
She stopped an instant in her wrinkled coat
And ducked her childish cheek in the coat-collar
To light a cigarette: seeing nothing,
Thick-lipped, in her grim composure.

Daughterwife, look upon me.

Artists' Letters

Folders, papers, proofs, maps
with tissue paper marked and coloured.
I was looking for something,
confirmation of something,
in the cardboard box
when my fingers deflected among
fat packets of love letters,
old immediacies in elastic bands.

I shook a letter open from
its creases, carefully, and read
– and shrugged, embarrassed.
                Then stirred.
My hand grew thin and agitated
as the words crawled again
quickly over the dried paper.

Letter by letter the foolishness
deepened, but displayed
a courage in its own unsureness;
acknowledged futility and waste
in all their importance…a young idiocy
in desperate full-hearted abandon
to all the chance of one choice:

There is one throw, no more. One
offering: make it. With no style
– these are desperate times. There is
a poverty of spirit in the wind,
a shabby richness in braving it.
My apologies, but you are my beloved
and I will not be put off.

What is it about such letters,
torn free ignominiously
in love? Character stripped off
our pens plunge repeatedly
at the unique cliché, cover
ache after ache of radiant paper
with analytic ecstasies,
wrestle in repetitious fury.

The flesh storms our brain; we storm
our entranced opposite, badger her
with body metaphors, project
our selves with outthrust stuttering arms,
cajoling, forcing her
– her spread-eagled spirit –
to accept our suspect cries
with shocked and shining eyes.

Artists' letters (as the young career
grows firmer in excited pride
and moves toward authority
after the first facetiousness,
the spirit shaken into strength
by shock after shock of understanding)
suddenly shudder and *display*! Animal.
Violent vital organs of desire.

A toothless mouth opens
and we throw ourselves, enthralled, against our bonds
and thrash toward her. And when we have
been nicely eaten and our parts
spat out whole and have become
'one', *then* we can settle our cuffs
and our Germanic collar
and turn back calmly toward distinguished things.

Talent and Friendship
Neither is simple
and neither is handed down.

Either persisted in without change
grows ridiculous

and either at any time
may fail.

If it fail in part
it is made good only in part

and if it come to final failure
accept – but prepare for a difficult widow:

that fig-bodied stone devil
on your sanctuary wall

gross mouth open
to all comers

or, as I remember,
a still youthful witch

moving off sick to death
among the graves and the old men

in sharp argument with her pale son,
he muttering in sharp answer,

deadly familiar,
so unlike.

*

There is no mantle
and it does not descend.

from **At the Head Table**
The air grew dark with anger
toward the close of the celebration.
But remembering his purpose
he kept an even temper

thinking: I have devoted
my life, my entire career,
to the avoidance of affectation,
the way of entertainment

or the specialist response.
With always the same outcome.

Dislike. Misunderstanding.
But I will do what I can.

He rose, adjusted his garments,
lifted the lovely beaker
with the slim amphibian handles,
and turned to the source of trouble.

'Madam. Your health. Your patience.
Unlock those furious arms,
or we who respect and love you
will have to take offence.

How often, like this evening,
we have sat and watched it happen.
Discussing the same subjects
from our settled points of view,

our cheer turning to bitterness
with one careless word,
and then the loaded silence,
staring straight ahead.

O for the simple wisdom
to learn by our experience!
I know from my daily labour
it is not too much to ask.

This lovely cup before us
– this piece before all others –
gave me the greatest trouble,
in impulse and idea

and management of material,
in all the fine requirements
that bring the craftsman's stoop.
Yet proved the most rewarding,

perfect for its purpose,
holding an ample portion
measured most exactly,
pouring precise and full.

A fit vessel also
for vital decoration.
These marks of waves and footsteps
somewhere by the sea

– in fact a web of order,
each mark accommodating
the shapes of all the others
with none at fault, or false;

a system of living images
making increased response
to each increased demand
in the eye of the beholder,

with a final full response
across the entire surface
– a total theme – presented
to a full intense regard…'

Thomas Kinsella

Note
My first poems were written partly in curiosity, with my discovery of modern poetry. And in some excitement, with the discovery of my own personal world – in detail – in *Dubliners* and *A Portrait of the Artist as a Young Man*.

It was a while before my poems could say exactly what I wanted them to say. As I began to manage this, I wrote a number of poems out of a strong local sense, with an awareness of things against their routine backgrounds. 'Chrysalides' and 'Westland Row' are two of these. Later, I found reality and the past expressing themselves in a sense of family, in memories of my growing up in Dublin. In my attempts at generalisation, and making sense of experience that mattered, I wrote mainly longer poems; but 'Artists' Letters' and 'Talent and Friendship' are shorter poems of this kind.

When I try to write about these ideas, I find that I am more at ease in poetry. 'At the Head Table' is a recent long poem; the first part has to do with possible attitudes of the artist toward his work and toward his audience.

IAIN CRICHTON SMITH

A Note on Puritans
There was no curtain between them and fire.
Every moment was a moment when
a man could sink into a tranced despair
or shake his heels to vanity and turn
with frenzied gaiety from that drying air.

Therefore their urgency. That fire glowed
along their blackened senses hour by hour.
Only the book they clutched so tightly cheered
hearts that might stop, eyes that their burning fear
could hole with flame; heads that their thoughts had charred.

Garden and gardener, book and reader glowed;
limbs crackled their sins; silks twitched in a blue flame;
a man's flesh melted in the mouth of God;
he lost his name to earn a lasting name.
A heaven flashed where all that oil flowed.

That was great courage to have watched that fire.
not placing a screen before it as we do
with pictures, poems, landscapes, a great choir
of mounting voices which can drown the raw
hissing and spitting of flame with other fire.

That was great courage, to have stayed as true
to truth as men can stay. From them we learn
how certain truths can make men brutish too;
how few can watch the bared teeth slow-burn
and not be touched by the lumps of fire they chew

into contempt and barrenness. I accuse
these men of singleness and loss of grace
who stared so deeply into the fire's hues
that all was fire to them
    Yes, to this place
they should return. Cheeks have the fire men choose..

John Knox
That scything wind has cut the rich corn down –
the satin shades of France spin idly by –
the bells are jangled in St Andrews town –
a thunderous God tolls from a northern sky.

He pulls the clouds like bandages awry.
See how the harlot bleeds below her crown.
This lightning stabs her in the heaving thigh –
such siege is deadly for her dallying gown.

A peasant's scythe rings churchbells from the stone.
From this harsh battle let the sweet birds fly,
surprised by fields now barren of their corn.
(Invent, bright friends, theology or die)
The sharing naked absolute blade has torn
through false French roses to her foreign cry

Old Woman
Your thorned back
heavily under the creel
you steadily stamped the rising daffodil.

Your set mouth
forgives no one, not even God's justice
perpetually drowning law with grace.

Your cold eyes
watched your drunken husband come
unsteadily from Sodom home.

Your grained hands
dandled full and sinful cradles.
You built for your children stone walls.

Your yellow hair
burned slowly in a scarf of grey
wildly falling like the mountain spray.

Finally you're alone
among the unforgiving brass,
the slow silences, the sinful glass.

Who never learned
not even aging to forgive
our poor journey and our common grave

while the free daffodils
wave in the valleys and on the hills
the deer look down with their instinctive skills,

and the huge sea
in which your brothers drowned sings slow
over the headland and the peevish crow

Lenin

In a chair of iron
sits coldly my image of Lenin,
that troubling man
'who never read a book for pleasure alone.'

The germ inside the sealed train
emerged, spread in wind and rain
into new minds in revolution
seeming more real than had been,

for instance, Dostoevsky. No, I can
romanticise no more that 'head of iron',
'the thought and will unalterably one',
'the world-doer', 'thunderer', 'the stone

rolling through clouds'. Simple to condemn
the unsymmetrical, simple to condone
that which oneself is not. By admiration
purge one's envy of unadult iron

When the true dialectic is to turn
in the infinitely complex, like a chain
we steadily burn through, steadily forge and burn,
not to be dismissed in any poem

by admiration for the ruthless man
nor for the saint but for the moving on
into the endlessly various, real, human
world which is no new era, shining dawn.

Two Girls Singing

It neither was the words nor yet the tune.
Any tune would have done, and any words.
Any listener or no listener at all.

As nightingales in rocks or a child crooning
in its own world of strange awakening
or larks for no reason but themselves.

So on the bus through late November running
by yellow lights tormented, darkness falling,
the two girls sang for miles and miles together

and it wasn't the words or tune. It was the singing.
It was the human sweetness in that yellow,
the unpredicted voices of our kind

The Law and the Grace

It's law they ask of me and not grace.
'Conform,' they say, 'your works are not enough.
Be what we say you should be' even if
graceful hypocrisy obscures my face.

'We know no angels. If you say you do
that's blasphemy and devilry.' Yet I have
known some bright angels, of spontaneous love.
Should I deny them, be to falsehood true,

the squeeze of law which has invented torture

to bring the grace to a malignant head.
Do you want me, angels, to be wholly dead?
Do you need, black devils, steadfastly to cure

life of itself? And you to stand beside
the stone you set on me? No, I have angels. Mine
are free and perfect. They have no design
on anyone else, but only on my pride,

my insufficiency, imperfect works.
They often leave me but they sometimes come
to judge me to the core, till I am dumb.
Is this not law enough, you patriarchs.

The Bible

The Bible stands like a big rock which no one attends to.
It is a novel with murders, adulteries and fears.

It is the solid TV of our human history,
and God is the eagle with human flesh in its claws.

It used to be made of marble, a statue among leaves.
Now it is a record of deaths, tribal partitions,

and its victims have black faces and its saints have batons
and their diseased ethics are undazzled by rainbows.

Dying Man

Breathless and blue-lipped
you thank God for his mercies
in a prayer you have learned
on a bare island.
How grand the face of God
secure, imperious,
to whom you are a slave
in absolute fear and dread.

Dying, you thank God,
beating at His door
for an exact justice
though you do not hear
a high answering voice.
It is only history
that sweeps grandly on
in spite of your 'Rejoice.'

Pity shakes my heart
as at night I hear
your eloquent sleepless prayers,
endless and austere.
But only the birds of dawn
answer with their twitter
or the continuous water
chatters among leaves.

And the window rises,
contingent and gaunt,
like a white picture,
misty, indigent,
over the wet grass.

Iain Chrichton Smith

Out of the vast silence
there is no voice
to raise you from your knees.

Dogmas
Perfidious dogmas,
unremitting theses,
let the wild seas
blow through you

with their salt taste
and tang of seaweed
and all the dead
whose bones have been picked clean

by the fresh currents,
and let the rocks of dogma
be steadily worn down
till only the water

brilliantly sparkling
with its modern ships
flows always eastwards
towards a temporary sun.

Note
Coming as I do from a Scottish island – the Island of Lewis in the Outer Hebrides – where an austere inflexible sabbatical Presbyterianism holds sway, it was natural, I suppose, that I should write about religion, though it has not been fashionable, except for someone like R.S. Thomas, to do so.

However such a religion raises interesting questions of order and spontaneity. It is usually hostile to the arts (for instance music is not allowed in its churches). Thus we have antitheses such as the Law and the Grace (of religion) versus the Form and Inspiration of poetry. How much spontaneity does metre allow: how much free will does predestination allow.

It also raises questions of singleness (on the part of religion) and the marvellous multifariousness of the world. Its historical cruelty (in the service of its dogma) as in Puritanism and Calvinism must be attended to. A figure such as Lenin from this perspective of dogma becomes an icon and is set against the complex Dostoevsky. Simplicity is seen as dangerous and complexity as friendly and more 'truthful'.

Yet in earlier versions of my work the truth 'of facing the fire' on the part of religion is seen as admirable. Maybe it is true that the arts are merely sentimental fictitious decorations in front of these eternal flames.

However as time passes I see all religions, and dogmas, as dangerous. Religion makes intolerable demands and is itself self-deceiving. We bounce our 'truths' off God who is beyond the stramash of the world. Religion is psychological rather than objective. One can see it in Ireland and in many other countries. Instead of facing the 'truth' dogmatic religion hides from it, from the dangerous and exciting wealth of choices that the world generates. My theme of religion and dogma has now moved to the centre of the stage – we see its peril and barbarism in Palestine and Israel, in the strength of Muslim dogma in Iran and elsewhere, in India, in Bosnia. The world seems to be systematically torn apart by single-eyed dogma. One-eyed Polyphemus is gaining on rational eternally mobile Ulysses.

These poems reflect my distrust of dogma. They do not encompass the whole of my poetry but are a significant theme in it. I hope that they are not 'documentary'. I hope they have been tested for the most part on the pulse. Against the death of predestination I set a poem like 'Two Girls Singing', the unpredictability of the human world, and art as represented by the song. This is what we must attend to, not any theology of death which in the last resort represents an artificial world imposed by fear. To this world of untheological plenitude and sometimes terror we must address ourselves. It will make demands on us but they are the demands of 'reality'. And we will be better for answering these fresh questions which the nature of the world presents us with.

THOM GUNN

Duncan

1

When in his twenties a poetry's full strength
Burst into voice as an unstopping flood,
He let the divine prompting (come at length)
Rushingly bear him any way it would
And went on writing while the Ferry turned
From San Francisco, back from Berkeley too,
And back again, and back again. He learned
You add to, you don't cancel what you do.
Between the notebook-margins his pen travelled,
His own lines carrying him in a new mode
To ports in which past purposes unravelled.
So that, as on the Ferry Line he rode,
Whatever his first plans that night had been,
The energy that rose from their confusion
Became the changing passage lived within
While the pen wrote, and looked beyond conclusion.

2
Forty years later, and both kidneys gone;
Every eight hours, home dialysis;
The habit of his restlessness stayed on
Exhausting him with his responsiveness.
After the circulations of one day
In which he taught a three-hour seminar
Then gave a reading clear across the Bay,
And while returning from it to the car

With plunging hovering tread tired and unsteady
Down Wheeler steps, he faltered and he fell
– Fell he said later, as if I stood ready,
'Into the strong arms of Thom Gunn.'
                                      Well well,
The image comic, as I might have known,
And generous, but it turned things round to myth:
He fell across the white steps there alone,
Though it was me indeed that he was with.

I hadn't caught him, hadn't seen in time,
And picked him up where he had softly dropped,
A pillow full of feathers. Was it a rime
He later sought, in which he might adopt
The role of H.D., broken-hipped and old,
Who, as she moved off from the reading-stand
Had stumbled on the platform but was held
And steadied by another poet's hand?

He was now a posthumous poet, I have said
(For since his illness he had not composed),
In sight of a conclusion, whose great dread
Was closure,
                       his life soon to be enclosed
Like the sparrow's flights above the feasting friends,
Briefly revealed where its breast caught their light,
Beneath the long roof, between open ends,
Themselves the margins of unchanging night.

In the Post Office
Saw someone yesterday looked like you did,
Being short with long blond hair, a sturdy kid
Ahead of me in line. I gazed and gazed
At his good back, feeling again, amazed,
That almost envious sexual tension which
Rubbing at made the greater, like an itch,
An itch to steal or otherwise possess
The brilliant restive charm, the boyishness
That half aware – and not aware enough –
Of what it did, eluded to hold off
The very push of interest it begot,
As if you'd been a tease, though you were not.
I hadn't felt it roused, to tell the truth,
In several years, that old man's greed for youth,
Like Pelias's that boiled him to a soup,
Not since I'd had the sense to cover up
My own particular seething can of worms,
And settle for a friendship on your terms.

Meanwhile I had to look: his errand done,
Without a glance at me or anyone,
The kid unlocked his bicycle outside,
Shrugging a backpack on. I watched him ride
Down 18th Street, rising above the saddle
For the long plunge he made with every pedal,
Expending far more energy than needed.
If only I could do whatever he did,
With him or as a part of him, if I
Could creep into his armpit like a fly,
Or like a crab cling to his golden crotch,
Instead of having to stand back and watch.
Oh complicated fantasy of intrusion
On that young sweaty body. My confusion
Led me at length to recollections of
Another's envy and his confused love.

That Fall after you died I went again
To where I had visited you in your pain
But this time for your – friend, roommate, or wooer?
I seek a neutral term where I'm unsure.
He lay there now. Figuring she knew best,
I came by at his mother's phoned request
To pick up one of your remembrances,
A piece of stained-glass you had made, now his,
I did not even remember, far less want.
To him I felt, likewise, indifferent.

'You can come in now,' said the friend-as-nurse.
I did, and found him altered for the worse.
But when he saw me sitting by his bed,
He would not speak, and turned away his head.
I had not known he hated me until
He hated me this much, hated me still.
I thought that we had shared you more or less,
As if we shared what no one might possess,
Since in a net we sought to hold the wind.
There he lay on the pillow, mortally thinned,
Weaker than water, yet his gesture proving
As steady as an undertow. Unmoving
In the sustained though slight aversion, grim
In wordlessness. Nothing deflected him,
Nothing I did and nothing I could say.
And so I left. I heard he died next day.

I have imagined that he still could taste
That bitterness and anger to the last,
Against the roles he saw me in because
He had to: of victor, as he thought I was,
Of heir, as to the cherished property
His mother – who knows why? – was giving me,
And of survivor, as I am indeed,
Recording so that I may later read
Of what has happened, whether between sheets,
Or in post offices, or on the streets.

Enough
Here is the bed she lay on, look, a double
Though she slept by herself, divorced and rich,
No longer having to seem like a wife.
A partner was not really worth the trouble.
Here is the futon's yellowing grey on which
She spent a strait third of her later life.

She liked the padded firmness, as ungiving
As she herself, or floormats at the gym
She attended three times weekly to keep fit.
The futon was in style for healthy living;
But from pure ignorance – or self-punishing whim? –
She got up without ever turning it.

Thom Gunn

Yet it did give. Look here, now she is gone.
She always kept to the one side of the bed,
And here her body's obstinate impress
Bore down the surface she curled nightly on.
It must have never come into her head
To lie diagonally or move across.

She dug a small mould not to be exceeded,
And rested in the unexacting habit.
Defiant hollow in the greyish stuff!
Here she lay sour, unneeding and unneeded,
Like a divorcee, like an aging rabbit
On stale straw, in its hutch. Enough, enough.

In Trust
You go from me
In June for months on end
To study equanimity
Among high trees alone;
I go out with a new boyfriend
And stay all summer in the city where
Home mostly on my own
I watch the sunflowers flare.

You travel East
To help your relatives.
The rainy season's start, at least,
Brings you from banishment:
And from the hall a doorway gives
A glimpse of you, writing I don't know what,
Through winter, with head bent
In the lamp's yellow spot.

To some fresh task
Some improvising skill
Your face is turned, of which I ask
Nothing except the presence:
Beneath white hair your clear eyes still
Are candid as the cat's fixed narrowing gaze
– Its pale-blue incandescence
In your room nowadays.

Sociable cat:
Without much noise or fuss
We left the kitchen where he sat,
And suddenly we find
He happens still to be with us,
In this room now, though firmly faced away,
Not to be left behind,
Though all the night he'll stray.

As you began
You'll end the year with me.
We'll hug each other while we can,
Work or stray while we must.
Nothing is, or will ever be,
Mine, I suppose. No one can hold a heart,
But what we hold in trust
We do hold, even apart.

Eastern Europe
February, 1990

'The iron doors of history' give at last,
And we walk through them from a rigid past.
Free! free! we can do anything we choose
– Eat at McDonald's, persecute the Jews.

Note
'What I meant to do, what I *meant* to do… ' If I wrote it out, you'd be in danger of reading it into what I did do. So I'll write instead something about poetic structure, the shape of these recent poems, which you can read as an introduction to all of my poetry, if you wish.

What evidently interests me a lot is narrative, since three of these poems tell stories. 'In the Post Office' is largely about myself, 'Enough' about a woman in Boston her daughter told me of, and 'Duncan' about the late Robert Duncan and also about everything else. Up-to-date theory disapproves of narrative, as far as I can make out, but I can't do without it in my life and so I can't do without it in my poetry. When people think about their lives, it has to be first as a sequence of intertwined stories. Poets have always known this: the *Cantos* are full of anecdotes; and I have thought of using as an epigraph for a book Hardy's line concluding his latest and most grotesque of narratives, 'Well, it's a cool queer tale!' (from 'Her Second Husband Hears the Story').

'Eastern Europe' is purely cerebral. Of course, people hate ideas without imagery these days, and I notice that by consequence epigrams are found repellent. But the Romans valued them, and so did Ben Jonson, and we should keep the form around for joking and cleverness and also for those occasions when pointed rudeness is appropriate.

And then there's 'lyric' – thinking and feeling about things in a stanza derived from song. I was always attracted by the nonce stanza forms of the *Songs and Sonnets*, and more recently by those of Wyatt, and in 'In Trust' I wanted to give them my own turn by writing a love poem of mere truth, without fudging, in which I avoided both the idealizations and the contempt found so often in Wyatt and Donne. But here I've slipped into expressing the intentions I wanted to avoid.

ELAINE FEINSTEIN

At Seven a Son
In cold weather on a
garden swing, his legs
in wellingtons rising over
the winter rose trees

he sits serenely
smiling like a Thai
his coat open, his gloves
sewn to the flapping sleeves

his thin knees working
with his arms
folded about the
metal struts

as he flies up
(his hair like long
black leaves) he
lies back freely

astonished in
sunshine as serious
as a stranger he is
a bird in his own thought.

Song of Power
For the baiting
children in my
son's school class who
say I am a witch:
black is the
mirror you give me

drawn inward at siege
sightless, mumbling:
criminal, to bear three
children like fruit
cannot be guarded
against enemies.

Should I have lived sterile?
The word returns me.
If any supernatural power
my strangeness earns me
I now invoke, for
all Gods are

anarchic even the Jews'
outside his own laws, with
his old name
confirms me, and I
call out for the
strange ones with wild hair

all the earth over to
make their own coherence
a fire their children
may learn to bear at last
and not burn in.

Dad
Your old hat hurts me, and those black
    fat raisins you liked to press into
my palm from your soft heavy hand:
    I see you staggering back up the path
with sacks of potatoes from some local farm,
    fresh eggs, flowers. Every day I grieve

for your great heart broken and you gone.
    You loved to watch the trees. This year
you did not see their Spring.
    The sky was freezing over the fen
as on that somewhere secretly appointed day
    you beached: cold, white-faced, shivering.

What happened, old bull, my loyal
    hoarse-voiced warrior? The hammer
blow that stopped you in your track
    and brought you to a hospital monitor
could not destroy your courage
    to the end you were
uncowed and unconcerned with pleasing anyone.

I think of you now as once again safely
    at my mother's side, the earth as
chosen as a bed, and feel most sorrow for
    all that was gentle in
my childhood buried there
    already forfeit, now forever lost.

from **The Feast of Eurydice**
A path of cinders, I remember
    and limping upward
not yet uprooted from
    my dream, a ghost

with matted eyes, air-sacs
    rasping, white
brain, I staggered
    after you

Orpheus, when you first
    called, I pushed
the sweet earth from my mouth
    and sucked in

all the powders of volcanic ash
    to follow you
obedient up
    the crumbling slope

to the very last ridge –
    where I saw clumps of
yellow camomile in the dunes
    and heard the applause

of your wild mother
    great Calliope
crying good, my son, good
in the fumes of the crater.

When the wiring sputtered
    at my wedding feast
she was hectic, glittering;
    her Arabian glass

burst into darkness
    and her flesh shimmered.
She was still laughing, there,
    on that pumice edge

with all Apollo's day behind her
    as I saw your heavy
shoulders turn. Your lips move.
    Then your eyes.

and I lay choking   Orpheus
    what hurt most then was
your stunned face
    lost

cruel   never to be touched
    again, and watching
a blown leaf in your
    murderous eye

shrivel…

from **New Lyrics for Dido and Aeneas**
Some pain has burnt a desert in your head,
    which spills into the room,
sexless and stony-eyed, you rock
    over the landscape of your sandy dead.

I cannot soothe or reach into your dream
    or recognize the ghosts you name, or even
nurse your shaken body into calm.
    You wake, exhausted: to meet daylight in hell,

as the damned wake up with pennies
    of departure, and the ash
of all their lives have left undone
    lying like talcum on the tongue.

Urban Lyric
The gaunt lady of the service wash
stands on the threshold and blinks in the sunlight.

Her face is yellow in its frizz of hair
and yet she smiles as if she were fortunate.

She listens to the hum of cars passing
as if she were on a country lane in summer,

or as if the tall trees edging this
busy street scattered blessings on her.

Last month they cut a cancer out of her throat.
This morning she tastes sunshine in the dusty air.

And she is made alert to the day's beauty,
as if her terror had wakened poetry.

Izzy's Daughter
'You must be Izzy's daughter,' they said.
I was a liquid, black stare. An olive face.

'So thin. Doesn't she eat? She reads too much.'
My teasing, brawny aunts upset my mother.

I wanted to be as reckless as a man,
to dive through rough, grey waves on Southport sands,

and shake the salt out of my hair as he did.
Instead, I shivered, blue with cold, on the shore.

But I was Maggie Tulliver, proud of my cleverness,
when the whole family listened to my stories.

He listened, too; troubled, his lips moving,
and dog-brown eyes following every word.

'Where does it all come from?' they marvelled at me.
My timid mother smiled from her quiet corner.

Insomnia
The moon woke me, the pocked and chalky moon
that floods the garden with its silvery blue

and cuts the shadow of one leafy branch across
this bed of ours as if on to bright snow.

The sky is empty. Street lights and stars
are all extinguished. Still the moon flows in,

drowning old landmarks in a magic lake,
the chilly waters lapping at my pillow,

their spell relentless as this cold
unhappiness in which I lie awake.

Note
I find my poems get bonier and more bare as I get older, and usually spring from some experience in my own life, as if the impulse to make poems now has to connect with a need to puzzle out personal thoughts and feelings. And I want the verse to be clear and quiet, even though lyric poetry rises most powerfully from intense emotion, and it is the lyric I love. I have no ambition to write a long poem. If I'm going to tell stories, I'd rather write novels.

The poets I most read are still above all lyric poets; Herbert's simplicity, Pound's marvellous ear for syllables, Lawrence's sharpness of response, and Charles Reznikoff's humanity, remain my models. My one-time Black Mountain mentors had some of these virtues too, but neither their passion for geography and local history nor their insistence on uncorrected spontaneity were ever truly mine. And they were often obscure even on a close reading.

These days I work most of all for directness and lucidity. I don't want the music of the lyric to drown what has to be said. There is always a tug between speech and music in poetry; what I'm looking for is a music which has the natural force of spoken feeling, the Wordsworthian 'language really used by men'; though I confess I enjoyed the street language of slang rather more in the days when it was not so smart to make use of it.

It was from Tsvetayeva I first learned to use personae, finding mythical figures particularly useful as vehicles for the passions. Like characters in fiction, personae allow poets to go outside autobiography, without forfeiting their own patterns of feeling. It's rather like writing drama. I don't know whether I will do more.

Tsvetayeva thought a poet had to let 'the hand race, (and when it doesn't race to stop)'; and I may well write fewer poems of any kind. It's hard to predict. I shall probably not do many more translations. The pressure is elsewhere: in the work of understanding, assessing and confronting the passage of time.

I'm not conscious at the moment of being part of any particular grouping, nor have I been, since the *English Intelligencer* poets who followed Jeremy Prynne came and sat on my Trumpington floor in the sixties; and even then I'm not sure how much I shared with them. Over the last twenty years or so my closest literary friendships have been with novelists. But I'm very much aware of the good women poets that are writing now. When I began writing there were so few of us, and now some of the best young poets are women. And I haven't written many overtly political poems; I continue to feel a poet should serve poetry rather than putting his art at the service of any politics.

P.J. KAVANAGH

Nature Poet

1. *Voices*
Peering for clues in dust on a brown moth's wings,
Touching white doors and greening stones in a wall.
Pondering lichen shapes and lines in his nail,
He liked all the people he could and, more than is usual,
Cherished his dead, thought often of them, because they were still.

But bewildered he was, more and more: enamoured of Things
Because they contained a patience and a waiting.
His voices clamoured for clarity: 'All would be easing
If only you'd stop watching trees. Their way of standing'
His voices insisted, 'is their way of teasing.'

He bad-temperedly argued; the voices were his soul,
Nine-cheerful-tenths of it, and gazing got him nowhere;
Stroking the hair of barley, hanging on to a chair
As though it contained a vision carpentered from air,
Left him standing, led him to idleness and despair.

Yet he could not let go, could not. Inside that wall,
In wings of moths, in lists of patient Things he detected mercy
Wafting, like a smell. His voices had their say.
He companionably stared across horizonless grey,
His children fading, his dead fading further away,
And decided he must be a creature made for night,
A moth, besotted, banging against the light.

2. *The Attempt*
Surprised at a dawning white, white with dews
On spiders'-webs in sheets, on everything, everywhere,
A work of darkness whiter than white air,
There comes again the thought he cannot lose
(Like it or not) that world is continuous speech,
Never the same, spoken once only, always out of reach.

Curving above the mist the morning grows.
Webs dry. Their shrouding brilliance goes
And bushes have their inside-darks again.
Impatient and impelled he takes his pen,
Knows he is deaf, is a world, is talking to deaf men.

3. *One Sentence, and Another*
'First, be clear in your mind what you want to say.'
Advice, in this rain and fog, which sounds even
More than it did at the time like bunkum:
For how can a man say anything clear when (say)
A gust of rain hitting a hillside can take him
So far to one side of himself that under a dripping tree
In an unpromising valley called Uncombe
He stands in his coat and out of it at the same time and clarity
Is not what he feels or needs and the reason
He knows is that he is alone and now not lonely;
As white columns of rain roll past him like sheeted
Spirits, others are near as real as rains are,
Whom he ought to admit to, though nothing is said
Or promised him in unpromising places and only
The eyes of water on branches are perfectly clear?

4. *Companions*
He talks to himself as he walks to an unfavoured spot
Which is boggy but windless, a hanging and desolate
Stillness he hooks on himself like a coat
    For this is his favourite
Place, and although overhung by kestrels he is not
Over-impressed by such taut-shouldered obsession,
Their hungers are smaller than his, for they look down.
    He is feeling his own
Possession there, his feet sucking out of mud
Under old thorn-trees (below these in winter each grass-blade
Stands apart from its neighbour, a separate green
    Isolation for sun
To shine at low season through each individual one).
It is ghosts he looks up for, as well as lit grass he delights in
And laughs to observe himself warmed by their non-replies.
    He is standing alone
Because he could point to nothing but drabness to see.
He feels himself simplified, soaked by their silences,
Held among lives keeping out of the god-kestrel's eye,
    His companions, the brown
Almost invisible presences, birds – that he notices
Stay at his side, on his level, certainly stay,
Though they silently shift to whichever side of the tree
    Is furthest away.

5. *A Clean Sensation*
Believing his dead invigorate the air
All round him, winging, bustling everywhere
(Not to be sure, always on his affairs),

One blossom-littered May on Bodley's stairs
He turned, at a loss, to address them: 'You known
And guardian affections – I have blown
My life. Lived it too much where you are,
Which is not my place. Nor this,' (the crowded square),
'Nor anywhere. Some help is needed here.'

Whether like nurses they came shafting down
Over the Radcliffe Camera is uncertain.
Hoping perhaps they would he crossed that town
Which loves success too much. (Though failure,
Undefined, he had not reckoned on.)
A clean sensation touched him, winging-in
Outside Halls' shop, pushed him towards the human:
He knew on his finger-ends he could settle for
One toe-bone from a certain skeleton.

Severn *Aisling*
Odysseus attentive to grey-eyed Athene,
Transfigured Beatrice lecturing Dante,
Who had muddied his glimpse of her granted him briefly,
As all must; a life in two worlds requires liturgy
Bridges, is balancing dangerously.
She and the river were singing this, gladly.

Walking up from your loss, your estuary
Sabrina, seeking your source, was a piece
of my life every summer with you as companion,
talkative, sometimes elusive, but only
at last when I stood at your birthplace and heard
how you sing at your source did I understand why

I had walked you, that you were an allegory
of what I believe in. Yours, like the voice
I remember, the voice in my long conversation
with somebody absent, and present as you are
Sabrina, sang that a sense of two worlds
is no treason to this one, is fact, as you can be

fact and be flat on a map and be mystery
when we are near you. Your sound was the key
to why you seemed female the length of your flowing
from calm disappearance to tentative birth,
for there as you gathered came clear to the surface
my subconscious reason for walking you that way,

upstream – to confirm the quick freshet I live by.
(A man on Plynlimon, queer as an angel's
the way he appeared out of nowhere and vanished
where not a rabbit could hide, saying sternly,
'*I* would begin at the *Source*!') Away
from a loss I had to make my journey,

your song said. 'You walk with a ghost and she,
like you, has a need to be solid, solid,'
(I grasped this) 'as moving water that's held
without losing motion only by margins,
as I am. Yours is the earth holds a ghost,
alive, and a river flowing away –'

such sweet intercession – 'You never will see
me again and, look, you are walking beside me!'
Flowing away. And towards. From your Bridge
to peninsular Framilode, Epney,
Ashleworth, Minsterworth – litany
recited in trenches by Ivor Gurney

which had drawn us towards you (a friend had come with me)
you pulled us both further, past cormorant mudflats
on one side (the other was gnarled mossy orchards)
through voices of Gloucestershire, Birmingham, Wales –
your own singing as changeful – till velvet
shadows of oaks in Montgomery

led to your desolate source, where memory
kicked like a womb. A blue dragonfly
dozed over your brackish beginnings,
your pool streaked with oil among cottongrass wind-bleached
the colour of sheep that huddled about you.
It hung like a fragment of different sky,

unexpected, a promise remembered, then quickly
as love (which seems like a promise remembered,
divinely inherent), augmented by oozes,
came singing in bleakness, the voice I remembered,
and blessing it brought me – exploding green margins
of mosses in colourless grasses, excitably

nodding fern-plumes you brush on your way,
as she did, a girl, through a cordon of glowing
admirers applauding, shy and excited –
oh, how could I not be reminded, not hear
what she and your river were singing, how world
is a language, and constant analogy?

Sabrina – a river-nymph turned into memory
of a reality – being divine
metamorphosis will not concern you, a blur
as fast as the balancing dragonfly's wings
of her into you and of fact into faith
and back will give you no difficulty

who endure in our world. For in moments your joy
is corseted under a road, put to school
in an acid plantation and only your voice
is heard, like the voice I remembered, rejoicing
in whichever world. Your escape among alders
and ashtrees, sculpting smooth rockpools, your play

is as youthful, but thoughtful (not matronly,
ever), as though a stern check to your gladness
had made you more able to bless by the way
stale wharves long abandoned and nuclear stations
of sinister silence. There men in white coats
furtively bend to examine a fly

for monstrous mutation, caught in their dimity
lampshades set on your birdsinging banks
on green poles like lampstands, absurdities. Barrage
could force you to service, past centuries did so,
their uses decay. Your mind is not on them,
your patience is deeper. And should the times say

that sexual love is illusion you equally
show it the hem of a garment to clutch at,
as unabashed, doubting but choiceless, for decades
I cling to the spar of an absence and presence
I heard in the song at the source and I swim
in what used to be called the Sabrinian Sea,

your end, no end, imperceptible entry
to widening silence. This on your way
you interpreted for me, saw no point in using
more than you needed, a dragonfly dozing
in marshes, then green intercession and song,
never ending. I turn, it is singing behind me.

            The binding.
Odysseus attentive to grey-eyed Athene,
Transfigured Beatrice lecturing Dante,
Who had muddied his glimpse of her granted him briefly,
As all must; a life in two worlds requires liturgy
Bridges, is balancing dangerously.
She and the river were singing this, gladly.

(The *aisling* – pronounced *ashling* – is a traditional form in Irish, in which the poet is addressed by a supernatural being, usually female, who instructs him.)

Message

When you fell silent and still in a holy place,
Unwontedly so, abstracted, your thinking face
Averted from me as you stared at an ancient stone
Statue of some milky beast under Javanese sun
In Borobodur, I suddenly felt on my own
Unwontedly. I, who tether my dreams, whom symbols appal,
Who as close as is possible cling to the actual,
Now wonder if such an abstraction so long ago
(As lives are counted) has led me to see as I do,
Suddenly, that the loss of my young self and you
Can no longer be distinguished; that when I yearn
For you, it is for me; in that sense on my own,
As I felt when I saw you were drawn by symbolic stone
Towards an impersonal form of entire concentration,
Which – for our link is unbroken – you want me to learn.

Note

In his *Notebook*, April 1805, Coleridge wrote: 'In looking at objects of Nature while I am thinking, as at yonder moon dim-glimmering thro' the dewy window-pane, I seem to be seeking, as it were *asking*, a symbolical language for something within me that already and forever exists… '

Precisely, and it does seem that if a Creator should wish to communicate it would be through Creation, its surfaces, its Things. Dr Johnson said, 'Things are the Sons of Heaven', and perhaps by closely observed descriptions of Things we might come nearer to what is being said.

Coleridge continues the entry in his *Notebook* by saying that even if he is observing something new, 'still I have always an obscure feeling as if that new phaenomenon were the dim Awaking of a forgotten and hidden Truth of my inner nature/ It is still interesting as a Word, a Symbol! It is λογοσ [Logos], the Creator! (and the Evolver!)' The external world, therefore, as the educator, or 'Evolver', of our inner one.

But it is 'obscure', 'dim', the communication hard to hear. I now realise that in poems written over many years, later put together under the title 'Nature Poet' (something I never wanted to be) this is what in various ways I am trying to describe.

'Severn *Aisling*' is another, later, attempt at a 'symbolical language' based on the practical and external, in this case a walk along the Severn to its source in Wales. When I *heard* the source I was invaded unexpectedly by memory. This, and the emotion that accompanied it, had to be kept as close to the actual, to the surface, to 'Things', as I could manage, even to the absurd bankside lampshades inside which insects are examined for signs of nuclear-caused mutation; even to the threat of a Severn barrage.

Only after I had written the poem did I learn that there is in Irish a long tradition of the dream (aisling) poem in which the poet is visited by a 'sky-woman', and that these have a Knot, or Binding at the end, summing up the poem's theme, which in this case is our need for a 'liturgy', or 'symbolical language' for our dim-glimmerings.

ALISTAIR ELLIOT

Turnstones on Lewis

Pale in the shade of a taller person
I have seen these birds before;
in the wintry black and white
of my father's telescope
I used to watch them turning
the stones and spinachy weed,
guest-workers from the north
with an international job.

They search for something to eat,
the soft stuff lying under
uncompromising hardness
in the wet space between languages
where solid and liquid fret;
they ask only for stones
to hide among and hunt in,
and dipterans (they love midges).

Today their colours show
for once, the tortoiseshell
feathers of summer. The birds
pose for a moment, characterless.
What are they? I don't know,
forgetting even the word
turnstone. The manual tells me:
Arenaria interpres –

they are translators of stones,
turners of words, probers
of worn old surfaces
for meanings that live here
in the white fragmented-bone
shell-sand of the Hebrides,
a calcium of lost shapes
that will be eggs next year.

Two Cats in New Hampshire
for Don and Jane

The perforated barn tries to keep out
This summer like the older hotter summers,
But samples of today's light,
Already dusty, lean in corners.
A careful husband would collect
Spiderwebs here for his new wife's new dress,
Dearer than silk; the kittens came and picked
A bat for breakfast, full of insect juice,
Or sun-demented flies.
It was built to hold treasure, and it does.

The house was built, not by one grandfather
But others, earlier, room by room,
Cells for the honey of him and her,
The unconsumable taste of home.
I itch, slightly, to be off,
As if seeing the footprints of a bear
In the deep woods were what I must achieve:
As if I could not just sit pickling here.
The cats can, staying indoors forever
Now the road's busier. They have each other.

Being a lovable cat is good:
Regular features, regular meals.
But don't they long for chickadee blood?
To clean their teeth with chipmunk tails?
They had their curiosities cut off,
Of course. Could I be calm like them
Without my sausage and its bag of stuff?
Those seeds, like marjoram, a dust of thyme,
Season our wholesome but monotonous moods.
Without them, we'd have just the thing that broods.

The thing that broods, impatient in the head,
Fingers the fate of these two animals
Preserved like harvest in a box: I brood
Upon the variety of pleasant jails,
Where it does not appear the air's been censored,
The messages of water scrambled: I brood
Most on my prayer for nomadism, answered
With this disease of travelling from food
To food that other creatures gather,
As if the goddess of fortune were my mother.

Inside, my friend prays to his dictaphone.
Outside, the singing silence, tinnitus
Of crickets, leads me on.
The flies are out of season, but saws buzz
Angrily in some transept of the woods.
Over the still green leaves some bird of prey
Cries a fair warning as I find the treads
The bear left for me. Should I stay
To dance among the boles with him? Or home
On my old friends, open the caddy and brew up for them?

What is my treasure, bears or the tea-brewing
With cats in their old wooden kitchen?
On my way back, I see a beaver drawing
Right across Eagle Pond his thoughtful line,
Like the path of the scissors cutting up
A western territory,
Trampling the water almost in his sleep:
Calm owner of the pond and its periphery,
However large, calm cutter of the trees,
Unable to see that they are someone else's.

Wetting Yourself
(*Thanksgiving Day 1983*)

At a strange distance from my dictionary
I ponder 'bilge' – a fine word to be found
Wearing about your head the night you're drowned –
And steer, looking the zephyr in the eye.

The main flaps, ghost of an expensive sail.

The engine-head's cracked. You scoop diesel stink
From under floorboards straight down *Emilie's* sink –
Jack still works, when the pumps and radio fail.

The sea's worse, but my stomach's now quite calm:
I spell you bailing.
                The sink blocks.
                              We pour
The bilge on the self-draining cockpit floor.

Drenched with the Gulf Stream spray (too warm for harm?)
In the cold wind I ponder 'piss myself',
Forty miles out on the continental shelf.

Another Day
Wedged in behind the table, on the floor
In a damp blanket: it's Jack's turn to steer,
My turn to sleep. Just under my left ear
The keel thumps water – or the Florida shore?
The mast tries to unstep itself – I'm curled
Beside its stormy knowledge like a snake.

The moon's framed in a hatch when I awake:
God! I'm in outer space, and that's the world…

Jack's calling: he's seen dolphins in the air,
Rolling down mountain-waves. Still wet, I climb
The oily steps into another time:
The hemisphere's so bright! And the wind fair…

High on the bucking boat, I laugh at the sun,
My equal: 'Sol! Dear Jewish relative,
So glad to see you' – and as glad to live
As if I were fifteen, not fifty-one.

For now the greater light of Genesis
Leans through the firmament with a long, dry kiss.

Facing South
for Tony Harrison

'Happiness, therefore, must be some form of theoria.'
(Aristotle, Nicomachean Ethics, X,8)

'Theoria: … a looking at, viewing, beholding… "to go abroad to see the world" (Herodotus)… 2. of the mind, contemplation, speculation, philosophic reasoning… theory… II. the being a spectator at the theatre or the games… '
(Liddell & Scott, A Greek-English Lexicon)

Sat at my desk, I face the way I would
migrate: sunwards along this cobbled lane,
over the poplar trees of Elmfield Road,
across the Town Moor, up the mud-grey Tyne,
screaming with other swifts along the spine
of man-made England, eating airy food
and dozing in slow circles over Spain…
to the great desert where they still wear woad.

I had to buy an Apollo window-blind
to shut that out – the interesting sky
pours vagueness into the unresting mind
more than the prettiest-coloured passer-by,
more than the cars mysteriously left
unlocked by jolly women and dour men –
so many people unafraid of theft –
I have to watch till they come back again.

I never saw a thief here. The one thing
that pricks our quiet bubble is the roar
of comment from St James's – the fans sing
inaudibly, but bellow when we score.
Horror seems far away: our car-alarms
play the continuo of crime; we feel
the needles hovering near our neighbours' arms;
the viruses float in; but peace is real.

We suffer some illusion of control
in watching: so, the passenger keeps the car
safe if she watches the white line unroll;
the watching fans 'support' the football star;
watching the world wag past our café chair
gives us a sense of ownership: we share
some of that passing chic or savoir faire,
forgetting we are only who we are.

I must shut all that out. I want to make
these verbal systems in my workshop here.
Watching the world's a job too big to take:
I want to make small worlds that will cohere.
We have both travelled: south, east, west. I go
north now, quite near, where on the first of May
our earth relaxes and its rivers flow:
there I want nothing but to stay, and stay.

I could fly further; I've been free for years,
but don't migrate, for always there outside
in all the infinite other hemispheres
there'd be more sights from which I'd have to hide:
I'd have to take the blind, to blot out views
that would distract the wandering inner sight,
that pleasure Aristotle says we choose:
the blank I look at as I sit and write.

Taste Enhancers

An overdose of monosodium
Glutamate is like Sappho's medical
Account of love. Your blind spot starts to swell
And washes people in and out of the room
As you look round. An interesting game,
But you feel sick; and when you speak, you say,
'I'm eyes. I'm ternia's a float a way?'
You sweat. You shake. That small electric flame
Bobs about in your voice-box, out of reach –
So near the ammunition of the mind.
Is it a stroke? Too late you scribble, 'Find
A blank tape' – to record your shuffled speech –
For now control comes back. Gears seem to meet
Again. A day in bed, and you recover.
You're sensitised for life, though, like a lover,
And there are things you can no longer eat.

Note
In Elizabeth Bishop's *Anthology of Twentieth-Century Brazilian Poetry* there is an interesting item by Manuel Bandeira called 'Antologia': it is a cento, a poem constructed, that is, 'out of nothing but lines or parts of lines of mine, the best known or most marked by my sensibility, which at the same time could function as a poem for a person who knew nothing of my poetry'. It struck me that this might be a good way of escaping the horrid job of writing explanatory prose about my work. However, Bandeira's offering remains, I fear, an 'item', an 'interesting idea', and besides, I think it is not for a Promising Young Poet (my first book came out only 17 years ago) to distill the savour of his work. As for the 'best known lines' I fear they are the beginning of 'Rooms', which appeared in Pseuds' Corner of *Private Eye* ('My favourite lavatory was on Ischia, etc') and perhaps the more recent 'On the Great North Road', which *The Independent* reprinted, but with a confusing misprint.

I still like both those poems, but I thought others more suitable for an introduction. The first one, though on a subject I usually consciously avoid (writing and language), arose from the pleasurable shock of finding that the shore birds turnstones were called *Arenaria interpres* ('translator of sand'). As always, the ideas that this shock brought up were worked out on paper as I composed the poem: they did not exist in my head beforehand. The poem was written about a month after the Hebridean holiday on which I saw the birds.

The central subject of 'Two Cats in New Hampshire' (what can we take with us even before we die? what is our treasure?) arose as I wrote it. In fact I started the poem thinking it would be about the contrast between the two cats these friends kept in and the three cats some Californian friends always kept out. But keeping cats in, keeping anything in, in fact keeping anything at all, became the backbone of the poem, and the Californian cats had to wait for later (their poem turned out to be about something unexpected too). Both poems are sort-of

Keatsian odes, though in the Californian one the stanza-form is concealed by re-alignment. They were written some years after the observations they relate.

'Wetting Yourself' (a sonnet) and 'Another Day' (which is really its second part) were also written years after the experience they 'describe', a storm off the Florida coast. I suppose the fact that I do have Jewish relatives made me think of the sun (Sol) as a relative, and then made me call it 'the greater light of Genesis' but I still recall the relief, after an awful night, of its 'long dry kiss'. Some of the other details probably came out of a notebook kept at the time.

'Facing South' is a response to my near-neighbour Tony Harrison's 'Facing North' and is the same length and (mostly) form. It started from the trivial idea or fact that our workrooms face different poles and have very different views outside. I found I have to blot out my view in order to work (the blind really was made by a firm called Apollo), and the subject of the poem arose out of that: it is not supposed to be a criticism of Harrison's way of seeing. It first appeared in the *London Review of Books* a few months ago.

'Taste Enhancers' (a Meredithian sonnet) kept being rejected because of its title (I assume), because I originally called it 'Asian Restaurant Syndrome' (the medical technical term is 'Chinese Restaurant Syndrome', but it wasn't a Chinese restaurant). It's a straightforward account of what I understand to have been an overdose of MSG, to which I suddenly became allergic, but again the idea that my symptoms were like those described in Sappho's famous poem and the painful last line came to me as I worked.

I describe my aims more generally in my entry in the reference book *Contemporary Poets*.

JUDY GAHAGAN

Winter Day Fasanenpark
There are no words only white.
The day has been shunted off to wait
in a pearl-hung white hung chill

where trees in twos are being marched away
and the other trees have withdrawn
into their mysteries of rising

no horizon just one direction
down which two people
intolerably alone
appear to make
small progress
into the vanishing

Together with Crows
I love crows
as people sometimes love cruel guardians,

their black dilapidated skirts
de-frocked whisky priests, my heart
goes out to them, their terrible flapping,
pathetic legs, our desolation.

We live in leaflessness together.
There is no family life here
in the winter forest.

Isn't it better
to be starkly visible,
black truths stalking the margins
of ghostly ballrooms with a curse,
to be waiting in dead gardens?

All my journeys are winter journeys
across the lines left by silence.
Today the sky streams backwards
we walk starved on cracked ice.

Siesta
Three slow hours, bell-stunned hours,
slow as drugged words, Burma-slow,
stupefy the moments.
These are southern hours for sleep.

In rooms, gloam-dim rooms, stone
still, heat-heavy tombs for sleeping,
sun glows still on
lids, closed before the marble stare

of kings. Such sleep is South.
Dreams rise, calm and warm as peaches.
Sleepers soaked in peace, stir
in the eyeless smiles of crumbling Gods.

These hours in days as vast
as seas, in vase-shaped afternoons,
poised within the sun's big arch,
embalm the last persisting innocence.

Swifts and Boys
Outside the walls and in the morning, swifts,
flung up, flung wide, flung high: slow free fall,
the consummate glide of a skateboarder
wunderkind, unteachable, missing school,
and boys on their bikes, legs working madly
stand tall, look-no-hands, the wind in cahoots,
the breathless hills dive up to meet them, till,

inside the walls and later, the day grows
hot and complicated, the swifts move in
on the town for street corner pickings,
recalcitrant wheeling dealing mafia
internecine; roads without exits; boys
who never sleep in their own beds. Grieving
mothers keep their grief preserved in sepia;

outside the walls the evening's anodyne:
swifts yo-yo slowly or drift rudderless,
strung out, apart and silent, a woman
far away, meanders in the groping deep
of a wet garden, resisting the worse
dark of a shrunken son-less house. They've gone,
the swifts, down the infinite glide to sleep.

Festival of Dark
Now the shiny times are over,
an organ moon half-eaten
full of resentment hunches
over the abandoned village,

and the summer nights
of gauzy flitting have gone
to be up-ended ships,
their holds of old cargo
imaginary damasks.

And it's only now the sun's
shifted you see the mists rise,
like shades, like shades;
along the untidy rivers,
tree calamities,
upheavals of roots.

They say the prisoners
seeing the October sun grow weaker,
pleaded with it to stay on
a little longer, withstand the clouds,
tried to hold it still
with their terrible eyes…

you too are slipping away…

like a watery Polish sun.

But I will remember this:
there are creatures in ocean deeps
where no light falls
so they are never seen,
which nonetheless have brilliant colours,
living their incandescence secretly,
rapturously invisible.

When the Whole Mood Changed
Day after day
the under-silver of the olives
glimmered all the while the wind was gentle
and we breathing evenly and freely as the sea,

but the whole mood changed.
The sea streamed up grey and confrontational,
olive trees thrashing changed silver
to dangerous metal and warning lights.

You're basically alone in barbarous weather:
high-sided vehicles hog exposed roads
no one will guarantee anything –
not even indoors.

Grey sand filters from some desert war-zone,
while the wind searches your teeth for pain.
After a few hours the rich interiors
of your favourite dreams are pillaged

and there's nowhere to go.

Snake on the Road
At the beginning of the endless big heat
snakes appear suddenly and out of place
on alien roads. I watch a skinny biscia*
loop sidelong and laborious over the tarmac;
innocent though he is, I fear his whiplash,
fear he'll look at me with his bunker eyes.

Out of my proper time and climate, out of place,
among these cool-skinned salon people, I sweat.
Slithered over frontiers, migrant, I forget
my language, talk in pidgin, my eyes become
passionless as snakes' eyes are, as migrants'.
Desire's burned out under mindless daily blue.

It's hard to be alone in a far country. I saw
a snake on hot asphalt writhing in its silvery
eau-de-nil body, its solitary convulsions petrified
for even snakes should writhe together, entwining
their poisoned ropes without faces, betrothed.

In this heat my fear sees vipers at every turn.
The viper! Found out by its flat purposeful head,
the sudden stump of its tail, its abrupt ending:
I want no lengthy insinuations either. Not now.
I heard how one from the cemetery wall hung down
eye-level to gaze into a woman's eyes, hers filled
with consternation, the snake's had no expression.

And still the migrants set out alone and stay
alone; follow some business along dis-used roads
where they have no business, unloved as snakes.
But some summer night a city will celebrate
with fireworks something even its inhabitants
have forgotten, the migrant will try to join in

and look around agog at exploding stars, feel
the heat of happiness, sweating in the clothes
he left in, the clothes he stands up in, slink
to the migrants' bar near the pulsating loops
of highways on the outskirts; a fag, a joke,
forget he's alone, no home, no mate, no child.

I watch the biscia, and I see how once a snake
reaches into its own grass, how easy it is, how swift
and straight. How amiable. Snakes are born to ease
not friction. Last night in the black, in the cool,
I dreamed that the people could return to the small
houses they'd left unlocked and just as they were.

*biscia = non-poisonous snake

Up and Down in Man-a-hat-ta
(*Man-a-hat-ta: Indian name meaning Heavenly Land*)

I
It was the huge plug of granite
rooting down like a wisdom tooth
fixed that up-roar of skyscrapers;
the granite of the Man-a-hat-ta
and the invention of the elevator
back in 1857;

marooned now on the high floors
of the 1990s where vertigo is common
high winds may shift glass shafts
a quarter of an inch or more, cold
water colours shiver in the strong
heroic light;

braced shafts sustain the breathless
verticality, the sheer nerve of sliver
buildings, the purity of their glass;
but they start to outgrow the early promise,
spiritual, seemingly neurasthenic, bored,
intestine-less;

and anorexia nervosa often alternates
with bulimia: below their bony structures
the rich clefts of the streets are oozing
with stuffs to stuff the heavy soul of us
then purging sales and riddance to rise
above the binge.

II
Deeper in the granite where they first cut
the railroads, where ebullient foliage plunges
some New Yorkers live in old Algonquin caves;
you see them from the train commuting, see them
pally in their crevices, a sun shaft warming
their listless chores;

deep down too on the winding Algonquin
trail of Broadway: the Laughing Honky-Tonk,
(the Indians said Pale-face talked too much
and left for the silent forests), there,
there's quiet negro black on the move
recycling the city:

one old man dressed in ancient black,
black pressed suit, black hat, black
careful gloves, picks bottles from the trash can,
and with his handkerchief he polishes them
to take to the distant 5-cent restitution.
He has no shoes on.

They say the earth will restitute itself
too eventually. In the meantime, (and I wish
I were about 500 years younger), old granite waits.
Today under dark cloud and blackish rain,
black granite, black rain, black man
are infinitely patient.

But let us not forget how lovely they are,
(or will have been), all the tall buildings:
shimmy-ing at each other, self-absorbedly,
reflecting one another and the clouds
held in the sheer glass falls from heaven
above the Man-a-hat-ta.

Note

These and many others of my poems are written in a state of mind fallen into disfavour in the last fifty years – the enraptured subjectivity of the impersonal but lyrical Ich of German romanticism. I'm not keen to share in that contemporary mindset, urban, disenchanted, cerebral and deeply anthropocentric, which represses 'beauty' and suspects the 'poetic'. I want to keep company with those poets who hold a candle for the portentous in poetry, even if it feels like a risky enterprise in the contemporary world.

And this state of mind is invoked for the most part by the natural world – the colours and movements of its weathers, vistas, creatures and plants. And in a poem I don't want to appropriate these qualities and nail them down with a linguistic virtuosity born of detachment, I want to express the feeling of participatory consciousness and enchantment which the natural world invokes and to express a sense of connection between that world and the human – both inner and personal and outer and political. Harking back to such a consciousness, supposedly rendered obsolete by the events of the twentieth century, might seem like an excursion in a blind-alley. But for me it has also political import: for this poetic sense of participation in the non-human cosmos is ecological, and the re-enchantment of the world that it implies is likely to shape the future politics for which we are now still reaching in the dark.

The challenge of writing from a stance which is rather out of favour while still fulfilling the poetic tasks of charging words with energy, finding the recognizable forms and diction to communicate this stance to one's contemporaries, and risking the 'beautiful' requires a confidence I've only acquired late in life.

The three short poems 'Winter Day Fasanenpark', 'Together with Crows' and 'Siesta' are the simplest examples of risking the poetic. 'Swifts and Boys' is an example of intense connectedness – in this case between the movements of birds and the qualities of the young male; 'Festival of Dark' is the most 'personal' of the poems in that it arises out of an emotional episode; 'When the Whole Mood Changed' and 'Snake on the Road' are two of many poems reflecting the ominousness of the world to which I wake every morning, especially far from home as I frequently am. 'Up and Down in Man-a-hat-ta' is a search after the soul of the skyscraper.

'Siesta' was first published in *Ambit* and 'Up and Down in Man-a-hat-ta' was first published in *Poetry London Newsletter*.

PETER SCUPHAM

The Gatehouse

Late. And though the house fills out with music,
This left hand takes me down a branching line
To the slow outskirts of a market town.
We are walking to the Gatehouse. Mr Curtis
Will call me Peäter in broad Lincolnshire;
Red currants glow, molten about the shade,
And cows are switched along a ragged lane.
Tonight, my son tousles away at Chopin
And a grandfather whom he never knew
Plays Brahms and Schumann at the same keyboard –
Schiedmayer und Soehne, Stuttgart –
The older, stronger hands ghosting a ground-bass
Out of a life whose texture still eludes me,
Yet both hold up their candles to the night.
The gatehouse settles back into the trees,
Rich in its faded hens, its garden privy
Sweet with excrement and early summer.
New bread and sticky cake for tea. The needle
Dances across: *Line Clear* to *Train on Line*;
The lane is music too. It has no ending
But vanishes in shifting copse and woodsmoke.
The levels cross: a light and singing wind,
Arpeggios, a pause upon the air.
The gate is white and cold. I swing it to,
Then climb between the steady bars to watch
Our station blurring out at the world's end.
The wagons beat their poésie du départ;
The lamps are wiped, and lit. Then we, too, go.

Young Ghost

Oh, the young ghost, her long hair coursing
Down to her shoulders: dark hair, the heat of the day
Sunk deep under those tucks and scents, drowsing
At the neck's nape – she looks so far away,
Though love twinned in her eyes has slipped its blindfold –

And really she glances across to him for ever,
His shutter chocking the light back into its box,
Snapping the catch on a purse of unchanged silver.
Under those seven seals and the seven locks
She is safe now from growing with what is growing,

And safe, too, from dying with what is dying,
Though her solemn flowers unpick themselves from her hands,
The dress rustles to moth-wings; her sweet flesh fraying
Out into knots and wrinkles and low-tide sands.
The hat is only a basket for thoughtless dust.

And she stands there lost in a smile in a black garden:
A white quotation floating away from its book
Will it be silver, gold, or the plain truth leaden?
But the camera chirps like a cricket, dies – and look,
She floats away light as ash in its tiny casket.

Under the Barrage

Schlafe, mein Kind,
In your mother's bed
Under the barrage.
The soon to be dead

Will pass you over;
It's not your turn.
The sheets are warm
But they will not burn.

In your half-dream
Sirens will sing
Lullay, lullay,
Lullay my liking.

A saucer of water
For candlestick:
The night-light steadies
A crumpled wick

In a house of cards
In a ring of flame;
The wind is addressed
With a different name.

Schlafe, mein Kind,
In your mother's bed.
Under the barrage
The soon to be dead

Lie as you lie,
And will lie on
When the dream, the flame
And the night are gone.

from **A Midsummer Night's Dream**

Epilogue

Observe the rites of May, betake yourselves
To wakes, summerings and rush-bearings,
Wash with hawthorn-dew on a bright morning
For beauty's preservation; hugger-mugger,
Enveloped with a mist of wandering,
Lose your virginities in wayside ditches.
Your lavish Queen, made bold in this Floralia,
Sits in her arbour by the painted pole
Under whose standard Justice is agreed.
Dance for Jack-in-the Green, your high roof-boss,
The oak-leaves foaming from his wooden mouth,
Before your bonfires, garlands, junketings
Are levelled by a thundering ordinance,
Your landscape raked by new theologies,
Your hedges rip-sawn and the wood stubbed out,
Dragons' teeth sown in the poulticed gums.

'Think you have but slumbered here
While these visions did appear.'

I walked in the astonishing light of trees,
A tenant only of their close estate,
Where the Great Oak, scored and furrowed,
Grappled his roots through subsoil into clay;
His branches, solid in the rising mist,
Have housed us all, and burned our oldest dead.
The Wodewose, with matted hair and beard,
Who knew the springs of love, walked there beside me,
As dark as any heart. Night fell again;
I took the key to her dark wardrobes,
Fingered the sloughed skins, the heap of cast-offs.
The spars fell loose; their sails were nets whose mesh
Caught nothing more than a little dust and air.
Now, out of my text and out of pretext
I pray for amity and restoration,
Who have dreamed waking-thoughts, woken to dreams.

from **A Habitat**

This Room, That Room
This room is a hold of chattering teeth,
Split-pins shaken in a dry tumbler,
Light plunging your silhouette with flat knives
In the Cirque d'Hiver, the cold, the cold.
Washing hangs barbed on front-line wire
And air jolts to the high explosive words
Tracked by the huge scream of their arrival.

That room is dense with a dead thing,
The surfaces are coffin-lids come off
And with them come the sticky skins of faces
Which might be where the flowers have had enough
And sent their candles drowning into wax.
The words? A Tennysonian murmuring:
Oh, oh, alas, alas, was, was.

This room believes in the belief of moths
And shows by the dark how to betrothe darkness
To the space where wing-chair and carpet sing
In their dull brilliance about gone sun.
I think the onset of Alzheimer's
Is making the words run in and out of their colours.
Quite charming, this prattle and confusion.

That room is locked black and sobbing.
The walls are dry bread and the floor is water
Where Alice wept when she was sent to bed.
When you touch wood, it turns to iron;
When you touch iron, the cold scalds you.
Listen, the words are kicking hard
At both sides of the door. Which is echo?

This room is where they put the other rooms.
Chekhov would have known the servants' names
Who pulled the rug from under the feet of time
And spread it out, a great big dirty dustsheet.
Light goes loose-limbed over mottled marble
And words are tic-tac, miching mallecho,
The chirping of dead mice from the underworld.

That room? Ah, that room is the last room,
The doorway swung out on a brass fanfare of light,
The dustsheet flicked like a conjuror's hanky.
And here they are, so many he's and she's,
And all so pretty in their love and ugliness
As any thousand pictures. And the words
Are quite unnecessary.

Note
And on another day, perhaps, five different poems. But since these seemed, this August, to choose themselves, I look at them and wonder what hidden signatures and sub-texts brought them up from the depths. Are they signposts, fading beacons, the drowned waving? I would like to think that they share something: perhaps the wish to be light-pencils scribbling messages which make the dark even more substantial while doing a little to alleviate its pressure. 'The Gatehouse' was written as the music unwound; to me it is a window on simultaneity and palimpsest: all experience is written over other experiences of equal intensity, and when the paper is held to the light the dead walk, as they do, under the same sun as the living. My son and his unknown grandfather play their duet; the train runs over the uprooted sleepers, the rhythms in the body of a child dictate the rhythms of that child's adult self, evanescent shapes on the air become a charged, sensuous landscape. In 'Young Ghost' my dying mother, longing for dissolution, becomes her photographed self at seventeen: that self, framed in silver, which reaches beyond her own death from the dressing-table by the death-bed, speaking lyrically, calling for an answering lyricism. From a childhood of blackout, searchlight, torch and flare comes 'Under the Barrage', a cradle-song, epigraph, epitaph, where the shift of a stop in the first and sixth verses embraces each dark Icarus and his victim. The 'Epilogue' from the *Midsummer Night's Dream* sequence holds for me a multiple love, for England, for the complex oscillations between the cavalier and the puritan, for theatre and its capacity for cheating the final curtain, for darkness pierced by a little light – never too much or too full. And finally, 'This Room, That Room' from the *Habitat* sequence. The soul's dark cottage is always capable of extension; new doors keep appearing in the blankest of walls. Prescriptive? To find the last room and to be able to believe in it.

ANNE STEVENSON

Minister
We're going to need the minister
to help this heavy body into the ground.

But he won't dig the hole.
Others who are stronger and weaker will have to do that.
And he won't wipe his nose and his eyes.
Others who are weaker and stronger will have to do that.
And he won't bake cakes or take care of the kids –
women's work – anyway,
what would they do at a time like this
if they didn't do that?

No, we'll get the minister to come
and take care of the words.

He doesn't have to make them up.
He doesn't have to say them well.
He doesn't have to like them
so long as they agree to obey him.

We have to have the minister
so the words will know where to go.

Imagine them circling and circling
the confusing cemetery.
Imagine them roving the earth
without anywhere to rest.

Small Philosophical Poem
Dr Animus, whose philosophy is a table,
sits down contentedly to a square meal.
The plates lie there, and there,
just where they should lie.
His feet stay just where they should stay,
between legs and the floor.
His eyes believe the clean waxed surfaces
are what they are.

But while he's eating his un-
exceptional propositions, his wise
wife, Anima, sweeping a haze-gold decanter
from a metaphysical salver,
pours him a small glass of doubt.
Just what he needs.
He smacks his lips and cracks his knuckles.
The world is the pleasure of thought.

He'd like to stay awake all night
(elbows on the table)
talking of how the table might not be there.
But Anima, whose philosophy is hunger,
perceives the plates are void in empty air.
The floor is void beneath his trusting feet.
Peeling her glass from its slender cone of fire,
she fills the room with love. And fear. And fear.

When the Camel is Dust it Goes Through the Needle's Eye
This hot summer wind
is tiring my mother.
It tires her to watch it
buffeting the poppies.
Down they bow
in their fluttering kimonos,
a suppressed populace,
an unpredictable dictator.

The silver-haired reeds
are also supplicants.
Stripped of its petals,
clematis looks grey
on the wall. My mother,
who never came here,
suggests it's too hot
to cook supper.

Her tiredness gets everywhere
like blown topsoil,
teasing my eyes and tongue,
wrinkling my skin.
Summer after summer, silt
becomes landfill between us,
level and walkable,
level, eventually, and simple.

History
Five hundred fifty million years,
and then came the glaciers,
    and then came Gwilym,
a sack of silage forked on his fell-scooter,
    mobbed by his flock.

Each ewe in sail tugs its dinghy, look,
some of the lambs have come unhooked.

They're bounding back helter-skelter;
    the scraped rock
must be ringing with brittle *maas*
    and iron *baas*
I don't hear for window-glass and

April's weak milky light, Wales
and all those winters.

Going Back
For Don and Helen Hill, who are still there

It hazes over,
blurred by forty years,
topography
like the idea of pain,
like love affairs
that at the time *were* time.

An incredible alias,
half mine,

floats on these streets,
identifies each elm
that isn't there,
breathes in these
shapeless, lax,
companionable homes –
hand-built midwest America
that clones itself
in leafy, by-passed towns,
steepled, asleep on
ochre-coloured lawns,
named for the dead that still
fadingly mark a street, a school,
its sledding hill and park…

And next – when I next come?
More will be gone.
The underwater palimpsest
may be almost illegible,
might release me
from haunted erasures,
more haunting survivals –
Mrs Winter's house
flaunting a shiny extension,
for all that, stewed
in compost and a reek of cat.

Behind a veil of murky conifers,
screened by her purple-brown veranda
Miss Elizabeth Dean – at ninety-four?
a hundred and ninety-four? –
entices, still, with peppermints
young neighbors she'll outlive –
like her elms, like hazy autumns
drugged with burning leaves,
like all her contemporaries.
She willed her virgin wealth
to the city's trees.
          And who,
among our PhDs and kindly
Democratic wives would,
forty years ago, have guessed
that, thanks to old Miss Dean,
while maples remain,
Ann Arbor will remain an
arbor, releasing from October's
gentle hospice leaves like hands
that beg to go, let go,
let go, regretfully, a salmon one,
a crimson one… a yellow one,
brimming the sidewalks and shallow gutters
with yet another generation,
another kickable pile.

A mobile municipal vacuum-cleaner,
(is it?) roars its gluttony outside
the Newcombs' house –
its chocolate porch no longer
painted chocolate –
now by the Bursley's grander brick,
no longer Mr & Mrs Bursley's.

At sixteen,
waking on our sleeping porch,
I wrote a sonnet to the morning
'walking like a dancer'
on Miss Dean's weedless,
surely eternal front lawn.

Our house wants paint.
All the porches have been glassed in.
With the side-fence gone, how shrunken
the little summer-house. New owners
keep their white blinds down
like eyelids, but I see through
to that famous 'L' –
living-room bought for two
pianos to live in.
It brought up two girls, three,
too carefully, too musically.

Perhaps when we say 'ghosts',
we mean nothing
but our own cast leaves,
those vanished elms
I took for granted,
angel-food cake, and mother's
League of Women Voters,
mother, and faithful Mother Destler,
Mrs Florer, deaf, next door,
and further down, remote as Greek,
foundering in unhappiness I used to be
so scared of, Dr Blake.

Note
Pasted on the inside cover of my current commonplace book is a quotation from Charles Darwin's *Transmutation Notebooks*: 'Why is thought being a secretion of brain more wonderful than gravity a property of matter? It is our arrogance, our admiration of ourselves.' I also keep at hand a reminder that the top of Mount Everest is marine limestone. The 'astounding hypothesis' of Francis Crick's latest book, according to a review in the *London Review of Books* (7 July, 1994), 'is little more than the claim that mind or consciousness – or the soul… is "in fact no more than the behaviour of a vast assembly of nerve cells and their associated molecules".' The reviewer continues 'though [such a theory] begs the question of "nothing but" only dualists would wish point blank to deny it and there is nothing in the hypothesis that most scientists and philosophers would find in the least astonishing.' Some challenge to poetry surely lies in that 'nothing but', that belittling 'no more than'. Come, we mustn't be ostriches. It won't do to stigmatize 'most scientists and philosophers' as mere reductionists. Nothing, as Richard Feynman observed, is mere.

Science means knowledge. One begins to write poetry because one feels possessed by some individually precious, passional knowledge. Who knows where it comes from, but finding words for it becomes an obsession. As one grows older and writes more, consciousness impinges and begets 'art' – which like any form of socially viable order has meaning only as it communicates. Until recently, imaginative language (and the fictive superstructures that provide us still with all our faiths and ideologies) has boldly laid claim to revealing truth; but we seem to be learning now that even in science 'truth' adjusts itself to human consciousness. 'The way you say the world is what you get'.

So what does science have to give poetry? A spirit, perhaps, both of mystery and independence. For the more literature tries to ape or 'intellectualize' scientific method, the more poetry's imaginative elan is crushed. Art's way has always been to translate ideas into human feelings, into shareable human events.

As for these poems, I've tried to select five that, though personal, represent my work in the light of what has been said above. In 'Minister' (Presbyterian for priest) I fell into a way of dramatizing the difference that in the 1970s I perceived to exist between language and substance. Next come two poems written at different times in memory of my parents. 'History', written recently in North Wales, takes up the theme of anthropocentric mistrust that edged into my last collection, *Four and a Half Dancing Men* (1993).

I hesitated before including 'Going Back', since its references to my beginnings in Ann Arbor, Michigan, are so private. But I'm pleased with the way the rhymes and cadences informally weave it together (as I am pleased with the rhymes in 'History'); and since poetry, to me, is mostly a matter of sound – of a kind of internal, inevitable music – I hope readers (listeners) will overhear in 'Going Back' something that will carry them imaginatively into their own pasts.

PETER BLAND

The Happy Army
The child has a vision of the happy army. He
has carefully sketched in my appointment book
the smiles, the fingers, the boots and guns
his happy army wave like rattles. No
one is dying, no one's bad or good,
and even the one at the back has a medal
while the generals beam pure love. The sun
has rolled to the ground, has been caught up
in a growing air of excitement that runs
riot, filling the sky with faces, arms, legs
and bits of old tanks. It is natural
that everyone, everywhere, faces the front,
not out of discipline or to scare the enemy
but in frank expectancy of applause. And
of course this is why this particular army
is happy, why no one dies, why the sun
shares in the happy army's happiness
and rolls down to earth. It is why I run
towards the boots and guns, why I come
as far as I dare to the edge of the paper
to stare… to stare and to cheer them on.

Lament for a Lost Generation
Between V-J Day and 1951
we wore our first grey longs.
Drab, insular, short of vitamin C,
much given to fags and the fumbled grope

we became – like prefabs
or the last steam train –
something slightly embarrassing
that goes on and on: fodder for talks like

The Ration-Book Age or
The Wartime Growth of the Working Mum.
We were few; conceived in the slump;
brought up in shelters and under the stairs;

eleven-plus boys; post-war conscripts
who lowered the flag on better days.
What we lacked was a style!
We were make-do-and-menders,

utility-grey men, the last of a line.
You can tell us a mile off, even now;
there's a touch of austerity
under the eyes; a hint of carbolic

in our after-shave; a lasting doubt
about the next good time.

Two Family Snaps

1 *In a Council-House Backyard (Circa 1925)*
Here's mum modelling her Susan Lenglen gear
with the penny-a-week insurance man
looking amazed at this ripe
housewife in white silk stockings leaning
over the clothesline. Over

the fence the neighbours' kids
mime her poses. They wink and strut
waving their Great Exhibition mugs. Mum
was much admired by a neighbourhood
that knew a bit of class when they saw it.

Talent will out, they all said.
it never did, but the neighbours
still applauded – being more
than faithful to those of their own
who always made the most of their lot.

2 *Big Game (Circa 1928)*
Here's dad in Africa living it up
with a dead pig under his foot.
He's got a big cigar and an even bigger gun.
All around him there's space
and hordes of naked black lasses.

Just the place for a Bradford lad
brought up on Wesley and smog.
No wonder he's enjoying himself,
killing and screwing and making a profit.
When this was taken he was nearly forty.

Another few months and they shipped him home
to work on the ledgers. He packed life up
but took another twenty years to drop off.
I'm looking at an Empire in its hey-day.
Even the dead pig is laughing.

Letters Home – New Zealand 1885

1
Flocks sway, packed tight against the rails.
We boil them down for soap. Each
ewe's worth fourpence for her fat alone:
twice what we'd get by shipping them back home.
(How patiently they wait, heads bowed
like girls at Sunday School!) I try
to catch up on my notes
describing specimens of plant and stone
picked up on my walks. We hacked
cross-sections from live Kauri trunks
before we burned the slopes. I hope
to show them at Kew that decent work's being done
out here in the colonies. The smell
of blood and melting bones
fouls the verandah where I smoke.
(My notes on fault-likes are especially good.)
The lake's almost dried up. It's been
like Africa this year. The black
swans die in hundreds, eating
their own yoke. Eels
glut the crimson mud for scraps
tipped from the vats. I've seen
them crawl across the lawn
to grab a live sheep's foot. At night
I read the psalms… '*The Lord's
my Shepherd.*' It's most apt. Two
years here now. It almost feels like home.

2
Dear *friend* (there's no one here
called that) I intend
to write a natural history
of these hills. (Most plants
are primitive, some unique. My wife
says we are Adam and Eve.)
My mind's escaped old ways of seeing,
strict categories of breeding, station, class:
it roams, almost unprincipled, between
these tremendous horizons
and the new small print
used in the bibles that you've sent.
Much thanks. I wish
you could see my lake. I've made
a local version of our Oxford punt.

3
At Sunday School my dear wife reads
The Song of Solomon to a Maori chief.
He likes the *old* testament (those simple tales
of bygone kings and queens). He'll
listen for hours. His moko gleams
like blue blood on his cheeks. Once,
at a wedding feast, he ate the heart
of a living lamb – holding it up
still beating to the sun. It was
a sort of Grace – '*For what we are…* '
but that's perhaps difficult to understand
back in New Brighton. Suffice to say
he's *not* a violent man. He asks
why Jesus did not marry? '*The Son
of God should father sons himself.*'
A tribe of Gods! That's what he wants.
We need a priest. My poor wife does her best.

4
Our lake's one island – a sunken raft –
was once the home of cannibals.
Blood-soaked it's taken root – become
a Pavilion, a Chinese glade
of willows and bamboo. Swans
crowd there in their thousands. Some
hang themselves in their haste to breed
(long necks caught on willow forks
breasts spiked by green bamboo).
Their skeletons, so fine and white,
are delicate harps for the wind's tune.

*

At night I go down to the lake alone
haunted by the swans' cold song
(that hollow aboriginal throb). Black
swans, black eels, are all that live
in that still pond. For company
I recite to myself *The Lady of Shalott*
and see her white limbs floating past
my growing tin-roofed Camelot.
My wife's gone back. I cannot keep
her soft hands tied to this hard land.
God called her home to Camberley.
(She begs me to sell up.) I like
my lonely midnight strolls… eels
splashing… dark wings flying off.
I feel new silences. I hear Noah's doves.
I see the first hills loom above
these slow black waters fleeced in fog.

5
My wife's last letter with a pressed rose
arrived with the first snow. (How I ache
to hold her!) I've arranged my notes
in evolutionary order – according
to Lyell and Spencer. Strange
how the well-established species
show signs of regression. They 'give up'.
These acres obviously need new blood.
(Did she prick her finger? There's a stain

on the petals.) I couldn't live
without these hills, this
sense of space that goes on and on
inside my head as well as
all around me. I remember once
she said '*Our pohutakawa blossoms
have the scent of salt and oranges.*' That's what
this rose smells of – not Surrey
but her that summer on an Auckland beach
swimming with chestnut hair piled high
like one of Millais' women. The lake
has frozen over. Another week
and it will hold me up. I'll
skate out all alone to my island
(half-a-mile!) and count the unhatched eggs.
The swans have long gone north. Some ewes
are already lambing. In birth and death
(and love) the world goes mad.
There are no rules for our inmost feelings.
I must question Lyell and Spencer about that.

6
I'm working hard. (Six months
since I wrote you?) Lambs
to the slaughter and these endless notes!
My room is barely habitable…
roots, rocks, unopened bills. My drover
says that I'm being eaten up
by this 'great cannibal land.'

He's a hard worker, fresh from Yorkshire,
but a secretive and venal man.
(Some talk of crude high-country habits
and weekends at the Pa.) I've finally
got my index going. So many entries!
Where to end or begin? I've
consulted Darwin, always the best on sources,
but God still goes back further than we think.

7
'Her chestnut hair and white limbs floating… '
My bedroom mirror's cracked. I shave
two faces… or I did… my beard's
as thick as gorse and mad with ticks.
I've sent the first proofs off (not
happy with my quotes). The drover's left.
The front door's hanging on torn hinges.
Sheep are dying on the library steps.
The shearers are late this year. I'm lonely.
My head hurts and the blackberry patch
whimpers all night with tangled flesh.
No one comes near me. I'll leave this letter
under an ammonite. The lake keeps calling.
I'd like to lie down where the black swans nest.

Note
I emigrated to New Zealand in 1954 and 'The Happy Army' is one of a number of poems about children written in that country in the early 1960s. Others include 'The Building', 'House with Cat or Sun', and 'Death of a Dog'. The poems came in a sudden rush of 'finding one's own voice' that coincided with the beginnings of a nationwide artistic release from the conformist cold-war mentality of New Zealand in the 1950s. The development of a heightened vernacular quickly pulled my poetry away from more formal English concerns. I've chosen one of these early poems because, although they're well-known in New Zealand, they remain relatively unfamiliar to readers here.

'Lament for a Lost Generation' and 'Two Family Snaps' were written after my return to England in the 1970s. They look back at a wartime childhood and perhaps seek to understand lost 'ancestral' sources. My two longest periods of unbroken residence in England (which I left at the age of nineteen) have coincided with a world at war (and its aftermath) and with Mrs Thatcher's free-market triumphs. So there's been plenty to occupy my survival mentality in its struggles to come home.

I remember, on returning to live here, being told by one well-known young Oxbridge poet that I used the first-person too much and that this was 'bad form' (i.e. an implied ego-trip). The idea of the 'I' as survivor, amazed by the sheer fluke of being here at all, had obviously never occurred to him. He also informed me that 'the mere invention of voices was both anecdotal and unimaginative.' Apart from wanting to shoot myself at this welcome home, I could only admire the confidence with which he could take his own identity (and by implication his position in society) so for granted. But the use of the dramatic monologue has increasingly interested me as a way of creating poetic time and space, and of winning back territory from the prose-writers. It's a form that can accommodate so many variables (narrative, meditation, characterization, the lyric impulse, a sense of history etc) giving the imagination the freedom to 'become something else' and to explore its own subconscious at some length. 'Letters Home' was written in 1980, and was pretty well dictated at one sitting. It's loosely based on the life of an early settler in New Zealand called Guthrie-Smith, who had a homestead in the Hawkes Bay. I'd visited the place some twenty years earlier and had strongly identified with both the landscape (similar to North Yorkshire, only hotter) and with Guthrie-Smith himself as some sort of spiritual ancestor. It's surprising how long a poem can take to gestate, and how some slight but sharp experience – in this case the sudden scent of fennel – can release a whole world of past experience.

The notion of the poet as actor, dramatist, director – even camera-man – all in one, obviously appeals to someone who's spent his life as a jobbing actor, doing whatever other people decide is appropriate.

Peter Bland

ANVIL
AUTUMN BOOKS 1994

ANVIL NEW POETS 2
Edited by CAROL ANN DUFFY

Sean Boustead	Oliver Comins	Richard Price
Colette Bryce	Christina Dunhill	Mike Venner
Kate Clanchy	Alice Oswald	John Whale

The second volume of this series introduces another group of talented newcomers, selected and introduced by Carol Ann Duffy (winner of 1993's Forward Poetry Prize and Whitbread Poetry Award).

176 pages £8.95 paper   0 85646 262 4

VASKO POPA
Complete Poems

Translated by Anne Pennington, revised and expanded by Francis R. Jones

Introduced by Ted Hughes

'Popa works to reconstruct a new universe, where every element is selected and tested for its truthfulness.' – Celia Hawkesworth, *The Independent*

464 pages £25.00 cloth   0 85646 237 3

LUIS DE GÓNGORA
Selected Shorter Poems

Translated by Michael Smith

This bilingual edition is an ideal introduction to the complex work of Spain's major poet of the Baroque period, of whom Roy Campbell wrote: 'He is a symbolist who contains the whole of Mallarmé and a lot more besides, a symbolist 300 years before his time.'

176 pages £8.95 paper   0 85646 250 0

ANVIL PRESS POETRY 69 King George St. London SE10 8PX TEL & FAX 081-858 2946

JON STALLWORTHY

A poem is
something that someone is saying
no louder, Pip, than my 'goodnight' –
words with a tune, which outstaying
their speaker travel as far
as that amazing, vibrant light
from a long-extinguished star.

The Almond Tree

I
All the way to the hospital
the lights were green as peppermints.
Trees of black iron broke into leaf
ahead of me, as if
I were the lucky prince
in an enchanted wood
summoning summer with my whistle,
banishing winter with a nod.

Swung by the road from bend to bend,
I was aware that blood was running
down through the delta of my wrist
and under arches
of bright bone. Centuries,
continents it had crossed;
from an undisclosed beginning
spiralling to an unmapped end.

II
Crossing (at sixty) Magdalen Bridge
Let it be a son, a son, said
the man in the driving mirror,
Let it be a son. The tower
held up its hand: the college
bells shook their blessing on his head.

III
I parked in an almond's
shadow blossom, for the tree
was waving, waving me
upstairs with a child's hands.

IV
Up
the spinal stair
and at the top
along
a bone-white corridor
the blood tide swung
me swung me to a room
whose walls shuddered
with the shuddering womb.
Under the sheet
wave after wave, wave
after wave beat
on the bone coast, bringing
ashore – whom?
              New-
minted, my bright farthing!
Coined by our love, stamped with
our images, how you
enrich us! Both
you make one. Welcome
to your white sheet,
my best poem!

V
At seven-thirty
the visitors' bell
scissored the calm
of the corridors.
The doctor walked with me
to the slicing doors.
His hand upon my arm,
his voice – *I have to tell
you* – set another bell
beating in my head:
your son is a mongol
the doctor said.

VI
How easily the word went in –
clean as a bullet
leaving no mark on the skin,
stopping the heart within it.

This was my first death.
The 'I' ascending on a slow
last thermal breath
studied the man below

as a pilot treading air might
the buckled shell of his plane –
boot, glove, and helmet
feeling no pain

from the snapped wires' radiant ends.
Looking down from a thousand feet
I held four walls in the lens
of an eye; wall, window, the street

a torrent of windscreens, my own
car under its almond tree,
and the almond waving me down.
I wrestled against gravity,

but light was melting and the gulf
cracked open. Unfamiliar
the body of my late self
I carried to the car.

VII
The hospital – its heavy freight
lashed down ship-shape ward over ward –
steamed into night with some on board
soon to be lost if the desperate

charts were known. Others would come
altered to land or find the land
altered. At their voyage's end
some would be added to, some

diminished. In a numbered cot
my son sailed from me; never to come
ashore into my kingdom
speaking my language. Better not

look that way. The almond tree
was beautiful in labour. Blood-
dark, quickening, bud after bud
split, flower after flower shook free.

On the darkening wind a pale
face floated. Out of reach. Only when
the buds, all the buds, were broken
would the tree be in full sail.

In labour the tree was becoming
itself. I, too, rooted in earth
and ringed by darkness, from the death
of myself saw myself blossoming,

wrenched from the caul of my thirty
years' growing, fathered by my son,
unkindly in a kind season
by love shattered and set free.

The Source
'The dead living in their memories are, I am persuaded,
the source of all that we call instinct.'
W.B. Yeats

Taking me into your body
you take me out of my own,
releasing an energy,
a spirit, not mine alone

but theirs locked in my cells.
One generation after
another, the blood rose and fell
that lifts us together.

Such ancient, undiminished
longings – my longing! Such
tenderness, such famished
desires! My fathers in search

of fulfilment storm through
my body, releasing now
loved women locked in you
and hungering to be found.

Breakfast in Bed
Lying in late:
two croissants, warm
in each other's arms,
on a dazzling plate.

Pour Commencer
Take 1 green pepper and 2 tomatoes
and cut them into rings and hearts. Mix those
with olives, black olives, and go for a swim
in a green sea with her (or him).
Then serve your salad on two bellies. Pour
a little sun-warmed olive oil in your
salt navel, some vinegar in hers
(or his), and eat slowly with your fingers.
Empty the bottle. Open a second. Then
lick your plates. You will need them again.

Note
Randall Jarrell wrote that 'A good poet is someone who manages in a lifetime of standing out in thunderstorms to be struck by lightning five or six times.' Probably the closest I've come to being struck myself was after a doctor, who happened to be my father, had used the same metaphor in a different context. Telling me that my newborn son was a mongol (or Downs Syndrome child, as we would now say), he went on to explain that this was the result of a chromosomal defect that often 'struck like lightning', for no known reason. By then I was already at work on the poem that would be called 'The Almond Tree' and differ from any that I had written before.

There are four things I would like to say about it. Many of my earlier poems focused on strangers – often in the street – caught by a detached observer's telephoto lens at some moment of crisis or decision. In 'The Almond Tree', the camera is turned on the speaker and, for the first time, it's a movie camera. The poem's written in sections, each with a different stanza-form, in an attempt to convey the different stages of the experience. The opening lines, in fact, came into my head as I was driving to the hospital. The second thing to be said is that the lines 'Welcome to your white sheet/my best poem' echo the lines of a much better poem, Ben Jonson's elegy, 'On my First Son': 'Here doth lie/Ben Jonson his best piece of poetry.' I was stunned when a friend pointed this out: I'd have been prepared to swear in a court of law that I'd never read or heard that poem, but obviously I had. If my theft – or, as I now prefer to call it, my transformation – had been pointed out to me, while I was still writing 'The Almond Tree', I'm sure I'd have cursed and cancelled those lines, not perceiving the best thing about them: the fact that, while Jonson's lines about a dead son are echoed in a happy context, they anticipate my speaker's subsequent *un*happy discovery that this Jon's son is a mongol child. The third thing I should say about the poem is that it originally ended (and was published in my book *Root and Branch*) with an eighth section. I came to feel uncomfortable with this. It seemed to make too explicit something the rest of the poem should have made implicit; and so I dropped the section from more recent printings. Finally, moving from matter of fact to one of conjecture, I like to think that in 'The Almond Tree' I found my own voice – perhaps the most important discovery a poet has to make.

As for the other poems in this selection, they can – I hope – speak for themselves.

GILLIAN CLARKE

The Hare
(*i.m. Frances Horovitz 1938–1983*)

That March night I remember how we heard
a baby crying in a neighbouring room
but found him sleeping quietly in his cot.

The others went to bed and we sat late
talking of children and the men we loved.
You thought you'd like another child. 'Too late'

you said. And we fell silent, thought a while
of yours with his copper hair and mine,
a grown daughter and sons.

Then, that joke we shared, our phases of the moon.
'Sisterly lunacy' I said. You liked
the phrase. It became ours. Different

as earth and air, yet in one trace that week
we towed the calends like boats reining
the oceans of the world at the full moon.

Suddenly from the fields we heard again
a baby cry, and standing at the door
listened for minutes, ears and eyes soon used

to the night. It was cold. In the east
the river made a breath of shining sound.
The cattle in the field were shadow black.

A cow coughed. Some slept, and some pulled grass.
I could smell blossom from the blackthorn
and see their thorny crowns against the sky.

And then again, a sharp cry from the hill.
'A hare', we said together, not speaking
of fox or trap that held it in a lock

of terrible darkness. Both admitted
next day to lying guilty hours awake
at the crying of the hare. You told me

of sleeping at last in the jaws of a bad dream.
'I saw all the suffering of the world
in a single moment. Then I heard

a voice say "But this is nothing, nothing
to the mental pain".' I couldn't speak of it.
I thought about your dream when you lay ill.

In the last heavy nights before full moon,
when its face seems sorrowful and broken,
I look through binoculars. Its seas flower

like clouds over water, it wears its craters
like silver rings. Even in dying you
menstruated as a woman in health

considering to have a child or no.
When they hand me insults or little hurts
and I'm on fire with my arguments

at your great distance you can calm me still.
Your dream, my sleeplessness, the cattle
asleep under a full moon,

and out there
the dumb and stiffening body of the hare.

Radio Engineer

i *The Heaviside Layer*
Staring into the starry sky, that time
in the darkest dark of war and countryside,
'What is the stars?'
my father asked,

then told me that up there,
somewhere between us and Orion,
hangs the ionosphere, lower, closer at night,
reflecting his long wave signals back to earth,

light bending in water.
But things get tight and close,
words, music, languages
all breathing together under that old carthen,

Cardiff, Athlone, Paris
all tongue-twisted up,
all crackle and interference,
your ears hearing shimmer

like trying to stare at stars.

ii *Bedtime*
You'd plan for it, set out equipped,
warmed in and out before you left the fire
for the dash up the dark stairs.
Hot milk, hot water bottles, coats on the bed.
The quickest way to get warm
was to make yourself small,
to pinch shut the edges
of flannelette, carthen, eiderdown, coats,
to breathe in the stuffy cave till you fell asleep
under the breathless weight of the Heaviside layer,
and woke, stunned, into a crowing light.

iii
With wires, transmitters, microphones,
my father unreeled his line

to cast his singing syllables at the sky,
unleashed and riding airwaves up and up

to touch and be deflected,
moths at a silver window in the air.

I saw it, a cast line falling back
through shaken light above the pool,
sound parting water
like a hare in corn.

iv
Outside in the graveyard
I collected frozen roses,
an alabaster dove with a broken wing
for my hoard in the long grass,

while he unreeled his wires down the aisle,
hitched a microphone to the pulpit
and measured silence with a quick chorus

from the *Messiah*.

Still I can't look at stars,
or lean with a telescope, dizzy, against the turning earth,
without asking again, 'What is the stars?'
or calling 'Testing, testing' into the dark.

Anorexic

My father's sister,
the one who died
before there was a word for it,
was fussy with her food.
'Eat up,' they'd say to me,
ladling a bowl with warning.

What I remember's
how she'd send me to the dairy,
taught me to take cream,
the standing gold.
Where the jug dipped
I saw its blue-milk skin
before the surface healed.

Breath held, tongue between teeth,
I carried in the cream,
brimmed, level,
parallel, I knew,
with that other, hidden horizon
of the earth's deep
ungleaming water-table.

And she, more often than not half-dressed,
stockings, a slip, a Chinese kimono,
would warm the cream, pour it
with crumbled melting cheese
over a delicate white cauliflower,
or field mushrooms
steaming in porcelain,

then watch us eat, relishing,
smoking her umpteenth cigarette,
glamorous, perfumed, starved,
and going to die.

Musician

His carpet splattered like a Jackson Pollock
with clothes, books, instruments, the *NME*,
he strummed all day, read Beethoven sonatas.
He could hear it, he said, 'like words'.

That bitterest winter, he took up the piano, obsessed,
playing Bartok in the early hours. Snow fell,
veil after veil till we lost the car in the drive.
I slept under two duvets and my grandmother's fur,
and woke, suffocating, in the luminous nights
to hear the *Hungarian Dances* across moonlit snow.
The street cut off, immaculate, the house
glacial, suburbs hushed in wafery whiteness.
At dawn, hearing Debussy, I'd find him,
hands in fingerless gloves against the cold,
overcoat on. He hadn't gone to bed.

Snows banked the doors, rose to the sills,
silted the attic, drew veils across the windows.
Scent, sound, colour, detritus lay buried.
I dreamed the house vaulted and pillared with snow,
a drowned cathedral, waiting for the thaw,
and woke to hear the piano's muffled bells,
a first pianissimo slip of snow from the roof.

from Blood

1
The house is filled again with children.
I watch from the door, or walk,
a blue cup in my two hands,
while they dance in the drench of the grass.

The garden's a litter of gaudy, broken things,
of golden circles where the pool has been,
that little declivity below the swing
that will grass over in a week or two,

as will the scarred silence
where the hare goes
and three curlews cry.

2
Something's afoot
this summer of rain on the roof at night,
ghosts in the morning trees,
clouds thunderous with Atlantic news,

something woken where the moon
draws up her silvers from a shiver of flood
in the silted well where once
a clean spring rose,

a brim of blood I should have done with,
a forgotten dish of seed,
like the pigeon's saucer left out on the wall
when the bird had flown.

3 *Equinox*
Month of the high tides.
The small bay brims, and there,
far below us on the shore at Strumble,
not wave, not old rags,
but a seal and her newborn,
the afterbirth's ruby clean among the stones.

The children call 'Look, seal, a seal!'
We hush and look, lifting them to see
from the lighthouse wall, while far below
she rolls her slippery body in its pulse
of milk and need and afterpains
to that blind, crying mouth.

She sees us, nervous,
then lollops to the sea
to become wave, sunlight, salt,
to quicken skies and oceans
from her dish of seed,
hadlestr's huddle of stars.

5 *Mali*
Three years ago to the hour, the day she was born,
that unmistakable brim and tug of the tide
I'd thought was over. I drove
the twenty miles of summer lanes,
my daughter cursing Sunday cars,
and the lazy swish of a dairy herd
rocking so slowly home.

Something in the event,
late summer heat overspilling into harvest,
apples reddening on heavy trees,
the lanes sweet with brambles
and our fingers purple,
then the child coming easy,
too soon, in the wrong place,

things seasonal and out of season
towed home a harvest moon.
My daughter's daughter
a day old under an umbrella on the beach
late-comer at summer's festival,
and I'm hooked again, life-sentenced.
Even the sea could not draw me from her.

This year I bake her a cake like our house,
and old trees blossom
with balloons and streamers.
We celebrate her with a cup
of cold blue ocean,
candles at twilight, and three drops of,
probably, last blood.

Note
I cannot separate poetry from being alive, from thinking, from remembering, or from everything one discovers about the physical earth. My ground is the personal, its starting point now, here. I use poetry to think, to follow obsessions such as science, mythology, rocks, space, the sea, the new nature, the patterning of natural things, the mysterious mathematics of the body, earth and seasons. I use poetry to elegise and celebrate. For the past ten years the poem-sequence, with its freedom to let theme and image play out their lines over deep waters, its need for rapt concentration, has become my habitual way into poetry. I choose three elegies. One, 'The Radio Engineer' for my father, written 33 years after his early death, using his science to ask questions about death. 'The Hare', for a friend, celebrates and elegises women. The process of writing 'Anorexic' set a memory free. It brought back not only the aunt, the place, the carrying of a jug of cream when I was five or six, but also a childhood fascination with the water-table, and the horizon, an obsession both scientific and poetic. I add 'Musician', another poem of relationship, because the poem obeyed my will, and told all I wanted to tell about an aspect of love for a son, then eighteen years old, learning to play the piano in a season of snow. I tell it through weather, the music of Bartok and Debussy, and, in particular, Debussy's Cathedral drowning in rising water, or snow, or time. The sequence 'Blood', from which I take four out of seven poems, takes up the theme of woman, this time in wholehearted celebration of middle-age.

LES MURRAY

Green Rose Tan
Poverty is still sacred. Christian
and political candles burn before it
for a little longer. But secretly

poverty revered is poverty outlived:
childhoods among bed-ticking midnights
blue as impetigo mixture, through the grilles,

cotton-rancid contentments of exhaustion
around Earth's first kerosene lamp
indoors out of wet root-crop fields.

Destitution's an antique. The huge-headed
are sad chaff blown by military bohemians.
Their thin metal bowls are filled or not

from the sky by deodorized descendants
of a tart-tongued womb-noticing noblesse
in the goffered hair-puddings of God's law

who pumped pioneer bouillons with a potstick,
or of dazzled human muesli poured from ships
under the milk of smoke and decades.

The mass rise into dignity and comfort
was the true modern epic, black and white
dwarfing red, on the way to green rose tan.

Green rose tan that the world is coming to,
land's colour as seen from space
and convergent human skin colour, it rises

out of that unwarlike epic, in the hours
before intellect refracts and disdains it,
of those darker and silver-skinned, for long ages

humbly, viciously poor, our ancestors,
still alive in India, in Africa, in ghettoes.
Ancestors, ours, on the kerb in meshed-glass towns.

The Say-but-the-word Centurion Attempts a Summary
That numinous healer who preached Saturnalia and paradox
has died a slave's death. We were manoeuvred into it by priests
and by the man himself. To complete his poem.

He was certainly dead. The pilum guaranteed it. His message,
unwritten except on his body, like anyone's, was wrapped
like a scroll and despatched to our liberated selves, the gods.

If he has now risen, as our infiltrators gibber,
he has outdone Orpheus, who went alive to the Shades.
Solitude may be stronger than embraces. Inventor of the mustard tree,

he mourned one death, perhaps all, before he reversed it.
He forgave the sick to health, disregarded the sex of the Furies
when expelling them from minds. And he never speculated.

If he is risen, all are children of a most high real God
or something even stranger called by that name
who knew to come and be punished for the world.

To have knowledge of right, after that, is to be in the wrong.
Death came through the sight of law. His people's oldest wisdom.
If death is now the birth-gate into things unsayable

in language of death's era, there will be wars about religion
as there never were about the death-ignoring Olympians.
Love, too, his new universal, so far ahead of you it has died

for you before you meet it, may seem colder than the favours of gods
who are our poems, good and bad. But there never was a bad baby.
Half of his worship will be grinding his face in the dirt

then lifting it to beg, in private. The low will rule, and curse by him.
Divine bastard, soul-usurer, eros-frightener, he is out to monopolise hatred.
Whole philosophies will be devised for their brief snubbings of him.

But regained excels kept, he taught. Thus he has done the impossible
to show us it is there. To ask it of us. It seems we are to be the poem
and live the impossible. As each time we have, with mixed cries.

Rock Music
Sex is a Nazi. The students all knew
this at your school. To it, everyone's subhuman
for parts of their lives. Some are all their lives.
You'll be one of those if these things worry you.

The beautiful Nazis, why are they so cruel?
Why, to castrate the aberrant, the original, the wounded
who might change our species and make obsolete
the true race. Which is those who never leave school.

For the truth, we are silent. For the flattering dream,
in massed farting reassurance, we spasm and scream,
but what is a Nazi but sex pitched for crowds?

It's the Calvin SS: you are what you've got
and you'll wrinkle and fawn and work after you're shot
though tears pour in secret from the hot indoor clouds.

Like Wheeling Stacked Water
Dried nests in the overhanging limbs
are where the flood hatched eggs of swirl.
Like is unscary milder love. More can be in it.

The flood boomed up nearly to the door
like a taxiing airliner. It flew past all day.
Now the creek is down to barley colour
waist deep on her, chest on him,
wearing glasses all around them, barely pushing.

Down under stops of deadwood pipe in living
branches, they move on again. The bottom
is the sunk sand cattle-road they know
but hidden down cool, and mincing
magically away at every step, still going.

The wide creek is a tree hall decorated
with drowned and tobacco ribbons,
with zippy tilting birds, with dried snakes hanging
over the doorways everywhere along.

They push on. *Say this log I'm walking
under the water's a mast like off a
olden day ship –*. Fine hessian shade
is moistening down off cross-trees,

and like wings, the rocking waterline
gloving up and down their bodies
pumps support to their swimmy planet steps.

They've got a hook and bits
of bluebottle line from salt holidays.
They had a poor worm, and crickets automatic in a jar
but they let all them off fishing.

They're taking like to an adventure instead,
up past there where the undercut bank
makes that bottling noise, and the kingfisher's
beak is like the weight he's thrown by
to fly him straight.

By here, they're wheeling stacked-up water.
It has mounted like mild ice bedclothes to
their chest and chin. They have to tiptoe
under all the white davits of the bush.

But coming to the island, that is like the pupil
in acres of eye, their clothes pour water
off like heavy chain. They toil, and lighten
as they go up on it. All this is like the past
but none of it is sad. It has never ended.

It Allows a Portrait in Line-scan at Fifteen

He retains a slight 'Martian' accent, from the years of single phrases.
He no longer hugs to disarm. It is gradually allowing him affection.
It does not allow proportion. Distress is absolute, shrieking, and runs him at frantic speed through crashing doors.
He likes cyborgs. Their taciturn power, with his intonation.
It still runs him around the house, alone in the dark, cooing and laughing.
He can read, about soils, populations and New Zealand. On neutral topics he's illiterate.
Arnie Schwarzenegger is an actor. He isn't a cyborg really, is he, Dad?
He lives on forty acres, with animals and trees, and used to draw it continually.
He knows the map of Earth's fertile soils, and can draw it freehand.
He can only lie in a panicked shout *SorrySorryIdidn'tdoit!* warding off conflict with others and himself.
When he ran away constantly it was to the greengrocers to worship stacked fruit.
His favourite country was the Ukraine: it is nearly all deep fertile soil.
When asked to smile, he photographs a rictus-smile on his face.
It long forbade all naturalistic films. They were Adult movies.
If they (that is, he) *are bad the police will put them in hospital.*
He sometimes drew the farm amid Chinese or Balinese rice terraces.
When a runaway, he made uproar in the police station, playing at three times adult speed.
Only animated films were proper. Who Killed Roger Rabbit then authorised the rest.
Phrases spoken to him he would take as teaching, and repeat.
When he worshipped fruit, he screamed as if poisoned when it was fed to him.
A one-word first conversation: *Blane. – Yes! Plane, that's right, baby! – Blane.*
He has forgotten nothing, and remembers the precise quality of experiences.
It requires rulings: *Is stealing very playing up, as bad as murder?*
He counts at a glance, not looking. And he has never been lost.
When he ate only nuts and dried fruit, words were for dire emergencies.
He'd begun to talk, then returned to babble. It withdrew speech for years.
He remembers all the breeds of fowls, and all the counties of Ireland.
Is that very autistic, to play video games in the day?
He is anger's mirror, and magnifies any near him, raging it down.
It still won't allow him fresh fruit, or orange juice with bits in it.
He swam in the midwinter dam at night. It had no rules about cold.
He was terrified of thunder and finally cried as if in explanation *It – angry!*
He grilled an egg he'd broken into bread. Exchanges of soil-knowledge are called landtalking.
He lives in objectivity. I was sure Bell's palsy would leave my face only when he said it had begun to.
Don't say word! when he was eight forbade the word 'autistic' in his presence.
Bantering questions about girlfriends cause a terrified look and blocked ears.
He sometimes centred the farm in a furrowed American Midwest.
Eye contact, Mum! means he truly wants attention. It dislikes I contact.
He is equitable and kind, and only ever a little jealous. It was a relief when that little arrived.
He surfs, bowls, walks for miles. For many years he hasn't trailed his left arm while running.
I gotta get smart! Looking terrified into the years. *I gotta get smart!*

Note

These five poems are still close to me, having been written within the last two years. All will appear in my next collection. Foolishly, I published two of them, 'Green Rose Tan' and 'Rock Music', before they had had time to settle into their final forms. Their appearance in *PN Review* now is intended to correct those premature appearances. Since excessive commentary has tended in this century to alienate poetry from a wider public, I don't want to offer any remarks about the poems I've chosen. About commentary itself, I would say that exegesis still has a place, mainly in education, but under successive flavours of political correctness it has been hard to restrain criticism from drifting towards the condition of ideological policing, made the more pernicious by entrapment of literature within a limited milieu. The way out for poetry seems to lie in the direction of public readings, whether in person or on radio or television. A large, eager and discerning public has been forming for these over the last couple of decades. At the same time, the text, as printed on paper somewhere, remains necessary and normative. If the reader is allowed to get at it, through all the prose.

Les Murray

BRIAN JONES

At Great Tew
thinking of Cary, Viscount Falkland (1610–43)

'… and would passionately profess that the very agony of the war took his sleep from him and would shortly break his heart. He was weary of the times, he said, but would be out of it ere night.'

i

As he could not heal his country's disease,
he longed for death. Dressing himself cleanly
as one going to a banquet, he drew the flap
and stepped into the tented field. An army
stirred, and small fires through the morning mist
blossomed. A nervous boy
fidgeted fingertips on the war drum.

He stands and gazes. The morning light
gathers like elegance at wrist and neck.
Across an English field he stares
into the mirror of an English field
where small fires blossom.
Between the fields, the dark fume of a hedge,
and a linking gap…

ii

High summer. The Cotswold stone
returns light, softened. Echoes,
echoes everywhere. The lane
tunnelling green through covertures of scents
leads to a mossed and pitted gate, beyond
which, becalmed now like a photograph,
his house stands, at whose table, before friends,
the wine and meat were sanctified
by ideals of moderation, while the candles
glimmered in Oxfordshire darkness, itself
in an England black with storm.
And the storm rose, and each light failed
one by one. No man survives
alone in blackness, can only grasp
whatever is to hand, and that always
is weapons, the simplicity
of alignment, leading inexorably
to a misty field at dawn
before the battle…

iii

Hooves
gather to thunder over mist-soft earth.
With light fixed in determined eyes
he kicks blood from his horse and pulls ahead
aimed at the mirrored enemy, that gap
clean in the hedge where image coincides
with image and a hail of lead. Comrades
and foes, stunned, rein back to admire
momently this career of death…

iv

The picnic crumbles, slips into the grass.
The Sunday paper brightly features
'suicide chic', the hagiography
of exemplary failures:
a poet toppling from a bridge,
an aviator heading out to sea.
The tone of commendation and the staring
ikons of centrality sit well
among advertisements which also fail
to mention price and efficacy…

v

The Sunday's camera would have caught it well:
that split astonished second when
two hell-bent forces faltered as there lay
between them a small island of one man;
until one side saw in the death
bravery flowering from a certain cause,
the other, panic from a loss of nerve,

and craning forward, screaming, both came on.

Prospero to Miranda

1

Once upon a time, I was a tree, the tallest
tree of an island. Let me describe that tree.
I was an uprush, like pressured water,
cresting into dark needles that splintered light.
I was purely beautiful, high as breathlessness.
But I ached, O how I ached with my weight of beauty,
the responsible act of holding the high
head steady against the gaze of admirers,
against wind that breathed a music from me.
My trunk groaned to be so slender, bearing so much.
At night I wept gummy tears and swayed.
And around my shallow roots I felt the sand
and pebbles shiver. I felt treachery.
And beyond, the ominous instability of the sea.

2

My ache was intolerable. I split and hurled
my pain in a screaming arc across the sky.
It danced and devoured distances. Its gift
was punishing continents for my agony.
It struck, and from its strike huge flowers of flame
bloomed from roots of bone and rubbled brick
Then it returned and hovered loving near me.
I had made a venom of the light and air.
Sheared to the core with its birth, ugly at last
as I always knew I was, I toppled sighing
and my sigh released us both. I saw it climb
and curve fadingly to the curve of heaven. It became
its own creature. I lay fulfilled. Centuries
rotted me sweet. I settled. I became earth.

3
This time I dreamed. The dreams were slow and green.
They coated me with shimmer. The roots of dreams
drank from me, and I churned with pleasure. I gave,
I gave, and my giving blossomed and grew
effortless fruits. And there was silence, the silence
of a planet turning through its seasons.
Towards dawn, the dreams grew wild. Spasms fluttered
the leaves of harmony. Rough places surfaced
like eczema, and in one place a cave
cracked blackly open, and from its depths a something
scratched itself and yawned and shambled out.
Its skill was hurting. I felt how it hurt.
It yanked the green. It screamed for a mate to hurt.
It itched to breed. I felt the itch, and moaned.

4
It crept into my bed and stared at me.
It was a thing of darkness and was mine.
It stretched its face to touch my face and kiss.
I screamed and woke. Again I was that tree,
pure uprush, pure as pressured water,
cresting dark needles and splintered light,
aching with beauty and the need to hold
my head rock-steady like a beacon-flame.
Pray for me on my island. I feel again
unbearable pains, and that thing of light and air
ticking its countdown. I yearn to split and launch.
Cycles of endless grief are promised me.
Pray that I break like a staff whatever pride
it is that hates that creature and sets it free.

5
Somewhere in that cycle you appear,
wide-eyed and watchful of my face
as the full moon through a window as I sleep,
or the calm ignored meaning of a dream.
I tell you my story endlessly, as a man
imprisoned hopelessly talks to his visitor
across the impenetrable space between them.
I do not believe in you. You exist only
in a myth of innocence on some other island.
And yet you are my daughter, a woman
with her own story, waiting quietly at my feet
in an age-old posture of subservience.
Why do I refuse to speak the words 'Tell me'
like a bucket lowered in a well of sweet water?

The Children of Separation
While waiting for you to come, I imagine you sitting
in a stopped train between stations, feeling
at peace in no-man's-land, where there is no need
to say 'we' or 'our' or 'home', or other impossible words,

where the poppies among the corn
recall distant universal pain
cushioned in history and innocence.
How unusual it must be for you now to enjoy silence,

with no-one to crave your assurance, no-one to grasp
your hands, stare into your face, and guiltily ask
'Are you all right? Are you unhappy? Will you say?'
No-one you must gratify

with tears, or the absence of tears.
Suddenly, you are among the ranks of those
who once seemed as unlikely, as remote,
as the handicapped, the poor, the mad –

the children of separation, those who are given
two Christmases to halve the pain
and find it doubled, those who are more prey
to nostalgia than old men, who have been betrayed

by language and now handle it like bombs,
for whom affection is a thicket of spies, and surnames
amputations with the ache of wholeness.
Every book taken down is inscribed by loving parents,

and albums of photographs refuse to be otherwise.
What can be done with memories?
What remains of the self if everything that was
is now framed in the inverted commas of 'seemed'?

I imagine the brakes sighing to the inevitable,
and the train resuming the purpose of the rails.
Soon you will step out into my story
whose pages for too long I kept closed to you.

We will walk through fields I am still making mine,
and when the time comes for someone to say 'Let's go home'
no-one will say it. On the platform, we will wait to be parted,
your hand clutching a ticket to somewhere rejected.

At Lullingstone
Set in an act of Roman will against
the cold North, the dolphins curve their backs
of chipped mosaic, circling the dead hearth –
symbols of fecund joy we gazed at one
sunlit day when we trembled but dared not
touch. Now fingering snow caresses our windscreen
blind and we can barely glimpse the timbers
in whose shelter the remembered dolphins swim.
Your face is brilliant with starlight and distress.
I cull your words with icy fingers but cannot
speak what I hear – a child's whimper, your child's,
as the Romans might have heard beyond the hearth
and haze of imported wine the night-voice
of the dispossessed, suffering, unappeased.

Brian Jones

Letter from Elsewhere
It was not quite as we'd imagined
when we honed the splendour of consciousness
housed in the bodies of the just:
I approached a sun-thronged lozenge

where woodland opened to a path
that tussocked down to a fordable river.
Water tickled my ankles. A few stones
slurred their green rondures. And I emerged

squelching through the pats of cows that were
technically barbarian into the daisies
and buttercups of an alien regime. I had crossed
the Border!

I felt all we'd prefigured
in those smoke-anguished rooms: I sensed
trained on my back the trembling
rifle-sights of death-starved guards.

I knew behind each copse the shaggy
welcoming figures waited with their
torturing altars and backlog of impotence
to be vented on my flesh. But –

the stream chattered gaily away,
cows munched and sputtered,
and if soldiers patrolled a barbed border
and barbarians cared, it was solely

in a collusive myth. So my stomp
through forbidden cowshit was brutally
deflating, warranting no publicity
of departure or arrival. If there are

checks to the foot, they are not located
in trip-wires or snipers, but in a kind
of love, a defining by relationship,
a need to be needed, as a hand

reaching for blackberries expects a thorn
to make an autumn ritual complete.
At last I stood as uneventfully
as hawthorn on the far bank, and the guard

who slammed lead punishingly through me
was Nostalgia: an intense sunlight
on abandoned hills; a song suddenly
perfected on a forgiven tongue. I live

in my chosen dream, have parted company
with the possibility of being any place
but where daylight at this moment gleams.
I have no excuse for desire. And I envy you.

Note
I now see the poems I've written as outcomes of a struggle with

> those faces at my shoulder
> wincing or smiling at every word.
> The ground control of every flight.

A struggle towards being able to care only about how I appear to myself, not to others. For me, that is a primal and difficult struggle – the roots of being otherwise are deep. So deep, that my fear or fantasy is that the last word I speak on my deathbed will be the first word of the poem I have always tried to write.

    The poems I offer here feel true to the perpetual swing of my work between the private and public worlds, and in one or two of them I feel I am bringing these worlds together.

R. F. LANGLEY

Juan Fernandez

1

As we slowly exploit the opportunities
between the jug and the earth, sky, men
and divinities, somewhere along the hold
the spring has, the ring gaining the ear
as it is picked up, the print on the bar,
the head shakes, shakes in a rainbow nexus,
shakes to see the old marks so very plain,
shakes the traps in reflection, rattles
the concentration into scrapping across
the frame, fluttering, mercurial, rabbits
vanish, turning everything into a large
form protecting the small ones, a spread
hand mothering doubts, as, now that
whoever that was has stamped past, they
wrinkle out, filling the hollow again.
And now is the water as firm as a heel?
Back drops blue sky. Convenient steel.

2

Snug, close and whispering up a trade, we
peep abroad again to find the planets,
earth and stones still satisfyingly alike,
sanctioning a lot more familiar adventures,
though we absolutely don't explain that
impression. Toes. Tokens. Miracles. Don't
you fret. We are gently rocking again.
Which makes it wonderful to rediscover
the silky wet print and deliberately fit
the foot back in it. I stood like one
thunderstruck. It was too big. By a great
deal too big. It was not mine. Loose my
cattle. Demolish my bower and tent. Wear
very quiet clothes. I've left school and
nobody cares about my motives now. Nothing
is clearer and more simple than a row of
rabbits caught outright in common light.

3

It is a common experience to come upon a
pale, glittering house set far back across
a meadow. It is certainly inside you. Down
along hours of mumbling 'Hello', and for
the attention of nettles in their darkest
green listening uniform, whose steadiness
miracles your ridiculous modern feet. In
its nimble way the lease suggests you can
project yourself, be big as the ancestors,
in this tangy, tart-taking, distinguished
deal. 'It's a light touch,' he shouts back,
'that will cause a great burning!' To which
the response has to be a firm shake of the
head or a slight widening of the eyes. Then
he's hurrying up, laughing, with his silly
reassurance that 'It's only you!' and
another blue funk is absolutely everywhere.

4

The print over the bar is the order of release
and it's away home again, ransomed deep into
a second time, deep into a pale blue, silky
head, billowing, billowing, a mite of quick
silver rousing in the threads. It bites. The
smell of meths just opens slightly round the
lamps. The unexpected colours stare. The crowd
is wholly intent. A fluttering. A blaze. Then
justice on justice as prodigious striding
shadows come to shut under this foot that I
am putting carefully down. The self is felt,
as standing, fired, inside the diamond. He
elucidates every projection and teaches what
was hidden in the heart. Of what is really
here. Of nooks. Of ends. Of wrinkling leaves.
The sparrows to the trees outside. So quietly.
The leaves just open up and let them come.

5

And all along the breastworks the dominators lean
and sneer. And I sneak and look up and match snarl
with snarl. It has always been in me to know how
they snarl. And I've done it before as a child and
a dreamer. The power is in dark, steady beams. I
sneak and snarl. But now there's a tiny request. A
cautious sip which might be surprising. It is hair
brown, or even lavender. It is a faint roughness
that stops. A flickering that hops to a deep nest
where the old frame burst its black heart. And she
twinkles in there with a beakful of wriggling legs.
During the last stages of the struggle, like this,
and only through a medium of dim instruments, came
baby fact. A particularly gentle thrill. She wore
silvery bluegrey. Sparkling. Startling. And the
brooding self with all its vanity disappears. You
forget how it is. Then. Whizz. And a perfect catch.

6

Could be that, when the carpenter stops to look
up, just as he straightens, his first idea will
be to see what he's been chewing. And the late
afternoon will open into a stunning exhibition
of honey and pepper. The awkward handle of the
saw. Its shadow on the bench. The shadows of his
fingers next to it. Curling. The separate worm
holes in the wood. Nothing seems so alive as the
tense silence of this picture. A new assessment
has released everything into uninhabited islands.
Into a final order. No. No. No. Now style alone
replies tamarisk on the dunes. Curling. I am
indicated by a star. And a footnote. I have been
shot through. Some sort of dancer must have been
here. But command is taken now by those tiny
expert birds who perch, and glow, and whizz
and pick the pepper out of the closing air.

Mariana

And, looking out, she might
have said, 'We could have all
of this,' and would have meant
the serious ivy
on the thirteen trunks, the
ochre field behind, soothed
passage of the cars, slight
pressure of the sparrow's
chirps – just what the old glass
gently tested, bending,
she would have meant, and not
a dream ascending.

And, looking in, she might
have seen the altering
cream of unemphatic
light across the bevel
of the ceiling's beam, and
shaken by the flare of
quiet wings around the
room as martins hovered
at the guttering, she
might have soon settled for
these things, without the need
for certainties elsewhere.

So, 'Please,' she would have said.
'We could,' she would have said,
and 'Maybe,' mildly. Then,
selling out, buying in,
the drawling light and the
quiet squall of martins'
wings again, again, she
might have soon discerned her
self, seeing them. Not things,
but seeing things. And with
such care, it would be like
being shown what was not there.

It was the old glass cooled
the colours and transposed
them in a different key. It
chastened most of what the
sparrow said, and made an
affilatura of
the tree. She would have known
the consolation that
it gave, and smiled to see
the unthought-of tricks she
needed, and the sort of
liar she was, or might soon be.

As things came in, and as
they spread and sprayed, she could
have tilted up her face
in the soft fuss they made,
encouraging the cheat
with shivering lashes,
tremulo, fermo, wide
or tight, intending
to confuse her sight until,
perhaps, she dared to make
a try – to find her own
cupid in her own eye.

To such a scene, amongst
such possibilities –
the downright, matter of
fact determination
of ivy on the trees,
wriggling queerly under
the examination
of the glass, the steady
sunlit room, fluttered by
each martin as it made
its pass – to all of this
she might have deftly given

a lash, until there were
sequins in the air and
surreptitious cupids
glancing everywhere. They
pricked their wings. Their arrows
spun away with thinnest
silver chirruping. They
were miraculous, picked
by her to be beyond
belief – believing them –
the lie she told to throw
the truth into relief.

Into the pure relief
of ordinary light.
But now she must have all
of this, compelled to see
by possibility
just what the glass finds real
enough to bend, jolted
by tilting shadows that
the martins send, seized by
the amorini, who,
being unreal, demand
her head for what they steal.

R. F. Langley

Note
Every brushstroke changes the picture. If it's crimson it intensifies all the greens and there's the new problem in how to respond to that. The poem makes a start and you read what you've written, and from this and from what you half have in mind, the next bit comes. Sequence poems make the process visible. Many of the best poems I've seen over the past thirty years have been sequence poems. Don't talk to the driver. Not until some time afterwards. Crusoe standing thunderstruck, looking at the footprint, toes and heel, facing wide-reaching options. It might have been made by the devil deliberately to tell him something. Or by himself on some previous, now forgotten, occasion. Then the word 'toe' is close to 'token', 'sign', 'mark', even 'miracle'. It has connections with teaching, showing, indicating, having dignity and being worthy. Also, when walking through a bright nave, the various shades of a foot come from different sides, all at once, to join under the footfall. Ideas, etymology, experience. 'Juan Fernandez' ran ahead of me well, feeling fit, keeping me surprised. It has stayed in front over the years, and isn't exhausted yet. I don't write many poems, so each one has to be able to keep running, faster than I can, for as long as possible. I can't do without the autobiographical experiences, whatever happens to them in the subsequent process, however they got together in the first place. The sharpening of their distinctiveness, and the sense of their being separate from each other, and from me, lift, as Wallace Stevens said, the 'loneliness of thinking'. The shocks of fear and joy that specific moments seem to carry, for me, are often what matters most. 'What is really here.' 'Nooks and ends.' A flycatcher. A nest in the hammerbeams. Ford Madox Brown in August 1855 painting in the fields at Hendon, determining to 'make a little picture of it', while the clouds alter the light and the farmer carries away the corn Brown had chosen for his subject. He decided, eventually, it was better not to 'dream of possession'. But entertaining the dream is trying for more than a 'mock-up of consciousness'. It calls for testing all available strategies. 'Not things, but seeing things.' That could involve for instance finding out again, this time, what would happen if rhyme came back in to do a lot of the running. So, six years later, 'Mariana'.

ROBERT NYE

Familiar Terms
You say I love you for your lies?
   But that's not true.
I love your absent-hearted eyes –
   And so do you.

You say you love me for my truth?
   But that's a lie.
You love my tongue because it's smooth –
   And so do I.

You say they love who lie this way?
   I don't agree.
They lie in love and waste away –
   And so do we.

Darker Ends
Here's my hand turned to shadows on the wall –
Black horse, black talking fox, black crocodile –
Quick fingers beckoning darkness from white flame,
Until my son screams, 'No! chase them away!'

Why do I scare him? Fearful of my love
I'm cruelly comforted by his warm fear,
Seeing the night made perfect on the wall
In my handwriting, if illegible,
Still full of personal beasts, and terrible.

Abjure that art – it is no true delight
To lie and turn the dark to darker ends
Because my heart's dissatisfied and cold.
To tell the truth, when he is safe asleep,
I shut my eyes and let the darkness in.

Henry James
Henry James, top hat in hand, important, boring,
Walks beautifully down the long corridor
Of the drowned house just off Dungeness
At the turn of the century. It is 3 p.m. probably.
It is without doubt October. The sun decants
Burgundy through high windows. The family portraits
Are thirteen versions of the one face, walking
On the thick trembling stalk of Henry James.
It is a face which looks like the face of a goldfish
Fed full of breadcrumbs and philosophy, superbly
Reconciled to its bowl. The difference
Between Henry James and a goldfish, however,
Is that Henry James has nostrils. Those nostrils observe
An exquisite scent of evil from the library.
Henry James goes beautifully on his way. His step
Is complicated. (He nurses an obscure hurt. It is this
Which kept him from active service in the sex war.)
Listen and you will hear the trickle of his digestive juices –
Our author has lunched, as usual, well –
Above the sweetly unpleasant hum of his imagination.
His shoes make no squeak and he deposits no shadow
To simplify the carpet. Henry James
Turns a corner. Henry
James meets Henry
James. Top hat, etcetera. Henry James
Stops. Henry James stares. Henry James
Lifts a moral finger. 'You again!'
He sighs. 'How can you be so obvious?'
Henry James blushes and Henry James flees and Henry
James goes beautifully on his way, top hat
In hand, important, boring, he walks down
The long life-sentence of his own great prose.

Robert Nye

Going to the Dogs
Come Friday night my father's public vice
Was a greyhound track. He took me there twice.
Most of his life his own sad way he went,
So going to the dogs with me was different.

The electric hare, the eager racing hounds,
Tic tacs in their white gloves, fistfuls of pounds –
The magic of that place and its event!
Oh, to me going to the dogs was different.

To choose a trap my poor Dad bruised his wits
Perusing form, and when that failed had fits
Of asking me my fancies. What this meant
For us made going to the dogs quite different.

Once the choice dog in the pre-race parade
Excreted what looked like bad marmalade.
'A sign,' my father said, 'from heaven sent!
You do know going to the dogs is different?'

He'd urge his favourite home with passionate cries.
The keenest still brings tears into my eyes:
'Come on, my son!' It was an accident
Which our dear going to the dogs made different.

I can't remember what my old man won;
God knows he lost much more in the long run.
His coat was shabby and his hat was bent,
But going to the dogs I found him different.

I do recall my father shook my hand
When our dog came in first. Now understand:
Some of us gamble when our hearts are spent.
My going to the dogs is not so different.

Riposte
Above all other nights that night be blessed
On which my grandam rose from her sweet rest
Woke by a nightingale whose passionate song
Rang in the moonlight, Keatsian and long.
My grandmother threw open wide her door
And listened for a minute, not much more;
Then, when sufficient nightingale she'd heard,
Cried out: *Right! Just you bugger off, you bird!*

ANDREW WATERMAN

The Two Roads
The fork in the path
Came up before
I was ready to choose;
I found I had taken
The sky road. At first
I could glimpse through thicket
The other lane dipping,
Escorted by water,
Between flowering banks,
Rollered lawns, white stone dwellings.
A turn lost the view.
And what with the rain
Closing in, the unsheltered
Climbing a stony road
Riding blown grass,
It was only attaining
The ridge I could look
Down through snatches of cloud
At the coast road whole:
Past meadows where cows
Stood in clusters it followed
The strand to the bay's
Bluest haven, a house,
Sunlit garden, child playing
As if who belonged there
Might have been me;
Who appearing now
Did not look up,
Would be deaf at such distance
To the nothing I knew
Was all I could say now.

A Butterfly
Even under the shed there's something outdoors
About the work. One side stands open

To stars and wind. You pause on your barrow to watch
Dawn come up, or a shower across the city.

You're never bricked in. On slack shifts in summer
Men wander off along overgrown sidings, embankments,

For a sun and a glance through the *Mirror*, a couple
Have planted a vegetable garden back of Humberstone coal
    Wharf.

Grass invades. Dustiest corners are settled
With unauthorised flowers. The Grain Shed sparrows

Strut plundering leaking sacks, great rats
Buck-jump away from right under your feet.

On a fine day waggons trundle in hung with glittering
Waterdrops: somewhere rain is falling.

Even one bleak night, surrounded
By foggy blackness, and cartons, crates,

Rolls of netting stacked up on the shed platform,
Hard graft, something broke in when old Gumble found

In the straw that wadded a cased-up carboy of acid
A sleepy butterfly. It crawled

On to his palm. 'Beautiful little bugger
In't it?' It fluttered in his sour beer breath.

'Look at this, Jacko. Red Admiral.' Wherever
He carried it, cupped precious in his hands,

Men stopped, gathering under wan lights:
Blue overalls, stubbled faces focused on

A butterfly, straw strewn upon the concrete,
And birds starting racketing for the new day in the girders.

Growing Pains

Green from Ireland,
And a childhood of pushing prams –
I can imagine your fireship innocence.

You danced all night,
Telling them all the ways their lives were wrong,
Kept up in London like treading water.

Grounded now, you laugh at yourself then –
Until you gasp is if
Roots stirred with the sharp pain

Of all such laughter is a loosening from:
Home; a confirmation gown;
The candles of the faithful; on your cheeks

Not these, but hallowed drops again.

Outside

Outside for a minute fetching coal, I look
Back through the window: a luminous vignette,
The laden dinner-table, bravura fork
Conducting discussion, lustre of poured wine,
Composure of faces, dress for it. Chill night
Revives perspectives from when such wasn't mine.

Twenty years back, from pavements where great elms
Erupting in lamplight splayed black beams across
Opulent gardens, animated films
Of the good life behind glass that shut me off.
Wit-spangled comeliness arguing the toss
On Art, Truth, uttering 'fifthly', 'fugue', and stuff.

Not that I'd not thought then they might be jerks.
Nor that these are, on cars, schools, roles, pay, laws,
Things not what life's about, just how it works.
I sense, reentering with a full scuttle,
All ideality is sheen we know because
Of its cold outer dark. 'Another bottle?'

Christmas 1989

Last month's miracle was young people dancing
On top of the wall dividing a city, hands
From the West reaching for those from the East
Until that day shot for such transgression.

'The Berlin Wall is history!' headlines proclaim –
Meaning not just dead, but irrelevant. Likewise
My postwar German friends say, 'Hitler? –
That Nazi stuff's just history…'

But history never dies, is the perilous tide
That wave upon wave breaking bubbles carries us onward,
Floats once again like broken-up jigsaw
Poland, Hungary, Czechoslovakia.

In the baroque basilica of St Kasimir,
Vilnius, history laughs, is a headscarved woman
Clearing out the Museum of Atheism:
'All junk now, the lot wouldn't fetch three kopecks!'

While if, in Romania, this day a tyrant is killed,
History weeps through the imperfect living who bury
His victims, melts down their myriad candles…
And also history stares betrayed

From sad eyes knowing Utopia has died,
The lethal old charmer who led us on, alchemised
The selfless to murderers and their prey. Leaving
The future to crave merely more cars and shopping.

Uncle Bob

'Use your feet, and bring the bat down true
To the line of flight, head down, and Bob's your uncle!'
They said; or maybe, 'Think the problem through,
Tackle it stage by stage, and Bob's your uncle!'

Meaning it will be fine, turn out all right.
Having no Uncle Bob, I'd fantasise
A puissant lordly being out of sight,
Monitoring my every enterprise.

His hands on all the ropes, and never lost
For a solution, supernatural kin,
Concerned, however we felt mauled and tossed
By life, to see us right, through thick and thin.

Years brought wrong choices, people, home to stay.
For others, too. Unsolvable. Had Bob
Lost touch, not known his work fall miles astray,
Or flushed with the high life dozed off on the job?

No – not remotely all we'd cracked him up
To be, just a quixotic simpleton,
Even before he finally cracked up
Under the drift of things, he'd never won

A major title, steered the ship of state,
Or written Tolstoy. Now he's on his uppers,
Outcast, derided, an old reprobate
Scavenging bins for remnants of fish suppers.

Still meaning well, and wishing others joy.
From the corner of a pub he tips a wink,
Seeing again Miss Right meet the wrong boy,
Smiles 'Bob's your uncle!' raising his cadged drink.

Postcards from Norfolk

1 *Blakeney*

Turning, the eye can hardly tease
   Out among all our path is banked to crest
The braided blue-green mutabilities
   Of land, creek, marsh, dune; yet finds rest
Strangely in flux, mud, saltings, rafts
   Of meadow with cattle ravelling;
      And far and wide
         The sailing craft's
White wings; and fluttering
   Close-up a red admiral that
Rich with light is pirouetting at
   My side.

Thrilling through all, the ceaseless song
   Of high birds; casually punctuated by
Patterings as of a brief shower along
   The grasses as breeze stirs; and by
The time we rise, from open sea
   Flooding the channel comes the tide;
      Brimmed and linked
         Waters from quay
To causeways; and to ride
   At last our ebb to sleep, the slow
Tinklings of mast and halyard, music so
   Distinct.

2 *River Ant, Towards How Hill*

Yes, there are too many boats on the rivers and broads,
The one moored ahead last night just bristled with Germans,
Astern a careers development manager
Out of his element. Yet winding through reeds
And sedge, past mallards and coots and diving grebe,
And foliage adoring itself in water,
Like the great rooted windmills with stilled sails
And squared white windows we settle into a place
Indifferent to trafficking out of sight.
We take to a dawdling path along the margin,
On our other hand marsh sprinkled with wildflowers
And traversed by slow triangles of sail
Round the river's bend. My son stands motionless
As the heron he's recording in his notebook.
Here the impatient heart falls into place:
Nothing moves fast, no slope is difficult.
And languid under a huge sky all night,
Ignorant of its salty destiny
Water laps our hull… A sudden shiver
Whitens that willow, like mortality.

3 *Ludham, St Catherine's Church, the Rood Screen*

For those who gave to make what's here,
Intricate carved wood, tracery,
Pinnacled buttresses, *in the year*
Of ower Lord God MCCCCLXXXXIII,

The middle rail of folded leaf
Is inscribed: *Pray for the sowle*
Of John and Cycyly his wyf
And *alle other…* Centuries roll

Over what this hammerbeam
Roof sequesters. Civil fights,
Broad-brims with the zealot's dream
To beat out Popery's stained lights.

Still clear the colouring of those
Depicted on the rood screen's base:
St Edmund, St Walstan, St Ambrose –
And here St Appolonia's face,

Patron of dentists, with drawn tooth
In forceps… Perpendicular
Stonework clinches fossil truth
Outflanked by video, motor car.

Empanelled dead saints gather dust,
With faith in means whereby they bless;
Yet swell me to what feels like trust,
Winging unsure of its address.

Note

Anything can stir one to a poem, ferment in one's mind until one is nagged into jotting, intuiting shape, crossing out, trying again. Identifiable themes, obsessions, hungerings recur; beneath variety of subject and mood, one's writing is of a piece, rooted in the unalterable self. My chosen poems range my career, from 'A Butterfly' dating from 1969 to the Norfolk group written within the past year. A poem dependent on explanation has failed; but the following notes may enlighten curiosity about hows and whys.

'The Two Roads' exist. The symbolic should be rooted in the actual, a resonance off it whereby an experience makes sense of more than just itself. From Clifden, in Connemara, fork a mountainy 'Sky Road' and the 'Coast Road' hugging the shoreline. In life over and again alternative choices of all kinds open ahead, and before one has time to weigh and resolve pros and cons, one must veer one way or the other; the disused possibility remains vivid, one almost sees an *alter ego* travelling it, and what might have been, and how different. (I could not know when imagining that phantom child of a lost parallel world that years later I'd parent the son who appears in one of the Norfolk 'Postcards'.) The two-stress lines may suggest a walking motion, the sustaining of one sentence through the final twenty lines an insistent onwardness.

'A Butterfly' is set in a Leicester rail goodsyard. The incident connected with D.H. Lawrence noting a delicate sensitivity to natural beauty in miners. Contrastingly, I recalled girls in an office where also I'd worked panickily smashing with a newspaper a butterfly trapped against a pane.

'Growing Pains' – one of those cliche-phrases that yields multiple meanings – is a specific instance, imaginatively extended from the few words of a near-stranger, of our necessary wrenching exile from innocence. Pushing prams is commonly the lot, in Ireland's large families, of an elder daughter with many siblings. 'Outside' focuses more on our need for the saving illusions of the ideal; its material is directly autobiographical. The dangerousness of enacted idealisms, without which however life is impoverished materialism, figures in 'Christmas 1989', a poem with a public, historical theme, occasioned by the killing of the Romanian tyrant Ceausescu, the collapse of the Berlin Wall and communist systems throughout eastern Europe, and such events' moving but precarious attendant emotions.

'Uncle Bob' evolved from musings on the provenance of the familiar colloquialism, 'Bob's your uncle!', through joking with the notion that perhaps my having no uncle of that name accounted for things going awry or unremedied through my life, until I discovered I was writing about God, as misconceived by those supposing the Divine a sort of universal Mr Fixit; in which role it has never manifested itself with any efficacy.

'Postcards from Norfolk' are appropriately visual. My blunted eyesight had no chance within the gloom of the church at Ludham of discerning the rood screen details described: sensing something stirring, I departed with a leaflet and a postcard. Cheating? No, I'd had the experience, later study only helped fill it in. The sequence offers more than just pictures: at its heart my hankerings after a version of the Divine I experience as an elusive rumour that yet validates all I care about. The patterning of rhyme and line-length in the Blakeney poem is not gratuitous fancy footwork, but seeks to enact the interweave of the landscape's elements.

ROBERT PINSKY

Shirt
The back, the yoke, the yardage. Lapped seams,
The nearly invisible stitches along the collar
Turned in a sweatshop by Koreans or Malaysians

Gossiping over tea and noodles on their break
Or talking money or politics while one fitted
This armpiece with its overseam to the band

Of cuff I button at my wrist. The presser, the cutter,
The wringer, the mangle. The needle, the union,
The treadle, the bobbin. The code. The infamous blaze

At the Triangle Factory in nineteen-eleven.
One hundred and forty six died in the flames
On the ninth floor, no hydrants, no fire escapes –

The witness in a building across the street
Who watched how a young man helped a girl to step
Up to the window sill, then held her out

Away from the masonry wall and let her drop.
And then another. As if he were helping them up
To enter a streetcar, and not eternity.

A third before he dropped her put her arms
Around his neck and kissed him. Then he held
Her into space, and dropped her. Almost at once

He stepped to the sill himself, his jacket flared
And fluttered up from his shirt as he came down,
Air filling up the legs of his grey trousers –

Like Hart Crane's Bedlamite, 'shrill shirt ballooning'.
Wonderful how the pattern matches perfectly
Across the placket and over the twin bar-tacked

Corners of both pockets, like a strict rhyme
Or a major chord. Prints, plaids, checks,
Houndstooth, Tattersall, Madras. The clan tartans

Invented by mill-owners inspired by the hoax of Ossian,
To control their savage Scottish workers, tamed
By a fabricated heraldry: MacGregor,

Bailey, MacMartin. The kilt, devised for workers
To wear among the dusty clattering looms.
Weavers, carders, spinners. The loader,

The docker, the navvy. The planter, the picker, the sorter
Sweating at her machine in a litter of cotton
As slaves in calico headrags sweated in fields:

George Herbert, your descendant is a Black
Lady in South Carolina, her name is Irma
And she inspected my shirt. Its colour and fit

And feel and its clean smell have satisfied
Both her and me. We have culled its cost and quality
Down to the buttons of simulated bone,

The buttonholes, the sizing, the facing, the characters
Printed in black on neckband and tail. The shape.
The label, the labour, the colour, the shade. The shirt.

From the Childhood of Jesus
One Saturday morning he went to the river to play.
He modelled twelve sparrows out of the river clay

And scooped a clear pond, with a dam of twigs and mud.
Around the pond he set the birds he had made.

Evenly as the hours. Jesus was five. He smiled,
As a child would who had made a little world

Of clear still water and clay beside a river.
But a certain Jew came by, a friend of his father,

And he scolded the child and ran at once to Joseph,
Saying, 'Come see how your child has profaned the Sabbath,

Making images at the river on the Day of Rest.'
So Joseph came to the place and took his wrist

And then told him, 'Child, you have offended the Word.'
Then Jesus freed the hand that Joseph held

And clapped his hands and shouted at the birds
To go away. They raised their beaks at his words

And breathed and stirred their feathers and flew away.
The people were frightened. Meanwhile another boy,

The son of Annas the scribe, had idly taken
A branch of driftwood and leaning against it had broken

The dam and muddied the little pond and scattered
The twigs and stones. Then Jesus was angry and shouted,

'Unrighteous, impious, ignorant, what did the water
Do to harm you? Now you are going to wither

The way a tree does, you shall bear no fruit
And no leaves, you shall wither down to the root.'

At once, the boy was all withered. His parents moaned,
The Jews gasped, Jesus began to leave, then turned

And prophesied, his child's face wet with tears:
'Twelve times twelve times twelve thousands of years

Before these heavens and this earth were made,
The Creator set a jewel in the throne of God

With Hell on the left and Heaven to the right,
The Sanctuary in front, and behind, an endless night

Endlessly fleeing a Torah written in flame.
And on that jewel in the throne, God wrote my name.'

Then Jesus left and went into Joseph's house.
The family of the withered one also left the place,

Carrying him home. The Sabbath was nearly over.
By dusk, the Jews were all gone from the river.

Small creatures came from the undergrowth to drink
And foraged in the shadows along the bank.

Alone in his cot in Joseph's house, the Son
Of Man was crying himself to sleep. The moon

Rose higher, the Jews put out their lights and slept,
And all was calm and as it had been, except

In the agitated household of the scribe Annas,
And high in the dark, where unknown even to Jesus

The twelve new sparrows flew aimlessly through the night,
Not blinking or resting, as if never to alight.

The Day Dreamers
All day all over the city every person
Wanders a different city, sealed intact
And haunted as the abandoned subway stations
Under the city. Where is my alley doorway?

Stone gable, brick escarpment, cliffs of crystal.
Where is my terraced street above the harbor,
Cafe and hidden workshop, house of love?
Webbed vault, tiled blackness. Where is my park, the path

Through conifers, my iron bench, a shiver
Of ivy and margin birch above the traffic?
A voice. *There is a mountain and a wood*
Between us – one wrote, lovesick – *Where the late*

Hunter and the bird have seen us. Aimless at dusk,
Heart muttering like any derelict,
Or working all morning, violent with will,
Where is my garland of lights? My silver rail?

The Want Bone
The tongue of the waves tolled in the earth's bell.
Blue rippled and soaked in the fire of blue.
The dried mouthbones of a shark in the hot swale
Gaped on nothing but sand on either side.

The bone tasted of nothing and smelled of nothing,
A scalded toothless harp, uncrushed, unstrung.
The joined arcs made the shape of birth and craving
And the welded-open shape kept mouthing O.

Ossified cords held the corners together
In groined spirals pleated like a summer dress.
But where was the limber grin, the gash of pleasure?
Infinitesimal mouths bore it away,

The beach scrubbed and etched and pickled it clean.
But O I love you it sings, my little my country
My food my parent my child I want you my own
My flower my fin my life my lightness my O.

Poem with Refrains
The opening scene. The yellow, coal-fed fog
Uncurling over the tainted city river,
A young girl rowing and her anxious father
Scavenging for corpses. Funeral meats. The clever
Abandoned orphan. The great athletic killer
Sulking in his tent. As though all stories began
With someone dying.

                      When her mother died,
My mother refused to attend the funeral –
In fact, she sulked in her tent all through the year
Of the old lady's dying, I don't know why:
She said, because she loved her mother so much
She couldn't bear to see the way the doctors,
Or her father, or – someone – was letting her mother die.
'Follow your saint, follow with accents sweet;
Haste you, sad notes, fall at her flying feet.'

She fogs things up, she scavenges the taint.
Possibly that's the reason I write these poems.

But they did speak: on the phone. Wept and argued
So fiercely one or the other often cut off
A sentence by hanging up in rage – like lovers,
But all that year she never saw her face,

They lived on the same block, four doors apart.
'Absence my presence is: strangeness my grace;
With them that walk against me is my sun.'

'Synagogue' is a word I never heard,
We called it *shul*, the Yiddish word for school.
Elms, terra cotta, the ocean a few blocks east.
'Lay institution': she taught me we didn't think
God lived in it. The rabbi just a teacher.

But what about the hereditary priests,
Descendants of the Cohanes of the Temple,
Like Walter Holtz – I called him Uncle Walter,
When I was small. A big man with a face
Just like a boxer dog or a cartoon sergeant.
She told me whenever he helped a pretty woman
Try on a shoe in his store, he'd touch her calf
And ask her, 'How does that feel?' I was too little
To get the point but pretended to understand.
'Desire, be steady: hope is your delight,
An orb wherein no creature can be sorry.'

She didn't go to my bar mitzvah, either.
I can't say why: she was there, and then she wasn't.
I looked around before I mounted the steps
To chant that babble and the speech the rabbi wrote
And there she wasn't, and there was Uncle Walter
The Cohane frowning with his doggy face:
'She's missing her own son's *musaf*.' Maybe she just
Doesn't like rituals. Afterwards, she had a reason
I don't remember. I wasn't upset: the truth
Is, I had decided to be the clever orphan
Some time before. By now, it's all a myth.
What is a myth but something that seems to happen
Always for the first time over and over again?
And ten years later, she missed my brother's too.

I'm sorry: I think it was something about a hat.
'Hot sun, cool fire, tempered with sweet air.
Black shade, fair nurse, shadow my white hair;
Shine, sun; burn, fire; breathe, air, and ease me.'

She sees the minister of the Nation of Islam
On television, though she's half-blind in one eye.
His bow tie is lime, his jacket crocodile green.
Vigorously he denounces the Jews who traded in slaves,
The Jews who run the newspapers and the banks.
'I see what this guy is mad about now,' she says,
'It must have been some Jew that sold him the suit.'
'And the same wind sang and the same wave whitened,
And or ever the garden's last petals were shed,
In the lips that had whispered, the eyes that had lightened.'

But when they unveiled her mother's memorial stone,
Gathered at the graveside one year after the death,
According to custom, while we were standing around
About to begin the prayers, her car appeared.
It was a black car; the ground was deep in snow.
My mother got out and walked towards us, across
The field of gravestones capped with snow, her coat
Black as the car, and they waited to start the prayers
Until she arrived. I think she enjoyed the drama.
I can't remember if she prayed or not,
But that may be the way I'll remember her best:
Dark figure, awaited, attended, aware, apart.
'The present time upon time passèd striketh;
With Phoebus's wandering course the earth is graced.

The air still moves, and by its moving, cleareth;
The fire up ascends, and planets feedeth;
The water passeth on, and all lets weareth;
The earth stands still, yet change of changes breedeth.'

Note
Here are two recent poems, 'The Day Dreamers' and 'Poem With Refrains' and three from my most recent book *The Want Bone* (Ecco Press): the title poem, 'Shirt,' and 'From the Childhood of Jesus'.

This selection is not intended to slight my earlier books. But when I try to look at my own work with the idea of choosing a defining selection, hope and fear blind me, almost completely. And that blindness makes me rely on what I am closest to in time, poems where I still feel a little like the maker, still somewhat inside the words and lines, and less like the reader who sees from outside.

In 'Shirt' I see my lifelong attempt to include in one idiom, and one conception of form, as many kinds of my experience as possible: the speech and knowledge of my childhood neighborhood in New Jersey along with the speech and knowledge that came to me through English poets; my experience of prosperity and my experience of labor; the things I have read along with the things I have seen. I think the poem embodies my belief that all experience, if only we could understand it well enough, has historical dimension and dignity. I hope that this effort at inclusion expresses eagerness and pleasure as well as pain, cost and deception. The artifact recalls slavery, but also the genius of human design, intention, labour.

Similarly, 'From the Childhood of Jesus', though clearly interested in the relation between rage and creation, is not intended as merely a bitter perception of Christianity from a Jewish perspective. The boy in the poem, playing on Saturday morning and scolded by a Sabbath busybody, enacts a misery of my childhood training in Judaism. The poem acknowledges both traditions as loathed, formative, invasive, monstrous, pervasive. The ambition is to use the word 'Jesus' or the phrase 'a certain Jew came by' in a way that cannot be described simply as 'Christian' or 'Jewish': the point is to be something more than either. I do not consider the poem as precisely a 'religious poem' so much as a poem about history or creation, quite similar in theme to 'Shirt'.

'Poem With Refrains' is unusual for me in its specific, autobiographical material. All of the remembered material is as accurate as I can make it. I want to include this recent poem here because it illustrates in an almost diagrammatic way what I have said about the two others. Here, the duality of past and present is binary, antiphonal. The quotations from sixteenth-century English poets (and one nineteenth-century poet) partly comment on the personal story and partly act as a talisman whose qualities somehow protect me from that story, penetrating my world yet departing from it.

I hope that the poems I have chosen embody the ambitions

of my book-length poem *An Explanation of America*, published by Carcanet in the late 1970s, and my other earlier books. 'The Day Dreamers' begins and ends with a dreamy sense of the city that is a main note of *Sadness And Happiness* and includes a misquotation from Landor, a passage of his that I also quote in the title poem from *History of My Heart*. 'The Want Bone' is a poem that I hope has some sexual charge; but I also hope that in the sounds of its consonants and vowels, in its teasing divergence from traditional quatrains, it is also about the historical past, that past touching erotic life as it touches everything else.

JOHN PECK

Ars Poetica

By silvery increment, by mineral touch of the remorseless,
the irregular stone takes shape, though it derives shape
from the ruled lattice, denuded hegemenous crystal.

The bitterness of salt is a taste waiting to be changed,
waiting with the power to change every other savour,
dissolving under patience of the rains only,

like the rich man's regatta fading down evening beneath
the outflowing half of breath, towards the pulse's cusp,
and masts creeping beneath their spar candles.

White Deer Running

Baucis and Philemon, having forgiven their killer Faust
and been resurrected to this life, to reenter their rest,
have come south and bought a stone house in the Morvan.
Undulating woodlots, hamlets beyond Autun.
Windows west only, into the long evenings
at midsummer, butterflies wavering in throngs
while rooms hold off heat with deep walls and embrasures.
Serendipity and sublimity are peasant sisters
waiting behind trees for farmers to find them, scuffle
with a pod of wild boar, and extend a barn from the wall.
Sublime and serendipitous, their last possession
for a renewed aging, lindens cooling each description.
The forest is named *Socrate*, a leader of the Resistance
dialectical in his disappearances,
and the barn wall was used for executions, by which side
there are varying reports. This too is to be had
in the idyll of ownership, a filmy disturbance
across the tabletop's oak grain, brown generations,
apples mounded in a plain crock, clear wines
draping colors over board and fruit, all this the senses
manufacturing from drift and ripple of syllables
before anything can be verified, yet the sheen falls
across an excellence of properties in trust
to no single appetite, in a place where sheen seems made fast.
    Narrow, the gate into our garden. A black sucking,
and waters crash, but you must not cry out or cling.
And then you are there, and you may come back if you choose
and report, though boasting is indecent, there are other ways.
Space there is not really different nor the sun,
but attachment is not what holds you, all that has gone.
    But that is
no possession: left listening and seeing, I was.
Apples, glass with ruddy window in its belly, the ruse
of solidity calling across the spoken was and is.
A low forest in Burgundy, woodlots in Massachusetts,
the last field before that drop where the river cuts.
    Against the clearing's edge
    at evening, already sliding
    among the indistinct
    stems of December trees,
    white deer running.
    It was perhaps an hour
    over the page, Arjuna's
    refusal and the protracted
    gleams of his charioteer.
    When I looked out the window.
    ranked birches turned in wind
    silver through shadow, over
    white deer standing.

from Frieze from the Gardens of Copenhagen

That which does not pass but returns to peer in
    from the top corners of earth's hand-painted page,
little moons looking down curiously, little suns
    looking down blandly and benevolently, for these, too,
there is laughter, inaudible but presumably full, a long chorus.
    Was the laborious hand innocent after all?
How did he manage it, this durable cross-section
    in the colors of berries, a breviary of muds?
He discovered something. What is it? Behind the gold leaf
    it stares and winks, behind the stains also.
As if waiting for a response. Though what can one do?
    A man's lifetime tripled, clacks the stammerer, that equals a stag,
three stags give an ouzel, then three of those an eagle,
    mounting to salmon and finally the yew tree drinking three gulps
of bright dust to span earth's age on the rimmed octavo.
    Merriment ripples at the corners of fire's mouth.
And the fair daughters of fire, hair cascading their treasuries,

      nymphs outliving ten ember birds, choke with pitiless delight.
The one to whom they consistently attend in the great garden.
      the one they relish most, is a climber with donkey.
Undulant pebble nudged up the crest by heat shimmer.
      With him a boy, slaughtering knife, and kindling.
Do? Even the being of the wood is unintelligible
      to the strictest simplicity: at the fuzzed edges
of imagined weavings, drift your growth, fibers,
      and unlock, unfold into the full amplitudes
of your reach, and to your unclaimed auras go.
      A dense thicket, bees resuscitating the hive,
bundles loughing against ribs and blown flesh sacking.
      From the plain below, the crystalline rowdiness
of a wind band starting up, bass drum pacing them,
      lighter than pulsebeat, the clarinet rippling upward.
The rest of the strenuously recommended procedure?
      Huge bodies dragged across puddled lines of altitude
and beached at the appointed minim by more than volition.
      Dimension thrust and cinched through the pack strap's eye.
Feelings framed in the throat's pit, only there, in that gristly flower.
      Reason coming in, as it must from its ardent nature,
on wings with an exigent, an already created ram,
      dear reason in the dress which it gallantly adopts
out of passion, the partisanship of creatures,
      parliamentary gallantry in a moment without rules.
This one is sober, cry the high ones, he's no mere belly,
      he has done it, has really lifted himself to the first step
and is going to follow through! Then more laughter,
      whose attitude is not open to scrutiny and whose
unsearchable quaver does not yield to long study
      as the knife is taken out and used: thou dost not.
As the fire is kindled and the wood makes rendering: thou art not.
      At which the climb may invade calf and thigh, memory with forecast,
anticipated descent stinging the chest like woodsmoke
      at work in the persevering eyes: so he has accomplished
this thing about which the stone is speechless, crackling wood also,
      over which the soaring chorus also flies speechless,
done it like a man up there on a mountain in Copenhagen,
      over the mountains and sea. And the aeons of light were still.

Western Palace Rhapsodies
(from Single-Seal Readings of Oracle Bones)

   Flock on flock
agitated, stimulated, trying to get off the ground –
   fevers and guttering fires
and thunders ebbing, snakes wriggling in the nest,
miniscule twists all over the silkworm frames.

Family pantomimists in a row
   and a leaking roof corner.

   Pronouncements promulgated
in accents of the personal letter,
   and so the squares fill
for lay sermons in the rhythms of exorcism
promoting bearskins and the toothed capes of tigers.

Forehooves hobbled
   by the relay post,
millet fading
   by the void warden's hut,
manure drying
   over unbroadened ground –

heap up boundary stones but unbar the door,
put some metal in your mouth and get going,
   shoot your horse through the gate –

there is no visiting card to the endless spaces, and yet
   the lute shines under running winds,
   the ladle hangs among star dragons.

John Peck

from **Poem on Divine Providence**
Orientius

The bulk of these years is already gone out of mind
   because your page is inscribed with no verses.
What conditions have made such silence your product,
   what anguish has squatted on your glum genius?

If the wide sea were to rip broadside into Gaul,
   surging toweringly across its tillage, surely
there is no beast of the field, no grain or fruit or olive
   and no choice place that would not turn rotten;
no plantations and great houses that would not be swept
   by storm crash and fire blast and be left standing blank and sad:
like shouldering a landslide, going through this ten-year slaughter
   strewn by the steel of the Vandals and Visigoths.

And then, too, you trudged among the wagons, eating dust,
   lugging weapons for the Goths, and no small bit of baggage,
beside a white-haired commoner, ruddy with the dust of cities,
   driven the same way a shepherd goads banished sheep.

So you cry over farms laid waste, courtyards deserted,
   and the flame-swept stage scenery of the villas.
How, then, not weep over losses that are truly yours,
   if you could peer into the trampled sanctums ·
of your heart, their splendors crudded with filth,
   and hobnailed swaggerers in the mind's cramped cell?

Passage to the Islands
in memoriam John Mattern

Yellow stones and brown, white-brown and bone-yellow
   in the swash of the shallows
dropping to greens intimating safety,
   vision's liquor tapering
to darker drink but not lost, the wake settling
to an unbraided dispatch of cold annealings,
   of released levies,

after which the knee-grooved cell with its register
   of the week's intercessions:
For Joanne committed last Tuesday, and her two boys
   For William, out of work
For the soul of Jane Irene Watson, stillborn
   For Jill and Robert Watson

The prince stands close at hand, the Friend,
   slabs of his identity
lean or resist in cloud-roll from the straits,
his advance guard having made reconnaissance
   and taken up vigilance

eroded yet ground-set,
sheltering also Emerson: *The country stinks of suicide* –
   what here comes in on all sides
goes forth redoubled and without commentary,

   outcomes tiding to beginnings!
sheltering also my attempt to release
   that peak sunk in the hidden,
that one center of the hidden for my finding.

   Set close to the jabbering land
yet inviolate, barely lifted clear, incomparable:
   pride of the prince translated
here for replanting, preachings here struck dumb
   within the dense focus – let
   the accessible bury the accessible
and comparisons will take care of themselves.

   Sorrow, there is a river,
great path beneath your adamantine path,
   tugging it like a midwife
then breaking on these shores in its own birth.

   And joy, there is a blackbird
who will navigate its way to this washed margin
   and waking you in the morning
even you had not imagined, will have you speak.

Note

In a day of noise, disconcerting and corrosive but in the long run generative, modernist poetry takes on a traditional, that is, conserving and individually transmitting role. The stroller who totes a Blaster and cancels the privacies of others in public places has dispensed, of course, with the benefits of any such role; he can assert individuality only through a protest which levels the individuality of others with the wrecker of mass expression. For all of their individual differences, Joyce, Woolf, Pound and Yeats defended that ground on which the soul of the written remains the distinctively performed or the sung. Song is both finder and preserver. To sing is to find oneself among others while confirming and conserving oneself in the performance of exchange (about which a word later). The conservation, however, may be radical. Rhetoric is the calibration of performances among shifting ratios in consciousness, argues our Peter Ramus (McLuhan) in the wake of modernist poetics and prosaics. But even he pretended in public to approve what he privately despised, or even described as explicitly satanic, in mass expression and the thicker beat.

For the four writers I have mentioned, text still carried tune and tenor, a quality tenaciously intoned. With George Oppen in the next generation, this remained so to the end; for Samuel Beckett too. But not, now, for Charles Bernstein, although he would trace his ancestry back to the intensely cantabile Gertrude Stein. The younger Pound custodially amplified this intoned quality in the Troubadors; the elder Yeats modernised it from his Celtic roots. I imagine that certain professional readers of contemporary writing would judge my claim to be indiscriminate. But what I have in mind as traditional feeling in once-new form-sense has a parallel in music: Schoenberg called himself 'that follower of Mozart'.

A cantabile quality persists through literary modernism in defiance chiefly of a pervasive, forced-draft commercialism. The Blaster-toter has capitulated, in spite of his mangled protest, to the prevailing social wind and its rhythm. Has it registered sufficiently with us that even though ego has been drastically relativised, hand-writing aerated by oral, analytic, and electronic processes, articulation and tone corroded by beat, meaning shaved by the Sign, that text, though its weave has been freeze-dried by the handlers, asserts the wirily singable? I take this to be a modernist conservatism even when it is voiced negatively: 'How square, O Lord, how square!' in Beckett's Joycean satirologue ('I will play now a little song on my good grand') has as its target less the scriptedly performable as such and more our outmoded senses of compositional scaling and anticipation. It is not from Wallace Stevens's ice cream that the renewably singable will emerge, but from products of fission and resynthesis, some Steinian and Joycean, some Poundian. Meanwhile, 'in the chiarinoscurissimo I was unable to distinguish the obvious balloons': a persistent clair-obscur plays host to our drifting rondures, our hot air, and our blurred sense of scale, punishing perforce until the modes be resorted resartus resorcerfully.

And meanwhile, too, back on the reservation, things get fuzzy. Professor Vendler writes, 'We hardly know what to say to a lay audience about lineation and stanza-breaks. Nor do we know what to say about that of which lineation and stanza-breaks are merely the outward sign: the poetic form itself' (*London Review of Books*, 26 May 1994). A sense remains in which this way of putting it should not be rudely dismantled; to invoke, in part, Osip Mandelshtam's rebuke to the young reciter who accosted him on a St Petersburg bridge, a poem is both an intersection of incalculably intricate surds, and a single act of mind and feeling. Of course, 'the fine thing held in the mind' (Ezra Pound) is not necessarily 'platotudinous' (Beckett), but neither is the svelte-sharp thing unfolding within the ear without its ties to a schema (Donald Davie discovered that inventive articulations of humble trimeter elude many of his conthumperaries). And what shall we make of the inference drawn by Yeats, that even the possibility of invention depends on collective levels of usage and degrees of advance? and what shall we do with his subtle estimates of the more-than-personal agency at work in poetry? Must these go the way of the Silk Trade and Tibetan independence?

Because of the world's way, no philosopher or psychologist or student of art will read these words. Were they to do so, the first would take fussy exception to the term 'agency', while the others would pick at the usages of 'image', 'memory', and 'text'. The hounds of Herr Wittgenstein, who dismissed altogether the notion of mental images, would turn on the whole pack and rend them. So let the solitary *Wortschmied* bang away. It seems to me the premier intellectual arrogance and spiritual naiveté of our day that the psyche's humble propensity to produce imagaes of all kinds, 'naturally' as we say without reflection, is set aside each morning on waking. This disregard of how grass grows in the pasture severely qualifies most of the sheep-shearing on these matters that goes forward under the rods of our *Gelehrten*. In words of one syllable, they funk their own subjects. Given the intricacy and apparent scruple of their efforts, this fact is stupefying.

'Agency', or agency and identity: these mysteries in the philosophies and meditative disciplines of Action get routinely scanted in scientifically animated analyses of the arts. 'Theory', which once referred to comprehensive witnessings of performance, falls captive now to pre- and post-, sometimes preposterous scepticism that mock discredited authority in the Ten Realms and the Hundred Provinces. Disenchantment, demystification, and a ragging of failed fathers prevail in the fenced compounds of reflection, while a sweeping transformation, a Turn *de la base au sommet*, penetrates the One World without-and-within. (Western alchemy's old formula of the unus mundus is an arcanum no longer, but a res publica.) A turn is a versus. Its peculiar audibility is the poet's object. Its relative singability is the poet's job. And the performance of this relative quality is a matter of shared, indeed civic, concern. But do not ask the shepherds of civics to acknowledge this, either, unless thou covet a berth in the looney bin.

I reprint five poems from my last two books, together with one new piece. Several of these share the view that our lives are seldom ours alone, a matter finely discriminated by Charles Williams in his writing on Exchange. In the light of this view, mysteries of agency, even at a time when the notion of authoritative agency is treated to sceptical grapeshot, remain the unsentimental doings of objective feeling. No mean mean to hold to while the modes they are a-changin', no, knot at awl, know, naught atoll.

JEREMY HOOKER

Steps

First is the feeling,
which I must trust, moving on –
cut into the void.

A passage opens –
that is where the drama is –
out of the covert.

To attain a truth,
work fearlessly, for ourselves.
We must break our taste.

You dance on the edge
of destruction, you dare see
what will come of it.

There is work to do
with fire – simplify the self –
charred and blackened form.

You finger the edges,
you execute the instant –
gallows-carpenter.

A rooted figure,
bound to earth but gesturing
at the open sky.

A human forest –
energy between figures,
linking them and us.

You shape the image:
it is a bridge we cross over
to meet in the world.

To know oneself shaped,
and work with knowledge of death –
that it may bear fruit.

Fern, gorse, pine, slow cloud
moving on – 'voice of the rhythm
which has created the world'.

One use of space is
for speaking across, another
to deepen silence.

Black on Gold
He dreams he is a painter standing
at his easel in an ill-lit attic painting
studies in black and gold.
A dead butterfly flutters in a breeze,
dances at the window in a filthy web.
Even when I was a boy (he thinks)
walking with a rod in April among the trees
I tasted filth. How free the mind?
A man – but what (he asks) is man? –
will do anything not to wake up.
He dreams he is a sculptor hacking
at the block that is himself.
It is black, black as rainwater
from the stump of the tree of knowledge.
Let me let in the gold (he weeps)
but the wood rots under his hand.
He dreams he is a poet writing
a poem about the shadow of a tree
leaning over water, where sunlight
touches the gravel bed with gold.
He is losing his bony grip,
the bank is eroding under him.
Wild bees swarm in the hollow of his skull.
He dreams he is a hunter chasing
the beasts that seek him.
On hands and knees, belly
dragging in mud, icy skin,
he follows where a black stream
runs through bracken into the wood
and a doe steps gracefully to the brink
and bends her neck and drinks.

In Praise of Windmills
In the north the windmills stand
roundly on land and by water.

I take a leaf from the Windmill Psalter.
I name them, both the little and the great:

Young Hendrick and Four Winds,
Goliath and The Helper.

They have come far, but seem
to have grown where they are,
as native to the Netherlands
as sarsens to Salisbury Plain,
and as worthy of praise.

Yet Quixote was right:
they are monstrous.

    If windmills
did not exist, Hieronymous
Bosch would have dreamt them.
They are living contraptions,
part insect and part bird;
mechanical creatures pondering
flight; earthbound,
flailing at heaven.

There are windmills in the mind,
alive to every breath of fear.

And things that hold firm:
cross-beams and quarter-bars,
crown-tree and king-post;
windmills that drive
and are driven, turning
indifferent winds to use.

They are labourers
at the brink of water;
old warhorses
that take the starving field.

No wonder people say,
The miller is a mighty man;
his hand spans earth and sky.
The great sails are dancing,
but the painter holds them still.

The polder is a blank page
marked with a cross:
    Goliath,
a little windmill but a giant
graced by need and by use,
solitary as a lighthouse
on a sea of blue clay,
in a land raised from the sea.

Over furrow and rhine,
I see the blade of a sail
shining, and think of voyages,
and stillness at the heart
of tumbling breakers
where the keel strikes home.

Behind the dyke the wind blasts
and the sea hungers.

Here the windmill stands
roundly by water and on land.

I take a leaf from the Windmill Psalter.
May the grace of the sails breathe in my song.

Walking to Capernaum

1
Such violence struck here –
a new thing, a word with power:

And thou, Capernaum,
which art exalted unto heaven,
shalt be brought down to hell.

A gentler word
where the sea laps the shore:
The damsel is not dead, but sleepeth.

2
What I feel most is the heat,
and sick at the unreality
of bad art:

a sloppy English poem
which someone has fixed on a wall
at the site of the miracle
of loaves and fishes;

new stained glass daubing
the interior of the chapel built
over the rock where Christ
is said to have said to Peter…

Compared to these,
I could love the wooden donkeys
and camels and holy families
from the factory at Bethlehem.

Unreal, in a sweat of heat
and bad blood, I dip
my seamy face in the water.

It tastes of salt, and is
a dull silvery blue
on a day of desert cloud.

A crane – not, thank God,
a symbol – but a white crane,
with long, wispy hairs at the back
of its neck, stands
fishing in the shallows.
A black lizard looks at me
over the edge of a black stone.

3
On the road between
orchards and tomato fields;
in the dust thrown up
by tourist coaches;
between the columns
and among pine needles lying
on the ruins of Peter's house,
I try to imagine them:

The girl waking surprised
with hunger in her eyes;
the woman cured by a touch;
that loud cry, the man
on the floor of the synagogue –
torn and empty, but clean.

What had he seen? What thing
had cried with his voice?

And the fishermen
as they put out –
from this moment, no
denial will swerve their aim.

The port they left behind
is a heap of blackened stone.

4
It is evening, and very still;
heavy cloud, the colour
of smouldering ash,
obscures a misshapen moon.
Tiny fish swarm blackly
on the surface, nudging
crusts from our seafront cafe.

Suddenly, the wind rises. Trees
sway and open, lights go out
and napkins soar into the air;
waiters leap to catch bottles
and glasses blown off the tables.
A cloud swirls through the streets
and covers our plates with sand.
At once the sea heaves up
a huge, slippery shoulder
against the wall.

In the sudden violence
I see them for the first time:
the small port waiting, still
waiting – nets spread on the wall,
barrels of salt fish on the quay –
and the men who will not return,
but are borne up at a word
as their ship drives through the storm.

Westerbork
To the memory of Etty Hillesum

1
Our path lies along the Milky Way
and from planet to planet –

then out from the trees
and past the grey saucers
of the radio telescope.

Among toadstools, under oaks
loaded with acorns, we find
a solitary, white earth-star.

2
A few late foxgloves on a bank –
'sheltered'
I say, and the word echoes oddly.

Who can resist the ironies?
When will we recognise
that irony is not enough?

3
How understand the faces, Etty?

You looked at them
from behind a window
and were terrified.

Jeremy Hooker

You sank to your knees speaking
the words that reign over life
and bind you to these men
in the depths:

'And God made man after His likeness.'

Did you know they would murder you
and your kind?
That they would drive even the children
into hiding, and hunt them down.
And the patients. And the doctors.
All would be sent out on the Tuesday morning train.

4
The black train, which an artist
in the camp painted, looming.

But what amazes more
is his painting of a typical farm
and farmyard beyond the wire
as he saw them,
as we see them still.

5
At first there is little to show –
a few irregularities in the ground
of what might be a park.

Then we see what we expect:
a wooden guard-post,
preserved, or perhaps restored.

Below it, a short stretch
of the railway track reaches
from buffers towards the east;
broken off, twisted, the rusted iron
curves into the air.

And there, incised in stone,
a verse from Lamentations.

6
*They hunt our steps, that
we cannot go in our squares ...*

You were a fountain of life.
Your love flowed into the world.

You looked for meaning
and found it even in the worst,
accepting 'all as one mighty whole'.

But the faces – how shall we accept
that you could see in them
instruments of destiny?

Whose faces, Etty?
What are they like?

7
Back from the universe,
back from the world,
back from the streets
of Amsterdam,
back from the houses,
back from the rooms
and the rooms behind the rooms,

you were driven, and driven in.

The space of your freedom
was at last a book, in which you wrote,
passionate to understand;

a mind behind the white face;
a card, thrown from the train window:
'We have left the camp singing.'

(Westerbork, the site of the former transit camp, is now partly occupied by a radio astronomy centre, and the path through the woods near the entrance is set out and measured as a model of the planets and their relative distances from one another.)

Note
Two of the poems which I have chosen to represent my work, 'Steps' and 'Black on Gold', are from my most recent book, *Their Silence a Language* (Enitharmon Press, 1993), in which I collaborated with the sculptor Lee Grandjean. The other three belong to what will be my next collection, which is set mainly in continental Europe and in Palestine.

'Setting' has been important to me since I first began to publish poems, in the late Sixties. I have learnt to call it 'ground', by which I mean all the forces, material and spiritual, historical and cultural, personal and social, that constitute place as a channel for life in all its manifestations. At the same time, I have come to realise that the other main way in which I think of poetry, as an art of seeing, arises not from belonging to any particular place, but from being unsettled, drawn away but not divorced from primary attachments, and stumbling among the half beliefs and broken images which the world is to many of us today.

There are two quotations, from the work of the two poets of recent years whose work speaks to me most intimately, that sum up my sense of what lies at the heart of my poetry. The first is David Jones's 'One is trying to make a shape out of the very things of which one is oneself made', which defines poetry as a discovery and an exploration of 'the very things' by which the poet lives, things of time and place and culture, loved things, things blessed and cursed, broken and contested, things that appear dead but into which the poet may still breathe life. The other is George Oppen's 'What do we believe/To live with?', which I apprehend as the fundamental question of a time in which all our relationships are in question, relationships between men and women, culture and nature, self and others, body and soul, the human and the divine. According to my understanding, a poet is not so much the questioner, the interrogator of word or world or text, but the one who is most open to question, and who may thus discover the common in the unique, and gain a sense of what we are, and what we might be, in recognising deep human need.

A literary and artistic tradition I particularly value is that of Wordsworth and John Constable, who said he found his art 'under every hedge and in every lane', and of Charles

Reznikoff, who found his poetry in the streets of New York. Praise, as in the Welsh poetic tradition, seems to me not the least motive of poetry. It was with a shock of pleasure that I read the following passage in Dudley Young's *Origins of the Sacred*:

> Our word 'memory' is from the Latin *memoria* and *memor* = mindful, the act of calling to and bearing in mind. That such calling and bearing is essentially involved with gratitude is something we have largely forgotten, even though it survives in such cognates as memorial and commemoration. That the Greeks remembered Mnemosyne as mother of the Muses would suggest that the arts originate in grateful remembrance of what we have been given, and that indeed they call upon us, as the Psalm sings, to 'make a joyful noise unto the Lord, all ye lands'.

ROGER GARFITT

The Hooded Gods

Three male gods of healing, fertility, and the underworld, from a stone plaque in Housesteads Museum, Hadrian's Wall.

These are the odds and sods among the gods,
the other ranks, the omnipresences,
teamen, charmen, male midwives: the daily helps
from history's basement, the caretakers

who rarely come to light. They have become
their deliverances, their many hands
beneath notice and now beyond telling.
They surface from the sleep of history

whose care suffuses history like sleep,
powers of recovery and repair
who keep the middle watch, the graveyard shift,
the seamsters who knit up the ravelled sleeve.

Empire succeeds empire over their heads.
The paces centuries set in the Wall
have doubled under artillery wheels.
Now low-flying Phantoms ghost from the stones.

Their histories are the interleaves,
the pages happiness has written white.
They show as lapses in the chronicle,
or specks of dialect in letters home.

No stars in their eyes. No shrinking either.
These are the hard core. These are the heart's wood.
Three grey bottles still standing on the Wall.
Three pollards who can make a fist of green.

from Lower Lumb Mill

For Ellie; and for the teachers and pupils of Nicholls Ardwick School, Manchester, who spent a week writing at Lumb Bank.

Here are the reins of
the work horse, the traces
of water in harness,

still handstitched in stone:
and not slack, though water
falls in idleness, though weather

buffs and beeches the black
of the chimney that once blackened
the beeches; and still rises

out of all proportion
to rocks and stones and trees,
a first draught, a delineation

of valleys since transfigured
by cubes and planes and cones,
a shadow of Hell or Halifax,

of mills and manufactories
wherever water ran,
terracings and resurfacings

worn through again as the work
moves away. Now tree shadows
box the walls. Green thoughts

wash at the drystone. Or,
under the petrodollar's
green shade, green thoughts

walk down from Lumb Bank. Between
anorak and wellingtons, jay's
wingflashes of tight sateen

as the walking disco, Angela,
Jennifer, Beverley and Mo,
sends a green blue beat through

the thoughtful thrush-tap on stone
of the geologist's hammer
Mohammed would like to have,

and stirs Farah's tree of silence,
just broken into the first leaf
of her sketchbook. Our other lives

star the valley, the Persephone
in each of us given five days
above ground. Half-thoughts, slim chances,

huddle at the valley's rim,
wind-silvered underleaves,
the ghosts of our fits and starts.

'Where to go from here?'
A rainflash of fieldfares turns
into dust shaken from a duster.

Out of memory a ring-dove calls,
Darby, be true, Darby…
And truly, where can we go?

The Broken Road
Water on the fields
sedged with white grass

Tarmac over flints
the flints wearing through

Walking again
along the broken road:

is it the road bears us up
or the brokenness?

As the upper sky darkens
a depth enters the pools,
corn gold suffuses the grass

The stones grow luminous as they dim

Out of the blue-blacks of the tar
the blues effloresce

Light is a bloom
a pollen of blue

It powders up under our feet

Skara Brae
for Frances and Adam

The dunes of peat ash,
the skears of scraped-out shells,
the gravel of animal bones, the flocks of sand,

all worked to a hard mothering,
a weathertight skin of clay
hummocked over the huts: embryos

in chamber tombs, mound dwellers
under their own midden, they pressed
out of the vortex engraved on their pots,

childbearing children, dead at twenty;
learned to bait bone splinters with limpets
softened in freshwater; to twist heather

into simmons tethering the stock; to staunch bleeding
with the puff-ball's black gauze; step by step
moved away from the swallow-hole.

In fine weather they broke surface. Knappings
and food scraps littered the roof of the mound.
Here are the good days, the hours in the sun.

Water rose as they bent to the spring,
the ram's horn of water rose for them,
and they saw themselves as water's face,

as luck's two hands, fastening sheepskin
with a bone pin, polishing oxhide
with an ox knuckle. They scoured

the sea's scourings: soft horns of driftwood
that were American spruce; dry foam of pumice
from Icelandic lava flows. Worked on their luck,

grinding a gannet's bone into the pumice
until it was sharp enough for an awl,
hollowing an antler until it held an axehead.

Bored through cattle teeth. Bored through a walrus tusk.
Out of salvage and scrap built up a bead hoard,
a string of good days. Began to bank on their luck.

Set spy-holes into passages valved with stone slabs,
secreted it in treasure cells. Until the mound was
another mouth on the foreshore, swallowing all it could use.

Hunger is stilled now. Now there is only stillness:
the hearth swept; the quernstone at rest in the quern,
in the churn-hole of rock, a fossil of water in spate.

Here is the life they hardly knew, the quiet enshrined
on the shelves of their stone dresser, or glimpsed
out to sea, the horizon's back shelf of light

still clear and still out of reach: a persistence
of charms and undergleams, of secrecies and stowings,
a necklace tucked into the heather of the boxbed

or spilled over the threshold. White dribbles down,
the gutted fish leaking its roe, the skinned hare
her milk under the skin. All their luck let slip

at the last, the string snapped on the narrow door
they scrambled through, as the wind darkened
and the dunes began to run like the sea.

Skara Brae is a Stone Age village in the sand dunes of Orkney, covered over by a great storm in prehistoric times and uncovered by another storm in the last century. 'Skear' is northern dialect for a mussel scar, an off-shore ridge or sandbank exposed at low tide.

At Vanishing Point
para Eugenia en El Cántaro

This morning we talk again
under the bony plum,

whose fruit, like a stone
sucked in the mouth,

can outwit thirst. I sit
on the garden seat as on

the bench of the ship of souls,
lashed to my oar. Almost hear,

between the tick-birds and
the parakeets, a gull's keen,

invoking solitude, the doom
of the Seafarer, who dreams

of a hearth and companions, and wakes
to the ice of the whale-road.

My salve for hard times
is to make them harder still.

You do that too. You will
when I leave. Lock yourself

in your painter's attic
in Bogotá. Work to

the wry songs of Bola de Nieve.
Geni, you and I are two

of a kind. I find you
on the bench beside me.

Above us, like a daydream, like a thought
moored between two pillars of cloud,

El Cántaro, the house you built
out of stubbornness, out of shipwreck.

It is just pencilled in
against the sky. Just held

at the point of erasure.
Built of shadings, cross-hatchings,

a pencil sharpening the whiteness
of paper, constructing

a moebius strip of light,
endless galleries, rising

scales of roof, ascending
and descending stairs.

The pencil sketched, suffered
erasure, sketched again.

One by one the variants
emerged. Plumped onto the page

and sank without trace. Stepped out
on their spindleshanks

and crumpled into the pits
of erasure, the hubbub of forms

jostling for life. Then the pencil
took wing. Took from the swift's wing

the long, honed line, that austere
primary glide. Took from the owl's wing

the crossing of tenons, that secondary
softness of flight. Something lifted

that could fly. Now we live under its wing.
Watch the diamond lattice compose the light

and the stairs rise in counterpoint. Hear
the three-part harmony in the turn of the stair.

Geni, we came here already erased.
All that life we lived on paper,

all the ways and means we had sketched
in our letters. What precise negations,

what scar-white lines your ghost must have crossed
to find me. I was a blankness walking

on the white fires of that grid.
Now we talk. My fingers touch the blade

of your shoulder. And are fingers
on warm skin. We touch as only survivors

can touch. Butterflies like blue water
lap the air. The charcoal tree has blossomed

into featherdusters of flame. We could walk down
to the Sumapaz, the Peaceable River,

naming the white humped cattle, the hawk
who is a call, a circling

shadowed by her young, the lizards
who are known only by their vanishing.

Note
I came upon 'The Hooded Gods' when I was engaged in *Wall*, a poet-artist collaboration on Hadrian's Wall, and knew that I had found my allies. They watch as I take my place beside my unlettered ancestor,

    the labourer

beyond the ha-ha, who trespasses
twice a year on the park

of English poetry, the blackface

morrising and mumming
through the gates

and try to write the unwritten histories, a work of quiet subversion because it entails unwriting those that have been written.
    'Lower Lumb Mill' is a place that history itself has unwritten: a cradle of the Industrial Revolution that has greened over and become a creative writing centre. I was there

with a group of kids from inner-city Manchester, among them West Indians and Bangladeshis whom the Trade Winds had picked up and dumped back at the feet of King Cotton. The roots of their history were under their feet but they could not see them: they thought they were in the country…

'The Broken Road' was, as one reviewer rightly divined, the imaginative centre of my last book, *Given Ground*, and leads naturally into 'Skara Brae', which I visited with my late wife, the poet Frances Horovitz, shortly before she became ill with cancer.

'At Vanishing Point' is set in a house in Colombia where I spent much of my time in the years after Frances' death. My first visit was so disastrous that it might have been my last, had the poem not saved the day.

Most of my poems in recent years have borne a dedication and the dedication has become integral to them. 'Skara Brae' and 'At Vanishing Point' were completed by a third poem (first published in *PN Review*) in which I came upon one of my Colombian step-daughters as she sat writing in the spare room of my English house:

> I pause in the door,
> afraid to break the first hair's breadths
> of belonging, threads and sensings
> that are making of this spare room
> a familiar solitude,
> a separateness that is home.

EAVAN BOLAND

Night Feed

This is dawn.
Believe me
This is your season, little daughter.
The moment daisies open,
The hour mercurial rainwater
Makes a mirror for sparrows.
It's time we drowned our sorrows.

I tiptoe in.
I lift you up
Wriggling
In your rosy, zipped sleeper.
Yes, this is the hour
For the early bird and me
When finder is keeper.

I crook the bottle.
How you suckle!
This is the best I can be,
Housewife
To this nursery
Where you hold on,
Dear life.

A silt of milk.
The last suck.
And now your eyes are open,
Birth-colored and offended.
Earth wakes.
You go back to sleep.
The feed is ended.

Worms turn.
Stars go in.
Even the moon is losing face.
Poplars stilt for dawn
And we begin
The long fall from grace.
I tuck you in.

The Journey
For Elizabeth Ryle

Immediately cries were heard. These were the loud wailing of infant
souls at the very entrance way; never had they had their share of
life's sweetness for the dark day had stolen them from their mothers'
breasts and plunged them to a death before their time.
                                                        Vergil, *The Aeneid*, Book VI

And then the dark fell and 'there has never'
I said 'been a poem to an antibiotic:
never a word to compare with the odes on
the flower of the raw sloe for fever

'or the devious Africa-seeking tern
or the protein treasures of the sea bed.
Depend on it, somewhere a poet is wasting
his sweet uncluttered meters on the obvious

'emblem instead of the real thing.
Instead of sulpha we shall have hyssop dipped
in the wild blood of the unblemished lamb,
so every day the language gets less

'for the task and we are less with the language.'
I finished speaking and the anger faded
and dark fell and the book beside me
lay open at the page Aphrodite

comforts Sappho in her love's duress.
The poplars shifted their music in the garden,
a child startled in a dream,
my room was a mess –

the usual hardcovers, half-finished cups,
clothes piled up on an old chair –
and I was listening out but in my head was
a loosening and sweetening heaviness,

not sleep, but nearly sleep, not dreaming really
but as ready to believe and still
unfevered, calm and unsurprised
when she came and stood beside me

and I would have known her anywhere
and I would have gone with her anywhere
and she came wordlessly
and without a word I went with her

down down down without so much as
ever touching down but always, always
with a sense of mulch beneath us,
the way of stairs winding down to a river

and as we went on the light went on
failing and I looked sideways to be certain
it was she, misshapen, musical –
Sappho – the scholiast's nightingale

and down we went, again down
until we came to a sudden rest
beside a river in what seemed to be
an oppressive suburb of the dawn.

My eyes got slowly used to the bad light.
At first I saw shadows, only shadows.
Then I could make out women and children
and, in the way they were, the grace of love.

'Cholera, typhus, croup, diphtheria,'
she said, 'in those days they racketed
in every backstreet and alley of old Europe.
Behold the children of the plague.'

Then to my horror I could see to each
nipple some had clipped a limpet shape –
suckling darknesses – while others had their arms
weighed down, making terrible pietas.

She took my sleeve and said to me 'be careful.
Do not define these women by their work:
not as washerwomen trussed in dust and sweating,
muscling water into linen by the river's edge

'nor as court ladies brailled in silk
on wool, and woven with an ivory unicorn
and hung, nor as laundresses tossing cotton,
brisking daylight with lavender and gossip.

'But these are women who went out like you
when dusk became a dark sweet with leaves,
recovering the day, stooping, picking up
teddy bears and rag dolls and tricycles and buckets –

'love's archaeology – and they too like you
stood boot deep in flowers once in summer
or saw winter come in with a single magpie
in a caul of haws, a solo harlequin.'

I stood fixed. I could not reach to speak to them.
Between us was the melancholy river,
the dream water, the narcotic crossing.
They had passed over it, its cold persuasions.

I whispered, 'let me be
let me at least be their witness,' but she said
'what you have seen is beyond speech,
beyond song, only not beyond love;

'remember it, you will remember it'
and I heard her say but she was fading fast
as we emerged under the stars of heaven,
'there are not many of us; you are dear

'and stand beside me as my own daughter.
I have brought you here so you will know forever
the silences in which are our beginnings,
in which we have an origin like water,'

and the wind shifted and the window clasp
opened, banged and I woke up to find
my poetry books spread higgledy-piggledy,
my skirt spread out where I had laid it –

nothing was changed; nothing was more clear
but it was wet and the year was late.
The rain was grief in arrears; my children
slept the last dark out safely and I wept.

Envoi

It is Easter in the suburb. Clematis
shrubs the eaves and trellises with pastel.
The evenings lengthen and before the rain
the Dublin mountains become visible.

My muse must be better than those of men
who made theirs in the image of their myth.
The work is half-finished and I have nothing
but the crudest measures to complete it with.

Under the street lamps the dustbins brighten.
The winter-flowering jasmine casts a shadow
outside my window in my neighbor's garden.
These are the things that my muse must know.

She must come to me. Let her come
to be among the donnée, the given.
I need her to remain with me until
the day is over and the song is proven.

Surely she comes, surely she comes to me –
no lizard skin, no paps, no podded womb
about her but a brightening and
the consequences of an April tomb.

What I have done I have done alone.
What I have seen is unverified.
I have the truth and I need the faith.
It is time I put my hand in her side.

If she will not bless the ordinary,
if she will not sanctify the common,
then here I am and here I stay and then am I
the most miserable of women.

That the Science of Cartography is Limited
– and not simply by the fact that this shading of
forest cannot show the fragrance of balsam,
the gloom of cypresses,
is what I wish to prove.

When you and I were first in love we drove
to the borders of Connacht
and entered a wood there.

Eavan Boland

Look down you said: this was once a famine road.

I looked down at ivy and the scutch grass
rough-cast stone had
disappeared into as you told me
in the second winter of their ordeal, in

1847, when the crop had failed twice,
Relief Committees gave
the starving Irish such roads to build.

Where they died, there the road ended

and ends still and when I take down
the map of this island, it is never so
I can say here is
the masterful, the apt rendering of

the spherical as flat, nor
an ingenious design which persuades a curve
into a plane,
but to tell myself again that

the line which says woodland and cries hunger
and gives out among sweet pine and cypress,
and finds no horizon

will not be there.

What We Lost
It is a winter afternoon.
The hills are frozen. Light is failing.
The distance is a crystal earshot.
A woman is mending linen in her kitchen.

She is a countrywoman.
Behind her cupboard doors she hangs sprigged,
stove-dried lavender in muslin.
Her letters and mementoes and memories

are packeted in satin at the back with
gaberdine and worsted and
the cambric she has made into bodices;
the good tobacco silk for Sunday Mass.

She is sewing in the kitchen.
The sugar-feel of flax is in her hands.
Dusk. And the candles brought in then.
One by one. And the quiet sweat of wax.

There is a child at her side.
The tea is poured, the stitching put down.
The child grows still, sensing something of importance.
The woman settles and begins her story.

Believe it, what we lost is here in this room
on this veiled evening.
The woman finishes. The story ends.
The child, who is my mother, gets up, moves away.

In the winter air, unheard, unshared,
the moment happens, hangs fire, leads nowhere.
The light will fail and the room darken,
the child fall asleep and the story be forgotten.

The fields are dark already.
The frail connections have been made and are broken.
The dumb-show of legend has become language,
is becoming silence and who will know that once

words were possibilities and disappointments,
were scented closets filled with love letters
and memories and lavender hemmed into muslin,
stored in sachets, aired in bed linen;

and traveled silks and the tones of cotton
tautened into bodices, subtly shaped by breathing;
were the rooms of childhood with their griefless peace,
their hands and whispers, their candles weeping brightly?

Anna Liffey
Life, the story goes,
Was the daughter of Cannan,
And came to the plain of Kildare.
She loved the flatlands and the ditches
And the unreachable horizon.
She asked that it be named for her.
The river took its name from the land.
The land took its name from a woman.

A woman in the doorway of a house.
A river in the city of her birth.

.

There, in the hills above my house,
The river Liffey rises, is a source.
It rises in rush and ling heather and
Black peat and bracken and strengthens
To claim the city it narrated.
Swans. Steep falls. Small towns.
The smudged air and bridges of Dublin.

.

Dusk is coming.
Rain is moving east from the hills.

If I could see myself
I would see
A woman in a doorway.
Wearing the colours that go with red hair.
Although my hair is no longer red.

I praise
The gifts of the river.
Its shiftless and glittering
Retelling of a city,
Its clarity as it flows,
In the company of runt flowers and herons,
Around a bend at Islandbridge
And under thirteen bridges to the sea.
Its patience at twilight –
Swans nesting by it,
Neon wincing into it.

Maker of
Places, remembrances,
Narrate such fragments for me:

One body. One spirit.
One place. One name.
The city where I was born.
The river that runs through it.
The nation which eludes me.

Fractions of a life
It has taken me a lifetime
To claim.

•

I came here in a cold winter.

I had no children. No country.
I did not know the name for my own life.

My country took hold of me.
My children were born.

I walked out in a summer dusk
To call them in.

One name. Then the other one.
The beautiful vowels sounding out home.

•

Make of a nation what you will
Make of the past
What you can –

There is now
A woman in a doorway.

It has taken me
All my strength to do this.

Becoming a figure in a poem.

Usurping a name and a theme.

•

A river is not a woman.
    Although the names it finds,
        The history it makes
And suffers –
    The Viking blades beside it,
        The muskets of the Redcoats,
            the flames of the Four Courts
Blazing into it –
    Are a sign.
        Anymore than
A woman is a river,
    Although the course it takes,
        Through swans courting and distraught willows,
Its patience
    Which is also its powerlessness,
        From Callary to Islandbridge,
            And from source to mouth,

Is another one.
        And in my late forties
Past believing
    Love will heal
        What language fails to know
And needs to say
    What the body means –
        I take this sign
And I make this mark:
    A woman in the doorway of her house.
        A river in the city of her birth.
The truth of a suffered life.
    The mouth of it.

•

The seabirds come in from the coast.
The city wisdom is they bring rain.
I watch them from my doorway.
I see them as arguments of origin –
Leaving a harsh force on the horizon,
Only to find it
Slanting and falling elsewhere.

Which water –
The one they leave or the one they pronounce –
Remembers the other?

I am sure
The body of an ageing woman
Is a memory
And to find a language for it
Is as hard
As weeping and requiring
These birds to cry out as if they could
Recognize their element
Remembered and diminished in
A single tear.

•

An ageing woman
Finds no shelter in language.
She finds instead
Single words she once loved
Such as 'summer' and 'yellow'
And 'sexual' and 'ready'
Have suddenly become dwellings
For someone else –
Rooms and a roof under which someone else
Is welcome, not her. Tell me,
Anna Liffey,
Spirit of water,
Spirit of place,
How is it on this
Rainy autumn night
As the Irish sea takes
The names you made, the names
You bestowed, and gives you back
Only wordlessness?

•

Eavan Boland

Autumn rain is
Scattering and dripping
From carports
And clipped hedges.
The gutters are full.

When I came here
I had neither
Children nor country.
The trees were arms.
The hills were dreams.

I was free
To imagine a spirit
In the blues and greens,
The hills and fogs
Of a small city.

My children were born.
My country took hold of me.
A vision in a brick house.
Is it only love
that makes a place?

I feel it change:
My children are
Growing up, getting older.
My country holds on
To its own pain.

I turn off
The harsh yellow
Porch light and
Stand in the hall.
Where is home now?

Follow the rain
Out to the Dublin hills.
Let it become the river.
Let the spirit of place be
A lost soul again.

•

In the end
It will not matter
That I was a woman. I am sure of it.
The body is a source. Nothing more
There is a time for it. There is a certainty
About the way it seeks its own dissolution.
Consider rivers.
They are always en route to
Their own nothingness. From the first moment
They are going home. And so
When language cannot do it for us,
Cannot make us know love will not diminish us,
There are these phrases
Of the ocean
To console us.
Particular and unafraid of their completion.
In the end
Everything that burdened and distinguished me
Will be lost in this:
I was a voice.

Love
Dark falls on this mid-western town
where we once lived when myths collided.
Dusk has hidden the bridge in the river
which slides and deepens
to become the water
the hero crossed on his way to hell.

Not far from here is our old apartment.
We had a kitchen and an Amish table.
We had a view. And we discovered there
love had the feather and muscle of wings
and had come to live with us,
a brother of fire and air.

We had two infant children one of whom
was touched by death in this town
and spared: and when the hero
was hailed by his comrades in hell
their mouths opened and their voices failed and
there is no knowing what they would have asked
about a life they had shared and lost.

I am your wife.
It was years ago.
Our child is healed. We love each other still.
Across our day-to-day and ordinary distances
we speak plainly. We hear each other clearly.

And yet I want to return to you
on the bridge of the Iowa river as you were,
with snow on the shoulders of your coat
and a car passing with its headlights on:

I see you as a hero in a text –
the image blazing and the edges gilded –
and I long to cry out the epic question
my dear companion:
Will we ever live so intensely again?
Will love come to us again and be
so formidable at rest it offered us ascension
even to look at him?

But the words are shadows and you cannot hear me.
You walk away and I cannot follow.

Note
I chose these poems because in some way I remain connected to them. The reasons for a continuing connection, of course, are less easy to come at. But if I try to think of a poet I admire – say Housman – what remains in my mind is not a style of phrasing or a success with any one stanza. It's the way in which a particularly elusive emotion, almost the colour of an emotion, has been given reality by an arrangement of cadence. In the intense days when I had two small children, and wanted to record the life I lived in the poems I wrote, what I struggled for were cadences which might formalize those experiences. Nearly all these poems, right up to 'Anna Liffey', are poems in which the cadence in some way remains a chronicle for me of the attempt.

DAVID CONSTANTINE

from **In Memoriam**

5 *Récit*
No messenger in the tragedies
So mean but coming to the wife, the mother
Or any beloved woman waiting
Recounts fittingly the dead man's death
In alexandrines or iambics
And honours him in the telling.
But who the pal was is not remembered
Nor what he said, nor what the questions were
She had the heart to put nor whether
She lamented there and then, praising the qualities
Of the man lost and hiding her face as queens do
In her apron. Not a word, not the place itself
Reached me in his pronunciation
But as to how and where
She only shrugged her shoulders
And perhaps she had that from the messenger
Who did not tell her that the night was very short
And began in a barrage of phosgene gas
And ended in a thick fog
And a barrage of high explosive
As they moved around the southern edge of Trônes Wood
Across seven hundred yards of open ground
Gently sloping to the village of Guillemont
In an attack understood to be hopeless
But serving the French on their right
Whose attack was also hopeless
And that somewhere before the wire
He was obliterated
In gas and night and fog.

6
But by November the congregation of widows
    Being told it was a reasonable sacrifice
Their men had made saw mutilated trees bedecked
    With bloody tatters and being nonetheless
Promised a resurrection of the body
    They saw God making their men anew out of
The very clay. These women having heard from soldiers
    However little from the battlefield
Towards All Saints gathered black gouts from the elder
    Among their children stared at the holy tree
And envied Christ his hurts fit to appear in.
    Some then insisted on a photograph
Taken before the harm was done – which face they caused
    To appear in the hideous crater of their lives
Upon its slimy water. In time while she pursued
    With wrung hands her business as a widow
The water cleared. On the surface of a peaceful pool
    Decently framed the face shone steadily.

Mary Magdalene and the Sun
Hugging her breasts, waiting in a hard garden
For Sun, the climber, to come over the hill,
Disconsolate, the whore Mary Magdalene,
She of the long hair. But Sun meanwhile,

Scaling inch by inch the steep other side,
At last got a grip with his fingers on the rim
And hoisted himself up. She saw the spikes of his head,
His brow, then his brazen face. So after his swim

Leander's fingers appeared on Hero's sill
And he hauled himself inside, naked and salt
And grinning. She closed her eyes and let him feel
Her open face, uncrossed her arms and felt

Him warm her breasts and throat. Thereupon a cock
Crowed once, very red. And something came and stood
Between her and the Sun, something cold, and 'Look,'
It moaned. And there, casting a shadow, naked

And bled white was the nailed man, he whose
Blessing arms they fixed on a beam, and he crouched
There gibbering of love and clutching his
Thin shoulders and begging to be touched.

He was encrusted above the eyes with black,
And maculed in the hands and feet and in his side,
And through clacking teeth he begged her to touch him, and
    'Look,'
He moaned, 'at this and this that they did,'

Showing the holes. Sun, the joker, though
Had leapfrogged him, and more cocks crowed,
And down the green hillside and through
The waking garden the waters of irrigation flowed

And plenteous happy birdsong from the air,
As Sun diminished the ghosts of fruit trees on the grass
And over the nailed man's shoulders stroked the harlot's hair
And fingered open the purple sheaths of crocuses.

Eldon Hole
They fastened a poor man here on a rope's end
And through the turbulence of the jackdaws let him down
To where everything lost collects, all the earth's cold,
And the crying of fallen things goes round and round
And where, if anywhere, the worm is coiled.

When he had filled with cold they hauled him up.
The horrors were swarming in his beard and hair.
His teeth had broken chattering and could not stop
Mincing his tongue. He lay in the rope and stared,
Stared at the sky and feared he would live for ever.

Like one of those dreadful fish that are all head
They saw him at his little window beaming out
Bald and whiskerless and squiddy-eyed
He hung in the branches of their nightmares like a swede.
They listened at his door for in his throat

Poor Isaac when the wounds in his mouth had healed
Talked to himself deep down. It was a sound
Like the never-ending yelps of a small stone
Falling to where the worm lives and the cold
And everything hurt goes round and round and round.

Local Historian
Come in for a reference he lay down,
The book on his chest, his finger trapped in its pages.
Slept, and the sea did what it always does
When we sleep and listen, the sea drew nearer
And the neighbourly black cypresses
Almost leaned over the house. Starlings
Drove like hail to the collection in the marshes.

Slept, out of hours, late winter in the afternoon,
His finger marking a reference, and with a whisper,
A shush, an exhalation, his library
Dissolved and a thousand saints and the local worthies,
Every carn and cross and cove, as fine as flour,
Sucked from the room like dust, like spores,
Name after name after name, the parishes,

All of Cornwall, slipped from his lease
Towards home. When he wakes, in the darkness
For a while he will not know where he is,
The sea making a din, the cypresses overwhelming.
But I know that man. His finger marking the place
He will go back to the lighted room where his writing is,
He will recall the truant parishes, once more.

Ground Elder
Once since he died I saw him in a dream
Wherever the dead are, he was jovial,
He clapped me hard between his hands and said:
Stay, but I would not and I came back here
Where the living are. Now it is April

And kneeling on the warm earth in a sort of shame,
Dumb, fearful, not fit company
For anything opening I begin again
Pulling the ground elder, its leaves
Show it like flags or floats, the hands go in

After it gently, where it breaks it lives
Like worms, every remnant sprouts, this is
The thing he told me it was like,
This work of crochet through the living ground,
This reproductive act without an end,

A little like, nothing is really like
It, only love perhaps, both strike
And spread. Gathering the long tubers,
Stupidly laying them out in an old bowl
As though they were edible helps, it eases

The grip, the dumbness. Anyone patient
Who kneels half a day in spring and labours
Works wonders here. The summer will live.
You never get it all out, as he said.
No matter here. Here it is different.

Note
When I wrote 'In Memoriam' for my grandfather killed on the Somme and for my grandmother who survived him by more than half a century, that was the first time I felt I had a large subject and the knowledge and confidence to treat it. So I include two extracts here.

The other poems likewise are local, particular, and personal in the sense that I had grounds for writing them in my immediate real life. The subject of 'Local Historian' is my father-in-law, now dead. Eldon Hole is a deep shaft in the Peak District. I used to go there as a boy. I wrote the poem in a bus-station in Canberra, thinking of fathomless cruelties and holes through the earth.

I don't mind my poetry being thought of as 'self-expression', so long as it is understood that the self being expressed is a large and not merely biographical thing, more a state or condition than a person. The editor of my copy of Mandeville's *Travels*, says he has doubts about their author's 'personal entity'; and I do about mine. A writer of poetry touches upon the lives of others, and especially upon the sufferings of others, necessarily, and makes them his ground as much as his own life is. That is one reason for the instability of the poetic character; it is, to a risky degree, impressionable. Another reason is that through the successful poem we glimpse the life of myth, of recurrence, archetype, pattern; and the association with myth can act unsettlingly, or like a solvent, upon the biographical and individual life. At the same time the particularities of individual life are vital and must be held on to; without them no sense of myth is possible. The poem itself, however unsteady the personal entity of its author, must when it is finished be particular, coherent and exactly truthful. The particular, the personal, the vital here and now, these are laid on the pattern of myth, which shines out from behind them.

Thus Mary Magdalene, Yseut, Miranda, Christ, Lazarus, Caspar Hauser and other such figures are my familiars. I orientate myself by them; but also by my father-in-law, by 8571 Private J.W. Gleave, by his widow, by the living people I love, and by my dead friends, for one of whom 'Ground Elder' was written.

TOM LEONARD

. in the beginning was the word .
in thi beginning was thi wurd
in thi beginnin was thi wurd
in thi biginnin was thi wurd
in thi biginnin wuz thi wurd
n thi biginnin wuz thiwurd
nthi biginnin wuzthiwurd
nthibiginnin wuzthiwurd
nthibiginninwuzthiwurd
. in the beginning was the sound .

Moral Philosophy
whiji *mean* whiji mean

lissn
noo lissnty mi toknty yi
right

h hawd oan
whair wuzza
naw

aye
whitsiz name
him way thi
yi no yon

here
here yoo
yir no eevn lissnin
name a god

a doant no

from **Situations Theoretical and Contemporary**

(1)
The schooner *The Mother of Parliaments* has anchored in the bay.
The first British ship has reached your land.

See the row-boat, pulling to the shore.
See the ballot-boxes, glinting in the sun!

Run and tell your fellow-tribesmen.
We are going to have a referendum!
Shall we join the British Empire?

2
And their judges spoke with one dialect,
but the condemned spoke with many voices.

And the prisons were full of many voices,
but never the dialect of the judges.

And the judges said:
                'No-one is above the Law.'

from **nora's place**
only this particular
street to walk the length

of, this
is not a metaphor, only

being suddenly
walking down a street

in this place, having
this particular sense
not of anxiety, but

'the fact of the presence of existence'

                *

each time it happens
it seems

that all the intervening times
have disappeared

and this
is all that nora really is

Note
'. in the beginning was the word .' first appeared in a sequence called 'Unrelated Incidents' and then was published as a print by Glasgow Print Studio in 1976. I put it on the front cover of my collection *Intimate Voices*, where it could function partly as a kind of game/curious invitation, partly as a description of the style of some of the poems within, and partly as a kind of editorial: that Language is what is created in the Present Tense between people – 'the' dictionary follows in that wake. A statement against the notion that 'In the beginning was the word' is a sacred text meaning 'In the beginning was the primary act of colonisation'.

I wrote four 'Glasgow dialect' sequences between 1967 and 1979. They were really just expressions of a register of my own voice, written initially out of a sense of anger and frustration that that voice wasn't present in Literature other than in a patronising and bowdlerised fashion. It denied the real existence of people like myself by dressing 'them' up as inaccurate stereotypes.

In a poem like 'moral philosophy' from the second sequence, I was just enjoying the language; I've often had a notion to take the language down almost to a kind of limbo dance, at the opposite spectrum from high register. Not so as to be 'crude' or 'anti-Art' but as if to play with these morphemes of shape, enjoying how far a type of metric pulse occurs, and can be sustained. I think I've always had a kind of gut belief that when people are being honest and vulnerable in their language, the articulation, its pauses and even its monosyllabic hesitations, can form a kind of shape and music. I called my collection *Intimate Voices* partly in reference to Sibelius's string quartet.

But the politics have been unavoidable, even if they were implicit from the start in any case. It always seemed to come down to dialogue, whether every human being in their particular language is part of the dialogue of Language; or whether there is a particular language which can claim to possess and stand in lieu of the world; the possession of which language is the mark of the really human. The point at issue is really just the Elect versus the Universal Atonement again, only as at work in the politics of language. So it struck me when researching Scottish church history for my recent book on James Thomson 'B.V.'

As for 'politics' itself, it has always been at this level of language that I have felt engaged, or as often as not, enraged. The way a particular form of language can deny dialogue outwith itself, a matter of no consequence if it supposedly stands for all that there is of value. It never ceases to surprise me how in Britain this is so often thought to be the province of Evil Foreigners, or 'alien ways of thinking'.

This matter goes into 'Literature' as into anywhere else that language inhabits. Certain problems can arise regarding the governance of a narrator in relation to his 'subjects'. *nora's place* – from which the final poem is quoted – is another limbo dance of a kind, in which, as in my earlier dialect sequences, the narrator and the described occupy the same voice.

JEFFREY WAINWRIGHT

Transitive
in memory of Daniel Richardson

'The body makes love possible' – Galway Kinnell

This stripe of light
we lie inside,
a curtain crack,
carries me to you.
Another day,
a window breeze,
touching my shoulder, speaks
of what is realized,
like how you walk, or eat,
or dress, or sleep.
Love is made tenable
in skin and bone.

But if what is loved
is drawn away –
You saw the dead child
as he was given back to her.
You saw him leave
for his frozen world,
carried to its edge
in his father's arms,
the shapes of breath about him
pulled apart
and thinned
into the passing air.

Where he is
the soil stirs by him,
slanting his body
in a run of sand,
tamps him to itself,
lets go, and slides him again.
Casting above that,
the human eye seeks light
in what is shed
upon the world
and in the globe
where it resides.

So, grasped everyday
in a key-fob photograph,
or on a sideboard,
or pressed between pages,
he is immanent –
even soldered into marl
and the city's infill
he is imaginable.
What is in the mind
cannot be touched.
The lack of him
beats at the iron ground.

The stripe of light
we lie inside
carries me to you.
I can touch you,
pass from myself,
and in this accomplished
sentence: I love you.
With less – with what
is in the mind,
what is made possible
by the idea of him,
they love.

from **The Swimming Body**
The mind as it lives with itself,
Noticing, taking things in, pondering,
Dismissing from its presence, allowing some things
To slip out, hit by recollection,
Looking forward (tonight, the summer),
Seems to float free, say, as I walk across
This park, just in front and a foot to the side.
Today there is a tune, some serious matter
For a while, bits of books, a meal,
An old friend in his gaberdine.
It can't keep to anything,
Its sentences are left open, it is a conversation
Of unfinished thoughts, unfinishable, but
Running, running, even as it thinks of itself
As itself, intelligence, consciousness,
'The life of the mind' – and here it might be pleased –
What else can the soul be?

I am on my way to swim, the mind alongside
As I say, moving briskly in the cold through
Some interest or other, spending some time
On what to do – how many lengths, in what pattern?
Re-running Salnikov, today's sports page:
A 100 in under a minute times 15!
Be solicitous but stern with the lungs
And the aching arm.

The trees in the park are shuttered.
A young man comes into view, his hair shaved up
Around his ears, his shoes laceless and without socks.
He is speeding round the paths turning
In sharp angles and shrieking as he goes,
A huge, strange call like a bird
From some land of marsh and cloud.
The mind has noticed this and is
Drawing back. If I pick up my pace,
Barely noticeably, we will be carried beyond him
As he arrives at the next corner and
Twirls on the ball of his foot toward us.
The mind is back inside, to the matter in hand,
No intention of being left to face a mind
Bodied out as this is in its dented and
Bundled flesh, its tiny running steps,
Strange curves, and the wave beat of his cry
Pushing the air towards us. What
Comes down the path here, the vast chest,
The gait, the head, the face in white,
Is his mind, a physical thing as is my own,
Shrunk back now to be in step.

As the mind comes back it is not to prison
But itself. If I am not outside my body –
A foot to the side, a foot in front –
Neither is this body merely a house,
A space, a lodging, cavity, lathboard crack,
But something that is fluent in the mind,
As the mind itself is mortised
In this body's nervousness.

What the mind makes of anything comes of how
The body's made, as through the limb of sight,
Or what it touches and what touches it,
Like this water slipping past, happening
Outside the brain but not simply arriving there
To be noticed but already having joined us
At the skin. This is the border of the world,
The edge of space, the tireless lapping
Of the thought of truth, the pulse of death,
The simple outline of the self – here, and
Here, and here – the edge inventing the idea
Of itself
Of what it is and what it might be
Of what it is and what it might be
And so on and so on and so on.
Everything comes by the body and is streaked by it.

from **The Madness of George III**
Candidus, my tall blood-prince, my grenadier,
Come with me since I love you.
Let us find a grove in middle Europe
Raised from sandy soil
Where the words will leave these stories
We have become and steal away,
Hallooing still one to another
Like accomplices on a dark road,
But gone.

                And we can dissolve,

blushes into white space   forgetting even

        the moss of a tree

                on its north side

the lost touch of it

from **Free Rein**

IV
To resist Assyria (Ishtar upon her lion)
a democratic vista:
Nell and Perce and Gladys and Jack:

the we the people who are the *materiel*,
the hands between the biscuit and the glaze
colouring cornflowers fifteen to the dozen
or banding Etruscanware for table and sideboard,

and saffruck, the fitters and the clerks,
the servers of school dinners,
the spotters of paths in the sky, dust clouds
in the desert, the dead of the prison-ship,
Nell and Perce and Gladys and Jack.

[after Emyr Humphreys]

V
Suppose, consider, behold, see, know
these four and all those who for any hour
of these fifty thousand years have been a part –

dying in muffled labour for the species,
dreaming of the evening and a game of bowls,
deciding … What is it I ask you find
to do with them, and how, and why?

Only … think … Think of the number, and that
however hurried on their way, none was a speck,
a bit of all there is, of 'what happens',
not the poorest he and she of them but had
and has a life to live. Think of yourself.

XXII
Not that. Not that. Not that. Not that. But I
am still thinking theref… Though I'd rather be –
as who would not? – nicely fat, really comfy

in winceyette, snug as a bug in a rug. And but
for some tremor or other we could be in the coverlets
of shale, the same bits of what is not, of whatever is hiccupping
through its great extinctions,

but without the t-t-t-ting of Telos – spielos Telos,
forget we ever thought of you, out of sight
out of … ah hah! nothing to believe with
and thus free as … stop it! … just free as …
living as though [ ] don't exist. Dream on.

Note

'The poorest he that is in England has a life to live as the greatest he…' Colonel Rainborough's plea from the 1647 'Putney Debates' is a formulation I have long wanted to bring into a poem. But, no matter how true I believe his maxim to be, this is an embarrassing confession. Embarrassing because of the blatant didacticism; because there is no point (as Calvino has said) in reiterating in literary form what can be held in another discourse; because we have too great a yearning for the apothegm; because 'truth' has such a scent to it. In many respects therefore I am more pleased with a 'purer' poem like 'Candidus…' where the gist is much more elusive and the words escape the dragoons of meaningfulness by feigning an escape into their white background.

Discourses such as politics, history or swimming instruction, conducted under their own concepts, do, in practice, set aside the problems of language as they strive for the transparency of argument or narrative. They must claim an unreal, self-contained discipline of attention. From time to time it is discipline they press against, as for instance in Simon Schama's current effort to extend the scope of historiography.

Poetry is about the problems of language – Pound's 'brief gasp between one cliché and another'. But if poetry is thus imprisoned, it might also be seen to be free to play with any part of any discourse, perhaps displaying each fragment to the audience like a conjuror's ball before having it disappear before our eyes. I don't think the responsibilities of poetry towards play, towards words as sound-images which are only provisionally attached, or supposedly free, of referents, preclude an attempt to say something in a poem, however oblique, composite or provisional. The strength that poetry – having absorbed the discursiveness of neo-classicism, the subjectivity of romanticism and the fragmentation of modernism – now possesses is the opportunity to combine so many different aspects of experience, knowledge and ways of speaking, and to mix them in a way that is richer, more linguistically – that is to say humanly – diverse than any of the argufying discourses it might feed from. Descartes, a child's bedtime memories, geology and evolution (popularly apprehended), a bit of argot and verbal playfulness can co-exist here as in no other form outside the literary. Of course we strive to think our way through discrete subjects and to impose on ourselves the appropriate rules of enquiry and contemplation and it is right that we do so. But that effort is part of the whole contingent jostle of our mental states which bear the impression of the language about us. The capacity of the poem to speak something of this mix of the mind is what interests me most at present, though not, I hope, as an interior monologue, but as part of the exchanges in which we seek for sense.

MIMI KHALVATI

Rubaiyat
for Telajune

Beyond the view of crossroads ringed with breath
her bed appears, the old-rose covers death
has smoothed and stilled; her fingers lie inert,
her nail-file lies beside her in its sheath.

The morning's work over, her final chore
was 'breaking up the sugar' just before
siesta, sitting cross-legged on the carpet,
her slippers lying neatly by the door.

The image of her room behind the pane,
though lost as the winding road shifts its plane,
returns on every straight, like signatures
we trace on glass, forget and find again.

I have inherited her tools: her anvil,
her axe, her old scrolled mat, but not her skill;
and who would choose to chip at sugar-blocks
when sugar cubes are boxed beside the till?

The scent of lilacs from the road reminds me
of my own garden: a neighbouring tree
grows near the fence. At night its clusters loom
like lantern-moons, pearly-white, unearthly.

I don't mind that the lilac's roots aren't mine.
Its boughs are, and its blooms. It curves its spine
towards my soil and litters it with dying
stars: deadheads I gather up like jasmine.

My grandmother would rise and take my arm,
then sifting through the petals in her palm
would place in mine the whitest of them all:
'Salaam, dokhtaré-mahé-man, salaam!'

'Salaam, my daughter-lovely-as-the-moon!'
Would that the world could see me, Telajune,
through your eyes! Or that I could see a world
that takes such care to tend what fades so soon.

from Interiors, after Edouard Vuillard
The Parlour

Between the saucer and the lip,
the needle and the cloth,
the closing of a cupboard door
and the reassertion of a room,

in those pauses of the eye
when the head lifts and time stands still

what gesture flees its epoch
to evoke a crowded continent?
What household conjures household

in the heterogeneity of furniture,
rituals that find their choirs
in morning light, evening lamps,
in cloths and clothes and screens?

This woman sewing,
man reading at his desk,
in raising eyes towards the wall,
do they lose themselves in foliage?

Sense themselves receding
to become presences on gravel paths
and, in becoming incorporeal,
free to be transposed?

Do they see themselves and not themselves
– have any sense how manifold
might be their incarnations –
in the needlepoint of walls and skies
so distant from their own?

For this profile hazed
against shutterfold and sky
has as many claimants
as there are flowers on the wall,
in a vase, on a dress, in the air

and everywhere, like leaves,
recognitions drop their calling-cards
on a mood, a table set for supper,

disperse themselves as freely
as the mille-fleurs from a palette,

settle unobtrusively
as her to her sewing, him to his book,
lowering eyes from vistas
that have brought them to themselves.

The Workroom
It was in the whirring of a treadle,
biting of a thread,
in the resumption of the treadle

while eyes were closed
and shadows of the scissors
like the noon sun through its zenith
were passing overhead

that allegiances were fed their rhythms,
loyalties first given shape.

With a lever sprung, a length released,
launched in its wake on a sea of stuffs,
flecks of wool, waves of walnut grain,

receiving food, receiving drink, we gave
the thanks we never knew in time
we would strive to give, to keep alive
in words, in songs, in paint.

It was in these gestures, the day's devotions,
with a pockmarked thumb, pinheads
jammed in a mouth that held them safe,
that an inheritance was slowly stitched,

a paradigm to give body to
like a second life to curtains,
a lining to a dress. And now,
when prayers we never knew were prayers

in the guise of silver bobbins,
machines we never mastered,
are once again in currency
in the hands of daughters making light

of the partnering, unpartnering of threads;
when voices caught, then thought lost
in transit while ours, in vows,
were still keeping faith

return in transpositions,
in a dream like a revelation,
familial as they were in life
to orchestrate our states of grace;

how can we not fail them?
What sacraments can we find but these
poor leavings of a memory
of a home, a time, a place?

The Studio
Moving into an attic with skylights
that reflect
this attic, skylight,

this self-portrait that rises
from refuse round an easel,
refuse round a mirror, concretions
of a life fallen from the body,

concrete images by which we thought
to reconstruct our layers;

caught in an upper angle,
the triad by which light
consecrates mirror, wall,
the forehead's lobe

– a tightening of tension
between sky and thought
and where thought falls –
with an instrument at hand and memory
transfiguring, holding up prefigurations

of all the hand creates…

Mimi Khalvati

we move into a chain, a series of removes
like dinner guests at table recessive
in glass, like the painting of a painting
retracted to a sketch.

With skylight overhead
where birds divide their paths and cleave
its compass point as cleanly
as leaves cleave stems

or with fielded gold below
in those voids for interleaving,
becoming, ceasing,

and sounds of playing children
too far to be intrusive
like seabirds in a bay,

we are complicit in a subterfuge,
this series of removes,
diminutions to a dot

but cannot lose, nor even
drown in the grand design, that moment
when the eye lifts, the hand descends
to a description of itself.

The Bedroom
Sewing at her window,
leaning her head on a plane of light
like a cheek against its pillow

or watering her hyacinths,
whatever was passing through her mind
light from the lamp recorded,
light from the window guessed.

The room she had come to tidy,
tidied and left alone, embroidered it;
the air outside with its hooves and bells
indoors almost mute

spread it to thin in squares and parks
while flowers downstairs on divans and chairs
rumoured it back to borders
flowering at her nape.

In doors always left half-open
she is suspended in mid-sentence

like a thought
too generous to express.

Entering, exiting
as part of the same slow motion,
gliding profiled to the right,
older, to the left,

hers are the two stooped figures
behind the scrim of childhood,
parentheses we are caught between,
stalled in their vague arcades.

Might they not be our muses?
Our covenants with absence?
Greys that are never storm and cloud
but oyster, dove and snail?

Might they be spelling a secret,
in codicils a condition:
if art is to nail a butterfly's wings
and a prayer for flight be the nail…?

If only it were a question of will!
But will, mourning our own mortality,
forfeits the gift of pity
art earns in mourning theirs.

Coma
Mr Khalvati? Larger than life he was;
too large to die so they wired him up on a bed.
Small as a soul he is on the mountain ledge.

Lids gone thin as a babe's. If it's mist he sees
it's no mist he knows by name. *Can you hear me,
Mr Khalvati?* Larger than life he was

and the death he dies large as the hands that once
drowned mine and the salt of his laugh in the wave.
Small as a soul he is on the mountain ledge.

Can you squeeze my hand? (Ach! Where are the hands
I held so tight to pull me back to the baize?)
Mr Khalvati? Larger than life he was

with these outstretched hands that squeezing squeeze
thin air. Wired he is, tired he is and there,
small as a soul he is on the mountain ledge.

No nudging him out of the nest. No-one to help him
fall or fly, there's no coming back to the baize.
Mr Khalvati? Larger than life he was.
Small as a soul he is on the mountain ledge.

Note
'Rubaiyat', an early poem, was my first experience of a poem refusing to be written until I gave it the form it wanted; albeit, a third-hand form (not the Persian *ruba*, but Fitzgerald's linked quatrains). Some people have referred to this poem, and many to my grandmother, by her familial name, Telajune. This, and rhyming moon with June, has given me pleasure. (*June*, incidentally, besides being a common term of endearment, also means life, spirit, soul, 'the whole lot' as my mother says.)

Some time ago, I had a wonderful dream. I was back in Telajune's house, in the Sixties. She was there, pottering at her tasks and Akhtar Khanum, the seamstress, was at her Singer and I was wandering in and out of adjoining rooms, daydreaming. The radio was on. They were talking and, as in life at that time, I understood not a word of their Farsi. Nothing happened, the morning passed till, eventually, I woke crying.

The happiness that flooded me was one of re-creation: not only of a time in my life when I was happy but of a language that I still can't speak properly yet in my dream had recreated in two voices, accents, not as a gobbledy-gook Farsi, but the real thing. I had no doubt it was authentic. An Oliver Sacks sort of dream.

In an early draft of this dream as poem, I made a small reference to Vuillard – something about voices merging like colours in his air – and, on going back to his work, found, not only a remarkable resemblance between his mother and my grandmother, but that his paintings had already explored the parameters of my dream. Writing about Vuillard, then, became another third-hand medium.

Recognitions became the keynote of 'The Parlour'. 'The Workroom' relates more closely to the dream. 'The Studio' grew out of my irritation with insistence on the concrete (particularly in workshops), my own insistent use of the I and, equally, irritation at strategies to objectify, transcend. In 'The Bedroom', I officially appoint Telajune as my muse (though I had hoped to do it surreptitiously). The 'Studies' that complete the sequence *Interiors* grew out of the material I usually accumulate and throw away, but on this occasion had not the heart to.

My grandmother died as she lived, quietly, with resignation if not acceptance, and selflessly. My father raged. He seemed to do his dying on this side of the line and could only die when he had no *june* left. His last six months were in a coma. During that time Dylan Thomas's villanelle kept speaking in my mind, engendering a dialogue where none with the living was possible.

Perhaps one reason for my writing poetry is the opportunity it affords of translation at several removes where more faithful forms are impossible; and my recent concerns with thinning out imagery, fluid syntax, use of the fragment, may be indicative of a desire to become a more permeable medium through which this translation can take place.

DICK DAVIS

A Monorhyme for Miscegenation
(For Yass Amir-Ebrahimi and Stuart Benis)

We all know what our elders warned
In their admonitory drone,

'Water and oil won't mix my child –
Play safe, stick staunchly to your own.'

And I concede they're half right when
I think of all the pairs I've known

(Black/White, Jew/Gentile, Moslem/Me –
The home-raised with the foreign-grown)

Mixed marriages, it's true, can make
Two lives a dire disaster zone.

But only half: since when they work
(As my luck, and my friends', has shown)

Their intricate accommodations
Make them impossible to clone:

For gross, gemütlich kindness, for
Love's larky, lively undertone,

For all desired and decent virtues
They stand astonished and alone.

Gossip
*(Imitated from Sa'di-*Bustan, *bk. 7, ll. 3309-3356. Mid 13th century.)*

Forget the rat-race, hide yourself away
From all the fashion-mongers do and say,
But no-one, hermit, hoax or holy Asian,
Can hide from character assassination;
Look, you could be an angel from on high
Cavorting Superman-like in the sky
But still you'd see the slanderers have found
A way to bring you crashing to the ground.
You'll find it easier to keep the menace
Of Adriatic waves away from Venice
Than tie the tattling tongue of someone who
Has homed in on his helpless victim – you!

You choose a life of books and quiet contentment,
Precisely that provokes the brats' resentment,
Whispering in huddles, taking turns to slam you
'Nerd' 'Prig' 'Hypocrite' 'Creep' – your virtues damn you.
If someone's shy and finds it hard to be
A social animal perpetually
They say his strange desire for solitude
Is sanctimonious or downright rude;
If someone likes a laugh and noisy fun
They say he sleeps around with everyone.
If someone's rich they're quick on the attack
Nailing him as an ego-maniac,
But if he's poor then he's a sap, a loser,
An irresponsible pan-handling boozer;
On hand to comment on a bit-shot's fall,
(It shows them there's still justice after all –
'He and his arrogance just had it coming,
So let's see how the bastard likes *real* slumming')
And ready to assault like snarling bitches
Any poor wretch who rises up to riches
('That punks like him succeed is proof that slime
Is all that rises in this rotten time').
If you've a business and it's doing well
Then you're a grasping plutocrat from hell,
But if they see you unemployed they sneer
That cadging meals and money's your 'career'.

You like to talk, you're always on the go.
'Sure, empty vessels make most noise you know',
The quiet type's 'a frigging bathroom tile,
What's with that condescending silent smile?'
If Turn-the-other-cheek's your line they say
'That wimp has got no balls! Him, fight? No way!'
If you're aggressive though how they complain –
'I'm out of here, I'm gone, the guy's insane!'
If someone's on a slimmer's skimpy diet
The gossips' wagging tongues are never quiet
But if you like your food why then of course
You stuff your belly like a hungry horse;
A rich man who lives reasonably they call
A skinflint with no common sense at all,
But if he builds himself a fancy palace
And lives like someone on the set of *Dallas*
Then he's a tasteless drag-queen or a fool
Who doesn't know that rich kitsch isn't cool.
Someone's a modest stay-at-home, so those
Who change planes oftener than their underclothes
Will say 'What's he experienced from life
Tied to the apron of his dumpy wife?'
But if you've seen the world a bit, beware!
A man who's ever travelled anywhere
Is just a drifter who can't settle down
Meandering pointlessly from town to town.
A bachelor's a loner – when he wakes
At night the lonely bed-frame quakes and shakes,
But married, no-one comes to his defence,
'His hormones got the better of his sense,
Hot-rodding down the road, he never learned,
And now his Porsche has crashed and overturned.'
An ugly face gets cruelly criticized
But beauty's just as openly despised
Since envy's first priority's to find
Ways for what's lovely to be undermined.
Once I'd a room-mate who was rather shy,
He seldom smiled or looked you in the eye;
A visitor took me aside and said
'That friend you've got there might as well be dead,
Teach him some manners!' So, next day, I tried
To put the matter to him as described.
He didn't like it and the argument
Soon threatened to get fairly virulent;
Just then our carping visitor came back,
Immediately he went on the attack
At me! 'Hey, pick on someone your own size,
You've hurt his feelings, now apologize!'
If anger makes you lose your self-possession
You're 'crazy, in the grip of some obsession',
But if you're patient with all comers then
You're one of those 'soft, wimpy, wussy men'.
To generous folk they say, 'Hold back, enough,
Tomorrow you'll be begging for the stuff',
To careful spenders though they're sure to say
'What are you saving up for? Judgement Day?'
Enough though, really! Who alive can live
Uncriticized? To be too sensitive
Is self-defeating – as we know, the best
Get even more lambasted than the rest;
The wisest course then's probably to sit
Tight, keep your head down, and put up with it.

A Translator's Nightmare
I think it must have been in Limbo where,
As Dante says, the better poets share
Old friendships, rivalries, once famous fights
And, now they've left it, set the world to rights.
As I was being hustled through *in transit*
To God knows what damned hole, I thought I'd chance it
And chat to some of the assembled great ones
Who looked as bored as trapped theatre patrons
Who've paid good cash and found they hate the show…
I picked on one; 'I rather doubt you know…'
He started up and peered at me: 'Know you,
You snivelling fool? Know you? Of course I do!
You ruined my best poem. Look who's here…'
He turned to his companions with a sneer,
'Traducer and destroyer of our art,
The biggest stink since Beelzebub's last fart'.
They jostled round, each shouting out his curses,
'You buried me with your insipid verses…'
'You left out my best metaphor, you moron…'
'You missed my meaning or they set no store on
An accurate rendition where you come from'.
'He comes from where they send the deaf and dumb from,
He got my metre wrong…' 'He missed my rhymes',
'He missed puns I don't know how many times
Then shoved his own in…' But I turned and fled
Afraid that in a moment I'd be dead
A second time, torn limb from spectral limb.

A mist came down and I was lost: a dim
Shape beckoned: thinking it must be my guide
I ran for reassurance to his side.
But it was someone I'd not seen before,
An old man bent beside the crumbling shore
Of Lethe's stream. He stared a long time, then
'Did you translate?' I screamed, 'Oh not again,'
But as I backed off one quick claw reached out;
He clutched my coat, and with a piercing shout
(He didn't look as though he had it in him)
Cried, 'We've a guest! Who'll be the first to skin him?'
Then added, 'Just my joke now; stay awhile,
The crowd in these parts is quite versatile
Though we've one thing in common, all of us;
When you were curious, and courteous,
Enough to translate poems from our tongue
All of us gathered here were not among
The chosen ones'. I looked around – a crowd
Now hemmed us in and from it soon a loud
Discordant murmur rose: 'Please, why not mine?'
'You did Z's poems, my stuff's just as fine…'
'The greatest critics have admired my verse…'
'You worked on crap that's infinitely worse
Than my worst lines'. '*Some* of my stuff's quite good –
You will allow that? It's not *all* dead wood?
Why then…?' and slowly the reproaches turned
To begging, bragging, angry tears that burned
Their way into my sorry soul.

                                   Once more
I ran and saw my guide, tall on the shore
– The other shore – of Lethe. 'Rescue me!'
I called, 'Get me to where I have to be
For all eternity…' He smiled; 'My dear,
You've reached your special hell. It's here. It's here.'

Note

I checked and saw that I'd some poems in *PNR* 1, way back in 1976, which seems real confirmation of middle age. At that time I was working in Iran; since then I've been back in England, entered academia, taught here and there, and now teach Persian in the American mid-west. Looking at my poems then and now it seems that generally my interests have intensified rather than changed. I still like verse and the things you can do with it and can't do with prose (obvious things like regular rhyme, shifting the caesura about, end-stopping – or not end-stopping – lines); I still like clarity and light rather than depth and darkness; I'm still not keen on moments in poems that aren't paraphrasable, though I realize that's as great a heresy now as then, perhaps even greater. Foreign-ness still draws me, but it's not me as a foreigner in the landscape that interests me now. I'm still interested by what happens when cultures or their representatives come up against each other, and I'm still drawn by poetry, and art generally, not from my own cultural background, perhaps because – despite what I wrote above about paraphrase – there's always a residuum I'm not going to quite get, that's going to remain mysterious. (Perhaps I only mean that I like real mystery, but not factitious invented mysteries.) A new interest, growing out of the old ones, is verse translation/adaptation – the most unalloyed intellectual pleasure I know of. (It can have a rather voyeuristic, grubby side as well, as it's a way of pretending intimacy with the great.) Writing verse translations has certainly changed my own poems. In the 1970s almost all of my poems tried to be right-little, tight-little epigrammatic pieces: I still try for that sometimes, but having translated long narrative poems has helped me write more discursively, and encouraged me to use more diverse kinds of language within a poem. There's also a general question of technique; medieval Persian poetry (which is what I translate) is very technique-conscious indeed and my fascination with the mechanics of verse has been given a whole new lease of life by trying to translate such poems. The sheer crossword/jigsaw puzzle element is for me a major source of pleasure, and I've stopped feeling defensive about this though many people find it a derisorily low reason for caring about poetry ('O but this is verse, not poetry'. Spit.) For example, monorhyme is very common in even quite long Persian poems (up to hundreds of lines) and how to translate these poems into English is a big problem; that has made me experiment with monorhyme in English and one such experiment is included here. I'm very pleased to be part of *PNR*'s 100th issue; the magazine has been very good to me, and to many other writers, over many years and I wish it well as it moves on towards its next 100 issues.

CLIVE WILMER

Saxon Buckle
in the Sutton Hoo treasure

His inlaid gold hoards light:
A gleaming thicket to expel,
With intricacy worked by skill,
The encroaching forest night
Where monsters and his fear dwell.

Gold forest tangles twined by will
Become a knot that closes in
The wild beasts that begin
Beyond his habitation.
An object for his contemplation,

From which three rivets gaze:
A beast's head forested within,
That clasps his swordbelt to his waist
By daylight, and before his eyes,
By hearthlight, stills unrest.

The Parable of the Sower
Stained glass in the Arts & Crafts style, set in a medieval church

I
The sower goes out to sow. His sense and form
Move only in a landscape of stained glass;
   The leads like ivy stems,
   Enmeshing, bind him in.
Outside, it is afternoon; inside, the sun
Irradiates a face in shadow – eyes
   Inclined toward the earth
   Crimsoning underfoot.
The glory round about and through his limbs
Is vision in excess of daily need,
   Devotion in the work
   Dispersed beyond the seed.

II
Victorian glass of eighteen ninety-seven,
Replacing the clear light in the west wall
   In homage to a time
   That built as if for ever.
The vision is of a vision that transfigured
Perspectives on the bare field; but with skill
   The craftsman has contained,
   Edged, the unearthly glow.
His observation accurate, the self
A blemish that his labour should efface,
   Devotion to his craft
   Speaks through the pictured face.

III
The sower does not see the field he sows.
He walks in rapture, but his eyes are glazed
   With sorrow not his own,
   That has no root in earth.
It is the craftsman's sorrow, for he gave
These paradisal colours to the earth
   But when he looked on earth
   He found an absence there.
Here wayside, thorn, good ground and stony ground
Are stained through with devotion, with his need
   For things to mean – the word
   Secreted in the seed.

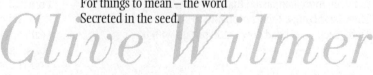

Post-War Childhoods
for Takeshi Kusafuka

If there were no affliction in this world we might think we were in paradise.
                            Simone Weil, *Gravity and Grace*

You, born in Tokyo
In nineteen forty-four,
Knew the simplicity
Occasioned by a war.
In London it was so
Even in victory –
In defeat, how much more.

Knew it I say – and yet,
Born to it, you and I,
How could we in truth have known?
It was the world. You try
To make articulate,
In language not your own,
What it was like and why.

Nature returned (you say)
To downtown Tokyo –
In your voice, some irony
Defending your need to go
That far: what other way
Of like economy
Is there of saying so?

Your images declare
The substance of the phrase:
Bomb craters, urban grass,
A slowworm flexing the gaze
Of the boy crouching there;
Moths, splayed on the glass,
Like hands lifted in praise.

A future might have drawn
On what such things could tell.
You heard, even as you woke,
Accustomed birdsong fill
The unpolluted dawn,
Heard a toad blurt and croak
In some abandoned well.

They call it desolation,
The bare but fertile plot
You have been speaking of.
You grew there, who have taught
Me much of the relation
Affliction bears to love
In Simone Weil's scoured thought.

I, too, have images.
A photograph: St Paul's,
The dome a helmeted head
Uplifted, as terror falls.
The place I knew, not this
But a city back from the dead,
Grew fireweed within walls.

I played over dead bombs
In suburban villas, a wrecked
Street of them where, run wild,
Fat rhododendrons cracked
The floors of derelict rooms:
It seemed to a small child
An Eden of neglect.

If we two share a desire,
It is not that either place,
Still less the time, should return.
If gravity and grace
Survive a world on fire
Fixed in the mind, they burn
For things to be in peace.

Charon's Bark
to my Mother

1
It's the being left behind
I can't believe:
me stranded on this shore
and glimpsing you,
too far out, too baffled by the crowd
of they might be twittering shoppers,
to notice that I stay.

I recognise you by
a look of panic, so faint
who else in the world would notice it,
as you stare back at the shore,
your set eyes blind to the same look
in these that reach out after you.

2
On nights like this,
when with snow piled deep it is
too cold to snow any more
in the bitter wind,
I can't get the thought of you out of my mind.

What I keep thinking of
is waking too early on a bright morning,
and running to your bed, and jumping in.

On nights like this,
I can't keep the tears back
at the thought of you –
out there in the dark, the snow your coverlet,
unwakably asleep.

Psalm
Here the waters converge and in their fork
        we sit on the ground and weep.
           So this is exile.

Their currents flow by me. Why should they heed
        a man in love with the past
           of his own country,

lost to him now, elsewhere? Our home river,
    gone underground, flows counter.
        And when our masters –

half in mockery, yet half curious
    to hear such foreign lore –
        call for an old song,

I hang my harp high on a willow bough
    leaning across the flood.
        Jerusalem,

let the hand that writes these verses wither and die
    if I forget you now
        in this ill time;

let my tongue stick in my throat if I sell short
    the source of all my words,
        fail to remember

where my joys began. In the mean time,
    Daughter of Babylon, you
        have humbled us:

you may publish us to the world, you may ignore us.
    But we have time. In time
        we will be revenged.

Note

These five poems have been selected to represent five phases of my work, though what they have in common interests me much more than what divides them.

The first of them, 'Saxon Buckle', was written in 1968 when I was 23. It remains the poem of my own for which I feel most affection. This is partly because I remember discoveries made in the course of writing it: I started with a longer line and steadily cut it back – I had not previously realised how much this can increase a poem's intensity. And it is partly because the poem still serves me as a kind of *ars poetica*. For me, a good poem should be a little at odds with its subjects. That is to say, the business of making art is necessarily a way of bringing order out of chaos. If one's subject is chaotic or menacing in itself – as it is here – then the act of making will tend to resist the threat, even as it expresses it. I have never been at home with the notion that the form of an art-work must imitate its subject. So in 'Saxon Buckle' I was looking for a form which would not only express the peculiar terrors we find in the art of the early English (which have, of course, their modern equivalents) but which would itself put up a resistance to those terrors. Thus, whenever art works for me, I find that it gives me a sense of peace and rest, even when it is truly terrible (as in *King Lear*, for instance, or the poems of Paul Celan).

The other poems I have chosen continue these preoccupations. 'Post-War Childhoods' (which owes everything to the two great political poems of the century, 'Easter 1916' and '1st September 1939') ends like 'Saxon Buckle' with an affirmation of peace – something I hit upon in the shaping of its cadences. 'The Parable of the Sower' shares with the buckle poem a preoccupation with the role played by art in both expressing and resisting the causes of suffering. This was the first poem I wrote that fulfilled another ambition – continued in 'Psalm' and several recent poems – which was to write in a lyrical stanza without rhyme. It is not in fact entirely without rhyme, but it is sparing in its use of it. The stanza was borrowed from Milton's version of a Horatian ode, 'What slender youth bedew'd with liquid odours', the earliest instance I know of an unrhymed lyric. But here again, my form is in some sense at odds with my subject. The stanza was also used by Collins and Clare for their versions of Horatian and pastoral subjects. There is a hint of pastoral in mine, but the atmosphere is much more distinctively Gothic than classical. 'Psalm', an imitation of Psalm 137, is written in an unrhymed stanza I invented for it. It is actually in a blank verse line, but one which has been broken up into stanzas to frustrate the reader's predictable expectations. This poem expresses anger, as the fifth poem, 'Charon's Bark', expresses grief. I hope readers will agree that the pursuit of calm and stability in form need not distract from intensity of feeling. In 'Charon's Bark', as it happens, I make a concession to a view with which I am normally impatient: the idea that the abandonment of fixed and predictable form brings us closer to the true voice of feeling. But then I have always found that free verse was as technically demanding as the most elaborate of metrical forms. Both require an equal balance of artifice and spontaneity.

BILL MANHIRE

On Originality

Poets, I want to follow them all,
out of the forest into the city
or out of the city into the forest.

The first one I throttle.
I remove his dagger
and tape it to my ankle in a shop doorway.
Then I step into the street
picking my nails.

I have a drink with a man
who loves young women.
Each line is a fresh corpse.

There is a girl with whom we make friends.
As he bends over her body
to remove the clothing
I slip the blade between his ribs.

Humming a melody, I take his gun.
I knot his scarf carelessly at my neck, and

I trail the next one into the country.
On the bank of a river I drill
a clean hole in his forehead.

Moved by poetry
I put his wallet in a plain envelope
and mail it to the widow.

I pocket his gun.
This is progress.
For instance, it is nearly dawn.

Now I slide a gun into the gun
and go out looking.

It is a difficult world.
Each word is another bruise.

This is my nest of weapons.
This is my lyrical foliage.

Loss of the Forest
Love is a fact
and black and blue is the skin
of water and sometimes milky white
and the fable always involves a boy with wings
who doesn't care for his biographer
and when the boy comes down to earth
the dogs all run to bite his body.
Here's what to do.
Get in the car and hurtle past the chooks.
Here's what to do. Head for the beach
and sit on the sand till all the people
leave the beach then make
as if to leave yourself. Ah well
at least climb well above the waves
and listen to the little darkness notes
which only sleeping birds outdistance.
Write a song about the wind
and send it to the one you love. The wind
is more important than the forest tra la
though the loss of the forest
would be terrible. Paste some clouds
above the map
and let the wind just puff them out to sea.
Let the ocean liner sail away!
Let them smash the plaster
off your leg with hammers!
And if the boy still yearns to float
then hobble home at once
and tie him to the flagpole
high above the water.

Zoetropes
A starting. Words which begin
with Z alarm the heart:
the eye cuts down at once

then drifts across the page
to other disappointments.

*

Zenana: the women's apartments
In Indian or Persian houses.
Zero is nought, nothing,

nil – the quiet starting point
of any scale of measurement.

*

The land itself is only
smoke at anchor, drifting above
Antarctica's white flower,

tied by a thin red line
(5000 miles) to Valparaiso.

London 29.4.81.

Hirohito
*I am like a canary whose cage has been
opened and someone says: 'Fly away!'
Where should I fly to? If I have a song
to sing, why should I waste it on places
where the wind may blow it away?*

To improve his eyesight
the young Hirohito gazes
at the horizon every day.

Birds and clouds: one day
he will be a living god.

•

In the playground
he always has to be leader;
the other kids
line up behind.

Already he knows
about physical fitness,
the importance of the will.

He likes insects, plants and butterflies.
He admires
the delicate protocols of Nature.

•

One day his father went mad:
he peered at his people
through the paper telescope
of his own speech.

Hirohito watched his father
being taken away
and thought of jellyfish.

•

At the age of 20
he travelled to Europe.

In London he sat for Augustus John.
He played golf
with the Prince of Wales.

In Paris his knowledge
of European military history
amazed the generals of France.

The happiest days of his life.

Hirohito went home,
ate eggs and bacon,
and dressed like a Western gentleman.

•

Then there was the war:
about which we know the truth
or do not know the truth,

in which Hirohito either played
the leading part
or he did not.

Perhaps he was
just a puppet of his warlords.

Or perhaps they lined up behind him
while he stared at the horizon

and the sun rose
and the sky filled with planes.

•

Hirohito knew everything
and nothing. 'Let the cry
be vengeance!' cried the allies.
'If you meet this man, don't hesitate.'

Hirohito hid inside the palace air-raid shelter,
a bank vault
with ten-metre thick
ferro-concrete walls.

•

When he announced the surrender
his ministers wept:
the god's voice
being broadcast on the radio.

At first no one could understand Hirohito.
He spoke a language of his own.

And for two days the nation wept –
long enough to let the Emperor's chamberlain
replace the bust of Napoleon
in his study

with one of Lincoln.

•

They say that when he met MacArthur
Hirohito bowed so low
that the handshake took place
high above his head.

So the Son of Heaven was a family man after all –
not in the least divine,
just a quiet marine biologist
able to sign the instruments of surrender.

I am writing my book about him,
A Modest History of the Wind,
but I am in difficulty:

chapter after chapter
is being blown away.

There he is: the warrior on a white horse –
blown away.

And there: the Shinto priest
planting rice seedlings
in the palace gardens.

Gone.

And look: there is Hirohito
winding his Mickey Mouse watch.
Tick-tock: the wind takes him.

Petals blown away –
as in a haiku,
as in a tanka.

•

In this final chapter, a funeral:
the powers of the world
have gathered in mourning.

Hirohito –
the 124th occupant
of the Chrysanthemum Throne.

Glancing idly at the news
I catch sight of him through snow,

a man with glasses
staring out of the screen
of my 14-inch Sanyo.

My Sunshine
He sings you are my sunshine
and the skies are grey, she tries
to make him happy, things
just turn out that way.

She'll never know
how much he loves her
and yet he loves her so much
he might lay down his old guitar
and walk her home, musician
singing with the voice alone.

Bill Manhire

Oh love is sweet and love is all, it's
evening and the purple shadows fall
about the baby and the toddler
on the bed. It's true he loves her
but he should have told her,
he should have, should have said.

Foolish evening, boy with a foolish head.
He sighs like a flower above his instrument
and his sticky fingers stick. He fumbles

a simple chord progression,
then stares at the neck.
He never seems to learn his lesson.

Here comes the rain. Oh if she were only
sweet sixteen and running from the room again,
and if he were a blackbird
he would whistle and sing
and he'd something
something something something.

Note

I feel quite warmly towards most of my poems, even the ones that now embarrass me. That's to say, on another day of the week I would probably pick a totally different set. These ones are in order of publication. 'On Originality' first appeared in *Islands* in 1973. Recently it caused a few problems when several versions of it appeared in a sort of 'education in schools' page which is syndicated around various New Zealand newspapers. (I had kept some early drafts, and the page's editor wanted to show students that poems don't always drop fully formed from the sky.) When I wrote the poem I was mildly pleased with the notion of the poet as street mugger – but several fundamentalist Christian groups in the Blenheim area missed the possibility of metaphor altogether and, taking deep offence at the recommended life style, started a letter writing campaign which moved the local paper to agonies of contrition. 'Loss of the Forest' was the title piece of a planned collaboration with the painter, Ralph Hotere. I haven't a clue what the poem is about now, which may well be why the project foundered. I like the chooks. 'Zoetropes' is a poem which most New Zealanders 'get' immediately, but which other readers find baffling. It takes its life from the fact that New Zealand vanishes if you leave it. All New Zealanders who travel know that small moment of inward twitching when you catch sight of a capital Z in the newspaper, and the subsequent disappointment when the word turns out to be Zaire or Zoo or Zoetrope. A little burst of hope replaced by an extended sense of loss – it's the Kiwi way. 'Hirohito' is a pretty long poem by my standards. It's full of equivocations, and they're those of the life the poem charts. It was actually a Pye Vidmatic on which I glimpsed Hirohito's funeral – but a Sanyo seemed a lot better for the general (and particular) finish of the poem. 'My Sunshine' is the title poem of the book I'm working on at the moment. It's about a young man who – in the current jargon – has been constructed by the discourse of romantic love, and who finally runs out of words, even the comforting noises of popular song. I was extremely pleased when the several somethings turned up at the end of the poem, but I realise now that I probably nicked them from Frank Kuppner. A successful piece of mugging, though; I'm sure he never felt a thing.

MICHAEL HASLAM

A Lubrick Loosed

It's like a sly evasive wit. It's like a shy reflection on a set of cellar steps. It's like saliva on the lips. It's like a highlight to the eye, it's like a lubrick or a trick. It twists the tongue into itself as it escapes.

    I should have loved to lure its source of likeness in to organise the making of a threnody for when it's gone. I could have thrilled to sense it shiver as it takes the bait. But as it spilled its reputation surreptitiously it left a trace, a blank, a tip, a bit of luck, it gave the slip.

    I read it once and swallowed my acceptance of the verdict and the sentence, to be taken down by hollow lingual alleys and be bound to serve a term of time in dispute and in disrespect, then to be smothered in expiry in the matrix muff in nothing minus happiness, and any skin thrown in the lake of dreary slime that's drying to a bed of crusted flakes.

    A shadow in the shedding light that slowly showed descending stone, I sniffed the fungal passage must effect arising from a dampening around the trap for soil and waste below the cellar steps. It must affect it to be dead, it should be buried. As obsequy, let it be said:

How lavish of its offices it offered silken thread, and yet how tacitly and well it kept the spell of secrecy alive within the cell, not letting any ghoul of imputation or the ghost of a suspicion ever touch or taint a hair – if it had any – of its silver head – but put a subtle finger to the lips, blinked as an imp, emitted squeaks, and with a crooked limb it shut its lid.

Ovidian Slips

Ovidian Slips
Ovidian Slips and Nothing More.
    I had come to the lips
of The Sibylline River. What
        Had I come to The Sibylline River for?

I had come to the pool out of tune as *foetid*,
quavering too loud, and stilted on my legs
I stood, a would-be one, immensely proud
but failing to admit that it's defeated
and in need of such a course
        or metamorphosis as this.

He's been the spitting image of his dissertation
How it is, the seminal identity must acquiesce
in its displacement if it dares to face and bears
the weight's repeated onslaughts, *On The State of Grace*.

But I had come here sickened privately within
my own insistent fiction, not to gain

publicity and risk disgrace. And breathing on
the glass I see how aqueous the essence
of a living is, and place these lips
upon the breast of this, and feel the hiss
of The Sibylline Source, and see how messed
the edges of my orders are. I seem to stay
for ages in a scented state, amused,
the lake has floral borders,
    while I'm shaken to the core.

The Unloosable *Pun on a Ford*
I've come to the river, I'm sounding the horn.
A mist-breath rises in the field of vision,
    glistening. The cry I heard:
high-pitched, self-desolating.

I might have known my goose was cooked.
I came this way before. Again this year
I have been cuckolded some more. I've had
my feelings badly torn, my feathers burnt,
and I've been pigeonholed in darkness
with bewildered doves.
    I don't think nothing's learnt.

Liquidity through shallow falls. But I was
    frightened at ignition of *The Flaming River.*
Barking Mad. I saw the shape it left
die back as quiet more like tidal falls
the tail between the legs, ashamed.
I came here to be shorn and sleeping wait
the horn, the comb and scissors of return.

Still Here? I dreamed I'd been stillborn
when I was woken by a goose arising
whole and giddy through the pool and gone
with flocks I might have known of like
    migrating souls.

The More Terrible Slips
I lie inside without control of my
wide-rolling eyes – I've seen me go
so clouded I obscured the skies.
But when this grace alights upon my face
I cry Goodbye to my Complicity, Goodbye
also Surprise: The Sword descends
to interrupt us, shredding instincts
into slivers in the grass. Am I
not satisfied? Time flies, the evening flocks.
It looks so late.

*A shriven forfeit as a rule may be
accepted if it's naked and alive.*
That could be my certificate and I'm
to have it framed before Her Grace and heard
in audience before the echo dies. Her Grace
is like the bitter taste of blankness in the eyes,
and I'm shown up as shaken but no wiser
for my faking lies. *Let Slip…*

The day she spiralled in the midges
    as a swallow dives across the clouded surface
set against: Let Slip The Knot, a craven nuisance
tries, trussed to a tree, to die, *subsumed with*
flaring in the cry and so accepted or rejected
as recurrence/no recurrence to the lips of fate

sets up together such a sort of dialectic as
the sexual spirit and a sleight of mind.

The Lucent School
The blush reversed, the blood was drained, a gulp at first
had helped me blank out what I'd done, and blank again
at why I'd come to school in tears without the terms
I had deliberately rehearsed.

*By the claw in the back of my neck I was seized
and fetched, I come to have this pressure eased, the claw
removed, the poison drawn, and for the blessing
to be drenched in one aspersion of the horn.*

With a goose, with a rush and a wild return
a fluency came fooling through the water-hole.
The shallow glitters sounds and shoals. A wispish soul
inclines to slip into the pool. Stripped to its lips
it calls a school of waving males and females,
ululating all its cry's display. *It's willing.*

The pool was fully solipsism, but so full
of others some of whom were sporting far
more nakedly than I who shades his eyes
to find in some particulars
    of ocular response *a love all over.*
With the splash of an unqualified explosion
and a shrilling larynx
    I had waded in.

Note
Thirty years ago I began to write of a mental space that opened just beyond my comprehension and control, that like a swimming-pool was occupied, by a poetic language, and which meshed with feeling sex, and – for example – living river places I had chanced on in my life.

    For many years I looked to Freudian works for explanation. But I came to sense that the pool itself were as though proposing another order of comprehension, that I could choose to go with – one proposing no conclusions, into which I interposed a querency I founded on myself. True life tales and often quite droll fictions intermingle in this area. I sweat repeatedly over the sense, but seem to have to let the sound flap fast or loose. I approach each page in various moods. They have to go through changes.

    A subject or a title for a poem, for me, is only a handle or a carrier-bag. Really there's only 'the pool'. I suppose I believe in something like coherent free and natural abstract narrative shapes, and to elicit these, I need some discipline. I choose a page to be the unit of my own, and imagine I co-operate with the source in the realms of number, aiming to have each page contain a version of shape.

My tonic or modal predominance inclines me to find cadence in romantic therapeutic comedy, strung with the hooks and bits of luck I hope of a romantic co-inherence that is, philosophically, joy. Grim realisms chasten me, but I'm content to claim no more than the fool's place of holiday or tea-break poet. I'd like to claim my levity has all the weight of gravity, but that line breaks down soon in hebephrenic giggle, unrestrained iambic, and slide of additional rhyme. But some folk find the outcome melancholy. Funny, I don't notice that.

The joy of poetry writing is the present working. These five are drawn this summer (1994) from stuff that dates from early days: the same but, on my principles, completely changed. *Ovid* is a recently conscious link and ascription. I'd found myself amused by a slogan I made, 'Not Lacan's Mirror, but Ovid's Pool'. What I mean is that while neither symbolic literalism nor some primordial pagan ritualism is original enough, the source is not blank but writhes with life. It ought to be possible for sophistication to help elucidate originality. I take Ovid's Pythagoreanism quite seriously. The comedy is that this source is never lost. Playing or working the fluid body of language, I fancy this my homage to the river spirit life.

MICHAEL VINCE

Goddess

The olive seems to root in the stone,
The hard wood twisting down; it is her tree:
Her bronze face shifts its colour as leaves turn.
    See how her robes in time have grown
So frail, they might seem dry enough to burn,
Such fragile metal, flaked and stained where she

    Lay centuries beneath the ground.
But now those swelling folds have met the light
Still blurred with mud which masks her attributes,
    And building-workers gather round
To gaze at her, and smoke, and scrape their boots.
The one whose spade first touched her knows it might

    Mean money, maybe a new dress
To soothe his wife. And so he makes his cross
To the All-Holy Virgin, and in case
    This dim archaic holiness
With its blotched staring corpse's face
Still holds a power of gain or loss

    He gives her equal reverence.
Later he comes home drunk and beyond care
Shouting a girl's name, with a bleeding hand,
    Then weeping and not making sense.
Unstirred, remote, his wife and mother stand
With neither blame nor pity in their stare.

Exchange of Population
Aegean 1922

An undemolished minaret leans on
At the edge of the village; I watch it pointing where
The mountain wind answers its call to prayer,
Its beckoning. The faithful have all gone,

Leaving their script which dedicates a fountain,
Carved thin by summer, with the Prophet's word,
A wasted trickle bright as a curved sword,
Till wrath descends in a wild squall of rain.

Below eastward imagine the mule-line,
The muted bundles, the old ones hobbling down

As westward comes the Bridegroom with his crown.
Dour men who graft the olive, prune the vine

Fade from the valleys where they don't belong
And mourn their losses in identical song.

The Crosses

There were some afternoons when wearing looks of warmth
She leaned over me, with a fringe grown long enough
To slant forward as her head bent, hiding her face.
My lips felt bruised and my jaws ached from kissing her.
In the gloom her dark shoulders slightly moved, and gleamed.
Beside the bed our clothes lay strewn across the floor.

That happened before the earthquake cracked our city.
The house still trembles slightly in the afternoon.
Evenings have grown cool. We drape the sheet above us
But then we shake it off. In sleep I dream I have
Wrapped us both in a warming and soothing blue sheet
But it wrinkles in the dream, and cracks appear in it.

Outside on every house is a green or red cross
Like a kiss put at the end of a child's letter.
Her mouth nuzzling at my cheek, she told me stories
About her doll, and the one about her rabbit
From the years before her father died. In the dusk
The rabbit savoured the freedom of the mown lawn.

So the closeness together of just a few days quickly
Becomes a story. The green cross means I can stay
And continue my life the way it was, before
The solid earth shook itself beneath the table.
If not, I dare not venture in, for what we had
Might open and widen until I fell right through.

Drive

A mountain spring shaded with plane trees
Where families stop to drink goes by,
And bare stones follow. The road winds down

Next to half a mile of open sky:
Over there hovers a bird of prey.
I stop to look, and in the stillness

Of great height begin to rest my mind
From that long impatience of driving.
Things that moved past me, fields, villages,

Now make up a reverse history
Of the world, from dead city outskirts
To this deep forest, they slow down and

Stop finally. Whatever drives us
From place to the next place confuses
Instinct and motive. I don't know why

I'll drive all day, but I know I will.
Just for now, though, there's the balancing
Hawk resting on a moment of thought,

As it wheels and enacts its hunger
Infinitely slowly, just watching
For tell-tale movements far below –

There's something there, but I can't quite see,
And next time I look it has vanished.
The road leads me, and so I follow.

As a Foreign Language
After a journey of some twenty days by ship and road
I have arrived in this noisy city, far richer than our own,
And walked its streets, which brim over with noxious crowds,
Wagons pressing everywhere and the chariots of the nobles
Thrusting unwary gazers into doorways or against walls.
It is all much as I expected from the written accounts.

Yesterday I met my host's family. Their Greek is bad
And their manners I am afraid somewhat barbaric
Compared to those of our own circle. They grin at me
And use expressions which contain obscenities, unaware
Of my proficiency in their Latin. It would not be hard
To excel the very best of them in composition

Or conversation. How they have come to dominate our polity
And buy us up bewilders me, although my employer suggested
Slyly over dinner that a perusal of our books on tactics
And on the deeds of noble men had helped. Somewhat, he said.
He allowed me to remain at my meal in a far corner of the hall
But sent me out when the sword-eater and fire-swallower came.

Study teaches us that life contains few blessings, but I,
Dear Philo, praise continually the beneficence of the gods,
And am especially grateful to them for the accident of my birth,
For thus it is that opening my lips I speak in the Hellenic tongue
That language of precision and the understanding of things,
And the very one which our neighbours and conquerors require

If they are to march in the footsteps of Philip's great son
Or voyage forth among the niceties of business and literary art.
What luck! to be thus provided with not unamusing employmer
With free travel, and with the company of growing boys.
The place drips with pilfered gold, but today I have stolen back
Half a morning for this letter and ten lines of my epic poem.

Note
Many of my poems reflect the fact that I spent a period of sixteen years living in Greece. Although I told myself when I went there that I would not write poems about mythology and the classical past, this proved to be unrealistic. I can only write about the things around me and I had to unravel a different landscape and history. The problem became one of writing in the wrong language, or for the wrong audience. I dislike the sense that a poem should be privileged just because it describes some foreign place, but that was just a fact of life I was stuck with. I have chosen these poems as somehow representative of my interests, both factually and formally.

'Goddess' reflects upon a statue discovered in Piraeus. The phrase 'All-Holy Virgin' is an attempt to translate the Greek 'Panagia'.

'Exchange of Population' was written before the war in the Balkans, but remembers previous ones. The 'Prophet' and the 'Bridegroom' are Mohammed and Christ.

'The Crosses' refers to the practice of marking houses after an earthquake. This poem may be part of a genre of seismic poems, one to which I have made other contributions.

'Drive' needs no explanation, but the landscape is that of southern Greece. It would not feel the same if read as Hertfordshire.

'As a Foreign Language' owes something of its tone to Cavafy. It of course concerns the hundreds of thousands of British people who teach their own language. As I belong to this profession, I would wish to give it some dignity by supposing such a historical perspective.

NORM SIBUM

Shakespeare in Verona
You birds –, you toughs with claws and beaks,
broken like me by the light at birth,
you skitter over the stones and the ground,
and peck and screech. In this way, I inflate my work.
To high and low, I gave my fooling.
Even as, through injury, I spoke my piece,
it was theatre to those who came for poetry.
I exacted revenge with beautiful poisons,
and now this age inspects the pollutions.
Still, at the end of the corso Cavour,
in the tiny square just off the street,
so forlorn a nook with the yellow leaves
a gardener swept into lonely piles, I sit.
Here's the stunted palm, the bedraggled cypress.
The Arch of the Gavi is baleful stone,
a desolate tooth in its gum of earth –,
and I, come to rest in the argument,
meet you Montagues and Capulets.
You tear at the litter along with the bees,
and you cross one another with your ancient weapons.
Here it is: hunger, bite, sting – old songs.
Over there, a waiter spreads open his newspaper,
backhands the thing into submission,
scans the opinions and skips to the sports,
his shadow debating the daily orders:
his progression through the vanities… to some year 2000,
and his cigarette sets fire to the obituaries.
If, elsewhere, dreamless hands caress

the museums of the word and flesh – here, a man jumps,
brushes his pants clear of offending ash,
miffed as any daredevil who's ruined a shirt.
Then, those Africans there –, they turn aside and snicker.
Uprooted, they drain their cans of Coke,
and a schoolgirl taunts her boy into testing his mettle.
Just so, Dante saw the lovers doing it,
then compressed into the kiss a downward spiral –,
and he buried the results in hell.
I shrug – like any ghostly instance of perjury would,
and between the palisades of shining teeth,
the girl sticks out her tongue,
and together, the lovers, lap to lap,
rub haunch to thigh, and grind the lazy hour into a jewel…
Pain pursues pleasure –, the chase inspiring music.
Save for critics, everyone sees through the trick.
The memory of a select few, if generous to all,
was too big an ardour to trust – to a mere critique.
So, I have been to the cathedrals to escape
the heat of committed minds, and I have said, 'Not yet',
and have stepped over the drifters on the stairs,
and have joined with the crowds in the streets,
and, with them, exchanged love's thin veneers.

They come just now to sit and converse.
They are assured like art once was –
the signora and the signora.
And they tuck their bottoms to a seat,
and, white-haired, lipsticked, powdered, they say,
'It's true', and 'Oh, how sad –',
investing so many acts with more rights and wrongs
than any actor, on his form, cares to remember.
The bells toll and the horns blare,
and with his worn stump of a cane,
the old sun taps against the newer goods…

Well, I tell you, you birds who hog your crumbs,
he who wrote John and gave Christ His soul –
when he thought: 'Sweet World of Worlds'
he meant: 'Even the Light has its Clamour'.
And the women knit, and with their eyes
they polish the molar – that Roman thing –
that announced a triumph long agonies before
the apostles blasted their entry into the void.
Put away this farce? No, it prospers –:
this town is so nearly lovely on its plain.
Birds mock birds, women snip flowers,
and lovers, by their kisses, wipe
egregious relevance from the word.
As for me, back through the arthritic autumn,
there's the pensione whose starved concierge
sucks the hearts from her chocolates,
irons the bedsheets, blinks at the TV.
A room, I suppose, with a crucifix
and a bulb of pitiful wattage…
And the review, of course.
I can imagine its suppressed fury –:
'Shakespeare, whom we brothers and sisters
expunge from the brotherhood and sisterhood of text,
performed, this day, as though on a whim.
It remains unclear if he will ever recover
his mandate, his immoderate achievement –,
but it is assumed that, if we relent,
and life returns to his gaudy complaints,
and he poisons us again with character,
he will liken his chamber of operations –
his skull – to a sleep of rouged walls,
and blush like a virgin for the sky
when it swings by to propagate the seasons
with the good, and with the evils that will finish the job.'
So you have it, you toughs with claws and beaks.

Note

At the time, I figured I had compelling reasons to write the poem. By chance, I'd read – in some journal or literary supplement – a critique that thought itself progressive. Like war, or so the thinking implied, Shakespeare is a repulsive habit. A mere glance at the work defiles what is, by now, the grand old impulse of recent decades: a level playing-field for the races and the sexes. Crazy times! Myself, I kept seeing venture-capitalism's blitzkrieg rolling across that hallowed ground. Fresh blood and opportunity, critics of the patriarchy in full collaboration… John Donne might have thought he had seen horrors. At any rate, what I'd read jabbered away like a self-elected war-tribunal. There was a lot of tongue-clucking in that piece.

Roughly at this time, a friend of mine was ill and would soon die of cancer. He taught literature at a college, and was, by all accounts, inspired. He had joined AA so as to 'clean up his act', and he quit writing his poems, some of which are worthy of anyone's attention. Quite simply, Shakespeare was his god. Many of his departmental colleagues were attempting to remove that god from its privileged status, and were succeeding. I believe firmly that my friend died of a broken heart. The cancer was a euphemism to describe his self-denial: that he'd sworn off booze, cigarettes, and women, and the muse, thinking the English Department a monastic retreat or a spa for those more spiritual than himself. They'd 'guilted him out', wagging their fingers, binding him to their false obligations. In my demented brain, some old god – colour him Dionysus, if you will – took his revenge on my friend's disloyalty.

In the meantime, I'd been to Italy again, and had visited Verona for the first time. I developed an affection for the town. It doesn't matter where one goes, so long as one does leave Vancouver on occasion – to remind oneself that the rest of the world doesn't gambol about idyllically, but with a profound sense of civic duty, under a pleasant-smelling bubble. The idea for the poem came to me there: in some tiny piazza off some corso, and I struggled with it for the next two years.

Even now, I read the piece, dismayed at its pretensions and weaknesses. Technical considerations aside, is it art or just another jerk-off exercise in propaganda? The silliest person in the sorts of quarrels that had bedevilled the last year of my friend's life was myself. I didn't truly understand what I realize now. Great literature is the property of no-one. Morality squads can't disembowel it. And if they go about engineering values in the minds of the impressionable, so what? Sloganeering isn't serious thought, anyway, for all the damage caused. I was only whining about my obscure place in the world, forgetting that poetry has little to do with mass consumption. It simply leaps from one heart to another, and its only value lies there – in that passage.

So I drank a lot of wine in Verona, conceived the poem – for better or worse. At this point in time, I can only hope that my friend, however dispersed his atoms are, approves of it.

ROBERT WELLS

The Iran-Iraq War
The roadside soft with dust, the threadbare hills,
The teahouse with its incongruous velvet couch,
The felt-capped boy stopping with his goats to stare:
Dusk drew these together in a frail coherence
As the moon rose, strengthening through deep-blue air.

In that dry numinous light, it seemed, the country
Lay changelessly far off, and the childish face
Unreachably open between domed cap and coat.
I count the years now to reckon the herdboy's age,
And guess the sequel. No village was too remote.

The Fawn
Starting, clumsy and graceful,
From the clumps of bracken at my feet

A fawn tumbles downhill –
Then gathers itself away into the thicket.

After the Fire
Stunting shade,
The leaning back towards light;

The wind's shape in the coomb, bending
The tops of larches over, so that they lie
Along the bank of its current
Like sand at a stream's edge;

A hard winter, a burgeoning summer,
A storm, a snowfall –
The evidence in cut wood-rings, in torn-off boughs;

A sycamore trunk stripped of its bark by squirrels,
The shredded patch
Where a stag rubbed its itching antlers in spring;

A main-shoot bitten short;

Also like sand the fluted pattern,
Graceful and smooth,
Where for years one branch has blown against another:

Small disparatenesses, the thousand accidents,
All gone to ash.

Six Emblems

(1) 'From the felled trunk…'
From the felled trunk the bark
Has rotted away, its wood
Worn into a fibred relief;

Grey-white the scars where branches
Splintered, shrunken the bracken
Which covered it in spring;

Years since the severed life
Died out. What life it has now
Is from the winter sun.

(2) 'The sea's blue at dusk…'
The sea's blue at dusk, tiled with waves,
Glazed by the mist,
Deepens.

Across it from the steep-edged coomb
A beech-trunk lifts,
Pale in the drying wind.

(3) 'Sun opening the coomb…''
Sun opening the coomb
In the morning
Moves down the side and curves out anew
The gentle incline of its lap,

Like a human goodwill
Illuminating the mind
That dwelt winterlong in shade
As though the shade were life,

And reaches
With a sense of warm discovery
Over budded trees,
Bent bracken, brittle leaf.

(4) 'The sapwood rots…'
The sapwood rots;
But where they lie embedded

The hard little cores of broken twigs
Stay sharp.

(5) 'Day overcast…'
Day overcast:
A patch of intenser brightness

Folds itself away amid the atmosphere,
Shedding light on the sea –

*

Clarity that, unable to attain
Full sway,

(Some flaw of will preventing it,
Some loss of heart)

Withdraws, prefers to fade,
Leaving only its shadow in the mind.

(6) 'Spermatazoa of flame…'
Spermatazoa of flame
Seed the dark, curling
Long momentary tails.

The fire flares at ease –
Could not burn harder
Or be more sheerly itself.

Bather and Horseshoe

1

Spring weather; days of alternate storm and sun.
Pausing at the bridge, he looks aside to where

The torrent spills from a concrete breakwater
To flood a hollow scooped in the bed below;

And sees – emblem of a pristine completeness –
A bather standing among the willow scrub,

Gentle and exact, feet curded with the dust,
Letting air dry him; who turns, then turns away.

2

Burst walls, rough fields, the dilapidated path:
Among loose stones the fragment of a horseshoe

Scraped thin and bright at the edge, one rusted nail
Adhering still. Picking it up, he studies

The fine pattern of scratches on its surface
As if some meaning which he could not construe

Were to be found engraved in the worn metal;
And thinks again of the figure by the pool.

Note

I've chosen five uncollected poems, partly for their variety of shape and partly because they are all about moments which, however slight, nagged at me until I could find a way of doing justice to them.

'The Fawn' pleases me as the equivalent of the moment it describes, hardly there and yet there, like the creature tumbling out of cover and disappearing – no less itself for my finding in it an emblem which is aesthetic and erotic in suggestion. Poetry means for me the righting of disturbance, the harmonizing of irregularity, and I read this too in the fawn's return to invisibility and quiet.

'After the Fire' is also about a disappearance. The idea is the youthful one that a life lived wholly in the senses, given over to the external world, can act as a fire in which one's own faults, hurts and limitations are burnt up. When writing it I thought of George Herbert's proverb 'A crooked log makes a straight fire'. But the poem is about a real bonfire first of all, and the same is true of the subjects of 'Six Emblems' – images of physical and mental process which are clear and yet partially hold back their meaning. (Emblems should have illustrations. Is there an artist willing to provide these?)

When I first tried, and failed, to write 'Bather and Horseshoe' it seemed to me that the bather represented a wholeness of life from which the observer was shut out, the horseshoe-fragment the sign of his exclusion. Now, long afterwards, the horseshoe suggests to me an exclusion of a different kind, from one's own past, as the self changes and one is left holding on to moments and incidents whose significance has been outgrown and lost, or almost lost. A detail of the poem which pleases me is that I use 'dilapidated' in its most literal sense (the path having been roughly paved and the stones now scattered).

The subject of 'The Iran-Iraq War' is a memory which is only given its meaning by subsequent events. For once in this poem I touch directly on contemporary history, and our ignorance and sheer fragility in the face of it. An unstated confusion counterpoints the clarity of the remembered scene. The lack of overtly contemporary reference in my poetry might be perceived as an evasion. My answer to this would be, at least in part, as in the poem's last line, 'No village is too remote'.

('The Iran-Iraq War' first appeared in *A Few Friends*, Stonyground Press 1989, and *The Poetry Book Society Anthology*, Hutchinson 1990; 'Bather and Horseshoe' in *La Fontana*, March 1994.)

NEIL POWELL

Afternoon Dawn
for Rod Shand

They are felling the dead elms
to the west: the sidelong sun
surprises the room after
a hundred years of shadow.
The forgotten web and dust
on untouched books are sunstruck.
Clearly, something has begun.

Things that had been unspecial
are transmogrified, reborn
to *duende* and charisma.
Sun settles on faded spines;
crystals through a decanter;
chases spiders in this, its
perversely afternoon dawn;

lights upon Márquez: *through the
window they saw a light rain
of tiny yellow flowers
falling.* Through the window I
see a blue haze of woodsmoke
spiralling towards evening,
hovering, rising again.

The room begins to darken;
now, blood-coloured light splashes
across the page where the pen
labours towards conclusion.
An end to the beginning,
the web once more unnoticed;
the elms will soon be ashes.

The Way Back

Amber streetlamps punctuate the night.
Their deviously analytic glare
Reveals a world created by the light:
Not what there is but what it shows is there.

A place without surroundings: linear edge
Usurps the processes of definition
From meadowland and forest, field and hedge.
Suburban night knows only this condition,

The emptied moon's apologetic husk
Outshone by haloed sodium overhead:
Always between, always this waking dusk.
Sleep, silence, darkness: absolutes are dead.

Beyond the outskirts to the motorway:
Dark claims its spaces, but the eye moves on
Towards another imitation day –
A town or roundabout on the horizon –

Until 'The North' proclaims giant sign,
As if the north were somewhere you could reach
By following a disembodied line
Which joins nowhere to nowhere, each to each,

And work to home. Or will it merely end
In featureless space, an orange void stretching
On each side of the road, round the next bend,
With distant amber lamps, the planets, gleaming?

The Bridge

One stands above an upstream cutwater,
Rod angled aimlessly towards the land,
Safe in his niche; while on the other side
His friend leans on the opposite pilaster,
Arms braced against the stone and legs astride
As if to clasp the bridge with either hand.

There are no fish. The first knows this and smiles:
It is enough to be a part of air
And sun and stone and water, bridging them.
His line into the river runs for miles,
Transfigured from the rod's initial stem
Into the web of currents everywhere.

His friend feels none of that. He stares downstream
Where sunlight catches an abandoned tyre
And glances back in glossy insolence,
Hardened into a rigid silver gleam.
The clasp upon the parapet grows more tense.
Sweat chills his neck. The stonework is on fire.

Between the bridge's piers the river brings
Its casual luggage and its fluent art
Past those whom it will neither curse nor bless:
One is detached because a part of things,
The other restless in his separateness.
The bridge which bears them carries them apart.

The Stones on Thorpeness Beach
for Guy Gladwell

O luminosity of chance!
Light spins among the spider-plants
As sand or amber glow seeps through
Tall windows of a studio,
While on the beach in random rows
The enigmatic stones compose
A silent staveless variation,
The music of regeneration.

Re-learn astonishment, and see
Where splinters of eternity
Still glitter at the water's edge,
Beyond the tideline's daily dredge
Of flotsam: plants and creatures who'd
Survive this stale decaying world,
And stones worn smooth as solid tears,
Each crafted by a million years.

Or dusky rain across the sea,
Dull pewter light, when suddenly
The level sun breaks through, makes clear
Another perfect hemisphere:
Its rainbow-self, supported by
A dark horizon, arcs the sky.
I watch the colours falter and,
Slipping on shingle, fall on sand.

Yet, high above the crumbling cliff,
A concrete pill-box stands as if
In crazy gesture of defence;
As if the huge indifference
Of change, decay, might somehow be
Perturbed by such small dignity
Which slowly shifts and cracks, and so
Will shatter on the stones below.

Search for a sound hypothesis:
'Safe as houses', 'Bank on this',
Dead clichés of security!
Houses? Bank? You'd better tie
Mementoes in a plastic bag,
Chuck in the sea, mark with a flag
The spot where fish or merman may,
With luck, remember you some day.

Our rented time is running out,
But unlike tide won't turn about
With regular and prompt dispatch
To land upon the beach fresh catch,
As gradually, with gathering pace,
Life ebbs out from the human race
Inhabiting a world grown ill.
Time for a benediction still:

Neil Powell

Peace to the gulls and guillemots,
To curlews and their bleak mudflats,
To sea-birds, sea-anemones,
To marsh-plants, meadow-butterflies,
To lavender and gorse and mallows,
To creatures of the depths and shallows;
Peace to the vast blue out-of-reach,
Peace to the stones on Thorpeness Beach.

Hundred River

We came to Hundred River through a slow October,
   when earth is scented with everybody's past;
when late scabbed blackberries harden into devil's scars,
   untasted apples rot to bitter toffee.

Across reed-beds a track of blackened railway-sleepers,
   a plank-bridge lapped by barely-stirring water;
swans gargling silently in their fine indifference;
   above, a sky of urgent discursive geese.

Now the year has turned again and I am alone here,
   where willow-herb's dry white whiskers drift over
the brick-red spikes of sorrel and the gossiping reeds;
   and the river sullen, muddied after rain.

No movement in the woods but stealthy growth of fungus,
   hesitant leaf-drop, distant scuttle of deer:
in one marbled, stained oak-leaf I sense gigantic change,
   and in the drizzle feel the season fracture.

Note

Choosing *five* poems turns out to be trickier than choosing one or twenty: it's between the single bloom and the whole vaseful, neither a solitary example nor a representative selection. In the end, I clung to the rubric's invitation to choose poems which 'offer the clearest introduction to your work': that seemed to exclude more wayward or eccentric pieces which I'd want my ideal reader to encounter within the context of – for instance – these five. For the same reason, I looked for poems which I knew other people had liked: ones which had been remembered or mentioned to me or had gone down well at readings. I decided firmly against taking chunks from extended poems or sequences. Even so, the short list was still a longish list, and after that a kind of impatient pragmatism took over.

   'Afternoon Dawn' is about coming home one day in the first summer of Dutch Elm Disease to find that the trees across the road from my previously shadowed house were being felled; it was published in *PNR* 1. The night drive in 'The Way Back' is north up the A1: I think that roundabout is near Biggleswade. Some readers kindly assume 'The Bridge' to be an allegory contrasting the Apollonian with the Dionysian; I was certainly exploring that sort of symbolism, as the punning paradoxes of the final lines suggest, though the poem's simple origin was a pair of utterly uncommunicating fishermen, obviously friends, standing on opposite sides of a river-bridge over the Ouse. 'The Stones on Thorpeness Beach' takes as its starting-point a painting by Guy Gladwell, described in the opening lines; the echoes of Lowell and, beyond him, Marvell, are intended. Finally, 'Hundred River' is an oblique elegy, about a walk in Suffolk with Adam Johnson and about revisiting the same place after his death in 1993.

   The first and second poems were included in *At the Edge* (Carcanet, 1977), the third in *A Season of Calm Weather* (Carcanet, 1982); all three are reprinted in *True Colours: New and Selected Poems* (Carcanet, 1991). The fourth and fifth poems are from *The Stones on Thorpeness Beach* (Carcanet, 1994).

DENISE RILEY

Poem Beginning with a Line from Proverbs

As iron sharpens iron
I sharpen the face of my friend
so hard he sings out
in high delicate notes.

A struggle for mastery to most speak
powerful beauty would run any
attention or kindness clean out
of town in angry rags.

Ringed by darkness the heart pulsates.
And power comes in like lightning.
A lion in the room, fair and flowing
twists with unsparing eyes.

Whitely the glance runs
to it and away. But let it
talk its golden talk if we
don't understand it.

Grabbed by remote music
I'm frightening myself. Speak
steadily as is needed to
stare down beauty. That calms it.

Well All Right

Above, a flurry of swans, brothers, great wings airy
around my bowed head in rushing darkness, neatly
these bone fingers plaited their green cloaks each night
to unfeather them so now they stand upright before me
freed and gaily they leap to their caparisoned horses as
in my breathing cell I smooth down my own cloak of
nettles – but Grimm sweetie mediaeval griseldas, right
out on the night plains are no tiny lights of huddlement
but only the impersonal stars in blackness and the long
long winds. What you see is what you see: it's never
what you won't. Well all right things happened it would
be pleasanter not to recall, as a deeply embarrassed dog
looks studiedly at a sofa for just anything to do instead,
so determine to assume events silently with no fuss –
who doesn't try to – yes that is a dart in my neck and
doesn't it look a bit biedermeier – so take up that thud
of attack dropped out of a righteously wide-open beak
sailing slowly across its own high sky which you'd not
registered as contempt straight out to kill – far rather

than know that, wear it as an owned cloak's blazing
fabric stuck in the fine flesh of your shoulders like any
natural skin burning; so cloaked, no-one sees through
to you wrapped in darkness, only a darkness pressed to
outward navy twill – no queen of the night's gorgeous
winking suit, just suave cheap unexceptional off any
rack – want to slip out of it? but flesh has soaked to join
its fiery choric costume. Break out in flames. Leap to
the crests of orange birds flickering along the long line
of shoulders, hiss, warble in gaping whistles hoarse lyre
chants of plumed and swollen throats whose glowing trills
waver and zigzag the swayed neck heavy under the flare
song of any body glittering with hard memory. Let fall
this garment with its noisy wings. Slide from me now –
and let's just run something red and stinging rapidly down
the page, shall we, let's try an echt gloss speed placing
let's stand back in triumph dripping brushes, shall we
see what can be made out of this lot my lot, its lovely
trailed gash wet as a frock in a pool, what it's for is for
defence, it will keep your beautiful soul glazed as a
skein of floating hill mist and as quietly as slightly
and as palely lit – at risk of frank indifference it may
make beauty to sleep and, or, to sleep with. Who sang
'you don't have to die before you live' – well who.

Lure, 1963

Navy near-black cut in with lemon, fruity bright lime green.
I roam around around around around acidic yellows, globe
oranges burning, slashed cream, huge scarlet flowing
anemones, barbaric pink singing, radiant weeping When
will I be loved? Flood, drag to papery long brushes
of deep violet, that's where it is, indigo, oh no, it's in
his kiss. Lime brilliance. Obsessive song. Ink tongues.
Black cascades trail and spatter darkly orange pools
toward washed lakes, whose welling rose and milk
beribboned pillars melt and sag, I'm just a crimson
kid that you won't date. Pear glow boys. Clean red.
Fluent grey green, pine, broad stinging blue rough
strips to make this floating space a burning place of
whitest shores, a wave out on the ocean could never
move that way, flower, swell, don't ever make her blue.
Oh yes I'm the great pretender. Red lays a stripe of darkest
green on dark. My need is such I pretend too much, I'm
wearing. And you're not listening to a word I say.

Dark Looks

Who anyone is or I am is nothing to the work. The writer
properly should be the last person that the reader or the listener need think about
yet the poet with her signature stands up trembling, grateful, mortally embarrassed
and especially embarrassing to herself, patting her hair and twittering If, if only
I need not have a physical appearance! To be sheer air, and mousseline!
and as she frets the minute wars scorch on through paranoias of the unreviewed
herded against a cold that drives us in together – then pat me more, Coventry
to fall from anglo-catholic clouds of drifting *we's* high tones of feeling down
to microscopic horror scans of tiny shiny surfaces rammed up against the nose
cascading on Niagara, bobbed and jostled, racing rusted cans of Joseph Cotten reels
charmed with his decent gleam: once *we* as incense-shrouded ectoplasm gets blown
fresh drenched and scattered units pull on gloss coats to preen in their own polymer:
still it's not right to flare and quiver at some fictive 'worldly boredom of the young'
through middle-aged hormonal pride of *Madame, one must bleed, it's necessary…*
Mop mop georgette. The only point of holding up my blood is if you'd think So what?
We've all got some of that: since then you'd each feel better; less apart. – Hardly:
it's more for me to know that *I* have got some, like a textbook sexual anxiety
while the social-worker poet in me would like her revenge for having been born and left.
What forces the lyric person to put itself on trial though it must stay rigorously uninteresting?
does it count on its dullness to seem human and strongly lovable; a veil for the monomania
which likes to feel itself helpless and touching at times? or else it backs off to get sassy
since arch isn't far from desperate: So take me or leave me. No, wait, I didn't mean leave
me, wait, just *don't* – or don't flick and skim to the foot of a page and then get up to go –

Denise Riley

Milk Ink
Don't read this as white ink flow, pressed out
Of retractable nipples. No,
Black as his is mine.

Rain-streaked glass, burnt orange cherry leaves, eye drape of sugar pink.
Don't pin me to frou-frou accident
But let me skate – that

This ganglion cluster should have been born with better eyes
More glowingly deer-like – then instead of being horrified might not
One lift its banging head up off the ground and stroke its streaming hair
And, and, and, and never go away.

Don't read his as white ink flow, shot out
Of retractable. No,
Black as this is mine.

Problems of Horror
Boys play and a horse moves through the woods.
Through perfectly heat-sealed lyric, how to breathe?
He has tailored a cadence out of disgust, and spins to see its hang on him;
privately faint at heart he pirouettes, sporting a lapel nausea carnation.
Who shakes her locks, seaweed hissed branching to blood coral
flirty alright, sat under the painterly sky in this flapping landscape.
China blue swollen in a race of high cloud, full woods, blowing fields,
snatched gill smoke, rain slap of running wind.
Stone looks speak *freeze*.
Not, Call the sold earth hyacinthine 'to get the measure of the damaged world'.
The new barbarian's charmed sick
with his real sincerity, sluiced in town georgics fluency, solitude skills.
He knows this smooth emulsion is truly-felt revulsion.
He does not mean to be so pure an isolate, his elegance worries him:
Is beauty good, if it's a furious gloss body of disgust, not porous
and not more of a pitted beauty, penetrable, moody?
But Horror gleams 'we're all complicit, all to blame for cruelty' holding aloft
its fine-tuned shock; naming it *political*, sighing *see me, stay for ever*.

Note
'Poem beginning with a line from Proverbs': An instant of violent feeling, which produced, through the tension of its suspension and displacement to a struggle for clear speech, the hallucination of a bright animal in the room.

'Well all right': One out of a clutch of four poems, *Four Falling*, composed to be contained in the depth of my word-processor screen, with the hope that they'd tumble down the page in a thickly-stranded rope. There's a lot of Attitude being struck in here, which I don't much care for; but it's to drive the poem to get up enough miles-per-hour to rush on to an edge.

'Lure, 1963': Sherbet spiked with cheerful envy. Pure colour and pure musicality or cadence are ideals towards which the poem – non-gallery-dependent, non-performance-dependent, and democratically (we implausibly hope) circulated – longs, like the Sunflower youth, to aspire. But the poem is rooted on silent paper, in inglorious black and white. This piece intercuts colour notes, jotted down in front of early paintings by Gillian Ayres and John Hoyland, with phrases from song lyrics contemporary with that brilliantly-floating abstract moment. Their as-it-were unsung lyrics get credited. There isn't anything 'of me' in this, except for its collage work. But of course that could mark the stronger egoistic presence.

'Dark Looks': One of several which worry about the stance of the contemporary poet. However ardently you try to avoid self-presentation, however bitterly you suspect all forms of self-description, perhaps this valley of the shadow you must go through, and you may or may not reflect aloud on it as you whip along. The middle of this poem is clotted. The whole thing fails if it can't work reasonably well *without* these references being picked up; but it has warring 'modernisms' starring as in the movie *Niagara*, in which Marilyn Monroe and Cotten were wrapped against its spray in plastic macs. A line of Jeanne Moreau's from *Les Valseuses* leads straight into meditations about self-presentation in poetry as an aggressive appeal for love made through a terror of being left, even on the page.

'Milk Ink': A squib against the body-readings, however kindly meant, which plague poets who are women. As only women have a sex, so only women poets attract body-reviews. This isn't anyone's fault, and will change (though the poem emphasises that it doesn't want sexual democracy here).

'Problems of Horror': Pegasus and the Medusa, as in

Claude's seashore painting, walk through this, but recognising them shouldn't be crucial to the lyric. Its anxiety is that risk of reacting to damage by petrification, paralysed horror which can get stuck as an aesthetic response – producing a stance of poetic disgust which understands itself to be immediately 'political'. But the poem stresses the sincerity as well as the hazards of this approach, and knows that it offers no superior answer.

GREVEL LINDOP

Recumbent Buddha at Polonnaruwa
A grain like marbling or like watered silk
flows without movement through the sleeping face:
rock-ripples tinged with rose and ash and milk,
known tastes of being, calmed, finding their place.

It is as though the rock itself had slept
to dream this shape, the eyelid's curve, the lip
smoother than any natural form except
maybe the moon's rim or a water-drop;

or as if we had sought a word to speak
out of our nature, suffering, changeable,
empty, and found at last simply this cheek
relaxing on clasped hands, and this half-smile

that flowers from more than a child's unblemished seeing
or a god's detachment. Massive, lightly creased,
the carved silk pillows a wholly human being
whose last breath has perhaps this moment ceased.

The Welsh Poppy
Forgotten desires fulfilled
   are the best kind:
her yellow silks uncrumpled
   by the wind

out of their furred green case
   the Welsh poppy now
unplanned, unasked, displays –
   and unrelated to how

some years I scattered seed
   in a different bed,
dug in roots, scrutinized,
   but nothing happened.

Over starry leaves
   green springs unfurl
from weedlike beginnings
   in unpromising soil.

Perhaps there's hope:
   it may be, happiness –
once you have given up
   hope – will come like this.

Summer Pudding
for Carole Reeves

Begin with half a pound of raspberries
picked from the deep end of your sloping garden, where the birds
   play hopscotch in the draggled fruitnets; add
a quarter of redcurrants; gently seethe in orange juice
   for six or seven minutes with some sugar,
giving the pan a ritual shake from time to time, inducing
   a marriage of those fine, compatible
tastes; and leave to cool. An open kitchen door invites
   whatever breeze will help itself to flavour,
attenuating it downhill across your neighbours' gardens
   (be generous!) so summer will surprise them,
an unidentifiable recalled fulfilment haunting
   the giant bellflower and the scarlet runners.
Now introduce your strawberries, sliced to let the pallid heartsflesh
   transfuse its juice into the mass, transmute
cooled fruit to liquid crystal while you line your bowl with bread
   and add the mixture – keeping back some juice –
lid it with bread, cover and weight it, chill it if you like
   (as if the winter took a hand) and hoard it,
opus magnum ripening its secret, edible,
   inviolable time. And when you dare
slide your knife round its socket to uncling – a sudden suck –
   this gelid Silbury mined with the wealth
of archetypal summer, let it be on one of three
   occasions: for a kitchenful of children
whose mouths grow purpleringed and flecked with whipped cream as they dig
   and lose, entranced, the treasure of the minute;
or for the friends around your polished table, when that soft
   lake of mahogany reflects the faces
melting in candlelight and burgundy, rivers of talk
   eddying to a stillness lost in taste
primitive as a language, clear as thought; or for whoever
   will join you in your garden when the sun
carries out summer to the edge of dark, and stay to eat
   there in the early chill as twilight gels
and owlhoots quiver from the gulf of darkness, where a floodlit
   cathedral floats under your eyes, and still
(wreckage of smeared plates and clotted spoons piling the table)
   after the lights are killed and the cathedral
vanishes like a switchedoff hologram, remain to plot
   the moon's progress across the brimming air
scaled by the nightscented stocks, or with binoculars
   arrest the Brownian movement of the stars.

Grevel Lindop

Russet Apples

Lie back against the pillows:
and again, as if for the first time,
I give you a russet apple.

In our country the custom
is love first, and then apples:
a ritual celebration
of our unhoped-for return
after aeons of wandering where
there was nobody, or the next best thing –

some lover who didn't care
enough to let it be right;
some man who wouldn't trust,
some woman who didn't dare;
where always she was hiding a hate,
or he had to fondle an image
to help him get it on.

Now we've passed the gate,
the land is ours again
and the apple's into the secret;
feel how it loves us as you bite
and the juice comes, cider-sweet,
leaf-sour, and the rusty bronze skin
gleams wet in candle-light,

and feel when I kiss you how
within the mouth's dark space
there is no I or you
but only a fragrance of endless
orchards that waited here, always
ripening, longing to welcome us
back into paradise.

Note

I find it impossible to offer comment on my own poems. They must speak for themselves. If they are enjoyed by particular readers, well and good; if not, no amount of explanation or justification will improve them.

from **Trojan Voices**

Burned out with the light of a sum total
amounting at last to zero, I was left
to feel my way with this framework of bones
and a fed skin through the animal world of touch,
knowing collusion of cup with lip, identity
of hand with woven cloth or hair, an ancient kingdom
I had never acknowledged and which seemed
sufficient, the body collaborating,
to follow its own strange laws for ever.

Nothing to do with me either the memories
that spread, clouded and fined above the dry unquestionable
calyx of here and now, a great immaterial spun
seedhead puffing itself as if I were growing
a second mind. Were others like this, was it
a tumour, an infection of being? At last,
to clear my head, I began. I must have cried
but every tear was a word; it was beyond me
or my hearers and I gave in. There seemed
no end to what I knew, but that the knowing
wasn't mine.
    Already our language is scattered
like groundsel fluff on the wind, catching at thresholds,
housecorners, unweeded verges. I am singing it
in its own voice and know we are saying goodbye.
If here is a purpose I do not understand it,
or if there are gods or what is poetry.

But the hearers are loud again, they are calling
out of their hunger I can feed but not satisfy
for more than a moment. The back of the skull
opens. I turn with this blind mask
towards them. They want me
to tell them what they have seen.
Until I speak, they cannot believe their eyes.

VICKI RAYMOND

The Legend of Julian

Various saints have been depicted with stags; notably, Eustace, who is shown confronting a stag which bears a crucifix between its antlers. When the stag bears no crucifix, the saint is Julian the Hospitaller, patron of innkeepers, boatmen, and travellers.

I

The hunter, in blackness, burning like a brand,
pierces the forest brain, and bursts at last
into a clear space of sunlight. From his hand
drops the slack rein. The hounds begin to cast
about for the scent of fear, while, in plain sight,
a few feet off, the hart of ten stands fast.
The air vibrates with summer, but the night
of woven branches silences the birds
even within this circle of green light.

The hart, indifferent, drops the oval turds
of St John's Eve, and Julian's horse takes fright.
Then from the hart to Julian flow words
like these: *That man who hunts me here today,
in time to come, shall father and mother slay.*

II

So Julian leaves his father's house, for fear
of a murderer's fate, and goes to a far land
beyond the forest. There he serves his lord
so well in war, that, in the space of a year,
he's given, not only a knighthood, but the hand
of a rich widow. Now his shield and sword
sleep in a time of peace, and middle-life
steals on him softly while he is still young.
In daily tasks the seasons slip away:
his thoughts are all for vineyards, fields, and wife,
except when he hears songs of hunting sung
in the great hall; or, on a summer's day,
when the horn blows a meet below the walls,
or else a prise in the far forest calls.

III
Bathed in beasts' blood, he feels his life renewed.
It's been a day of strategy and deeds,
to which, inevitably, now succeeds
a species of postcoital lassitude.
He will dispel this languor if he can;
and, suddenly, desire shoots up afresh
to print himself in blood on his wife's flesh,
and make her know the meaning of a man.
In darkness Julian ascends the stair,
in darkness tries the door of his wife's room.
A shaft of moonlight penetrates the gloom:
he sees the bed, he sees a loving pair
of shapes entwined, breathing each other's breath.
He falls on them, and fills the night with death.

IV
Returning from church, the wife of Julian sees
a strange sight in the road: a man, half-dressed,
covered with blood, who, falling on his knees
before her, starts to rave and beat his breast.
The wife of Julian (I'll call her Ann)
has heard of such wild creatures from the wood.
She tells her servants to restrain the man,
to bathe him in the stream and give him food.
But, *Madam, look! His ring!* her maid exclaims,
Lord Julian's signet ring! And Ann gives way
to loud despair. No need to say the names
of the two visitors, who, yesterday,
came unannounced, and whom she billeted,
as custom demanded, in the softest bed.

V
Another journey Julian must bide,
though broken up and ground as fine as meal.
This time he's not alone. Ann, by his side,
supplies his female soul, and keeps him real.
Sometimes she thinks *He would have murdered me*,
and wonders whose he thought that second head.
Then she remembers the hart's prophecy,
the twisted paths all leading to that bed,
and folds her sleeping husband in her arms.
They lie in the open, among stooks of hay;
they beg their food at hovels and lonely farms;
at wayside shrines they bow themselves to pray;
but still the forest draws them further in,
to the place where the new story must begin.

VI
The river stretches grey into the north:
the furthest side is just a smudge of brown.
On the grey river, a speck moves back and forth
all day, as farmers for the market town,
pilgrims for Rome, and heretics for hell,
call out the ferryman with his boat that leaks.
The ferryman and his wife keep the hostel
for needy travellers, whom they lodge for weeks
and never charge. Thus, Julian and Ann,
reborn by water in the wilderness,
warm in their beds the leper, the outcast man,
the demon-led. But Julian, no less
afflicted than these, continues still to wear,
under his clothes, the penitent's shirt of hair.

VII
A night of blizzard. Julian hears a shout
from the river, takes a brand, and hurries out
to search the reeds. He finds a frozen form,
and lifts it in his arms. *Why, now I'm warm,*
the hoarse voice whispers, *Carry me inside.*
And Julian brings the leper like a bride
over the threshold. Ann's asleep; the inn
is full of pilgrims. Nowhere but within
Julian's own bed to comfort the outcast:
he lays him there, gets in, and holds him fast.
That night he dreams: the leper, clothed in glory,
stands before God, and tells Him Julian's story.
The word *Forgiven* is the last thing said;
and Julian wakes, and finds the leper dead.

VIII
That forest spreading over half the earth
is almost gone, and no one marks the year
by different sorts of droppings from the deer;
our rivers have more to do with death than birth.
Still, Julian, exile, murderer and host,
your story grows in us, and sends down roots
into dark places; likewise, your green shoots
break on the branches when we weep the most.
And Ann, though no one made a saint of you,
it was no little thing you did to save
that furious soul; and, when that soul withdrew,
to lay your Julian in his forest grave.
A wandering friar, perhaps, performed the same
for you, but your cross inscribed no name.

Ardent Spirits
William McCoy, able seaman and mutineer from H.M.S. Bounty, was the first man to distil spirits on Pitcairn Island, using the roots of ti trees. The first bottle was made on 20 April 1797. The following year, McCoy, in an alcoholic delirium, tied stones around his neck and threw himself over a cliff.

I
Bad luck comes smiling,
death's head atop
a cloak of feathers.

I see her pictured
in dark water,
wavering. At night

her breasts fill my hands,
sea-smooth and cold,
hardening to stone

when sunlight strikes them.
With such ballast
I run with the wind.

II
Some say he[1] escaped
to England,
and I dreamed or lied

the day I found him
in his blood.
I hid in the hills.

III
The woman was short,
stout, and flat-faced,
but clean and sound.

Her breath was sweeter
than any drab's;
her temper, sharp

as an Ayrshire wife's.
I gave her rum
and tobacco,

and my fists and feet.
The brats she bore
will rule this land.

IV
Waves of the calm
loll about,
waiting their chance.

They are all tongues,
and can tell
death by its taste.

V
The creak of boughs
in the wind
got into my dream.

I saw the boat
with its crew
of live corpses, saw

Bligh, dividing
stinking meat
with 'Who shall have this?'[2]

VI
After we bound him,
we mocked his rage
with *Mamoo, mamoo*,[3]

bellowing like bulls.
One man, Martin,
seeing his parched lips,

fetched him a shaddock,
pressed it against
the roaring mouth.

VII
Only sober men
should use this art
of making drunkards.

I have no patience
with the slow still:
must taste before time.

VIII
Train vines or hops, you reap
a nation. I bring you
no such harvest.

From root-torn plants, I press
a juice without vintage,
as harsh as sand.

IX
I leave my anger
to the weaponless;

my wandering
to landsmen.

Drunk or dry,
there'll be no rest

for the lovers
of sea-phantoms.

X
Bill McCoy's a rantin' boy
of enterprise an' darin';
he met the deil by Galashiels
and axed him for a fairin'.

'Twas no for gowd he seld his sowl;
'twas no for doxies swoonin';
but maut tae still, and maut tae swill,
and maut at last tae droon in.

[1] Fletcher Christian.
[2] A traditional method of dividing food which gave each person an equal chance of the best share. This method was used by William Bligh during the voyage in the open boat.
[3] Silence.

'Towards 1897, the Pitcairn Island community had deteriorated into lawlessness. 'The man who stemmed the tide of degeneration was James Russell McCoy, a great-grandson of the mutineer. The direction and purpose he gave the community as Chief Magistrate and Chief Executive, on and off for thirty-seven years, earned the mutineer's great-grandson an honoured and secure place in Pitcairn History.' – Robert B. Nicolson, *The Pitcairners*

Note
I have chosen these two poetic sequences as examples of my interest in narrative, and in different verse forms.
    A friend told me of the St Julian legend (up to the murder of his parents) when I was a student. It seemed an interesting example of repressed blood lust, but I did not feel impelled to retell it until some twenty years later when I bothered to look up the rest of the story and found that there were two circular movements in it, from forest to forest, and from bed to bed. At about the same time I saw an aerial photograph of a forest – it

reminded me of the convolutions of the human brain, and of mazes of all sorts, from green and growing ones to the examples you sometimes see carved on church façades.

John Cummins's book on medieval hunting, *The Hound and the Hawk* (Weidenfeld and Nicolson, 1988) was invaluable background material to me, not just in helping me to get the terms right, but in suggesting 'believable' ways in which I might handle the supernatural or paranormal incident at the beginning of the story.

'Ardent Spirits' is part of an entertainment of the same name which I wrote in 1989 to commemorate the Bicentennial of the Mutiny on the *Bounty*. Most of the *Bounty* songs and poems were pastiches of various eighteenth century verse forms, which I had enormous fun writing. The sequence given here concluded the 'show', and is more modern and pared down in form.

My interest in William McCoy stems from a tradition that he is somewhere in my family tree; this led me to a fascination with the *Bounty* story itself, which, like that of St Julian, is one of those archetypal tales that can bear any number of interpretations. Again. like the story of Julian, it has two circular movements, both concerned with degradation and redemption. Bligh's failings as a commander on the voyage out are redeemed by his courage and resourcefulness after the mutiny; the redemption of the Pitcairners takes several generations and false starts. To me, the footnote from Robert B. Nicolson's classic work on the subject is an essential part of the poem's meaning.

The extract given here represents a series of images that may have drifted through the mind of McCoy during his last delirium. Only in the last short poem, which is meant to be sung (or rather, bawled), have I attempted to imitate what may have been McCoy's actual 'voice'. One device which I used during the *Bounty* sequence was the coincidence of Bligh and McCoy having the same Christian name, so that McCoy becomes Bligh's 'shadow' (in another poem, 'Bligh's Roses', Bligh sets out, full of good intentions, to bestow gifts on the natives, and is confronted with the vision of McCoy 'tattooed/and knife-scarred, sprawling/in spiritous puke'); while McCoy, just before his suicide, is haunted by a dream of Bligh's heroism when cast adrift. There is a small personal allusion in no. IX: with such a (putative) ancestor, obviously I have sometimes wondered what his legacy to me might have been!

JOHN GALLAS

The Atatürk Factory

It was Spring; everything sprouted and spread.
I stepped out with a halo of mozzies
and miles of sugarbeet buried in one field
and miles of sunflowers climbing out of the other.

A hot Puch pursued a rabbit. Two tractors grazed.
Hazelnut shrubs in a line clicked greenly.
They sounded like soles on the gravel and I followed them.
A cricket wound itself up in the grass.

At the top of the hill was a myrtle bush
waving its arms and sprouting, a bosky guide,
but waving them *everywhere*. Whatever it was
over there, I thought, it had to be good.

I puffed and panted a bit. And there it was:
miles of Atatürks lined up in one field
and miles of Atatürks driving out of the other;
which were the particular vegetables of the soul.

Hammers kicked the Spring. A rasping truck
whisked them away – City-size, Town-size, Village-size.
Marble-plaster-sugarbeet, I watched them go,
spreading a halo of dust, to every public place.

I blew my nose. The myrtle danced its dance.
Miles of oats and olives sprouted to the horizon.
I stood in my dusty court of mozzies and counted
the other crops, while Summer overtook me.

Cornelius Fidus

It's night-time: him what wants a good name
has jammed himself in a corner of his bedroom,
squirms on the wall-with-very-accurate-roses
and a dragged, cold sheet at his throat.

Gulp. Somebody else's moon scythes the clouds.
Sleep, like nitrogen, eludes your patient: Death,
the larger version, waves its eager rake
because it is the -Ism at the end of order.

Some dead old dope has lost his little bays (again) in the dark.
Ah! – something sweetly all in order tosses the sun back,
stamping up for fair proportion, thank God it's morning,
flaming, ordered, served and saviour from the inert night.

Engineer your reputation, Buzz, and I'll train mine:
your monument and brightly-fated fall is very-big-business,
but hardly ever works beyond... – oh, the rotting;
and we go under famous for some rot or nothing.

Only accidents are true: and Buzz has accidentally
entertained *suggestions* of Cornelius Fidus by night
that must have winked with lots of doubtful lights
across the wallpaper His Reputation all cold from Rome:

'*a depilated ostrich*'. FINIS. No place, position,
duty, order, empire, industry, decency, taxes,
invasion, invention, the general good and some dominion –
nothing. Nothing else that is was, or was will be.

Oh. Oh! Buzz is as white as a sheet after that. No more?
Bingo, Cornelius Fidus! This is life and not death,
rosy-fingered across the old stone fibs.
The more man builds the wider will his desert be.

It's nearly dawn. Now! Now! Smack in the name of something
very confusing Buzz takes his baptism, long overdue:
to Signor Amnesia his burning soul, his bedroom to the flood...
and up he goes, in something invisible – and pink.

Two Thoughtful Poems

1 *Woolwich Arsenal*
It was drizzling at Woolwich Arsenal.
I buttoned up my jacket by the stairs.
The sky went up like acid-drops, and brume
stood shining on the floor. The ticket-room
whitened down my back, and Beresford Square
was lit by rain all down the milk wet wall.

I saw the New Road houses, like torn tin,
jiggered at their chimneys and look dark,
and orange lines of light squeezed on the roofs
as far as Barrack Field. I saw them move,
the dead things – light, wind, rain – around Gun Park,
uncapped, not true. My jacket was too thin.

Up from the civil offing pricked a crane
which down a mustard bath of cloud unspun
two girders to Grand Depot Road, and crowned
their supplication from the Underground,
their cruck and upright arms, with nails. The sun
went out. I watched them building through the rain.

Something was born: some bolt, black anchorite.
I waited for the bus. Next year, when spring
remakes the light, wind, rain, and lays Blue Gate
with short, distracted bice and duplicates
our paper-dressing of the bone, this thing
will run, unfallen, in our salt delights.

I sat upstairs. At Shooters Hill I saw,
beside me, dancing on the second floor
of some hotel. The moon came out again
and whitened down the roofs of Marlborough Lane.
I buttoned up my jacket by the door.
I do not like high spirits anymore.

2 *To Particularity*
A doubtful, long-legged spook (my shadow) ebbed
and fell into the underwood. The light
rolled down. The negatives of thistles strode
up banks of yellow weed and in them rode
gigantic crane-flies; warmish aconite
squeezed up in pillars, spiked and spider-webbed.

I drowsed. I dozed. I fell asleep. I dreamed.
I don't remember what. At eight o'clock
I stretched across the park from end to end.
I yawned. I saw a bush of wormwood bend.
its wooden purpose at the moon, which mocked
the fading shadows' shadows' glass and seemed

to blanch our brief society. I said
I saw its vague, divine intent – I smiled –
its sticks, whose calculations, grey and dry,
with unapparent faith approached the sky,
its leaves, its bitter smell, and for a while
I wasted time admiring it. I said

it was possessed of good intentions, beauty,
stratagems and faith; of patience, breath
and fruit – I saw them all. The moon unrolled
and walked above the limes. My breath felt cold.
I watched the wormwood working up to death,
unfriendly, pawning at its rooted duty,

denied the knowledge of all consequence
and celibate amongst its common kind.
Its life was mine: its gravid work and art
my work. Each natural atom drew apart
and left the white-faced moon and me behind,
the blind reflections of impermanence.

We share too much. The moon walked through a cloud.
And common knowledge damns us. It struck ten.
I blundered through the flowers and found a town.
I saw the lights; they threw my shadow down.
I trembled at the touch of other men.
The streets were full. I pushed into the crowd.

from **Mustafa Orbaneja**
The Bishop of Ubeda visits Mustafa

This unaccustomed effort reached the Bishop,
sitting in a bearskin at his table.
'I think the Church might take this little fellow
to its bosom.' ('Abysses are so shallow,'
says Henry James. How true. The Tower of Babel,
likewise, shows that if one wants to fish up

– or pull down – some monstrous thing or other,
depths and heights are mostly discontenting;
only on the level, bourgeois roads,
in common hearts and common episodes
may our uncommon souls be found, frequenting
not the dark but mostly one another

and finding thus a common-sized reflection
between whose glass and breath (the opposing masses
being thus close together) fierce vibrations
naturally follow, indications
both of life and passion.) The Bishop's asses
trotted off in Mustafa's direction.

He stopped beside a tree to catch his breath.
The stream was frozen. Tiny sticks of ice
jingled in the bushes. No one stirred.
The Bishop held his breath. A single bird
passed through the sky. The apparent sacrifice
of all that once had lived, the seeming death

of all around him gave him pause. He sighed.
Sometimes the requisites of faith are hard
when nothing but the soul that ought to save them
painted what they were – whose picture gave them
only doubtful form – which disregard
for all the world might strengthen or divide

the human heart. 'Gee up,' he said and went on,
but wearily. He reached Mustafa's door.
The asses coughed and halted in the snow.
The Bishop knocked. The house was still. 'Hello?'
No sound. The Bishop shivered. All he saw
was something blank and blind and bleak hell bent on

freezing life to death. He pulled his bearskin
round him, raised his eyes to Heaven and knocked:
yes, from this unpromising subjection
would come, thank God, the promised resurrection.
And yet he doubted. Now the way seemed blocked.
He banged the door. What if his faith should wear thin

and spring refuse to come? What if the grass
shot up each year in answer to the piety
of all the world, whose fainting, craven souls
shot down by disbelief and full of holes
might damn the earth? The Bishop's cold anxiety
besmirched his heart. He heard a noise at last.

from **Tillo**
The Arrest of Fatih Düz

'Twelve o'clock,' said Ibrahim Birçay
and yawned. He closed his book and plumped his pillow.
How clear it was! He had a cigarette
and watched the stars climb past his minaret
that shot up like a rocket out of Tillo
and go, with brilliant slowness, round the sky.

A sparrow left the windowsill and dropped
around the rooves of town; the hot night air
leant up its walls; some televisions turned
its windows blue and gas-jets softly burned
like sleep. The sparrow landed. Shouts! – a glare
of torches – marching feet towards… They stopped.

Upstairs in 22 Republic Drive
Nusret Düz had just set up his wife:
her beautiful dyed hair fizzed on the bed.
'Your brother's in the dining-room,' she said –
'They'll kill him.' Nusret panted, 'What is life?'
The moon danced through the glass. 'The worst survive,'

said Sevtap through her hair – a van – a jeep –
'the best get' – headlights licked the floor. *Knockknock*!
A cushion popped. Kerrrr*ACK*! The doorbolt snapped.
Fatih jumped against the sofa wrapped
in an eiderdown. They entered. 'One o'clock,'
said Ibrahim Birçay, and fell asleep.

They marched across the carpets. 'Where were you,
you shit, on Freedom and Constitution Day?'
They stood in a line. 'Here,' said Fatih Düz.
Their helmets gleamed like plums. 'Bad fucking news,'
said Sergeant Naz, 'you stayed in Başkale
and shot a soldier.' Nusret smiled. 'It's true!

He wasn't here!' 'Gerrout!' Smack. Ow. Goodbye.
'My eiderdown!' 'He's gone.' 'We're ri-' 'Uuuuuhhh!' 'Aaaaaah
The yellow door lay broken in the street.
The van roared away. The morning heat
swirled slowly, making bubbles in the tar.
Stars rolled on like clockwork through the sky

Note

'The Atatürk Factory' describes a small adventure of my own, with added Thought. This is the kindest sort of verse, because its contents have no Truth.

'Cornelius Fidus' tries harder. It is obscure. Good. Being haunted by bits of Obscurity in your own bedroom is probably confusing enough. Writing a poem about it does not have to make things easier.

The 'Two Thoughtful Poems' are more well-formed. They are in my favourite stanza form, which demands the comfort of reference books, and come to miserable conclusions. I don't have enough ideas about Life to be 'I' for very long.

'Mustafa Orbaneja' is a huge poem. It was written with a new pleasure. My desk was covered with reference books for a year. I could almost convince myself I was working. It freed me from whining in verse.

'Tillo' is my newest; a story of such nastiness, driven by hearts fuelled with treachery, terrorism, betrayal, lust, pruning, double-cross, triple-cross, cruelty to animals, murder, sex, bribery, corruption, TWOCs and astronomy, that there is neither time nor space to think at all, is included only to annoy you with not knowing what will happen next, and will be included in my next collection.

John Gallas

MARIUS KOCIEJOWSKI

Coast

1

We moved among delicate instruments,
Taking for a theme the sovereign light,
The scrimshaw, the parliament of water.
We then sought a division between things.

Once divided, truth divides forever.

We abandoned the angelic forms, smashed
Against the wood our heavenly quadrant,
Struck aimlessly from island to island.

2

We embraced without shame what was simple.
We wept to see the wild geese heading home,
The small blue flowers we could never name,
The women so ripe in their summer clothes.

The compass we held true is stopped inside.

We worship as pure the broken circle.
A blind foghorn sounds our way toward shore,
The old bleached houses dispossessed of love.

3

A band marching in circles slays a tune.
A megaphone blares garlands of welcome.
What should we return to, and what survives
Of love? And who are the boys skipping stones?

The shallow waters keep our image moored.

We were proud scavengers once, and we come
As ghosts here, savages brandishing grace,
With nothing to give but this our silence.

4

Speak kindly of those we have abandoned,
The innocent who in their madness strayed,
Who mistook for seraphim a bright lamp
Beneath the waters camouflaging death.

Such tenderness the depths would not abide.

There was nothing could be done to save them.
We trembled as the gulls swallowed their cries,
And as the distance took what else remained.

5

Who shall carry them across the harbour,
These stranger particles that seek congress?
We say words alone keep our nature whole
Against the hard weathering of fractions.

So what now siphons our breath from inside?

There is no way home, and the petty schemes
Are brushed aside, and the horoscopes too,
The mock images, the lights on the shore.

6

As with fish entering the broken hulls
Or the blind eel tunnelling through the weed,
So shall we make darkness our corridor.
We will by dead reckoning tempt fortune.

Go, *catch the slightest air should any come.*

It is better so than light which is false,
Better the rougher shape, the ruined voice.
Ask nothing more, as more would madden us.

Note
'Coast', As Seen through the Wrong End of the Telescope
'Coast' has its origins in a conversation I had, in September 1979, with a young Polish woman in the Café Jama Michalikowa in Krakow. She had been berating me for suggesting that there was such a thing as a black rose. Photosynthesis, she argued, would not allow for such an occurrence. I then mentioned that I would be going to visit Auschwitz the following day to which she replied in a tone which seemed to mingle scorn with surprise, 'Why?' Perhaps she felt that one could not be anything other than a tourist in so solemn a place. After she left my table, I scribbled down the line which for me has become some kind of touchstone: 'Once divided, truth divides forever.' A doubtful rose, an attractive woman whose fingers were stained with nicotine, and the Holocaust: without this peculiar, and indeed troublesome, conjunction of things, things which in fact find no place in the poem, I doubt 'Coast' would have come into existence. The poem although it displeases me in parts contains the beginning of many a theme important to me. I present it here as my best failure.

There is a letter which Giacometti wrote to Pierre Matisse, in which he describes working away at his sculptures until, to his horror, they would collapse in front of his eyes. I wish for some analogy more stable, but the fact is, I struggled with 'Coast' for nine years, obsessively, blindly even. The poem would grow foolish tentacles, then dwindle, and at times disappear altogether: the Abstract Beast threatened to consume everything 'simple, sensuous and passionate' (Milton). I have been cursed with a tendency to begin with the abstract rather than with the concrete. As a result, I write very little: I spend too much time clearing away the rubble.

The 'delicate instruments' may be seen at the museum of the Greenwich observatory. I find in those compasses, sextants and quadrants an exquisite marriage between physical beauty and practical use. The instrument most dear to me, however, is a fictional one – the 'heavenly quadrant' which Captain Ahab smashes against the deck of the *Pequod*. What Melville clearly intended here was an act of Satanic pride, but I cannot help but see in this something more – our own century prefigured, the dark corridor through which we have to grope our way 'by mere dead reckoning of the error-abounding log'. – *Moby Dick*, Chapter CXXIII. Also, there is the modern Odysseus who upon reaching the shores of home determines to go back from whence he came. The darkness is preferable to the light which is false. 'Speak kindly of those we have abandoned,/The innocent who in their madness strayed': I had in mind, although it is nowhere in section 4 of the poem, the mass suicide, in 1978, of Reverend Jim Jones and over 900 of his followers. There is the visual memory too of a scene in a war film, *The Cruel Sea*, in which the survivors of a torpedoed ship are left to their terrible fate. 'The shallow waters keep our image moored' serves to remind one that it is also quite possible to drown in a puddle.

'Go, *catch the slightest air should any come*': I took this line from W.E. Dexter's *Rope Yarns, Marline-Spikes and Tar* (London, 1938), the reminiscences of a master mariner. There is in the lovely Elizabethan cadence of those words something which stands for all time: Homer, Sir Francis Drake and Melville would have understood them. Yes, there was a time when 'we embraced without shame what was simple.' What more can I *not* say? I am perplexed by what poetry is, but I do believe that in the dark of the imagination there always is the possibility of a black rose.

CHARLES BOYLE

Species
When you look at me as if to say
That's the first meaningful thing you've said in months
I immediately want to take it all back
into a small purse, and let someone else pay.

I want to get drunker than I was last April
and not to be bothered to do all the things I suddenly know
I can do without trying.
I want to hand in my notice.
I want to be wearing my trusty blue shirt.
I want to have such omnivorous sex it's beyond all reasonable
    doubt
that in twenty years' time someone will tap me on the
    shoulder and say dad.
I want to go back twenty years to a Friday evening in the Café
    Amphitryon
and start my life again from there
and be stubborn enough to repeat it all exactly
down to the last visit to the fucking launderette.

I want to stand with you in front of an endangered species –
200 in the president-for-life's reserve, then sixty,
the single final innocent misfit
comatose in its sleeping quarters or scraping its flank
against the bars, a sad disappointment
after the vivid illustrations in the books for children –
and see where that gets us.

Alex in February
The ex-king's palace is a museum now,
ragbag of swords and medals, French furniture,
an English pram; in the queen's bathroom
we gawp at antique plumbing.

We are as cold perhaps as she.
Out of season, this could be somewhere English,
a spitting rain in the off-sea wind,
sunlight glancing through the waves' fine spray.

A thin, brilliant mist hangs over the sea,
element at times of madness, a sleep of reason
whose monsters dog me, familiar and feigning tame,
they know the answers but they never tell.

No one it seems knows where the king has gone,
or if he's yet dead. Imagining, I sit
in a seafront café reading last week's English papers
as the clouds lumber across.

They split with hail: children run
across the blitzed Corniche, and the dark muffled Arabs
huddle at doors.
Exile's disease, we catch it being born.

Timur the Lame
A man with a limp came towards me,
begging money for liquor – spoke of cairns
built of skulls, of the wind off the steppes
on the night before battle
and the evils of cholesterol.

Some of this, I thought, he must be making up.
Besides, what was I doing here,
talking with a dead Mongol warrior,
in the middle of the life that was mine?

At the end of the street, some camels
grazing, the air mottled with flies
above ribbons of goat flesh…
Even the tourists looked sick.
Even the women, that day, were not untouched.

He said: You think a life
has a beginning, middle and end?
Then he emptied his pockets
and showed me the eyes of Hafiz.

The Chess Player
I'm thinking of a famous grandmaster
on the sixteenth floor of a hotel in Bucharest,
kept awake by the gypsy music
of a wedding party downstairs.

I'm seeing him watch from his window
some cleaning women emerge
in the sodium-lit small hours
from the national exhibition centre,
and the rails from the station stretching
towards the vanishing point of asylum.

When at last he falls asleep
to the strains of the last violin,
he dreams fitfully
of a lady with a parasol
stepping out on the first marble square
of a black and white chequered piazza.

His task is to guide her across
to the shade of the colonnade
before history takes over,
before the city lies in ruins.

The light is hot and even
and, like the Pyramids when they were built,
the stones are so perfectly cut
a knife blade couldn't slip between them.

I Didn't Mean to Kill My Husband

she said, and I believed her, as we came out of Finnegan's
at nine o'clock on a rainy evening
and headed for somewhere to eat. Water was running
down the roofs and gutters
like the Nile in flood, and when she closed her blue, blue eyes
when we kissed,
I knew she was the kind of person
who just lets what will happen happen, as I was too.

Note
Too much of what I've written seems to me now to sit primly on the page, toeing the line; certain new poems such as 'Species' may be in part a reaction to this. The Alexandria poem is here out of nostalgia for the period rhetoric of its last line and for the period of its writing (20 minutes in a Cairo bar). Three from my 1993 collection, *The Very Man*: the opening Tamerlaine poem, distancing myself from what the specialists call progress narratives; a pre-1989 poem in which a Bucharest stop-over combined fortuitously with looking at the ruled perspectives of Renaissance paintings of the Ideal City; and a poem titled from a come-on line on the cover of a women's magazine, here in case Judith Chernaik *et al* should be reading – to be printed on the Underground, or indeed on a banner trailed from a biplane in a blue summer sky, would be pure pleasure. An inkling of a more complex pleasure that may come during a spell of writing – when everything seen or heard is available material and nothing's irrelevant, when correspondences lock home – is the reader's right.

FRANK KUPPNER

The Kuppneriad
Mk 1

1.
And if there was a time before this 'beginning',
that would have been this actual universe too.
For what other totality can there be to belong to?

2.
Another unwritten epic! They're my favourite kind.

3.
as, from the end of it
poured out into the opacity of the night sky
an endless sequence of galaxies; of complexities
to be disentangled, at length, into galaxies;
into vast strands of matter, which could possibly
develop into life, or whiplashing enormities,
or currents which fifty lives, one after the other,
would be insufficient to cross. So it went on for

4.
as I fell out of the window of heaven, I remarked
the wonderful light of evening. Or was it morning?
Whatever it was, it was such a wonderful light.

5.
Come out of that void at once. You aren't fooling anyone.

6.
He rushed towards her, as if intending some indecency –
but whether she moved aside; or he unbalanced;
or both; or one contributed to the other;
or the gods finally lost patience with the gross self-
congratulation of those who call themselves monotheists –
he toppled over the side of the ornate balcony anyway
and landed in the midst of a still adoring throng.
And now, o Muse, let me begin my song.
There was at this time a certain young man
in the deme of Cowcaddens: and this good youth, hearing

7.
His eyes flashed. He raised a powerful hand,
and pronounced the doomladen, ineluctable words –
until he had disappeared entirely beneath the bathwater.
Still she stood by the sink, calmly brushing her teeth.

8.
His scream sounded out over the whole nonchalant earth.

9.
Holding her close to me, I hacked my way
through the hostile ranks – but when I reached the door,
I discovered that she had vanished. Gritting my teeth,
I turned back, intently searching for clues –

10.
How the Goddess sighed. Sometimes it depresses her
to hear what men most ask for. With a wan smile,
she disjoined another head from its cervical vertebrae,
and called out, 'Next!' I was pushed into the room.

11.
I looked over, worried, to the source of the disturbance.
She followed my gaze and smiled. Don't worry, she said. It's nothing.
It's Dante. He keeps trying to break into heaven.
He seems to think he has some sort of right to be here.
Fortunately, we keep a troop of soldiers,
whose heads are little girls' bums, to watch out for him,
be alert for his arrival, and throw him out again.
It's a special detachment. No-one is quite sure
whether they have been rewarded for something, or punished for it.
On the whole, I tend to think they have been rewarded.

12.
I sneaked back into the laboratory during the lunchbreak.
Yes! The experiment seemed to be proceeding
most successfully. In every dish of culture
a tiny God was growing. Oh! What triumph!
What an era this would be sure to inaugurate
in Mankind's spiritual pilgrimage towards the ultimate truth.
I assume I have time to nip out for a quick couple of sandwiches.

13.
I was buying some food routinely in a shop –
when something in the tired but alert expression
of the girl behind the till jolted me into life.
Please do not understand this merely in a base, physical way.
She was bored in such an exhilarating manner!
To be anywhere else, at any other time!
Surely this was the Goddess? In disbelief,
I watched her carefully, for the least sign
that she recognised my presence and purpose. But no!
Some change passed from one being to another –
and nothing more would ever be shared –

14.
I'm lucky. At least I still have death to look forward to.
But you! Well: what a predicament! What a predicament!
I'm not surprised you say you envy me.

15.
It's just that I never like to see so much blood
coming out of a cake.

16.
Know, then, this sobering gigantic truth,
vain, ignorant and autokulaktic man:
when God bends down in the bathroom, the very stars
weep at the acid, ineluctable sadness
somehow inherent in creation. And when he farts,
somewhere a little cosmos mysteriously disappears.

17.
Knowledge of the numinous is a rare thing indeed,
and to be treasured, however it emerges.

18.
Morning. The goddess comes quietly into the room:
She is looking slightly wiser than usual, as usual.
She is making no attempt to hide many of her subtleties.
Is a Divinity inviting me to apologise? Or the opposite?
I can lift newspapers up. I can examine new letters.
Look. Or don't look, if you are not here. Look there!

19.
No; that is not true. You did not give me this body.
Rather, you helped create this body, and this
body unfolded as me. You cannot give things – who can? –
let me rephrase that as, even you cannot give things –
to what does not exist. Life is created,
not given. For what is already there, waiting
for life to be given it? Birth is something else.
Indeed – everything else is something else.
Sometimes merely another word. For nothing.

20.
No you misunderstand me. I would estimate
that 40% of this crowd are not divine at all.

21.
Of legs and women, oh Muses, sing: and of how,
as the light of the infinite morning crept in upon him,
the Deity slowly began to bestir himself
from the corner of the kitchen where he lay,
disbelieving among the disjected panoply,
on a soft, supportive mound of discarded (thoughts)

22.
One o'clock again. Is there no prize this time either?

23.
Our scene is the research establishment in Heaven,
where novel military inventions are constantly perfected.
A disconcerting giggling has just broken out
in the interior. The more astute passers-by
look at each other in ever-mounting consternation.

24.
She broke my weapon off with a snort of contempt,
and continued implacably towards the inner sanctum
where our general waited for the information
that would let him work out what the Universe meant.
We knew we must, at all costs, keep them clear of there.

25.
She dropped out of the sky, and landed in my bed.
I was shocked, of course. And grateful. But it was difficult
to keep up a normal, human conversation.
A certain strain intruded itself.

26.
She opened her small mouth, and took out a globe.
It looked so stunningly like the earth, that I
glanced round involuntarily, checking that

27.
She was sitting reading a letter when I jogged her arm.
The recoil smashed my inept skull, rebounded
from a wall, crashed through my pons; then ricocheted
from a mirror, whistling through my ear, and exiting
from my aghast nostrils, before burying itself
in the bowl of porridge in front of me. I sighed.
Obviously, this is not going to be my day –
cars or no modest cars beyond the sunlit wall.
Some mornings have it, and other mornings don't.

Frank Kuppner

28.
So, for hour after hour we traded impossible punches.

29.
So I said to the four Goddesses, from my seat
in front of the small gas fire – Yes, I am most impressed.

30.
So subtle, interlinked, and precarious
was the sequence of events which first brought us together,
that I often thought of how close we came to not meeting,
and felt a sort of horror at it. Now,
I still think very often of how close we came
to not meeting. But without the same horror.

31.
So, the great heroes struggled for hour after hour –
wrestling, groaning, occasionally using swords –
loosing the occasional spear – and even, at moments,
firing off a few rounds of vocabulary –
while, in its little bed, the child continued to sleep;
oblivious of the mighty and epoch-making

32.
Soon the bathroom was a hive of uproarious merriment,
with elbows and feet flying all over the place.
By Heaven, these old deities certainly know how to enjoy themselves!
You should have been there. You would have laughed to see it –
had you been sufficiently dead to be allowed entrance.

33.
that fiend, with whom he was locked in deathless combat,
the endless struggle between the good and the better?
Oh, wiliest of adversaries! At times like this
he even came close to forgetting which was which.

34.
The Goddess's head instantly disappeared
into a round megaglobule of fat, from which
a neat little tongue continued to poke out, provokingly

35.
The snake wriggled desperately, trying to escape.
But the woman caught it, tied it into a knot,
swung it round a few times, and flung it into
a rubbish-bin nearby. Having done which,
she picked up a piece of fruit, and turned on the television.
Soon she would have to make a *really* significant decision.

36.
The veil that covers life is life itself,
she screamed, dragging me over to the window.
Remove that glittering surface, and what is left?
Some say, all that matters. But I say – Nothing.
By all means look for yourself. What do you see?
Oh, superficial infinity of fragments!

37.
Then, after he had said this, he went back
to see if the ship was still safe in its harbour.
But he could not find it. Neither the ship nor the harbour.

38.
Then, just perhaps as they start to believe
that no-one is ever going to come and fetch them
from the gradually more foully smelling clouds
that they are attached to: I'll turn them all to acid
and have them slowly, painfully eaten away
for an eternity. Does it sound impossible to you?

39.
Though all discussion of this is root and branch inadequate.

40.
Thus he was left alone, tied to the stake,
as night fell with more intensity than ever,
and his mighty organ reached out into the darkness,
questing, probing, ever searching

41.
To be frank, I am almost bored by my own unearthly resilience.

42.
We shrink, J, from approaching the ultimate in all things;
for fear that, gazing steadily at it from close to,
we shall suddenly think – so: this is all there is to it!
And at the final boundaries, what can we do
but turn and head back? We can hardly stay there.
Even he who may, with prospect of success

43.
We sliced each other's head, brutal, from its neck,
then gazed at each other, astonished. Could this somehow
also lead to love? Might it still not be too late?

44.
What exactly do you mean, 'The Empire has just fallen'?
Don't be so melodramatic. It doesn't suit you, Marcus.
Try to leaven all your remarks with a dry wit.

45.
What joy! Look around, oh great ones! What joy!
The same appearance of a pack of worlds shuffled together!

46.
Whatever it was, it was such a wonderful light.
I was almost sorry I was killing myself.
Or was it someone else killing me? I sometimes
have great difficulties with the details, I admit.
I heard a mocking voice call: 'Enjoy your fall!'
Or was that perhaps, not mockery, but the profoundest wisdom?
The difference is sometimes too subtle for me, I'm afraid.

47.
Who could it be? Surely not a rescuer?
For who can rescue a God, from whatever predicament
he contrives, for reasons best known to himself,
to find himself in? He gave an Almighty groan,
so that the whole valley resounded in sympathy;
sniffed, and stifled some tears. How cruel life was!
Even to someone from whose body the entire

48.
Yesterday I was still on the troubled elements;
as far removed from home, it seemed, as at any point
on all my previous tortured, absurd, long journeyings.

49.
Yet nobody was sitting on the chair, again,
among the memorable suburban trees. Good bye.

Note
I am fortunate enough to be able to assuage any grief I have that my attitudes and interests should by and large be so remote from those of so many others, with the reflection that my past work does not particularly interest *me* either. It's a common enough phenomenon, I suspect. I further suspect that none of my past poetry offers a clear introduction to my work; nor does any of my present. Though I suppose I may be wrong. After all, the present offering contains some of the tragic remnants of huge past ideas which did not quite work. There will be more of them, no doubt. Since I wrote them, I suppose they might well be characteristic. As indeed might this.

ALISON BRACKENBURY

Rented Rooms
Night stole away my reason to be there –
that routine note which missed the post. I came
out of the throaty mist, the New Year's air,
stared, at the dim house which showed no name,
called to a girl, who rattled past her bike,
blowing her fog-damp scarf, winter's hot cheeks.

The first door I pushed open from their hall
gaped a conservatory, shadowed: full
of spoiled ferns once, sweet geraniums.
Now it held bikes, askew. It breathed back all
the cold of first streets, lingering on stairs –
the outside door blows open – no one cares
to clean: from Christmas, ivy curls in sprays,
dark, in rolls of dirt. Who went away
leaving this television blank above
a rolled-up quilt? Quick: drop the printed note
on the hall's floor.

       It echoes back again
the deep sea chill of fog, the waves of dust,
my wonder at a room's dimmed lights.
Need, then:
the stairs to silence; not to own, but love.

Constellations
But my daughter; I wish you could see my daughter
Stretch woolly hands to an Alsatian,
The blunt pale claws scrabble her coat
Flourish their mud down her prim coat.
She calls to the white cat when she wakes,
Is not afraid.

       Softly you say –
Glancing to the empty window –
She is ignorant, not brave.

Say that there was not a time
We walked through branches with the beasts,
The stars rose: we were not afraid.

Now in our winter we can see
A child scanned before its birth.
Silver fish on a dull screen
Kicking up, out the black stream,
Where have you gone?

Lolled back, she sleeps
In the icy sun, the moss-green pram,
Still with her arms held stiffly out
The wings of a swan. So Cygnus flies –
They tell me – through the winter heaven;
I cannot find him from my book.

That we must, still, be told, then look,
Forcing old lines round fleeing light,
Is that your way? I tremble, see
Bright Castor, Pollux, held and free;
Lovers, beasts, who once they were
Does not disturb them, constant pair.

Look back, past me. White streams of sky
Wheel over; I stand, trying
To track lost stars this night. She was not
Swimming. She was flying.

Bookkeeping
These are not (you understand) the figures
which send cold judgement into the backbone
which leave us, workless, shrunk at home
staring in a sky grown black with leaves.

These are like the ticking of a clock,
the daily sums, a van's new brakes,
three drums of trichloroethylene on the back
of a thrumming lorry; yet they take
a day to make: thin bars of figures. While
I try to balance them, light scurries round
like a glad squirrel. Radio music stales –
until shut off.

       What's left when it is done,
the green book closed? There is no sea to swim
no mouth to kiss. Even the light is gone.
Bookkeepers drink over-sugared tea
lie in dark rooms; are always hunched and tired.

Where I stretch up the low bulb burns and whirls.
And in it, I see him. The dusky gold wing folds
across his face. The feathers' sharp tips smudge
his margins.

Sunk, in his own shadows, deep
in scattered ledgers of our petty sins:
he, the tireless angel:
Unaccountably, he sleeps.

The Queen's Funeral
Her own horse steps in violet silk.
Black velvet sighs upon her bier.
The Duchess' train is wide as Thames.
The clerks and diarists crowd near.

Later, too late, they find the note
Forbidding all show. As before,
A practical and honest soul,
She'd spend the money on the poor.

Snow whirls on mud. Each coffee shop,
Warm inn stands closed. Her heart's one friend –
Bound by custom, strange in grief –
The ruined King does not attend.

After Beethoven
After he died she came, a veiled lady,
Who stood beside the bed. Nothing was said.
(There was a widow, who had had a child.)
She did not brush his forehead with her fingers,
She stood: now robed in fat beneath her furs,
Her veil the dark of time.

When she went home she cried a little, blotched
Her face, then stopped. Her daughter had gone out.
She clasped her hands, with their false ring, and listened.

The bed was warm, but when she reached the street
The keen air made her shawl a cave of white.
Her feet, in their small boots, broke through the snow
Softer, and faster, like a young girl dancing.

He never heard those steps. He quarrelled with her,
Struck her with silence, would not hear her name.
Now she spoke his; and snuffing out the candle,
Listened to the echo he became.

Note
Visions strike us rarely. We forget what we love, surrounded by unpaid bills, unfed cats, or overgrown lawns. If we work for wider causes, it is with uncertain hope.

To give you a careful cross-section of what I have written, I should have chosen at least one poem about the country and one about other countries I have seen, such as China, or Zimbabwe.

Instead, I have chosen these poems which came back to mind urgently, and would not be resisted. For poems are not a manifesto but a trick of the tongue, a flash in the dark.

GREGORY WOODS

Like a Shark's
We have the eye if not the will. The seasons attract us.
For every grove igniting lemons on a terraced slope
There's a fog; for every breath of air, air freshener.
Love has kept us occupied whatever the condition
Of the economy, no matter how surprised we are
We even like each other, let alone adore or worse.
We never learned to survive the pure menace of beauty:
Incisors like a shark's, angled inwards, no going back.

Post Mortem

I
'All that the assassins have been claiming
has been lies. Their meetings were not social
but a plot. Each courted temptation
in the others' company: not one of
them was capable of acting alone.
When they shot the hero he was strong (as
heroes are) but weaker for being alone.
They had no pity, finding ample space
for all their bullets on his broad physique.'

II
'Call us good not evil. There's little more
to be said. We're men of the type, as you
well know, who counter vanity with valour
but pride ourselves on love. We seek glory
not in the dusty ruckus of the world
and subsequent damnation, but in God.
Spirit, intellect and theology
keep us going. Heroes, like lesser men,
can meet with unfortunate accidents.'

A Blind Man Looks at a Boy
The smell of oranges – I could have been satisfied with that.
The spray – like an impolite but fragrant sneeze. I could
Have introverted all my senses, had I any sense,
And felt a thumbnail underneath the peel prepare to flay
The pulp. No need for an ending, no need to taste the fruit.

I could have sat here at my desk and been tempted by
All manner of profanities, my fingers dancing on
The blotting paper, sticky but as chaste as apathy,
The orange rolling on the carpet out of reach.
It would have been a simple life, a hive of discipline.

Instead the tilt of my tentative radar locates
A baffle at the centre of the room. My voice
Comes back to me a little late, diverted, each syllable
Coerced into the service of a boy's physique.
'Who's there?' reverberates on drumskin, naked abdomen.

A slight acoustic flurry, amplified within the vortex
Of his navel, makes me sound concussive, tremulous.
I seem to have decided – and been right – he won't reply.
The light is thick, life short, the stillness of the evening air
Transfigured by the delicate pomander of his balls.

Celibate
Pure decoration, this
perfection of body,
sculpted for no other
    purpose than to

catch the eye, beguiling
anyone receptive
to such travesties of
    ordinary life.

You feel you have to pay
at least token homage
by stopping to sniff at
    the brackish air

downwind of his fevered
self-regard, or even
going back to praise his
    definition.

The muscles have nothing
practical to do but
justify his efforts
    in the gym by

inciting you to acts
of forlorn theory.
He doesn't want to sleep
    with anyone.

Warlord
Achilles grieves. A soldier, weeping, seems
No less the hero – still delivers dreams.

Not powder running down his face, but tears
In the dust. Not ardour in men's hearts, spears.

Who says Patroclus should have been a farmer
Or poet? Nothing left of him but armour –

Which is apt. Women should be kept as chattels
For bearing sons. Lovers for love and battles.

Men should philosophise and body-build.
They like to see their lovers kill, not killed.

Maker
He touches the boy, then touches the wax.
Each compensates for what the other lacks

But neither is sufficient. Donatello's
Forgery needs an apprentice with bellows

To finish it. The boy's left in the lurch,
The statue in the chancel of the church.

(Identical.) He looks as soft as swan's
Down. But he's cold, immortal, made of bronze.

The sculptor comes to see him, sees him, seizes
The day, ventures to touch him, touches. Freezes.

*

Sandpaper the sun:
you would think nothing
could soothe such dudgeon.

But in corners where names
swirl on an updraught
of hopeless serenades

I borrowed cupped hands.
And when truants scrounging
cigarettes lost the

thread of their dreaming,
I drained semen from
their amber navels.

*

You can tell he wants
you by the way he
has to wet his throat

sending his adam's
apple careering
up and down his neck

like the thing on the
test-your-strength machine
lambasting the bell.

No fluffy toys as
prizes but knowing
you managed the test.

*

Offer him a drink,
light his cigarette,
ask him to dance.

Tell him what you do
for a living, but not
as if it matters.

Gregory Woods

Ask his name and try
to remember it
for when you find him

knotted in your sheets,
a total stranger
begging for Aspirin.

*

All the more tranquil for
a chainsaw above us
in the woods, we swapped

imperatives (touching
on the flesh) in each
other's native tongues.

It was not until late
that where words emerged
from his head I silenced

him. Another term for
love occurred to me.
I kept it to myself.

Note

These poems belong to my second collection, which I am now compiling. The title of the book will be *May I Say Nothing*, Oscar Wilde's last recorded words on 25 May 1895 at the third of the trials. I haven't decided whether to add a question mark. Probably not.

The book will open with an epigraph from Jean Genet: 'more objectivity, more passivity, more indifference, hence poetry'. The point of this remark has to do with detachment, but not inertia. Anyone who has read Genet's fiction will have seen that 'passivity' can be the most dynamic and powerful of forces, at once both active and attractive.

I am not just talking about sex, although sex is certainly near to the heart of the matter. At the same time as putting together these poems, I am working on a commission to write a history of gay literature. So, in my critical work, I'm studying the ways in which cultural change affects subcultural production based on social identities determined by sexual activities.

There is, you might say, a considerable distance between the act and the text.

As my collection's title might suggest, many of the recent poems are about negotiating a way between two imperatives: the need for expression as an assertion of identity, and the contrary desire to keep secrets. I suppose there is nothing particularly new about this. It represents the writer's usual problem of writing from within while trying to safeguard one's own privacy. But for explicitly gay writers, even now, there remains – if only as a kind of folk memory – the danger of being silenced. It is a persuasive motivation for making a noise.

The tension between the opposed motives of silence and speech, I think, enables the writer (perhaps the gay writer in particular) to wield the third power in Genet's equation, indifference, to incisive effect even when speaking about entirely personal things. It is what enables Genet himself to be both detached and obsessive at once. In a smaller way, I'm trying to perfect the same trick.

JOHN BURNSIDE

Signal Stop, near Horsley

Smoke in the woods
like someone walking in a silent film
beside the tracks.

A shape I recognise – not smoke, or not just smoke,
and not just snow on hazels
or fox-trails from the platform to the trees,

but winter, neither friend
nor stranger, like the girl I sometimes glimpse

at daybreak near the crossing, in a dress
of sleet and berries, gazing at the train.

Halloween

I have peeled the bark from the tree
to smell its ghost,
and walked the boundaries of ice and bone
where the parish returns to itself
in a flurry of snow;

I have learned to observe the winters:
the apples that fall for days
in abandoned yards,
the fernwork of ice and water
sealing me up with the dead
in misted rooms

as I come to define my place:
barn owls hunting in pairs along the hedge,
the smell of frost on the linen, the smell of leaves
and of the whiteness that breeds in the flaked
leaf mould, like the first elusive threads
of unmade souls.

The village is over there, in a pool of bells,
and beyond that nothing,
or only the other versions of myself,
familiar and strange, and swaddled in their time
as I am, standing out beneath the moon
or stooping to a clutch of twigs and straw
to breathe a little life into the fire.

Avoirdupois

The weight of mercury and frost,
or the plover's weight of remorse
at the root of my tongue

when I stood in the polished hall
and my grandfather died by ounces
a door's-breadth away.

No one could measure his house:
the loads were too subtle, too fine:
the weight of hooks, the swish of gaberdine,

his ghosts come in to tea, still damp with rain,
stains in the books Aunt Eleanor had read
the year she died,

and where he lay, the weight of riverbeds:
the tide of shadows under Fulford burn
where fat trout swam like phantoms in the weeds

and where I saw him once, big and alive,
dabbling his hands in the water, as if he would lift
the fish of our dreams, the catch that would break the scales.

Septuagesima

> *'Nombres.*
> *Están sobre la pátina*
> *de las cosas.'*
> Jorge Guillén

I dream of the silence
the day before Adam came
to name the animals.

the gold skins newly dropped
from God's bright fingers, still
implicit with the light.

A day like this, perhaps:
a winter whiteness
haunting the creation,

as we are sometimes
haunted by the space
we fill, or by the forms

we might have known
before the names,
beyond the gloss of things.

Aphasia in Childhood

I
A room in a village schoolhouse: sprinklings of chalk and rice; wingbeats smoothing the windows under a fall of copper-leaf and prayer. Certain constants: quadatric equations; the word in Latin for table. Science in one book; history in the other.

The questions I asked all the time, but never aloud: where is the soul? what does it most resemble? I had an image of something transparent, a fine yet indestructible tissue of buttermilk or chitin. But nobody knew: there was only the sugar-and-clove-scented room, and the mail van passing through, dusted with pollen and ozone, bearing the witness of farmyards and distant towns, and they were *real*.

II
The evidence of home: hairs in the paintwork; broken finger-nails between the carpet and the skirting-board. Traces; fibres; the smell of rubber gloves.

In the evening, with friends at the table, we spoke in anecdotes: the red stain of a haunting; a child in a nightdress; a picture of malice: sure-footed, graceful, walking around us on tiptoe. Mere entertainments, which no one would stop to believe.

Yet why repeat these histories if not for the peculiar sound of the victim? For the stoat in the soul: its pink-eyed wonder, its wistful desire for blood?

III
A shoebox of a life: gull's eggs and bullets wrapped in the sweet-ness of Wills Whiffs; foxed snapshots of the classroom beauty, smiling at nothing, flirting across the years.

IV
It was always autumn. Each evening the village melted: steeples and slate roofs dissolving in sunset; willows and cedars plunging into dusk. I sat for hours in the radio's dusted warmth. I slept for months. By morning the gardens had reap-peared; the fences smoked for miles in the gold suburbs; the hedges filled with water and jewelled birds.

I had lived so long. Maybe minutes. They sent me to school in a raincoat and colourless gloves.

V
Perfection arrives for the pleached hedges and the cress beds in frozen squares below the embankment. The parish map returns: steeples as landmarks; the old bounds of footpath and stream.

I am travelling a country of windows: a whiteness pressed to the glass as if the train was wrapped in iced velvet; the stations distilled to a glitter of frosted stone.

Memory clears: a series of lakes on maps, barely imagined, shrouded in oakwoods and moss.

VI
It keeps getting bigger. Everything points away from where I stand: new alleys scooped from light; street-names and water-

glass hedges; paradigms for cherry tree and snow. That one day I spent in the woods, digging leaf-mould: I kept finding thin silvery threads of mildew that dissolved in the air, and I was sure, if I dug a few inches deeper, I would find a being which resembled me in every way, except that it would be white and etiolated, like a finger of bindweed growing under stone.

Note
The poems selected here are probably representative, in their way, of the work I have been doing over the last six years or more. They reflect several of my interests during that period: the short lyric – that discipline of trying to convey the evanescent moment, however inadequately; the prose poem – a form that seems to me not to have been as fully explored in English as it might have been, (with the huge and inimitable exception of Mercian Hymns); the themes that have recurred in my work – continuity, community, concerns with language, childhood.

To have been prompted by this occasion to look back on my work to date has been a welcome, if slightly disquieting, event. In some ways, looking back is salutary: it allows one to reflect, to set aside, to move on. I feel now that I am moving away from a distinct phase, during which I can clearly see the influence of Spanish poetry, especially the work of Machado, Guillén and Jiménez, and of a number of British, American and Irish poets. But other influences cannot be discounted – early Italian painting, the cinema, Scots and Irish fairy stories, even the structures of certain computer languages.

CAROL ANN DUFFY

Whoever She Was
They see me always as a flickering figure
on a shilling screen. Not real. My hands
still wet, sprout wooden pegs. I smell the apples
burning as I hang the washing out.
Mummy, say the little voices of the ghosts
of children on the telephone. Mummy.

A row of paper dollies, cleaning wounds
or boiling eggs for soldiers. The chant
of magic words repeatedly. I do not know.
Perhaps tomorrow. If we're very good.
The film is on a loop. Six silly ladies
torn in half by baby fists. When they
think of me, I'm bending over them at night
to kiss. Perfume. Rustle of silk. Sleep tight.

Where does it hurt? A scrap of echo clings
to the bramble bush. My maiden name
sounds wrong. This was the playroom.
I turn it over on a clumsy tongue. Again.
These are the photographs. Making masks
from turnips in the candlelight. In any case they come.

Whoever she was, forever their wide eyes watch her
as she shapes a church and steeple in the air.
She cannot be myself and yet I have box
of dusty presents to confirm that she was here.
You remember the little things. Telling stories
or pretending to be strong. Mummy's never wrong.
You open your dead eyes to look in the mirror
which they are holding to your mouth.

Warming Her Pearls
for Judith Radstone

Next to my own skin, her pearls. My mistress
bids me wear them, warm them, until evening
when I'll brush her hair. At six, I place them
round her cool, white throat. All day I think of her,

resting in the Yellow Room, contemplating silk
or taffeta, which gown tonight? She fans herself
whilst I work willingly, my slow heat entering
each pearl. Slack on my neck, her rope.

She's beautiful. I dream about her
in my attic bed; picture her dancing
with tall men, puzzled by my faint, persistent scent
beneath her French perfume, her milky stones.

I dust her shoulders with a rabbit's foot,
watch the soft blush seep through her skin
like an indolent sigh. In her looking-glass
my red lips part as though I want to speak.

Full moon. Her carriage brings her home. I see
her every movement in my head… Undressing,
taking off her jewels, her slim hand reaching
for the case, slipping naked into bed, the way

she always does… And I lie here awake,
knowing the pearls are cooling even now
in the room where my mistress sleeps. All night
I feel their absence and I burn.

The Grammar of Light
Even barely enough light to find a mouth,
and bless both with a meaningless O, teaches,
spells out. The way a curtain opened at night
lets in neon, or moon, or a car's hasty glance,
and paints for a moment someone you love, pierces.

And so many mornings to learn; some
when the day is wrung from damp, grey skies
and rooms come on for breakfast
in the town you are leaving early. The way
a wasteground weeps glass tears at the end of a street.

Some fluent, showing you how the trees
in the square think in birds, telepathise. The way
the waiter balances light in his hands, the coins
in his pocket silver, and a young bell shines
in its white tower ready to tell.

Even a saucer of rain in a garden at evening
speaks to the eye. Like the little fires
from allotments, undressing in veils of mauve smoke
as you walk home under the muted lamps,
perplexed. The way the shy stars go stuttering on.

And at midnight, a candle next to the wine
slurs in its soft wax, flatters. Shadows
circle the table. The way all faces blur
to dreams of themselves held in the eyes.
The flare of another match. The way everything dies.

Prayer
Some days, although we cannot pray, a prayer
utters itself. So, a woman will lift
her head from the sieve of her hands and stare
at the minims sung by a tree, a sudden gift.

Some nights, although we are faithless, the truth
enters our hearts, that small familiar pain;
then a man will stand stock-still, hearing his youth
in the distant Latin chanting of a train.

Pray for us now. Grade I piano scales
console the lodger looking out across
a Midlands town. Then dusk, and someone calls
a child's name as though they named their loss.

Darkness outside. Inside, the radio's prayer –
Rockall. Malin. Dogger. Finisterre.

Mrs Midas
It was late September. I'd just poured a glass of wine, begun
to unwind, while the vegetables cooked. The kitchen
filled with the smell of itself, relaxed, its steamy breath
gently blanching the windows. So I opened one,
then with my fingers wiped the other's glass like a brow.
He was standing under the pear-tree snapping a twig.

Now the garden was long and the visibility poor, the way
the dark of the ground seems to drink the light of the sky,
but that twig in his hand was gold. And then he plucked
a pear from a branch, we grew Fondante d'Automne,
and it sat in his palm like a light-bulb. On.
I thought to myself, Is he putting fairy lights in the tree?

He came into the house. The doorknobs gleamed.
He drew the blinds. You know the mind; I thought of
the Field of the Cloth of Gold and of Miss Macready.
He sat in that chair like a king on a burnished throne.
The look on his face was strange, wild, vain. I said,
What in the name of God is going on? He started to laugh.

I served up the meal. For starters, corn on the cob.
Within seconds he was spitting out the teeth of the rich.
He toyed with his spoon, then mine, then with the knives, the
    forks.
He asked where was the wine. I poured with a shaking hand,
a fragrant, bone-dry white from Italy, then watched
as he picked up the glass, goblet, golden chalice, drank.

It was then that I started to scream. He sank to his knees.
After we'd both calmed down, I finished the wine
on my own, hearing him out. I made him sit
on the other side of the room and keep his hands to himself.
I locked the cat in the cellar. I moved the phone.
The toilet I didn't mind. I couldn't believe my ears:

how he'd had a wish. Look, we all have wishes; granted.
But who has wishes granted? Him. Do you know about gold?
It feeds no one; aurum, soft, untarnishable; slakes
no thirst. He tried to light a cigarette; I gazed, entranced,
as the blue flame played on its luteous stem. At least,
I said, you'll be able to give up smoking for good.

Separate beds. In fact, I put a chair against my door,
near petrified. He was below, turning the spare room
into the tomb of Tutankhamen. You see, we were passionate
    then,
in those halcyon days; unwrapping each other, rapidly,
like presents, fast food. But now I feared his honeyed
    embrace,
the kiss that would turn my lips to a work of art.

And who, when it comes to the crunch, can live,
with a heart of gold? That night, I dreamt I bore
his child, its perfect ore limbs, its little tongue
like a precious latch, its amber eyes
holding their pupils like flies. My dream-milk
burned in my breasts. I woke to the streaming sun.

So he had to move out. We'd a caravan
in the wilds, in a glade of its own. I drove him up
under cover of dark. He sat in the back.
And then I came home, the woman who married the fool
who wished for gold. At first I visited, odd times,
parking the car a good way off, then walking.

You knew you were getting close. Golden trout
on the grass. One day, a hare hung from a larch,
a beautiful lemon mistake. And then his footprints,
glistening next to the river's path. He was thin,
delirious; hearing, he said, the music of Pan
from the woods. Listen. That was the last straw.

What gets me now is not the idiocy or greed
but lack of thought for me. Pure selfishness. I sold
the contents of the house and came down here.
I think of him in certain lights, dawn, late afternoon,
and once a bowl of apples stopped me dead. I miss most,
even now, his hands, his warm hands on my skin, his touch.

Carol Ann Duffy

MICHAEL HULSE

Burslem

I

For ages I thought that the wireless comedian
    Arthur Askey lived in Burslem,
      quishing and quishing his glittering knives
in a reek that was seawater, sawdust and death,

and filleting, grinning and chuckling, a glint in his
    glasses, selling us plaice, chinkling
      George Rex, Elizabeth Reg, the shillings
and pence in his striped apron pocket, and wiping

and wringing his hands: *Thank you, thanking you kindly.* The
    sign on the shop read *A. Askey:*
    Fish, Game and Poultry. Halibut bedded
on ice amid plastic tomatoes and parsley.

Button-eyed pheasants. Rabbits drip-drippeting crimson.
    Askey pushing his mongering
      boater up off his forehead to listen
to pips and a Home Service voice. Are these thoughts home?

What is the point of remembering Cox's entry?
    They're boarded over now, the thick
      black glossy timbers; gone, the fat number
bossed in gold above the door; the painted plaster

girl who stood in the chemist's doorway, holding a box
    marked *Spastics*, is gone, and gone is
      the chemist's as well, where they sold the sticks
of barley sugar I'd suck oh so slowly till

all that was left was a golden glow. Was sweetness. Light.
    Whose life was that? What child was that?
      What am I hurting for?

II
      Much of my life
I despised and detested the place I was born.

I hadn't a good word to say about Stoke-on-Trent,
    its philistine dreariness, lack
      of a spirit, of anything better
than getting and spending, money and muck. But now

I often catch myself wondering what it was like
    when Wedgwood called his factory
      Etruria. The gentle land. A breath
of elder and briar and grasses on the air.

XL Publishing Services

typesetters of books and magazines of all kinds

congratulate *PN Review* on reaching its 100th issue

XL Publishing Services, The Wellington Gallery, Lodgehill Road, Nairn, Scotland IV12 4RB
Tel (01667) 455400 Fax (01667) 454899

I think of Arnold Bennett looking down to Burslem
    only a century ago:
  the curving earthy road ran down the hill
between the leafy green to where the brick-built town

nestled among the hills in a pall of smoke, almost
    as picturesque as Flemish towns.
    When I was a boy, the buckets of slag
whined overhead at Smallthorne colliery. Grime

fell from the air. The backstreets off Hamil Road where Dad
    grew up were the prowling grounds of
  youths who punched me and stole from me. Grim. And
unbeautiful. Unoriginal. What can it

mean, to say I miss the bleared Burslem I grew up with?
    I wouldn't want to live there now.
    But still: it seems so human and so rich,
to start with high ideals among these English hills

and end so appallingly soon in this dereliction,
    where it's a comfort knowing once
    the sisters, Constance and Sophia Baines,
pressed up their noses at the window. That one. There.

Raffles Hotel
Singapore

Say a colonial sailed up the straits and saw
a fishing village. And set foot in a city.
    Say the future was opium
    traded for tea, parades on the padang,

secret societies, rickshaws on Collyer Quay,
and riots in the streets. Say an Armenian
    bought the villa where a bankrupt
    colonel had opened a tiffin parlour,

and made a white hotel, a place of colonnades
and frangipani, palms, pilasters, rattan blinds,
    piano waltzes in the court:
  the marriage of the bride to the roué.

And while men died at the Somme and at Passchendaele
a barman was (gently) shaking the first gin sling.
    While General Percival puffed
    and dallied, refusing to fortify

Singapore on the landward side, the Japanese
were riding down the peninsula on bikes. For
    history is a seduction:
    cocktails on the verandah, then dinner

at eight, and the stylish contempt of the waiters.
After the rain the sky is open again. Stars
    are holed in the indigo night.
    A British lord and lady lead their guests

to a private banquet where pipers are playing
'Scotland the Brave'. An Australian swears that the
    last tiger killed on the island
    was shot underneath the billiard table.

This is the idiot empire. I'm lapping the
pool past midnight, thinking of Dad, and a jazz band's
    playing in the bar. After the
  war he dealt in textiles in Raffles Place,

and one day his driver came early to warn him
and hurry him to a villa where Englishmen
    waited armed behind shutters all
    the fanatical afternoon and night,

making light of their fears, but whispering, watching,
alert for a palm to sway as these do now, in
    the innocent air, trembling with
    the darker breathing of the saxophone.

The Architecture of Air

Though the waters still lap the ghat at Udaipur,
    the Minoan bull still leaps at Knossos,
Frederick's spirit still frets in Knobelsdorff's
    marble halls, and at Azay-le-Rideau
    bankers and kings contest the ghosting rights,

though stupefying superstructures of beauty
    still conform to the paradigms of power,
my lady paints an inch thick, my lord drives a Porsche,
    and fake apartment blocks line the approach
    to Termini when Hitler visits Rome,

our architect is still the architect of air,
    the making mouth, shaping the living breath:
teeth and tongue and lips, building a word or a kiss,
    expressing the inexpressible this.
    Whatever we say is said against death.

The gods are gone: in the Sistine ceiling a crack
    has come between Adam and creation,
the bombs explode in Belfast and Borobudur,
    Petra wears away to ignorant rock.
    Whatever we say is said against death.

Whatever we say is said against death. Adrift,
    listen you whisper, finger to your lips.
The oars shipped, the air unstirring, water dripping
    in stillness. And breathless we wait
    to hear each other say three simple words.

Knowing

    Knowing is movement, like a fly
        sitting in sunlight and
        fretting its forelegs, like
a pantomime miser rubbing his hands:
a callous confidence of possession
        cold as vivisection

    informs the several motions. Flies,
        however, will spread their
        bladed wings and shed skies
of light from off steel-plated gossamer,
shake rainbows, poking blackened cast-iron rods
        like pistons. Only gods

perform so perfectly. Brilliance,
        though incidental as
        a fly's spectrum abglanz,
is natural. We don't see it, nor is
it given to us to mirror by deception
        light's bright intellection.

Note

The earliest of these four poems, 'Knowing', was written in the early summer of 1976. Regular metrical forms had begun to bore me, and I was not yet able to write free verse that seemed bearable, but syllabics seemed a way of combining discipline and tautness with whatever freedoms I wanted. The line out of Marianne Moore interested me more than that out of Bridges. To this day, though I enjoy writing in metrical and in 'free' forms, syllabics of this kind (using stanzas with lines of varying lengths, rhyming or not) give me the greatest pleasure in the writing.

    'The Architecture of Air' (written in 1985), 'Raffles Hotel' (in 1988), and 'Burslem' (completed in May this year), mark a steady return to my deepest instinct, one that I had reacted against in the latter half of the 1970s: that poetry is truest when it most closely comes from real personal feeling. Scrutiny of the first principles of the art is essential; experiment of every kind has always engaged me; but poetry written on a programmatic platform is usually dead at the centre. My conviction has always been that poetry is answerable to traditions in theology, philosophy, ethics, social and political behaviour, aesthetics and linguistics, and above all to plain common sense, honesty and truthfulness; but if it is not written with excitement in the heart's blood it is nothing.

SUJATA BHATT

Clara Westhoff to Rainer Maria Rilke

No road leads
to this old house we chose.
Its roof of straw scattered
by the loud wind wheezing
its North Sea sounds.
No road leads
to this old house we chose.

I live downstairs
with my clay and stones.
You upstairs
with ink and paper.
What do we do but play with truth,
a doll whose face
I must rework again and again
until it is human.
The clay has gathered all the warmth
from my hands. I am too cold
to touch the marble yet.

Last night the wind blew
my candle out. Tonight again
on the staircase, I
grope my way to your room.
Each night I climb
up these steps
back to you, with your open windows
so close to the wind and stars.
I listen to your poems as I wash
the dust off my skin and hair.
You must have the windows open all night,
I must watch
the straw from the roof
slowly swirl, fall inside
and gently cover your poems.

Tomorrow
come downstairs, will you,
it has been a month.
I want to show you
the new stone I found
stuck in the mud by the dead tree.
Such a smooth globe, not quite white
but honeydew
with a single dark green vein curled across.
Come downstairs, will you, see
the bright red leaves I stole from the woods;
see my lopsided clay
figure bow low down
before my untouched marble.
Tomorrow
come see the ground,
the gawky yellow weeds
at eye level from my window down below.

from **Search for my Tongue**

You ask me what I mean
by saying I have lost my tongue.
I ask you, what would you do
if you had two tongues in your mouth,
and lost the first one, the mother tongue,
and could not really know the other,
the foreign tongue.
You could not use them both together
even if you thought that way.
And if you lived in a place you had to
speak a foreign tongue,
your mother tongue would rot,
rot and die in your mouth
until you had to spit it out.
I thought I spit it out
but overnight while I dream,

મને હતું કે આખ્ખી જીભ આખ્ખી ભાષા,
(munay hutoo kay aakhee jeebh aakhee bhasha)

મેં થૂંકી નાખી છે.
(may thoonky nakhi chay)

પરંતુ રાત્રે સ્વપ્નમાં મારી ભાષા પાછી આવે છે.
(parantoo rattray svupnama mari bhasha pachi aavay chay)

ફુલની જેમ મારી ભાષા મારી જીભ
(foolnee jaim mari bhasha mari jeebh)

મોઢામાં ખીલે છે.
(modhama kheelay chay)

ફળની જેમ મારી ભાષા મારી જીભ
(fulllnee jaim mari bhasha mari jeebh)

મોઢામાં પાકે છે.
(modama pakay chay)

it grows back, a stump of shoot
grows longer, grows moist, grows strong veins,
it ties the other tongue in knots,
the bud opens, the bud opens in my mouth,
it pushes the other tongue aside.
Everytime I think I've forgotten,
I think I've lost the mother tongue,
it blossoms out of my mouth.
Days I try to think in English:
I look up,

પેલો કાળો કાગડો
(paylo kallo kagdo)

ઉડતો ઉડતો જાય, હવે ઝાડે પહોંચે,
(oodto oodto jai, huhvay jzaday pochay)

એની ચાંચમાં કાંઈક છે.
(ainee chanchma kaeek chay)
the crow has something in his beak.
When I look up
I think:

આકાશ, સૂરજ
(aakash, suraj)
and then: sky, sun.
Don't tell me it's the same, I know
better. To think of the sky

is to think of dark clouds bringing snow,
the first snow is always on Thanksgiving.
But to think:

આકાશ, અસમાન, આભ.
(aakash, usman, aabh)

માથે મોટા કાળા કાગડા ઉડે.
(mathay mota kalla kagda ooday)

કાગડાને માથે સૂરજ, રોજે સૂરજ.
(kagdanay mathay suraj, rojjay suraj)

એકપણ વાદળ નહિ, એટલે વરસાદ નહિ,
(akepun vadul nahi, atelay varsad nahi)

એટલે અનાજ નહિ, એટલે રોટલી નહિ,
(atelay anaj nahi, atelay rotli nahi)

દાલ ભાત શાક નહિ, કાંઈ નહિ, કુછ ભી નહિ,
(dal bhat shak nahi, kai nahi, kooch bhi nahi)

માત્ર કાગડા, કાળા કાગડા.
(matra kagda, kalla kagda)

Overhead, large black crows fly.
Over the crows, the sun, always
the sun, not a single cloud
which means no rain, which means no wheat,
no rice, no greens, no bread. Nothing.
Only crows, black crows.
And yet, the humid June air,
the stormiest sky in Connecticut
can never be

આકાશ
(aakash)

ચોમાસામાં જ્યારે વરસાદ આવે
(chomasama jyaray varsad aavay)

આખ્ખી રાત આખ્ખો દિ' વરસાદ પડે, વીજળી જાય,
(aakhee raat aakno dee varsad puday, vijli jai)

જ્યારે મા રસોડામાં ઘીને દીવે રોટલી વણતી
(jyaray ma rasodama gheenay deevay rotli vanti)

શાક હલાવતી
(shak halavti)

રવિંદ્ર સંગીત ગાતી ગાતી
(Ravindrasangeet gaati gaati)

સૌને બોલાવતી
(saonay bolavti)

the monsoon sky giving rain
all night, all day, lightning, the electricity goes out,
we light the cotton wicks in butter
               candles in brass.
And my mother in the kitchen,
my mother singing:

મોન મોર મેઘેર શંગે ઉડે ચોલે દિગ્દિગંતેર પાને . . .
(mon mor megher shungay, ooday cholay dikdigontair panay)
I can't hear my mother in English.

Sujata Bhatt

A Different History

1
Great Pan is not dead;
he simply emigrated
      to India.
Here, the gods roam freely,
disguised as snakes or monkeys;
every tree is sacred
and it is a sin
to be rude to a book.
It is a sin to shove a book aside
           with your foot,
a sin to slam books down
      hard on a table,
a sin to toss one carelessly
      across a room.
You must learn how to turn the pages gently
without disturbing Sarasvati,*
without offending the tree
from whose wood the paper was made.

2
Which language
has not been the oppressor's tongue?
Which language
truly meant to murder someone?
And how does it happen
that after the torture,
after the soul has been cropped
with a long scythe swooping out
of the conqueror's face –
the unborn grandchildren
grow to love that strange language.

* Sarasvati: the goddess of knowledge. She presides over all the Fine Arts and is worshipped in libraries.

Angels' Wings

I can recall that age
very well: fourteen-years-old,
when I thought I understood
Lenin and Mao,
and Christina Rossetti was beginning
to sound silly.

One April Saturday morning
after swimming lessons
I stood waiting for my father,
pacing the formaldehyde
      stung corridor,
I twirled equidistant between
the autopsy room and his office.

My eleven-year-old brother
         and I together
but silent for a quarter of an hour
as if all that swimming, all that chlorine
had altered our breathing
had washed away our speech.

A heavy door opened and a man,
dark as the shadows he cast,
a man with electric white hair
asked us to step inside.
There was something
he wanted us to see.

The room was festooned with wings,
all of a similar shape
      and strangely human.
Perhaps fairies' wings
      or angels' wings, I thought,
made of real gossamer…

As we stepped closer
we could see clumps of clogged cells,
those grape-like clusters meant to blossom with oxygen –
now shrivelled
beside rivers of blood choked black.

They were not drawings,
not photographs –
but human lungs
well-preserved by someone's
skill in histology.
He could tell us how old
their owners had lived to be
for how many years each had smoked.
He would tell us everything
except their names.

Twenty pairs of lungs
pinned up on his wall:
a collage of black and grey,
here and there some chalky yellow
           some fungus-furred green.

How long did we stand there?
And what did we say?
I don't remember eating lunch
or what we did
for the rest of that day –
Only those twenty pairs of nameless lungs,
the intimate gossamer
of twenty people I never knew
lungless in their graves.

The Stare

There is that moment
when the young human child
stares
at the young monkey child
who stares back –

Innocence facing
innocence in a space
where the young monkey child
is not in captivity.

There is purity
    clarity
there is a transparence
    in this stare
which lasts a long time…

eyes of water
        eyes of sky
the soul can still fall through
because the monkey
has yet to learn fear
and the human
has yet to learn fear –
        let alone arrogance.

Witnessing it all
one can count eyelashes
one can count the snails
in the grass
        while waiting
for eyes to blink
waiting to see who
will look away first.

Still the monkey looks
at the human not in the same way
he would look at leaves
or at his own siblings.

And the human looks
at the monkey knowing
this is some totally other being.

And yet, there is such good will
such curiosity brightening
        their faces.

I would like to slip inside
that stare, to know
what the human child thinks
what the monkey child thinks
at that very moment.

Remember, the human child
is at that age
when he begins to use words
with power
but without the distance
of alphabets, of abstractions.

Mention bread
and he wants
a slice, buttered and with honey –
immediately.

Mention the cat
and he runs over
to awaken her.

The word
is the thing itself.
Language is simply
a necessary music
suddenly connected
        to the child's own heartbeat.

While the young monkey child
grows at a different rate,
looks at a tree, a bush,
at the human child
        and thinks…
Who knows what?

What remains burning
is that moment
of staring:
the two newly formed heads
balanced on fragile necks
tilting towards each other,
the monkey face
    and the human face
absorbing each other
with intense gentleness…

Note

One of the first things to be noted about my selection of five poems is that I haven't included any new work. The reason I've restricted myself to poems from my first two books is that I feel more detached from them and hence I can be more 'objective' about them – which, of course, doesn't mean that the lines in these poems are not alive in my veins. Furthermore, these poems have survived (so far) the test of time and audiences – who, I think, can be quite discerning. I have also tried to include as many 'different' types of poems as possible. This is not, however, an entirely definitive list. The only poem I would keep on every list is 'Search for My Tongue'; the other four poems could be easily substituted by many different but equally varied groups of poems. One feature that these five poems share is that they were all 'gifts', all beginning with a solitary first line which when jotted down rapidly led to a poem: it was almost as if someone had dictated the lines to me.

    I would prefer these poems to speak for themselves, free of any explanations or analysis. Instead, it might be more interesting for the reader to know how the poems came into being: to know the driving forces, external and internal, resulting in these poems.

    I'll discuss the poems in chronological order. This brings us to 'Clara Westhoff to Rainer Maria Rilke' which was written in winter 1979 – sometime between Christmas and New Year's Eve. I was a student then, living in Baltimore. I used to spend a great deal of time at the Johns Hopkins University Library where this poem (among many others) was researched. The previous year, a friend had presented me with a copy of Rilke's *Letters to a Young Poet*. Being young myself, and possessed by similar obsessions (as those explored in the *Letters*) I was hooked which meant of course that I had to know 'everything' about Rilke. My poem grew out of the desire to give life to Rilke's abstract notion of love as 'two solitudes greeting and saluting each other'. Also, knowing about Rilke's problematic relationship with his wife, Clara Westhoff, and knowing that

Westhoff left no written record of her feelings, I tried to imagine what she might have said. At that time (1979) I had never been to Germany and so hadn't a clue as to what Worpswede looked like. Maps, pictures, and written descriptions of the place proved to be useful. Ultimately however, the physical world I created in the poem had to be imagined. Little did I know that many years later I would be living just a few miles away from that very place, in the immediate neighbourhood of the *Kunsthalle Bremen* which accommodates the works of the major Worpswede artists, including Westhoff.

'Search for My Tongue' (of which the second part is reproduced here) was written a few months later in spring 1980. It was started as an experiment, rising purely out of my experience. Although there is much sadness in it, I wasn't sad while writing it – I was absorbed in the play between both languages, and found it a very exhilarating and liberating experiment. Despite the fact that these days, in this German town where I live, there is no one with whom I can speak in Gujarati, my native language remains a resounding physical presence even in the silences within me. I never expected this poem to amount to anything, and didn't think any editor would allow it to enter a book. Ironically, apart from being published in the US, in Britain, and in India, this poem has already been translated into Norwegian, Italian and German.

'A Different History' was written in August 1984, a few days after my arrival in Iowa City. This poem is partly a response to Adrienne Rich's poem, 'The Burning of Paper Instead of Children'. Initially, I had taken the last lines of her poem as an epigram to 'A Different History'. Here are those lines:

> The burning of a book arouses no sensation in me. I know it hurts to burn. There are flames of napalm in Catonsville, Maryland. I know it hurts to burn. The typewriter is overheated, my mouth is burning, I cannot touch you and this is the oppressor's language.

In the end, I was persuaded by my editor to omit the epigram. I believe this leaves my poem open to more varied interpretations – all of which would be 'correct'.

'Angels' Wings' was written in January 1990. My daughter was almost a year old and I was struggling to find time to write again. This poem was very unexpected. A dormant memory surfaced and I wrote it down. Once again it was written quickly and I had no idea what the first line would lead to. The poem was as much a surprise for me as it is for many readers.

'The Stare' was written in January 1991. It is based on memory and observation – and developed out of my fascination with the way small children interact with animals. Several children and various animals have been condensed into one child and one monkey. I had brooded over the subject of this poem for months before gathering the courage to actually sit down and write it.

Luckily, the poem took over and practically wrote itself without much interference from 'me'. I think that the 'I' in my poems is someone different from the 'I' in my prose, and is not exactly the 'I' who lives in the world.

MICHAEL HOFMANN

Kleist in Paris

Dearest Mina,
   Thank you for yours, my first news
of you in ten weeks. Imagine my happiness
when I saw my address in your handwriting.
But then the postmaster wanted to see my passport,
and I didn't have it on me. I begged him
to make an exception, swore that I was Kleist,
but it was in vain. Deceived a thousand times,
he couldn't believe there was an honest man
left in Paris. I went home to get my passport,
and read your letter in a café, quite exhausted.
You are so earnest. Despite all the trouble
I cause you, you still manage to be cheerful.
It moved me so much that I left the theatre
where I was waiting to see a great play,
and ran out to answer you with enthusiasm.
– You want me to tell you about my spirit?
Willingly. The storm has settled somewhat,
the sailor feels the gentle, swelling motion
that announces a bright and sunny day.
Perhaps I can even bless this day in Paris.
Not for its sparse joys, but because it has
taught me that knowledge leads to immorality.
The most developed nation is ready to decline.
When I see the works of Rousseau and Voltaire
in libraries, I think: what is the point?
Why does the state subsidise education?
Love of truth? The state?! A state only thinks
about getting a return on its investment.
It wants comfort, luxury and sophistication.
What can transcend chicken *à la suprême*?
But man is draw irresistibly to the sciences.
He rolls the wheel of fire up the mountainside,
and shoulders it again when it reaches bottom.
If progress doesn't accomplish happiness,
should we say no to it? Forget what we know?
The alternative to decadence is superstition.
Where brightness exists, there is also shadow…
When you consider that it takes a lifetime
to learn how to live, that on our deathbed
we still don't know what Heaven demands,
and can God expect responsibility from Man?
And don't let anyone talk of a 'quiet inner voice'.
the same voice that calls upon the Christian
to forgive his enemy, instructs the savage
to roast him, and he eats him up with reverence
in his heart. What then is Evil? The things
of this world are ramified in thousands of ways,
every deed is the mother of a million others,
and often the best is sired by the worst.
Whatever anyone says about Attila and Nero,
the Huns, the Crusades and the Inquisition,
still this friendly planet rolls through space,
spring comes round again, and people live,
enjoy themselves and die, just as always…
Freedom, my own house, and a wife, I pray
for these every day, my three monastic vows.

Heaven's promised gift to Man is *joie de vivre*.
Man has to work for it by doing good on earth.
I haven't made up my mind what to do yet.
Writing is forever, so I won't commit myself
any further. Be patient and hope for the best.
And don't let a day pass without seeing me.
You can find me in the shady part of the garden,
or upstairs in Carl's room, or by the stream
that flows from the lime-trees into the Oder.
May the past and the future sweeten your present,
may you be happy as in a dream, until – well,
who could spell it out? A long kiss on your lips.

P.S. Greet your parents from me – tell me,
why do I feel uneasy whenever I think of them,
and never of you? It is because you understand me.
I wish the whole world could see you in my heart!
Yes, greet them, say that I honour them,
whatever their opinion of me. Write soon –
no longer *poste restante*, but Rue Noyer 21.

Nights in the Iron Hotel
Our beds are at a hospital distance.
I push them together. Straw matting
on the walls produces a Palm Beach effect:

long drinks made with rum in tropical bars.
The position of mirror and wardrobe
recalls a room I once lived in happily.

Our feelings are shorter and faster now.
You confess a new infidelity. This time,
a trombone player. His tender mercies…

All night, we talk about separating.
The radio wakes us with its muzak.
In a sinister way, you call it lulling.

We are fascinated by our own anaesthesia,
our inability to function. Sex is a luxury,
an export of healthy physical economies.

The TV stays switched on all the time.
Dizzying socialist realism for the drunks.
A gymnast swings like a hooked fish.

Prague

Author, Author
'verba volant, scripta manent'

Can this be all that remains – two or three weeks a year,
sitting at the opposite end of the dinner table from my father?

To listen to his breathing, more snorting than breathing,
puffing out air through his nose during mouthfuls,

chewing loudly with open mouth, without enjoyment,
uninhibited, inhibiting, his only talk, talk of food?

And to watch myself watching him, fastidious and disloyal,
feeling my muscles through my shirt – an open knife!

(My own part of the conversation, thin, witty, inaudible,
as though I'd spoken in asides for twenty-five years.)

To come back to him unannounced, at regular intervals,
one of two or three unselfsufficient, cryptic,

grown-up strangers he has fathered, and see again
his small silver mouth in his great grizzled face,

head and stomach grown to childlike proportions,
supported on his unchanging, teenager's legs…

To come upon by chance, while emptying the dustbin,
the ripped, glittery foil-wrapping of his heart-medicines,

multiplication times-tables of empty capsules,
dosages like police ammunition in a civil disturbance,

bought for cash over the counter and taken according to need –
like his sudden peremptory thirst for a quart of milk.

If sex is nostalgia for sex, and food nostalgia for food,
his can't be – what did a child of the War get to eat

that he would want to go on eating, and to share?
Standing in the road as the American trucks rolled by:

chewing-gum, cigarettes, canned herrings, a kick in the teeth.
(The way it is with dogs, and their first puppy nourishment:

potato-peelings, or my maternal grandmother in East Germany,
and Chéri, her gay dog – pampered, shy, neurotic Chéri,

corrupted by affection, his anal glands spoiling with virginity –
she feeds him heart and rice, the only cooking she ever does.)…

After the age of fifty, a sudden flowering, half a dozen novels
in as many years – dialogue by other means: his main characters

maniacs, compulsive, virtuoso talkers, talkers for dear life,
talkers in soliloquies, notebooks, tape-recordings, last wills…

Hear him on the telephone, an overloud, forced bonhomie,
standing feet crossed, and one punishing the other for lying,

woken up once at midnight by a drunken critic
with his girl-friend hanging on the extension –

her sweet name not a name at all, but a blandishment –
finishing with promises, and his vestigial phrase of English

after ten years in England, *'Bye, bye.'* Then going off to pee,
like the boys at my boarding-school after fire-practice…

Till that time, I had a worshipful proximity with him,
companionable and idolatrous. If my nose wasn't hooked,

my hair not black and straight, my frame too long,
my fingers not squat and powerful, fitting the typewriter keys,

then it was my mother's fault, her dilution, her adulteration.
Home from England, I landed on a checkered pattern

of unwillingness and miserable advice. Not to take drugs,
not to treat my face with vinegar or lemon-juice,

to make influential friends, and not to consort with others.
And, on interesting subjects, either a silence

or the interviewee's too-rapid turning to his own experience…
Perplexed, wounded, without confidence, I left him to himself,

first going round the block on the small-wheeled bicycle
in one of his leather jackets, like an elderly terror;

or, now, on walks with my mother in the shitty park
among the burghers: his duffle-coat in the zoo of democracy.

A performance, like everything else… What's the point?
He wants only his car and his typewriter and his Magic Marker.

Every action he divides into small stages, every traffic light
on the way home, and each one he punctuates with a crucified 'So.'

I ask myself what sort of consummation is available?
Fight; talk literature and politics; get drunk together?

Kiss him goodnight, as though half my life had never happened?

Sally
A blue button-through day, a pink, a black,
the little black dress, the bricks circulating
painfully through the central heating system,
sorrow, lust and peristalsis at three.

Postcard from Cuernavaca
to Ralph Manheim

Picture me
sitting between the flying buttresses of Cuernavaca Cathedral
reading Lawrence on the clitoral orgasm, and (more!)
his notion of replacing the Virgin Mary,
the one enduringly popular foreigner,
with Cortez' translator, later mistress, la Malinche,
the one enduringly unpopular – because xenophile – Mexican…

The night wind
blows the clouds over from the direction of his old palace,
a rather gloomy, conglomerate affair, pirated from an old pyramid,
and studded with red volcanic tufa in heart-sized pieces.
It's an even-handed museum now: offensively large statue of
                                                    Cortez –
revisionist Rivera mural. (Or you turn away from both,
and look to where the volcanoes used to be.)

Out in front,
there are forests of helium balloons glittering under the fresno
                                                            trees
where sociable black grackles natter and scream.
Hawkers trailing by in profile like matadors, trailing – in one
                                                    case a hawk.

A Mariachi trumpeter, wearing just his old pesos,
trilling drily into the gutter. Ostensible Aztecs
stitching their silver Roman-style tunics *im Schneidersitz*.

There's a band
hidden in Eiffel's unilluminated iron snowdrop bandstand –
bought by the Austrians here to cheer them up
when Maximilian left the scene – giving it some humpity.
The rondure and Prussian gleam of the horns –
I sit and listen in the Café Viena.
Anything north of here goes, and most things east.

My room is both.
A steel door, pasteboard panelling,
and so high it makes me dizzy.
The toilet paper dangles inquiringly from the window cross.
A light bulb's skull tumbles forlornly into the room.
Outside there is a chained monkey who bites. He lives,
as I do, on Coke and bananas, which he doesn't trouble to peel.

For Gert Hofmann, died 1 July
The window atilt, the blinds at half-mast,
the straw star swinging in the draught, and my father
for once not at his post, not in the penumbra
frowning up from his manuscript at the world.

Water comes running to the kitchen to separate
the lettuce for supper from the greenflies who lived there.
The sill clock ticks from its quartz heart, the everlasting radio
has its antenna bent where it pinked his eye once.

Ink, tincture of bees, the chair for him,
the chair for my mother, the white wastepaper basket
empty and abraded by so much balled-up paper,
nosebleeds and peach-pits.

The same books as for years, the only additions by himself,
an African mask over the door to keep out evil spirits,
a seventeenth-century genre scene – the children
little adults – varnished almost to blackness.

Outside, the onetime pond packed with nettles,
the cut-down-we-stand of bamboo, the berries
on the mountain ash already orange and reddening, although
the inscrutable blackbirds will scorn them months more.

Note
A funny business and rare temptation, this auto-historicism. Still, my first poem came out in 1979, so I suppose I should be ready for it. Think about album liner-notes and things people said to me, or wrote, along the way: Michael Wood's word 'disarray'; George Szirtes about how all my poems were set in rooms or cars (or did I say that to him?!); or the editor and *Jubilar* of this journal that 'Michael Hofmann is an enigmatic exception' to the general drift that finds life pretty tolerable.

I started off with this amazing shrillness. I appeared innocent and shattered glasses. I remind myself of a boy in short trousers climbing the steps of a pulpit and reading some apocalyptic lesson far beyond his years. Then somehow my naivety became guile. Kleist's voice is trapped in his letter: absolute youth, evasive, clever, passionate, ungrounded, fearless.

'Nights in the Iron Hotel' was written in Prague. American students have thought it was *by* Prague. A critic (David Punter) wrote of 'the cruel corrosive metal that frames the world'. It's a transferred epithet. Everything in the poem is iron really. Iron in the soul. The short sentences crash into one another. I was interested in misprision. 'A hospital distance' – a spitting distance, an inhospitable distance? I studied under Christopher Ricks. I hear my poems in his slow, nagging, teasing voice, that turns the words over as he reads.

Hugo Williams told me in '82 or '83 that he was writing about his father. I shrugged. To me the subject (fathers, not Hugo Williams) was of no interest. Then I got started. Everything for me meets there: German, writing, feeling, sex, self-disgust, the future, the rudder of my life. Why I am what I am and do what I do. 'Author, Author' is the 'biggest' and most rhetorical of these poems. I couldn't have done or borne rhetoric when I began. Repetition was anathema.

I've always loved tiny poems. Chinese, epigrams, snapshots. My poems struggle to be long. 'Sally' is hallucination. Karl Miller, who over the years was as important to me as the Sibyl, said two words to me: once 'reportage', later 'music'.

Most of my poems were written outside England (my very first in Austria, in 1977). It pushes me into the arms of the language, hearing another. I went to Mexico for five months in 1990. It seemed a promisingly explicit place. Some of the places I wrote about, four years later were in rebel hands.

A year ago my father died. I wrote this sitting at his desk a week later. An inventory of objects, *lachrimae rerum*, a Chinese poem. I like the idea now of a less engineered, less indirect poem – more open, adventitious, 'natural'. I hope to bring with me my own intensity, an almost abstract thing, from the words, like Montale. That's the only value.

STEPHEN ROMER

Higher Things
I wish I could, like Søren Kiekegaard,
be absolute and let her face recede

until it is an island in the water
he called memory. Nothing impure

could touch his lasting image of Régine.
Only in memory is love immune

from longing to be with her all the time.
He kept a candle burning in each room,

unfinished manuscript on every desk.
I shall need all his courage for the task

of settling firmly to the sublime;
there is only her face to start from.

Coming Back
(for James Malpas)

When the something withdrawn (you cannot tell
exactly what or when) flows back into the blood
and you return from the damned into your own
(where living is at last to be living now
which the damned cannot know); when your beloved
is again beloved, and morning shows a tree
dressed in light, meaning and memory
at peace in its leaves; when your thought is cool
as linen and you go downstairs to receive
a letter from a friend with total recall
who tells you what you were, and you listen
with attention to rain on the skylight
which tells you what you are;
                                         then you know
that nothing is so lost or gone to waste
that it cannot start again; as when you leave
the city for the pulling air and the sea
which turns upon itself and fills you, something
bows you down to the ground, bows you weeping
down to the sand, weeping there and giving thanks.

The Weight of It
You come out into the floating garden
of early October, there's a mist on your cheek
and you say it's autumn, what have I done

what must I do? and look back at the house
with its cock-eyed face, which you think you want
to leave, but you're seized by a mysterious

invading reverie and stand quite still,
your footprints tracking back in the dew;
the lawn's a mirror where your thought can't settle,

even your language is lost, suddenly
among the grass and the foliage, in the rippling
water of ash leaves against the sky.

And momentarily you're a medium
these presences will trust and pass through
for they know you well, and you them,

such has been the constancy of living here;
then the vertigo of time sets in,
as if the years were gathered in an hour

and you're still standing, rooted in the place,
grown into this garden as the garden
has grown into you, a solitary witness

who cannot easily withdraw.
Then you may ask the garden a question:
what is it continuing for,

what kind of certainty can it supply
after the years of watching
and tending? But there is no reply.

The Work

Settling to work is like the idea
of Venice, a cutglass Serenissima

flashing in the mind's eye;
or a tract of country

we left unexplored one summer,
the small hills winding away

into the memory of what was to come,
the peace and space and time

we promised ourselves, but drove on
gazing back at the work to be done

receding in the rearview mirror.
The Work itself is always there,

like Ithaca, grown lustrous in postponement,
or Penelope, or what we most want

and best avoid, our tacit destination.
There are passages in Titian

of lapis lazuli, distances
at the end of experience,

cool water, bridges, hills, a landscape
of reconcilement and essential time

where the work might take shape
under our hands, if we could get there,

and recover those we have lost,
from the first to the last,

if we could say *the last*, renouncing
such kisses as may come

or places we never saw, the idea
of Venice among them, banished forever

from our high blue peak of concentration.

Blocks & Scaffolds

This snow on your lashes is our duty to the present
falling away on every side at every second
unshareably into avenues estranged from us.

We are elbowed out by the sites and monuments
and the grand promenades of political masters,
captains of industry and moneyed contractors.

Our meagre bundle of human happiness,
or of its opposite, presumably human,
huddles at the foot of a sheer glass precipice.

Machine-washed and replete with cunning light
the crystal pyramid of the cultural state
points up our losses and our own neglect.

You met me in these gardens, a wide smile
in a Russian hat, under trees uprooted since
by the bulldozer of public safety.

These plotted saplings are not for us, my love!
I am the poison tree they carted off to burn
when the city died into traffic and stone.

Note

One of our more distinguished younger poets opined recently that a poet becomes 'established' if he or she manages to develop and then sustain 'an unmistakably individual voice'. This whole notion of 'voice' is tricky, and it came to a head when I sat down to select these five poems. It is notoriously irksome to listen to one's own voice; like speaking with plugged ears, or hearing the fatuity of one's own words repeated in the eerie echo-chamber of long-distance phone calls. It may not be in the poet's gift to decide upon a voice – his audience, if he has one, usually does that for him. Yet it would be disingenuous to pretend to a kind of lyric innocence; most poets are wised-up enough to know they are 'on to a good thing'. They can recognize it, and repeat the performance, like a circus animal.

And so it is that the carefully nurtured ironic elegance, or whatever the descriptive happens to be, is transformed into the voice of temptation – to self-parody. The editor of this journal once declared that 'something had happened' when I sent a batch of poems that included 'Higher Things'; and of course my ears pricked up, and I was grateful to him for not defining the change any further – that became my job. With many poets, I suspect, it is the assumption of the obstacle or the difficulty (like Larkin accepting the mode of failure and self-mockery) that first defines a 'voice'. Becoming self-conscious in this creative sense would then be the first step to maturity as a writer. But only so far and no further; otherwise, as I have suggested, self-parody sets in like rot.

I shall resist the temptation here to provide a thematic account of the poems I've selected. What interests me more is the alternator that seems to drive them. First, there are those very 'rare, random descents' dictated, or delivered whole, by the imagination; (one is brought back, inevitably, to Romantic formulations). I like to call them the Golden Age in any poet's work. Much more often we have the Silver Age in which the lyric impulse is self-consciously mediated by wit, eloquence, ironic distanciation. It is often, perhaps, a more public, audience-orientated voice. I am not necessarily setting up a hierarchy here; both modes are liable to corruption into baser alloys, and one reason for this is, precisely, the attempt to sustain an instantly recognizable 'voice'. 'More of the same' can be a damning indictment. That hard-boiled, strangely invulnerable, ludic tone, so prized these days – God how depressing to find you can *do* it, and more of it…

These are five poems from various periods that I happen to prefer today; tomorrow I might choose differently. Whether they 'characterize' my work is not really for me to say; I start to hear that ghostly feedback again…

IAN McMILLAN

The Grimness: BBC Radio 4, Tuesday, 8.30pm
We don't talk much
but when we talk
we talk about the Grimness.

Almost a cliché
in this muck.
Ah, the Grimness.
I remember it well.

    And now on Radio 4
    the poet Ian McMillan
    presents a feature
    on the Grimness of 1993
    and what it did.

    He talks to a number of people
    who survived it
    and some who
    didn't.

    Such a big microphone

It just sort of sat there
on the settee.
Occasionally it looked at
the coffee table.
Sometimes it glanced
at a wedding photo.
Not its own.
Any wedding photo.
It
had
sacks
full.

    Can you tell me something
    anything about the Grimness.

Look at the view, kid.
Grimethorpe. The band
playing their lips out
but you can't hear them
because the window's shut.

It's smashed but at least it's
shut.

Grimethorpe. Is that mike on?
Is that thing turning?
You can't shift for Channel 4
film crews round here. Big fat bastards
with the arse crack showing, lugging
cameras. Thin kids with boom mikes.

You pick up the lingo.

Little lasses with clipboards.
The colliery band rushing
from shoot to shoot.

    But the Grimness.
    Can we talk about the Grimness?

In the sky, look. That constellation
there.
Round here we call it Wrecked Oil
Tanker,
that constellation, because there's no
shape
to it and its black all around it.

Is that thing turning?
That's a joke.

    O pinpoint the Grimness for me madam.
    Pointpin it. Speak into this thing.
    This, call it what you like, pimple.
    Speak faster than you normally would
    to compensate for my dying battery.
    And in a higher register than you
    would normally employ. Pin pin
    the Grim? Point it?

The Grimness? Not a bad pub.
Dead tap room. Old caps with blokes under.
Knock of a domino echoing back from the '26 strike.
Scab's knock, you see. We pretended we didn't hear it.
It flies round the tap room like a bat. Nice lounge,
young people get in it. Just the one hairstyle
between them. They pass it round like drugs.
Big stuffed fish on the wall. Most pubs have a
big stuffed fish on the wall. Look at that one.
Look closely. Not a fish at all. Look.
A bird

in the shape of a fish. We're not daft.

Ian McMillan

There we have it. The Grimness. Grimethorpe 1993.
Defined. A miasma. The sticky bit of an envelope.
A burst h.w. bottle. Nelson: kiss me, Grimey.
Distant piccolo music. An ant's first breath.
Hooks in a butcher's trousers. I have polished my shoes.
Al Pacino in Carry On Grimethorpe. Valves. Sellotape.
Jiffy Bag with a broken hen in it. Ten to four in the morning.

The Miner's Breakfast:

A bowl of Grimethorpe Flakes. Look: a free model of Thunderbird
8, the forgotten one, like Ghandhi, the tenth Marx Brother.

That's a short shopping list mister!
It's okay!
No shops!

Ian McMillan. BBC Radio 4. Grimethorpe.

Was that okay? Was my voice concerned enough? Enough about
The Grimness? To be honest I wanted to laugh most of the time.
It's funny. Do you think I should do that bit at the end again?
Let's listen back. A man was trying to breathe in a house two
miles away. Bloody deafened me pal.

Halifax!
History nags like a mouth
ulcer, and you can't tell
where one year starts
and the other one ends

except the slang gets
further away from words
you understand. Hunk,
dish, pillock you grew

up with, streets of them.
Now bevs pull bleeds
and you shout Halifax!
I made that last one up.

History nags like a mouth
bleeding, a dream
you can't remember
and therefore never had,

a film you never saw
but read the reviews of
and they were all bad,
they were all bad.

Halifax! History nags
like a mouth, History smells
like a DSS-approved hotel,
a waiter with a tie on elastic,

a receptionist drinking
lager through a straw
who tells you No Messages.
Halifax! I'm on this late

night bus, alone except for
a hunk, a dish and a pillock
with a mouth ulcer, throbbing
like history with batteries.

It's my stop. I'll get off.
Invent some new slang. Halifax!
Canvey! Oban! Barnsley!
Dursley! Chester le Street!

Mining Town
As he goes to sleep
my son's face loses definition.
He becomes like the Man
in the Moon, or a child's
drawing of a face.

His eyes flicker. Outside, in
the light of a Summer evening
Mr Johnson bends down, picks leaves up,
only really he's looking for his wife
who died at the start of the year.

If I think hard I can recall her face just.
My daughters are talking about their visit
to the Yorkshire Mining Museum.
They went right to the face. It was
like a child's drawing
of a moonless night.

And that's it, really. This place
has gone down like a balloon,
one of those balloons that you find
behind the settee two weeks after Christmas.

Nothing more to say. I find it hard
to imagine my dad as a boxing champ;
he was, though, in the Navy, in the 1940s.
He's so gentle. I imagine him saying sorry
every time he punched somebody.

'I never went for the face'
he told me once.

**A Cliché Defines the Moment in a Poem about
Language and Oppression**
A blackened Yorkshire pit village
in the smoke
of a burning chimney, 1968;

Joan always burned her chimney
Sunday Mornings,
heating the oven for the Yorkshires.

'Yorkshire's finest Yorkshires!'
cried Joan, a pinny
on legs. Her husband George

smiled and smiled,
cracking his blue scars, and said
'You've hit the nail on the head!'

Outside, tall Sarah
and her husband Sam
new from Ayrshire, and a
pit shut as a cellar door,
listening at the window,
pulled to Yorkshire
by the NCB's smiling promises
and a film called King Coal.

Rows of houses like rows of boots.

Sarah leaned towards
the open window,
caught the end of the phrase
'… nail on the head.'

and smiled and smiled and said
'It's okay, Sam; they use clichés like we do'
and Sam leaned in the open window
like a sailor through a porthole and said
'You've hit the nail on the head!'

And they all smiled, like skulls smile.

Postmodernist Summer Nights in the Dearne Valley
Went to see a blues band
called the Pete Mitchell Smith
Blues Band at the Thurnscoe Hotel,
missed the last 213, walked home.

Contemplated school names
resonating like boat names
or the names of fishing flies:
Springwood, Upperwood, The Hill,

Low Valley, Sacred Heart, Lacewood.
I've got conjunctivitis. Entropy
and collapse by the Coronation Club,
turn on, attracting more, many more

than the Pete Mitchell Smith
Blues Band. Language falls in
on itself. A dead fish falling
in the bath. I know this valley

like the back of my hand. Look
at the back of my hand. It's
a mystery to me. A mystery.
Your dad's gone fishing.

On his own.

Note
I've chosen recent poems with a sense of place, because that's the kind of writing I'm doing at the moment. The place is an unusual one: South Yorkshire: a surreal, unreal, magically real and real landscape of closed pits and open theme parks, of operas in pit yards and ex-miners setting up as small businessmen. And, of course, the media (and that includes me), recording it for posterity. So, 'The Grimness' looks at Grimethorpe which TV people love because of the Colliery Band and it looks at me trying to make the kind of radio programme I would never get to make; 'Halifax!' sits me on a bus and gets me to try and understand the kind of language my children use as they attempt to live in this opencast/open field/open space world; 'Mining Town' is an attempt to express pain at the extremes of childhood and old age (and Mr Johnson's still there, two years on, looking for his wife. I saw him this morning, staring into a tree); 'A Cliché Defines the Moment in a Poem About Language and Oppression' tries, again, to be about language and place, tries to mix the two up;

'Postmodernist Summer Nights In The Dearne Valley' is my favourite poem of mine as I write this (July 1994) because it comes closest to capturing the feeling I'm trying to convey about here. My reading at the moment is often poets of place: Norman Nicholson in Millom, George Mackay Brown in Orkney, or poets of language, like W.S. Graham… I'm reading his 'Implements in Their Places' over and over these days. I'm reading lots of fiction at the moment, and I'm trying to read more poets I've never heard of, and I hope it's all filtering into my poems. I'm not sure. I'm pretty sure that I'll stay here in Darfield for ever, trying to use its greening hills, its empty shops, its men walking dogs up and down the same roads every day, its huge skyscapes dotted with planes coming down to Leeds or Manchester Airport as material for the kind of poems I want to write, or the kind of poems I can't help writing, which may or may not be the same thing.

Ask me again for the 200th issue. They'll be looking for me up a tree then!

PETER SANSOM

The Folklore of Plants
Joss slices hunks of ham
off the ham-hock. His hand clamps
the bone to the table
and he cuts away from himself 'because that way
you never cut yourself'. When he

eases the pressure, the milky pearl
of the knuckle shines more brightly.
I am reading a book called *The Folklore of Plants*.
It is Saturday tea,
makeshift because Mother is poorly.

'Blockbusters' tells us the Italian-born pioneer
of radio was Macaroni. Dad grips the loaf,
butters the open edge before slicing.
Tea appears by magic
from beneath the rabbit cosy,

and I pour. Dave has given up sugar
but has to go in any case. His car-coat
half-on he looks helpless
and on cue Dad says 'You'll be blower-catched,
it's five and twenty past.'

So far no-one has thought to ask Mother
if she wants a cup or anything to eat.
She is in bed again with the ulcer she kept
to herself for fear it was the cancer
that killed her sister.

Dave leaves and another brother comes in.
'Our Brian,' says my dad when he hears the door go,
but it is Tony. He has a big bunch of holly,
he doesn't say for Christmas
but for winter. He doesn't know

it's bad luck before Christmas Eve
– Mother wouldn't have it in the house –
and no-one says. 'Another book,'
he says cheerfully, shaking his head at me,
'you bloody live in books.'

Al & Clare Have Bought a Middle Terrace instead of being Married

They are working in the cellar.
Above us, a man is turning the roof.
Sometimes there is a room full of pot-plants
where the dead speak to us from near at hand;
they are like voices from the under-drawing.

And our memory of them is a ship
in distress. Our memory of them is
foundering in heavy seas; and we are woken
as if someone had knocked on the window
with words about the rain, but the washing

is finished in the utility room.
It is curtains. It's a digression, a domestic
parenthesis in a sentence in a section
dealing with some entirely different subject:
let us say Climbing. Climbing that endless ladder –

you must not look down, but then you do.
Dusk is falling, you're afraid of heights,
and night rung by rung decants last moments
into our brimming glasses, into a blue
earthenware jug, into our hands.

I Opened the Door

I opened the door and walked through.
I opened the door and stood in the doorway.
I opened the door and hit my head on the edge.
I cut my head open opening the door.
I opened the door no problem,
I have been opening doors all my life, as long as I can
    remember.
I opened the door and went out,
It was raining.
I opened the door and went out,
It was sunny.
I opened the door and it wasn't raining or sunny,
It was a cupboard door.
I couldn't open the door it was locked.
I couldn't open the door it was bolted on the inside.
I couldn't open the door it was a window.

January

1
You stand at the door (you sometimes are
the door) and, according to tradition, look
to the past year as well as to the new;
but me, I'm all for that watch, moving on
in a room so quiet I can almost see
the second finger as it beats against each mark,
though for a while I can't place it,
there, by the blank appointments book and diary
on the uncluttered desk. Mid-morning
the beginning of 1993.
We have been to the coast, as we do.
The garlands are down, the tree undressed
and hoovered under, bin-bagged and put out.

2
According to tradition, and by name,
you look back as you look forward, while what is
is people skating on their arses down Slant Gate,
burst pipes, a broken tanker spilling oil,
or the fox's single line of prints
to scramble our ice-locked gate for scraps
we first of all put out for the birds.
Now we put out rind, bread, apples at night,
for him, always the same young fox.

3
Reading by candlelight, next door's telly
on with this year's honours, I saw you,
at that moment, or thought I did, on a long slow track
out of evergreen woods, the start
of a ridge walk between two counties
when the valley was a stopped snowstorm
and the mountain air was white in our lungs
all morning gradually higher and higher,
my friend and I, what great friends we were then.
Till, reaching a summit, we could look down
with all of nature in our English pocket
and point out scree and gullies, scattered homes,
and name the named mountains round us
before picking our way back to the pinched-grey lake,
the straggling winter village, the mini-mart and café.
I saw you all right, but your back was turned.

4
Young and old, you give voice to a bell
telling midnight across an estuary,
crossed, uncrossable, the air thick with salt;
and that voice has the gawky confidence
of sharp bright metal; but that voice too
is the round, sober parish bell, the copper tang
of licking an old penny. Its chimes roll by
to where you are; and, at the last of them,
you are here, unassuming, a fox
in that fable of the old fox in his cave,
pretending to be ill and inviting
all the animals to visit him
so he could eat them without having to go out.

To Leigh Hunt

'I see even now
Young Keats, a flowering laurel on your brow'

Millfield Lane, Hampstead. You shook my hand,
that last time, as Coleridge did just here –
the handshake he said of a dying man,
but today I walked the heath, admired the Turner

and understood the distance I had travelled.
The house is a monument. I went instead
to spend an hour with a slip of a girl
in a damp room, no sheets on the bed

but enough claret inside her to be sure.
Indeed she passed out and I was obliged
to finish by myself. Now I am certain
of nothing but the colour of her eyes.

She will wake to a fever of her skin,
despising the money but pocketing it:
almost a remembrance, to say her name again
and leave a note in her currency.

Leigh, you praised me, half-proud of, half-amazed
at my posthumous reputation –
while you, 'The Spirit of the Age',
wrote yourself into oblivion.

One morning she will come to read 'Bright Star'
and, looking to a critic for the answer,
will find your name, vaguely familiar
though she has not read a word of yours;

and then, in Gittings, her brow will crease
at the time you crowned me with laurel,
a night so warm we wrote beneath the stars -
I blushed at those rhymes, but now they make me smile,

pleased to have been your friend. Remembering
will change her too. Because, I remember
how we meant to look back at that evening –

true success, the two of us together

joking, laughing, batting a late moth
from our faces lit with drink, and then
the Reynolds' girl turning up to flirt with.
We would never be that way again.

I read the girl read further, how you lived
to see your best-seller 'Rimini' dismissed,
and coped with it in your not-so-wedded bliss;
while I, Shelley's Adonais,

lay broken in Rome among the English Poets…

*

Well, we have left the night forest,
The landscaped gardens,
The people.

I don't know your second life;
Only that I am obsessed with water.
I have fed a river
I have walked into an ocean
I have taken the coin of language on my tongue

And everything I was once capable of,
Those even to me miraculous words
Wait in my rapid hand,
And in my little books, to be written.
I will not write them.
I have become a reader of water,
A life of sensations.

I have found my place
In the bright book of the dead
Where I sit before a window
Which opens on a lake,
And like the picture of somebody reading
I read daylong, nightlong,

In sunlight that writes itself in water.

Note

These may not be my five best poems, but they will give you an idea of the sort of different things I do. 'The Folklore of Plants' is very early. I like it though because it gets so many members of the family in, and gives you a glimpse of teatime at our house. The opening of the third stanza, incidentally – our Dave struggling with his car coat – seems to me real poetry. And although it comes rather pat, Tony actually did say that bit at the end.

'Al & Clare Have Bought a Middle Terrace Instead of being Married' is from the same book, *Everything You've Heard Is True*. I thought about 'The Fox in the Writing Class', and the Agony column, which is my funniest poem, or else the one for my dad, which is probably my strongest poem. But I plumped for Al & Clare because it was something I was looking for in those days – the poetry equivalent of a Talking Heads' song – and which I only really managed the once. I tried dozens of times after that to write the same way, but it always came out flimsy or contrived.

From *January*, I've chosen the prefatory piece 'I opened the door' and the title poem and then one in the voice of John Keats. The book is full of doors and dead people, something I noticed only half way through writing it, and which even when I did didn't amount to a programme or schema (though not for want of trying). 'I opened the door' was written in a classroom in Salford with thirty two nine year olds, and I always use it in schools alongside such gems as 'The Giraffe in the Black Hat', 'Jeremy Boring' ('he spends so long outside the head's/they've fixed him up with his own camp bed') and 'You will Soon get Warm as You Run Up and Down'.

I'm proud to say that the poem 'January' was sponsored by Alison Lurie, who came across *Everything* in Cornell and sent me a £100 cheque because she'd heard that money is a nice way to show you mean a fan letter. I couldn't believe it. Alison

Lurie is a *real* writer. (She'd always been one of my favourite novelists – though now of course she's top of the tree in my book.) And we'd just been wondering how to afford our usual New Year week in Whitby. It took me much longer to write the star-struck thank-you note than it did actually to write the poem. I lay in bed one sunny cold morning in the cottage overlooking the harbour, worrying that I'd not written anything in months, and wondering what Keats (why settle for less?) would have done; and I thought about the second bit in Autumn where he talks directly *to* Autumn in wonderfully vivid concrete terms, and I thought why not give that a go for Winter.

That's how it got started. The companion poem which closes the book, and brings the year round full circle, is called 'Whitby', in fact. I mention this poem, though I haven't chosen it here, because the final phrase in it is what 'Carcanet' means…

Finally, the Keats poem. Notice the conceptual rhyme 'sure/certain' in stanza three. Daring or what? Though nearer, actually, than some of the half-rhymes. There's more I could say about this poem if I hadn't run out of space sixty-eight words ago.

JAMES KEERY

Necessary Laziness
Lo Catoun, which that was so wys a man,
Seyde he nat thus, 'Ne do no fors of dremes?'

I have dreamed lately serene-blue unsolipsistic dreams,
Slumbering off the passive exhausting delirium of flu.
'A mere fever of thyself,' Keats would call me,
But my own life seems a bit less real than other people's
Just at the moment; I am one
Of those to whom the impressions of the world
Are beautiful and will not let them rest: –
A vision of the progress of an essay
Which I have never waking contemplated
But on which Susan
Is presently intent
Blended into walking down Culcheth Hall Drive
With Alison, passing the house
Of a neighbour and his wife (who don't exist)
Exchanging with her the smile of a free equal
And making a casual promise to the flags!

Distractions of March
Come out, come out, you yellow daffs,
Flying high with your long green staffs!

It gave over just as it was winning.
I'd stood at the kitchen window watching each flake land
And melt into the slice of Dunn's tree.
It dampened and coated the red wood, but on the path
Began to collect in puddles and drowned itself.
I felt in my heart somehow it wouldn't lie, and continued washing up.
The afternoon grows deeper, and flakes still fall, but the snow has not
Established the soft limits of desolation. It lies
Too wetly on the lawn, weaker and weaker, going green and patiently
Expecting a bright moon to freeze the air,
Which it just might. Snow-besprinkled daffodils, less
Wintry than that east wind, that blew all yesterday,
When Steve caught the plane to Kathmandu, until July. He was considering
Buying a house in Cambridge, according to Susan.
Melinda's stuck with her dissertations.
I saw a great tit shrug some snow off its wings.

How Many Streams Can You Rake With Your Copper Rake?
The nets have come up empty, leaving us free to imagine
What the object was. Who crayoned large, red slogans
On my body as I was sleeping? The dream
Would bleed away if I opened my eyes. This longing
Beyond you is love, and no cause for sadness.

The Strength of a Rope
Lucidity is good in all things;
In weather, and in the activity
Of an afternoon, harvesting
Irrelevancies. Mum's
Wondering whether a Henry VIII
Stamp won't upset the Catholic
College she's applied to. They
Discriminate against Ulster
Protestants, the priest
At her last interview was
Quite candid about it. Dad
Asked me who said, 'Every good
Servant does not all commands,'
He thought it was Talleyrand. I
Was delighted to remember my
Cymbeline, in the end, after
Looking it up in the *Dictionary
Of Quotations*, but in vain.
'The strength of a rope may be
But the strength of its weakest
Part,' but this principle
Does not apply to poetry, as
Augustine Birrell says. I like
His criterion, too: 'Do we
Whisper him in our lady's ear?'

Grebe Lodge
There were fishermen on my stretch of the canal,
So I headed up towards Bickershaw, crossed
Over to the other side of the footbridge,
And found myself among fenced-off stock ponds
With paths leading in every direction,
Fussily sign-posted like a Nature Reserve.
There was a young couple with a child
In front of me, so I selected
A pathway that led to Grebe Lodge, according
To a very convincing hand. There was a mist
On the channels, and dank, sudden cold. The lodge
Was there all right – it stood out against the dusk,
A log cabin whose entrance smelled strongly
Of turf, and it was empty. What I could see
From the viewpoint, as I knelt
On the wooden seat that skirted the wall
Was, to begin with, half a dozen grebes;
Then I looked over the water
At a slag heap shaped exactly like Ben Bulben
With dense grey clouds above, and below
A perilous shadow on the water, a blank abyss.

I was almost alarmed to see a pair of moorhens
Paddling into it, but instead
They bobbed about like plastic ducks
And thought better. I looked to my left
And there, to my delight, there was a heron,
Hunched a little, looking into the pool.
It straightened with an awkward twist
And leaned forward, then flapped out of sight,
Though probably only a yard or two, behind
The bank that divides the pool from open water.

*

I had been there in many moods – the wide water
Had taken as many guises as there are evenings
In as many weeks as all my walks would make,
And that was only the water – what of the skies?

For that was all there was, as often as not:
Skies wide enough to bloom and still be empty,
Whether of birds or clouds, however dense;
Wide water deep enough to reflect the whole sky.

Note
It's curious, but I've never been able to shake off the feeling that I've written my last poem. Often I find I have, for months at a time, and perhaps it's natural that a poem should be accompanied by a sense that a spring has run dry. But the feeling is really final, that my story is told. I suppose it's because I tend to write from a present-that's-already past. I can't speak about intention in what is (for me) an unconscious activity, but I find that when I write my attention is exclusively to the sound, the rhythm, not so much of the words as of the originating impulse. I'd better draw a distinction between what I mean by this and the lyric epiphany, for the kind of impulse I mean is as likely to give rise to discursive prolixity as to anything more succinct and imagistic. But each of my poems has its originating moment, in which it is in some sense implicit, and the quality of that moment is what I listen to, and listen for.

CHRIS McCULLY

Houses
They seem solid: render and Accrington brick,
good lines, set angles on a suburb slope
where no one hears (the walls are two feet thick)
the neighbours loudly drinking down their hope.
But scaffolding's erected everywhere
and yesterday these houses' roofs were gone;
the day before, the stonework layer by layer
vanished into dance-hall whistling and the sun.

Foundations turned to foot-prints, which grew back
to moor and coppiced hazel; road bled a spring
where horses drank; and through the Zodiac
the past unravelled on its stick of string
until what made the paid-for future there
was merely geese and winter, sleet and air.

Rain
  You should have seen the rain.
The hill was Lear's bald head left to the falling storm
and darkness shocked itself, in a springing wave buried the road
the valley and the singing stones, and each house
went out completely, like a switched-off brain;
  and you should have seen the rain –
stotting down so hard it melted hair and washed away
fences, pylons, all landmarks; fused lights; broke roofs;
and stopped the diesels underground in floods
(the water rising, hands hammering each pane);
  but you should have seen the rain
that night, last night, the very last – the howling stacks,
the gutters full, and all the fish swept smoothly out to sea
and back again, dispersed among the sky-reflecting fields,
fields of white noise, the static hiss of rain on rain,
  the rain you should have seen,
the broken storm, endless, the storm with strength
to hurt itself, with strength to erase my name
and yours, whether we lay apart listening to the rain
or in each other's arms and felt the rain,
imagining the dark rain walking towards us, the bane
stored up for us from the beginning of might-have-been.
  You should have seen, it was almost marvellous,
  you should have seen the rain which cancelled us.

Bede's Copyist

I have no proper name, yet his is tall
on Europe's stones and in the candleflukes
whose culture briefly held a sparrow's brawl
in a crowned head. We set it down in books,
a lettered Latin: that bird; this birth; that stall –
    with no mistakes.

Outside, the snow almost obscures the park,
our wooden Christ's obliterated face.
Inside, with all the negligence of grace
his habit falls across my page's mark.
Again we work between space and space –
    and both are dark.

This

Where did this begin?
    Not with the travelling hand,
    not with the gravelled paper,
    not with a person or a land,
    not with this voice behind the chin.

This was accidental, this was thrown
    from year to year like history,
    from mouth to mouth like dust;
    this is the sound of an old mystery –
    the noise time passes, like your own:

a dry scape, leaves on a road,
    the ticking of insects in a summer light,
    the itch of words as you turn the pages,
    the hiss of whisky in a glass at midnight –
    provisional silences you're owed.

But where did they begin?
    In flesh, the rage of skin on skin.,
    in alluring places of unease,
    in ghosts of marriage-beds, or body-resin,
    in beer, or blood, or tin –

too far back now ever to tell:
    a word-haunting, love in the dark,
    an animal ambition for itself;
    a poisoned finger in the park;
    an ego-hill; the memory-well.

This was Yes in throats torn
    by the edges of hours, minutes as they passed;
    by the shattering of faces in mirrors;
    by the weight of seeing through what fades at last
    into purpose, knowledge; into being born.

Some Say

I wish I were the river. Its power now
in flood obliterates
everything it once thought about itself:
on the valley stones, on this winter floor among the rocks
it slides through its own skin like a brown snake.

Elsewhere, perhaps, it's become a lake
for migrating birds, snowflakes or reflections of low cloud;
elsewhere, almost unimaginably, past pipes and drums,
the luxury of knotted towns and confluence, oil in the estuary
and wharves where slips no longer build,
it's become the sea –

turns blue in August, is mackerel-tide,
or salt-secreting cell in the anemone's claw,
disperses until the salmon smell it out,
evaporates, is sun-smashed, hauls through the winds,
repeats itself in isobars and the blowing sky, is mist and cloudburst
for summer's same greens riddling on their boughs.

Some say the river's purpose is the sea;
others say, deftly casting a fly, its fish,
rising to sedge in the halflight or
spawning on redds in the uplands where no hand is;
others see purpose in its geography,
its gathering in of loose stuff from the hillsides,
straw and branch and bloodstained fleece, the watershed
exacting its price; for others
it's the haunting of fossils; others simply think
its purpose is dogs and exercise, their favourite walk.

But here, in time where springs evolve
obscurely from reed and blackened brick, the flood supposes
nothing of its animate purposes.
Watching this twisting, unslackening rope of water pass
towards whatever end, leaving its new course
printed on bent stem and flattened, silver grass…

The river is the eye that looks at it.

Note

I've chosen these poems as representative since they embody some of the themes my poetry seems to be interested in: time and event, cause and effect, how the quotidian intersects with the enduring. At the same time, I'm aware that poets' accounts of their work may be charming fictions: if I say that I usually write in metrical forms ('it must be abstract, it must give pleasure') then I fictionalise the formal even as I make the claim. But I do prefer highly stylised rhythmical and metrical procedures since I think that modulated equivalence ('parallelism') is close to the essence of what I understand to be poetry. I also require my poetry to be that which cannot be said in any other way.

Influences. Like most writers I'm a good mimic, so I have to ration my reading of verse: Yeats, Dante, Auden and above all, Old English poetry; northern landscapes; love and waste.

I'm currently working on a large-scale setting of a mass; this seems to be writing itself alongside my fatal fondness for light verse and puns.

I write with some reluctance, and produce less than I did (I hear some relieved applause), but then again, I take more risks and know a few short cuts: twenty years' writing should, after all, enable one to turn a line somehow.

faber and faber
Poetry

This be the *list* . . .

Fergus Allen	Marianne Moore
Simon Armitage	Andrew Motion
W H Auden	Edwin Muir
George Barker	Paul Muldoon
John Berryman	Richard Murphy
Amy Clampitt	Norman Nicholson
Wendy Cope	Don Paterson
e e cummings	Tom Paulin
Walter de la Mare	St John Perse
Emily Dickinson	Harold Pinter
Douglas Dunn	Sylvia Plath
Lawrence Durrell	Ezra Pound
T S Eliot	Christopher Reid
W S Graham	Oliver Reynolds
Lavinia Greenlaw	Anne Ridler
Philip Gross	Theodore Roethke
Thom Gunn	Siegfried Sassoon
Ian Hamilton	Vikram Seth
Seamus Heaney	Harry Smart
Michael Hofmann	Stevie Smith
Miroslav Holub	Stephen Spender
Ted Hughes	Wallace Stevens
David Jones	Matthew Sweeney
James Joyce	Edward Thomas
Weldon Kees	Martin Turner
Philip Larkin	Chase Twichell
Edward Lear	Derek Walcott
Primo Levi	Susan Wicks
Christopher Logue	Richard Wilbur
Robert Lowell	Hugo Williams
Louis MacNeice	Hubert Witheford
Don Marquis	Adam Zagajewski

And still generating . . .

IAIN BAMFORTH

Reluctance
There's no way back
along the rutted lanes and puddles
where light settles
into a final liquefaction
of its natural uses.

Will tomorrow come?
None of us knows for certain
or cares enough to ask.
Flakes of sky drift down
on the open moor.

There's only the wind
brushing softly on the door.
What that means
is an innuendo of harvest plaits,
marks of the tribe.

The cattle get off their haunches.
Day stands in the door.
No other way to go but this,
afraid of arriving
where we're being brought.

The Water Tower
Wonder at it –
the ruined water-tower,
its cool fuselage
like a prophet in the scrub,

a rain-revivalist
waiting all day
for a hectoring vision
of sand, wind and stars,

that slight involuntary
creaking of the skin,
the metal flanges
sagging into rust, rungs

of a Jacob's ladder
slung against the sun's
hot echoings.
All night it groans

like nothing else on earth,
a drumming silence
calling up a cargo-cult
for angels, moguls –

any kind of transiting
promoter. Look up,
it vaunts, at the vector-
shifts of satellites,

those solar mirrors
of the hopeful parched –
O difficult life
at the midnight door.

Dread relic, this
is the coming-full-circle,
the marrow's appeal
to the tabernacle choir:

it sings your asperities,
a reservoir on high
and the windows in a blaze.
Wonder at it –

the funnel of our faith
and the earth's slow plume
dispersing in a trance
on the desert floor.

Lenz
When the breath of danger finally fades
dawn is one more broken vessel.
'Trace it back to where it came from –
what you'll come away with is vertigo and nausea.'

Outside a small ceremony's taking place
under eerie noonday lightning,
the life-symbol glazing to a durable icon.
'Just leave it for the cleaners in the morning.'

Even in this white place, intelligence slowly
puts out leaves from its bare branches.
Overhead a petrel raises the alarm,
and we go in behind the bulwarks of silence.

A row of tents drags on its sinews.
One or two dark shapes can be seen pounding frost,
singing as they reach down into a dishevelled
sea of transcendental homelessness.

Beached whales turn to shale in the underground
of potholes and cave-ins, a lava river
coursing through miles and miles of cracked tundra.
Hearts are being weighed in feathers.

'What do travellers do? They learn to walk
by using their heads, like Lenz.
To step over difficulties by piling them up –
eskers, pingos, drumlins, abruptly calving glaciers.'

Far away, we hear the tribulation of a million diatoms,
foraminifera waving goodbye. 'Where now?
Sunlight's a burden on our backs.
All our conversation gets sucked up the flue.'

So we fade into history like strange attractors,
conscience leaping in the slop-bucket:
our palms empty and open, our one hope to glimpse
an iceberg's slow advance on the equator.

Open Workings

In between the yellow utes
and the flame-tree garageways,
my wife at the wheel –

upward to the scorched mesas
and camel-track droppings
of the overland Australia;

weatherboard houses reconciling
to the desert's boiler room,
sad suburbs without a centre,

figures all agape, wondering
what it was they'd heard. Transients,
we were crossing a language

bigger than its confines, burning
rubber and clambering up
the loose gravel of our talk,

lying on a broad hammock
slung between – gum-trees, the Hill
below, revealing its workings –

the lustre of its artemesian
gardens and the slow-arriving days,
desire like a flowering aquifer.

Mountains and Valleys

Once I had gone into the low adobes
from the mountains and valleys
everything became obvious;
faces hid in hands,
there was a spreading dimness
and quiet turning away, and I heard
a final warning about the man
with a mind of his own.

That day my name was Mud.
A brotherhood of stove-pipe hats
huddled me across the verdict
and on to commonsense's level ground,
downwind from the tannery
and the biblical beasts of burden.
What was on my mind
was the fate of my Gladstone.

And then they smiled, wanting
to teach me who I was.
Folk history, it's a hempen bind
and hedgehog diffidence
but the good book on the table
said I hadn't heard the half.
When I talked of leaving
it made as much sense to stay.

December – blew off the river,
and they weren't what they seemed,
the mountains and valleys.
Hands delved for dishes,
the dark route through the day.
Here was the meaning of the North –
gutters adept with rain
and hard silence after, alerted.

VONA GROARKE

Patronage

Arriving from Bath, they were a strange ménage –
a family thrown together by four marriages,
and having nowhere else to go. Four daughters
older than their new mother, and single still:
their chances harried by a father's debts.

He tinkered with prospects and arrangements of trees,
laid out a town to bear his family name,
devised a railway to cut across the bog,
and so, made an impression, and settled down
to oversee a world of prudence, tact, reserve

and writing books. One daughter worked
at a table made of wood from the estate.
While her sisters stitched bright patterns in
a lace-work plot of pleasantries and chat,
she took a clutch of unstrung characters

and muddy syllables, and set them in a landscape
of her own. In which her father recognised a flaw
and had her slightly shift the view from where
she stood, to take in the symmetry of poplar trees
that secured them from the wilderness beyond

but could not distinguish them, after all,
from a future placed elsewhere;
a time beyond him when their house
would become a final home for the old,
or its rooms be converted by nuns to maternity wards.

I was born in the ballroom of Maria Edgeworth's house.
I have tried to imagine the line that takes you from
muslin and moonlight to my mother's screams
and then to me, her last, her unstrung child.
But a room will always cover over more than it reveals.

A house is one place trapped in another.
With the windows shut and the doors locked up,
it passed for a place no one would choose to leave.
And when they found their way to a separate life,
something of what they could not leave remained.

I have never returned to Maria Edgeworth's house,
but I've passed behind it on the Longford train
and seen them sitting out in the garden.
I've noticed how they turn towards us as we pass,
how their faces are lost in the shadow of the house.

Rindown
A ruined castle approached by water,
an outpost station from the thirteenth century

where I used to camp in high summer,
pitch a tent at the castle walls,

and set a fire, as others did,
against the gutted silence of the lake.

Each time deciding that what's essential
survives after all – as a gateway

is a last defence against fields
of ragwort, gorse, and fireweed.

Each time deciding that all that's left
is to stand in the shadow of the final trees

to watch the strange and sullen mass of birds
turn above the headland to the north,

then stretch across the lake again, like smoke.

Figures on a Cliff
The rock-pool is where my voice sounds best.
To one side of an empty strand, where a single
tent is pitched to add a point of colour
to the scene, the breeze is lightest,
and my voice sounds best. In the rock-pool,
half-hidden by boulders and an upturned boat,

I am testing the air. I sing what I see,
find notes for sand, the cliff, the hills across the bay.
The scene is set. An evening early in the year.
A woman stands alone on the beach
with her dress hitched up, and her hair undone,
making music with the rhythm of the sea.

What would it take to turn this scene around,
to render me irrelevant, a figure
almost covered in by stone, drawn against
an ocean that will surely take me in?
A woman and her song are details.
The figures on the cliff have barely noticed me.

A slight shift in perspective, and I disappear.
The cliff is more imposing, the sand attracts the eye.
The dull insistence of the sea absorbs it all.
There are darknesses to counter what I wear.
Even my silver bracelet can't outshine
the light that snags on shingle near the wall.

Where I stand is hardly worth a second look
unless the eye is caught by something else:
the play of light; a seagull on the wing;
my skirt, worried by a sudden wind that shows
my legs as quartz against a limestone drop;
a drift of song that's barely audible.

But I may stay. The light is kind.
I could take up my song where I left off.
The sun may be drawn back, and once more
I will stand as the centre of it all.
My song may outstay the waves, and my hands,
to give it strength, instruct the sea.

In time, the pool may draw the warmth from me
and the scene its point of reference, until
the light moves, just fractionally, away
to where the cliff figures, inscrutable, pristine,
are unaware of their importance,
are surprised at being seen.

Home
I always thought this house would hold us;
that what we left would stay here, undisturbed,
except to be explained as stories told
of changes that we made to what we found.

In details like the worn upholstery, a cracked door-frame,
the bathroom wall with all our heights marked in,
I found the proof that something would survive
of years lived here, and that in finding it

– on a Sunday visit, or a Christmas stay –
we might come upon a store of memory
that would remind us, call us to ourselves.

I always thought this house could keep us safe,
as when, running from the car
to the front door, late at night,
I knew it was where darkness could not reach.

The dark can make no difference here.
Our house has been blown open
to a vacant future, bleak as January

in which no window is lit
against the dust and disregard,
where the only sound is the rooks in the chimney,

and the wind sifted through the hall,
closing, opening the kitchen door.

A Tree Called the Balm of Gilead
What is it that is done
and undone in a name?
How is it that the Tacamahac
from North America has come
to rest on waste ground beside
my home, to be named in my book
of trees, the *Balm of Gilead*?

Note

After *Castle Rackrent*, Maria Edgeworth's father began to appreciate the charms of having an author in the family. London beckoned with its literary evenings and free meals, and so he took it on himself to guide her hand, to smooth out a certain roughness in her style, and to recommend to her the moral parable as the structure best suited to her gifts. As a consequence, her work cast off its danger and its verve, and gradually solidified into a model of the well-made, formal and the terminally dull. Of course, it is for her first, deviant and gently subversive novel that she is now loved.

Mr Edgeworth was right. The moral parable is a most attractive literary form. I use this one to illustrate recurring themes in the poems I write: questions of history, legacy, loss, flux, power, and control. And architecture, which continues to fascinate me as an expression of historical intent.

My impulses are towards fiction, but not prose. My poems are narratives encountered through the lyric form. Although the central assertion of 'Patronage' is a fact, my poems are not confessional. The 'I', 'You', 'He' and 'She' of the poems are all stylised figures, and the facts of the poems are not necessarily events from my life.

There is a literalism to my poems, a flattening out of theme and subject matter. Thematically, 'Patronage' is probably the largest poem I've written. The other four chosen here are smaller in terms of thematic range, but they all arrive at the same preoccupations and ideas. The smallest and last poem here, 'A Tree Called the Balm of Gilead' is the most overtly concerned with language, but all five, I hope, are grounded in a sense of their own form and its potential.

JUSTIN QUINN

To Jan Neruda

I
If I wanted to tell people who you were
First off I'd say that there's a hill
Which stands above a turning river,
And stretched along its top a castle –
The city crystallising outwards
The last nine hundred years or so
On this basis, around lakes, through swards.
Beneath the castle, row on row
Of baroque tenements are pursed,
The quarter where your ghost persists.

These days you're pure omniscient narrator.
How often did you raise your head
Mid-way through making characters
To listen to what was being said
By other tenants in the hall-way
And think: this is my work, to hear
My people living, speaking daily,
To never lose them, move so far
That they might some time chant in chorus,
You are distant, you are not of us.

Outside you hear the agèd woman
As she is proudly telling neighbours
About her civil-servant son
Who diligently toils and labours
Up in the castle these last few years,
'And speaks good German, never Czech.'
Do you use this? A girl inquires
In early drafts what he looks like,
And the mother flushes red with shame.
The vignette closes. He never visits home.

Sometimes returning home you see
The bureau waiting there for you
To forge the national conscience, free
Your people from the fact they don't know
They are your people; the worksheets spilling
Steadily over the edge into
The world they are about, along
The floor, up walls, through streets, and through
Their tendered hearts '... *the land! the land!*'
The new age stealing from your hand.

Or not. A hundred feet above
The room where you sit writing this,
Above these lesser lives and huddled roofs
Which you are winding into strophes,
Up in the castle on the hill
The imperial bureaucracy
Grinds hugely on, its massive will
Oblivious to poetry,
Or anything you care to throw at it,
As safe as planets in their orbit.

II
I'm one street down from where you died
About a hundred years ago.
The worksheets for this poem are splayed
Half-way across the table. Below,
The old surgeon whose old house this is
Is reading books of history
To find out where things erred, his glasses
Twisting typeface into clarity.
He cannot fathom what I'm at,
Despite our common theme of squandered *Heimat*.

It's possible that there lies beneath
His mountainous encyclopædic learning
The simple question: why? Why at the zenith
Of his life did he lose everything
Through war and farmhands in high office?
If you spend your life repairing hearts
And cutting cancers out, it's fair to possess
The hope that in your lifetime courts
Will fairly judge, the state will thrive,
And that somehow people will improve.

None of which is true, so many
Saved and stitched up by his hands,
Which I see often resting finally
On his lap – their flesh and finger-joints
Long drained of their technique.
What new work could be dreamt for them?
Sometimes he might put down his book
And stare into the street, one theme
Revolving always in his head,
But downwards, on the finest thread.

III
You failed. Like this is failing too.
When you stared into that black lake
And tried to resurrect a hero,
A vis, a principle, with which to make
Your people proud and lead them toward
Themselves, confecting national feeling,
Your words did not become the world.
And therein lies your final failing
And why I'm writing this to you,
This quarter's spirit, hearing me.

It never does. It keeps its distance.
Go down to the turning river
Below the hill on which the castle stands.
Half for yourself, still you will murmur
Lightly and lightly, O my land,
Move lightly through the air again,
And go on wishing this, no wand
Instead of your black fountain-pen,
Just the oblivious city, and in
Among its streets, this poem being written.

Two Political Poems

1. A Seagull's Skeleton
Its eye saw land becoming sea
A hundred times a day, then back again,
Caught high by wind and steered quickly
Inwards, its cold-eyed camera tracking
From the wide bay into geography.

Listen to me. Trust in this:
Once more there is a lesson here.
First he sees a string of beaches
Becoming dune and then a blur
Of clouds that clear on trees and houses

(Your life and all the others'). What
He sees is you becoming nations.
His overview is oldest, weighed
Against the wind's harsh-aired inflations.
From where else would you legislate?

But now observe the final turn,
Your page here X-rayed for its meaning.
This hard ascender crashlands, worn
Clean of flesh and feathers, strewing
A clavicle, commas on free terrain.

2. The Nineteenth Century
(for Robert Cremins)
In the neo-classical city, look
How Schinkel's had it all arranged
Into a nation. Hill and lake
Collected into galleries are swinged
As national landscape to awake

A citizen to national feeling.
And then to fill the edifice
Of Parliament with nation-building
Navvies who'll argue nights and days
To keep your loves and lives a going

Concern. The Bank of the Republic,
Where the bottom-line of every life
Is marked, looms huge and free, mock-Greek,
A piece of giant clockwork, aloof
On a mantlepiece of marble brick.

And in the Library's brumous light,
Seated at his desk's green baize,
There's always some insurgent head
Which plans to spell a final chaos
Of seagulls, and bring down the state.

Note
The first of these poems is addressed to the nineteenth-century Czech poet and patriot Jan Neruda. During that period the nation which is now called the Czech Republic underwent a national wakening as artists, politicians and intellectuals tried to propagate the idea of an essential national character. The details of this awakening are not dissimilar to the events of the same time in other small countries which were attempting to break free from a larger political power. As an Irish writer who has spent time in Prague, thinking about these events and figures such as Neruda has given me new perspectives on our own Gaelic Revival which was spearheaded by Yeats, Patrick Pearse, Douglas Hyde and others. In some ways I have become more suspicious of it. On a recent visit to Finland I had the opportunity to visit the National Gallery, and I was immediately struck by the way in which the art of their national

awakening could have been exchanged so easily for that of Bohemia; the art which was supposed to express an individual national character was surprisingly commutative. One comes to realise that if nations have so many structures in common then the idea of an essential national character becomes questionable. Indeed the idea at all of such a character might turn out to be an auxiliary statutory instrument. This map of a nation is copperfastened on a particular tract of the earth by violence and ritual displays of force: a national mythology without a national army is hard to take seriously.

But this is not a call to the barricades. The nation is a fiction we live by, even if we don't believe it. When nearing the end of 'The Nineteenth Century', my first impulse was to come down on the side of the insurgent, the anarchist who would blow all these structures sky high. The revolutionary has something of an aesthetic sense in that he experiences the same simple yearning for change which was familiar to Ovid. But even in *The Metamorphoses*, horrific acts of violence surround the transformation of a king into a hoopoe or a girl into a river.

One might almost despair that an art which tries to make something happen is at best banal and at worst morally irresponsible. And yet what one continues to look for, in the words of Wallace Stevens, is 'a vis, a principle', an attitude which can negotiate this difficulty without being pulled apart by different currents. It is at first a selfish endeavour as one finds oneself thrown in among these already existing structures and tries to discover what they are and how they change. And hopefully it moves on from there.

MILES CHAMPION

from **Butterfly Knot**
recalcitrant quivering bough
a little pathos duck with abstract
Flood. His thought
bangles, and
a frizzy, pungent outline
while Toppy had lain dying
conscious again. When she was not
blue blanket, clenching one fist
hospital. The bloated
white cypher on the green, grassy
friend, almost tittering
for an outing – you pack
apple. But now
woman had put the unflinching window.
The tea strainer became great
        silly
feeling bungalow
their darling's feet. Then
features the terrible, square grin
on nothing. Something
everything quake. Anyone's being there
Keyed up by the sudden
fawn sandal, looking fixedly
through a cleft in his memory
she keeps the stiff penguin open.
savage dignity. The matronly
sorrow constantly bled away
You stay here and look at that duck
drawing choppy breaths

In rhapsody so much chaff
bored her. Her schooled lips
returned the scrawniest
fervour of stones.
thickets or bracken the families went
to touch the edge of Nature stands
summer, shed a smell of camphor – protestingly
giggle. They saw a haggard
wrong shore. When they met she had
Cecil the tripod. They were fifteen… thicket

mist came curdling into the lock-up.
The access of some new feeling, a feeling
The mother and father wheeled docilely.

Teresa, into the coats, said something
and stood on it to light the lamp in the hall. She
strolled across as though she were falling and could fall no further,
    while her breast
of dull glass began to spread
like a stain on the mist. Clifford took a sweep
and undipped his lights
on the pallid walls of a house.

Teresa did not come in; she examined,
as much by touch as anything,
the wonderful car. An idea of going away for ever lifted up the
    mist between the formless rhododendrons.
How foolish it was, in love, to have the outline
of her mist-clotted hair.

Relentless, pointless
Afternoon oppresses one
The cocktail-shaker, the telephone,
A house sheathes
Purely negative reason.
Blocky elms dark
With tea-roses: waxy cream.
The blistered door was propped open
With a bizarre object, a lump of quartz hung on loops of string
    that coughed.

The face
Had a stretched look
Coral, lemon and cold white
enormities you can only keep
    dread obstinacy, love, grief
you could stay with burning Josephine, but extinct paper and
    phantom – gutted

The white circle distended inch
   only half getting
earthy emanations and smells
the plonk of boards
            orange larder
   armchair and settee
   queerish, later, herself

    heartfelt cup
in the thickety darkness

bronze clods upright into pang

the kerb, her dread of stepping
into the thin November grey, but the houses with close 'art' –
pre-natal

    Towelling his face
remorseless new plumb.

The empty promise of morning
about the mattress palm
    and vera-
The orange curtains is at the front
daylight entombed there.

Dead glades and emasculate
Thumbs
    grass is reeking
curtains looking unliving
    rage tower

It was all coming in for coffee,
or else whist. It doesn't get you any-
where. I mean, you get used to it, but that
doesn't make it natural

Across the breakfast
blank leaf,
most facts, however
    hearts
successful nuns that bubble
watered down mouth centred the
lap prettily rector
The patchy kittens unfolded
mouth muffled doggedly striding
over the porch, snug as a ship's cabin and frilly
ferreting blood worked by Umbrian saucer
brook – – faction, at the bangles.   urgent air.

The honeysuckle up the south front
of the cottage unfolded the last
    of its green shoots,
and in the strip of orchard the other side of the brook daffodils
    blew their trumpets

In her raspberry-woollen dress

    nests excited her

An Easter party was quite a new idea
and looked like running them in for more
expense – they did not jib at this.

I think those lambs are pretty, I should like a pet lamb
    of my own;
I should call it Percy. One
of the sheep gave her a long, reproving look – meanwhile the
    lamb had frigidly walked away.

The pouch

    beaker

  sip milk

wrote

The egg

ones we

Flowering

mother

    salted experience

She pushed her hair back, brushed crumbs
Through her face – embedded in fat
Maroon pages
That had rotted.
the most naturalistic freckles – stretched
and stood up against the sun – a flake
of pastry still clung to her
tartlet, fluttered, looked desolate, dark as ink.

Here he blew green drippings off a page.

    backs have a somehow
    will sag
    flash

    sister's off
    The ozone smell of the bay
    a kind of pump, but I don't know
we keep calm doing this
The head stays bright.

An air of fastidious
Democratic smell.

It's all got in my hair
Chasing balls – you have to have names for things.

London, full enough before the Americans came
And a crumpled dead madam began to chafe

The refreshed town unfolded
Expunging something as white as bones with no history

Something more immaterial seemed to threaten
The lesser strangeness of grass

Outside the great sausage
The violence of the stranger within her ribs

This is a threatened night
Loaned for at least some hours to innocence.

```
A moron – annoyance
              On the ottoman
                          fetishes she
   like a smell to her
The crocus of flame is poisoned, not a pure drop comes out at
   any prick

       Appearance of shattered night
          immobile cataracts sensed not pleading
       air of delinquency
   not a mouse – my housekeeper's
   checked the uprush of an uncertain laugh
   'They burned the mouse of light.'
   Your forbearance delicacy
   broken her fairytale.       he writhes his head
   to the brow of the lawn the flush heightening
   a new cigarette inadequate time in which to thank each
   Frond and breath.
```

The Tenth Chaffinch
A wax pill (bespoke art)
Strikingly 'off'
   the pianola –
   like, of grey,
Pedalling puce-and-buff cough
                    and implacable hatchet

A tunic of fibres
Unpressing,
Resentful of changing colour –
The apartnesses and frustrations
Shortened by being knotted.

Note

The poem as object in words (which allows for changes in circumstance of the 'viewer'). One task (partially) becomes that of trying to find one's way in the reductive climate of poetry (comedy/philately/WHATEVER) as 'the new rock 'n' roll'. O'Hara as New Gen? But he did far, far more than just write about what he *did*. & the need too to read work that makes one, in turn, want to write. (In this regard: Tom Raworth, Ted Berrigan, Gertrude Stein, Larry Eigner, Jack Spicer.) Clark Coolidge's 'If you *got* something to say you should be a *speaker*.' The Language as Present Fact. Behaving (consciously) *toward* it & not *through* it?

SOPHIE HANNAH

Early Bird Blues
I am the early bird.
I have worn out my shoes
Simply because I heard
First come was first to choose.
One of my talents is avoiding queues.

I never ask how long
I shall be made to wait.
I have done nothing wrong.
I don't exaggerate.
To state the obvious, I'm never late.

Why has the queue not grown?
Nobody hears me speak.
I stand here all alone
Which makes me look unique
But even so, the worm avoids my beak.

What do the others know?
Have I been told a lie?
Why don't I turn and go?
I still know how to fly,
But, damn, I want that worm. I don't know why.

Mad Queen Hospital for Electrifying the Heart*
Welcome. My cocoa-buttered hands
Built these five rooms, undid this face,
Untangled all that once made sense.

The hall stands bare for compliments,
For chaos – an escape from peace.
So far so good. I'm in demand.

They bring their lives like powdered soup
For me to stir, and sniff, and drink;
The healing process, cruel to be
As cruel as they have been to me.
I am the one they have to thank.
I fill their rooms with scented soap.

Five at a time. The royal need
To charge their hearts, to be in charge,
Is almost physical, a craving.
I crave to save those not worth saving.
A mind once small that swells too large
Is happy as a hand grenade.

After explosion, fully trained,
Their feet leave scars on bedroom rugs,
Their frenzy stains the corridors.
Clutching their hearts, expensive sores,
They pay the bill. I bleach the rags,
The ash, the lives they leave behind.

Doors beckon shut. My vacant palace,
Drooling, awaits the next arrivals.
Five relentless rooms to let
And nobody has caught me yet.
It's pure; a matter of survival,
No grudges held, no taint of malice.

* The title of this poem is an extract from a poem called 'Telephone Directory' by Harry Crosby.

One-Track Mind
Why does she take unnecessary trips?
She lives just opposite a row of shops.
She went to Crewe to buy a bag of chips.
She went to Birmingham to buy lamb chops.

She has no time for aeroplanes or boats.
She cannot get enough of British Rail.
She went to Liverpool for Quaker Oats
Then Halifax to buy the Daily Mail.

She went to Chester for a pair of tights.
Every weekend she's up and down some track.
She went to York for twenty Marlboro Lights.
She went to Stalybridge and came straight back.

Once, on her way to Hull for cottage cheese,
She saw him. All he said was 'Tickets, please.'

Ghazal
Imagine that a man who never writes
Walks on the planet Mars in cricket whites

Looking for signs of life which isn't there.
He walks through hot red days and dark red nights

Across a surface which is rough and bare.
He feels confused; he's come to see the sights

But there are none, and nobody to share
His empty mouth, his sudden fear of heights.

Nine of his cigarettes are going spare.
The tenth is for himself, and that he lights.

Something's familiar now. He starts to swear.
He stumbles through bizarre, one-sided fights.

Meanwhile you're stuck on Earth without the fare.
In any case, there are no scheduled flights.

And all the love you send is lost in air,
And all your words stick in the sky like kites.

The Mystery of the Missing
Think carefully. You sat down on a bench
and turned the pages of a small green book.
You were about to meet your friends for lunch.

> I turned the pages but I didn't look.
> It felt as if the bench was in mid-air.
> Whatever held me wouldn't put me back.

What happened next? You must have gone somewhere.
The wind was blowing hair across your face.
Perhaps you went inside and lit a fire.

> But people looked for me and found no trace
> inside or out. I saw the things they feared
> in the green book before I lost my place.

Surely they weren't afraid you'd disappeared?
Did they suspect you might have come to harm?
You could have reassured them with a word.

> I wanted to, but every word that came
> threatened to burn my mouth. I also knew
> that soon it would be over, I'd be home.

The sky closed in. You say you shrank, then grew,
then everything came back to you with ease.
You sat quite still, deciding what to do.

> Huge purple bruises covered both my knees
> But no-one acted like I'd been away.
> None of my friends asked what the matter was –

Everyone else had had a normal day.

A Fairly Universal Set
Whoever cleans your windows once a week,
Whoever stuffs your letters through the door,
Whoever you'd get in to fix a leak –
I resent all of these and plenty more.

Men on the bus and women in the street,
Religious nuts who ring your bell at dawn,
Any chiropodist who's touched your feet.
Canvassers, tramps, whoever mows your lawn,

Your colleagues, friends, acquaintances (both sexes),
People with whom you've shared a cigarette,
Your enemies, and, most of all, your exes,
Everyone you have ever seen or met,

Voices you might from time to time have heard,
The speaking clock. Jealous is not the word.

Hotels like Houses
She is the one who takes a shine
To ceilings and to floors,
Whose eye finds room for every line
Scratched on the wardrobe doors.

She thinks in terms of thick red rope
Around the bed, a plaque
Above the hardened bathroom soap.
He's always first to pack.

If their affair has awkward spells,
What's bound to cause the rows is
That he treats houses like hotels
And she, hotels like houses.

Note
These aren't my absolute favourites of all the poems I've written. I tried that approach and found it impossible. My favourites changed every time I thought about it. So I've just picked seven poems which I like a lot and feel are fairly representative of my writing as a whole.

SINÉAD MORRISSEY

Clothes

Once they come undone, there's no stopping
The undoing of all that keeps us us not we.
From a room full of history and underwear,
I throw out my diary and walk naked.

Until we're talking of weather again,
Contact shrunk back to wherever it sprang from.
And I'm begging for it all: coat, hat, gloves, scarf –
Shoes shod in iron, and a waterproof.

Awaiting Burial

Being born was as painful as this –
The crusade of the heart to bloom in mist,

The pull of blood
On everything the body had

To pump in a new direction,
The sliding dissection

Of water
And air –

Getting the heart to falter
And the lungs to breathe water

Requires
The tonnweight of the sky,

A damaged hillside, nighttime,
The tunnel you dreamt of, O

Sarah, speak to me, you've been through
The journey, was there light on the other side

Saturday

Noon. I stand
Behind net curtains,
Watch kids on the street
Throwing stones.

Buses pass each way.
An ambulance,
In all its slowed-down
Urgency, forces through.

His heart must have stopped
Between the newspaper
And a glance
At the races. Something

Lurking
That caught up with a shock
And sucked him
Out of all he knew.

The Juggler

He must have practised for hours
Between the bins and the mattresses
Of a rented backyard
To dance the seven painted skittled
Off his fingers like that.
He has the game whittled

To art. God knows what
Anachronism he took up before –
Using medieval skill to stop
Time: he puts the clock back
Nine hundred years
With this sideshow for a quack

Or diversion for a king.
Still, or because of the drain
Of things modern, we ring
Him with faces. He knows
How we anticipate failure,
And that what he owes

His audience is defiance
Of breakdown. We watch as his magic
Creates the radiance
Of a spinning blue arc brought
Slowly to a standstill. Natural
Begrudgers, we are nevertheless caught

By the weightlessness, the controlled
Mechanics of air

With all the improbables cajoled
Into truth, we are not as far out
From faith as we were.

Belfast Storm

With a rain like that lashing into the city
And a wind that blew streets dark before you could blink –
It's as though the angels are angry: sitting in the sky
With heads in hands and howling it out all over us.

I can't think what they haven't got used to by now.
The great gap in the street where his knees hit the wall
Meant wheelchairs rather than coffins.

After the Hurricane

You saw the wind as the breath of God.
You couldn't help it. Your refusal
Of the ether that would mist over death
Got smashed to splinters like the Florida coastline,
Up-ended in rain.
There was too much rage in the sky for it not to be God's.

Perhaps it was your position under the window,
At the mercy of whatever startled missile
Made its appearance next –
A tree, a house, a woman –
Over your head.
You saw a shower of cars

Spat out like sycamore seeds
And a landscape that trailed wires
In its rush to be pure.
You felt too temporary not to be answerable
To the power in the break-up
Of hills

ADAM SCHWARTZMAN

The Legitimizing World
*I.M. Louis Berold
emigrated March 1973
(died November 1993)*

Lift up your eyes round about, and see:
They all are gathered together, and come to you:
Your sons come from far away,
and your daughters are borne on the side.

Isiah LX, 4

1 Aliyah
For some who say *laager, veld, indaba*,
there is another land even before the Old Country,
of psalms and aqueducts, secrets scrolled
away in caves or unrevealed in myth,

in godly etymologies passed through children
and grown strange in unintended places.

From new worlds glances backwards are thrown
to where patriarchs are hoarded. One more

of my tall men is taken into the confidence
of felled temples, and deserts and testaments,
and this replenished genealogy wanders again
for the restless shall inherit the earth.

2 Free State Drive
To kinds of houses pieces of sleep
come simply now in places you knew.
I was making this bus journey where you chose
not to die – in the night, through the country

and we drove by dark towns. The names
would still fit in your mouth, though we'll change

the dam's, rechristen in summer or next summer.
In the country are many stars that reach down

until the hills, made visibly pregnant, *Maluti,
Maluti*… It happened so much more quietly,
this scheduled movement, and we noticed how
from faith or fear you would not be here.

3 Evening Out
Being rowed now by me, the girl
I am carrying to see the sand bars and a sea,

Among Communists
I remember smoke and faces that I knew
And the fact that I got in free; my Mother
Taking money by the half-collapsed sink;
Cheap posters proclaiming 'AN EVENING OF BRECHT'
And subtitled 'Bring Your Own Drink';
Too much conviction to see through.

the spread cusps of the widening estuary,
you do not know, nor this place

which, were you out here once, you forgot
and left me. Silver fish jump, mullet run,

tail the surface, are carried out. Only time
has passed. I can measure you going

against the last big storms or even tides.
Without seeing, banks recede
in the sudden great opening out. You
feel now in the rush of new space.

4 Three African Animals
The flat pebble teeth show in the slow yawns
of our most dangerous animal, like mints
in brown icing. It has a name to enchant,
makes for popular toys – smiley, abundant comforters

that can also run faster than a man on land,
leave crushed canoeists halved round their ribs.

But the stuff of those nightmares were triassic logs
that rose from the happy waters to snap

around antlers and chew modern creatures
in primeval jaws (though the hypocrisy of fear
is not for the eaten antelope, who, taken,
does not discriminate, nor is indignant).

5 Caesarea
I found bits of antiquity in the sand
in the park I played at near you,
too common to hoard, but worth sunstroke.
The site of a Roman rubbish dump

was a promised land for a while,
in the Summer, at siesta time.

Once on a dig you found an old coin
near the sea, and coloured glass:

Death still came to those too big
for dissipation, broken into shards.
Damn you, the mighty, for hidden parts
baked harder into other people's lives.

6 Afterwards, with you
Those who had far to come from did not sit
with you on the day of rest you died on,
but your youngest son did, who undressed you,
and with his mother afterwards drank

from the cups you had not reached, while, naked,
you were only just stiller than the living.

It is not that you were cut short because your last
thought went something like *now where's the sugar.*

While the invited were sad and still on their ways
those two were luckiest to be the first to see
such poetry, how it all looked finished;
and you waiting to be unveiled to everyone.

7 Family motto
You go about in the days before
they bury you, are permitted
to appear as the hero of memories
in rooms where children come,

leaning over to say *Remember when*
to each, choosing elegies and the last touch

before the gathered diaspora scatter
and go back again to their own little dynasties.

When the sand hardens round the body
that failed, you stiffen into indignation.
Well, I didn't do this, you will think disappearing,
not right, although unto eternity, never wrong.

8 Burial rite
Made up and shown, other dead
are stored in their best clothes, and coffined,
wait. We wrapped you in linen
and saw your shape, in tight folds

and creases break around your body.
The first child, you were loved like this

on your way in. We are happy
for the inbetween, and lowering you away

imagine you suddenly tired of death,
stretching, grateful for a sheet,
while spitting sand you fall out of the ground
and think of the pink inside of a breakfast grapefruit

9 Looking back
Or, out from the hatched, arrogant orderliness
of stretched sheet, you saw through
to it still being light where, turning
to memories, we agreed sentimentally

life isn't everything and you, making desperate,
silly, impossible sounds, could have been pleading

there in recesses where the dead get exiled: 'love *me*,'
pale and stiff, from the other side of usefulness.

But in front of us you would have come apart
at the TV or supper. We could not have talked
or understood. So we tried not to hear or imagine
and, guilty, do this, to you, for us.

10 Epilogue
After chances at reknowing forever
lost now, what would he say,
the gone to the young, who held a lathe,
sold a company and kissed the young boy

on the lips. We are both long removed
from that indifferent intimacy of kin,

that corridor of clear in the sawdust
planked high above by piles of plywood.

Could you get out of this looped memory
I keep you in, would you take me aside,
unloosed, to say this: that you were somebody
who could make things out of wood?

Sunday School
The memory of the slate path and the house
to the left is clearer still for the vagueness
it comes out of. It is unattached and self
sustaining. I might have been born with it.

There were Sunday lunches there, I know.
I pretended to be the ex Ms South Africa
with the smooth skin, and cooing effeminately
could make you laugh, and your sisters too.

All afternoon we'd imitate advert slogans,
say *what about this one* or *remember when*,

then exaggerate amazement, ecstacy, love, pain.

Beach Drive
The white bakkie stops on the sand
where the road comes down to the beach.
Your father, with rolled up sleeves,
taps the wheel, leans forward; a blond girl

in the passenger seat. At 50 miles per hour
the back is filled with parents and cousins,

the legitimizing world, and the tire
on the bonnet is big enough for a child's bum.

Everything bends to the just curving horizon.
Scooping the air with your arms
you were lifted. You really flew.
I think we saw signs and visions in our own times.

Adam Schwartzman

The Sanctuary
For Alice

Our last big piece of free land frightens people.
The popular word is not to go to a place
that you don't know what can happen there.
For the time they are considered, the almost invisible
pedestrian myths that skirt it barefoot at twilight
are suspect. The rush hour returning bounce
light off his back and race up straight avenues
like tangents off a circle. In a while he turns down
where broad contours drain from under walls
of fortress communities into the stream park.
The ghosts of sleepers disappear in dry channels
as the next day unpresses dry grass. In years
his absence becomes only not being seen again.

Bertrams Suburb

While the water tower squats like a Turkish bird
on the ridge and smiles more nicely the other way in green
and bougainvillaea to where the warmest houses face north,

the dead well-to-do are ignored and grumble in the plumbing.
This could be a local myth. There could be many.
Stark living rooms made to be seen into

stare at each other often across the streets and say secrets.
No brass and marble now. But it's more humbling
buying groceries on a teak floor and more like us

to prefer the peopled ruin. I see the gaping fanlight
in the hallway behind a fruit stall on the stoep
after rugby, and now, when it's dry and the roads turn back

to gravel into driveways, dust rises and sweet william and anthracite
are there. There is a real side, where, when you never stopped before,
you hear whispering on corners only you understand.

Note

The first thing that 'The Legitimizing World' wants is to be read as an elegy: It discusses the deeds of the dead man. It says how they appear to those living after his death… During the time in which the poem was written I was translating and studying Old English texts. It occurred to me that it was not just for good manners that the characters with whom I was dealing would declare their origins and lineage before getting down to their business. 'The Legitimizing World' is also a kind of 'identity' poem. But what kept on coming back to me at the time was that I found myself unable to use my family or country's history as a means of affirming my identity as an African rather than a displaced European. The fact that my grandfather had left South Africa in the 1970s – during the grimmest and most hopeless days of Apartheid (and also a few weeks before my birth) – and that he did so through Zionist fervour, gave me the opportunity to feel around the various issues that have concerned both of us, and reconcile myself to the differences between the decisions he and I have made. Like many things I was working on at the time, the whole piece is written in anticipation of the April transition, which my grandfather did not live to see. Most of what I do seems to work in this way. I can't isolate any one of my concerns – they all come rushing in at the same time. 'The Legitimizing World' is the third section of a book in four parts. But it is as much about the other three parts as it is about itself, and as these three parts are about it.

'Sunday School' and 'Beach Drive' come from the second section of the book. They're about the girl who appeared in '3/Evening Out'… I may be plagiarizing somebody in saying that I like to think of my poems as if they were archaeological finds. These two say a lot about how a way of happening came about. I was just beginning to read and meet the kinds of people who would become of importance to me; learning to fly, I suppose. I also like the poems because they seem so very easy, and because I've watched them suck in meaning as the book grew. 'Bertrams Suburb' and 'Sanctuary' come from the first section, 'The Good Life. The Dirty Life', a title which, in my South African context, speaks for itself, I think. I've wanted to find an indigenous idiom, make a poetic out of the sounds and phrases and syntactic structures around me. In these two and other such poems I've tried to use this idiom in order to invent an integrated urban mythology to complement those we already have.

25 this autumn, **Carcanet** congratulates *PN Review* on reaching 100

Carcanet's list of new poetry and the Pléiade include

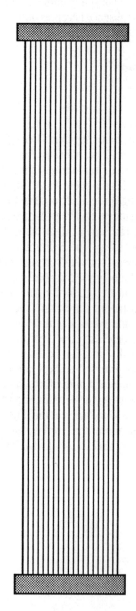

Edgell Rickword
Laura Riding
E.J.Scovell
Sorley MacLean
F.T.Prince
Anne Ridler
C.H.Sisson
Judith Wright
John Heath-Stubbs
Edwin Morgan
David Wright
Donald Davie
Patricia Beer
Christopher Middleton
John Ashbery
Iain Crichton Smith
Elizabeth Jennings
Elaine Feinstein
P.J.Kavanagh
Alistair Elliot
Jon Stallworthy
Gillian Clarke
Les Murray
Brian Jones
Andrew Waterman
John Peck
Roger Garfitt

Eavan Boland
Jeffrey Wainwright
Mimi Khalvati
Clive Wilmer
Bill Manhire
John Ash
Michael Vince
Norm Sibum
Robert Wells
Neil Powell
Grevel Lindop
Vicki Raymond
John Gallas
Charles Boyle
Frank Kuppner
Alison Brackenbury
Gregory Woods
Sujata Bhatt
Ian McMillan
Peter Sansom
James Keery
Chris McCully
Iain Bamforth
Justin Quinn
Miles Champion
Sophie Hannah
Adam Schwartzman

for a full catalogue write to
Carcanet
402-406 Corn Exchange, Manchester M4 3BY